HOLOCAUST

ALSO BY MICHAEL BERENBAUM

The Bombing of Auschwitz (ed. with Michael J. Neufeld), 2000

A Promise to Remember, 2003

After the Passion Is Gone (ed. with J. Shawn Landres), 2004

Murder Most Merciful (ed.), 2005

The World Must Know, rev. ed., 2005

Encyclopedia Judaica, 2nd ed. (ed.), 2007

Not Your Father's Antisemitism (ed.), 2008

Memory and Legacy, 2009

Witness to History (ed. with Ruth Lichenstein and Abraham J. Edelheit), 2009

Remembering for the Future (ed. with Richard Libowitz and Marcia Sachs Littell), 2016

ALSO BY JOHN K. ROTH

Holocaust Politics, 2001

Approaches to Auschwitz (with Richard L. Rubenstein), 2003

Ethics During and After the Holocaust, 2005

Genocide and Human Rights (ed.), 2005

The Oxford Handbook of Holocaust Studies (ed. with Peter Hayes), 2010

Encountering the Stranger (ed. with Leonard Grob), 2012

Rape: Weapon of War and Genocide (ed. with Carol Rittner), 2012

The Failures of Ethics, 2015

Teaching about Rape in War and Genocide (ed. with Carol Rittner), 2015

Losing Trust in the World (ed. with Leonard Grob), 2017

HOLOCAUST

Religious and Philosophical Implications

Edited by

JOHN K. ROTH
and
MICHAEL BERENBAUM

PARAGON HOUSE

Published in the United States by
Paragon House
St. Paul, MN
www.paragonhouse.com

Copyright ©1989 by Paragon House

First edition, 1989; 30th Anniversary (fifth printing), 2018

Grateful acknowledgement is made for permission to use portions of Elie Wiesel's
dialogues as epigraphs in this book. Excerpts from *Night* by Elie Wiesel, translated by
Stella Rodway. Copyright © 1960 by MacGibbon & Kee. Reprinted by permission
of Hill and Wang, a division of Farrar, Straus and Giroux, Inc. Excerpts from *One
Generation After* by Elie Wiesel, translated by Lily Edelman and the author. Copyright
© 1965, 1967, 1970. Reprinted by permission of Random House, Inc. Excerpts from *A
Jew Today,* translated by Marion Wiesel. Copyright © 1978. Reprinted by permission of
Random House, Inc.

Manufactured in the United States of America
Library of Congress Cataloging-in-Publication Data

Holocaust : religious and philosophical implications /
edited by John K. Roth and Michael Berenbaum.-1st ed.
p. cm.
Bibliography: p.
ISBN 1-55778-212-1
ISBN 978-1-55778-212-0 (pbk.)
1. Holocaust, Jewish (1939-1945) 2. Holocaust, Jewish
(1939-1945)—Influence. 3. Holocaust (Jewish theology)
I. Roth, John K. II. Berenbaum, Michael, 1945–
D804.3. H649 1989
940.53'15'03924—dc19   89-3174
                                                         CIP

To
Our Students
Who Have the Courage
To Go into That Darkness and Beyond
Against Despair

". . . Choose life, that you and your descendants may live. . . ."
Deuteronomy 30:19

Contents

Preface for the 30th Anniversary Printing

In the autumn of 1976, Richard L. Rubenstein, our mutual friend, introduced John Roth to Michael Berenbaum. Friendship grew, deepened through shared commitment to teaching and writing about the Holocaust. A decade later, on Thursday evening, December 10, 1987, we outlined *Holocaust: Religious and Philosophical Implications* during dinner at the Old Ebbitt Grill in Washington, DC.

Our outline emphasized writings frequently studied at the time, most of them authored by Holocaust survivors or pioneering scholars. Those writings, however, were scattered widely, some in books and journals no longer in print. We decided to make the reflections readily accessible to help students study the Holocaust.

Much has changed since the book appeared in 1989. For instance, we dedicated it to "our students." Primarily we had in mind the young women and men who had recently been in our classrooms. Now, those learners are no longer young; like us, they have children and grandchildren. But the original dedication remains fitting because we continue to teach and what we teach is still rooted in the book's contents. While they confront an event that took place decades ago, study of the Holocaust, its reverberations and implications, remains significant and timely. In our extremely dangerous world, such study is more urgently relevant than ever.

But hold on, not so fast—how can those claims be true? When another mutual friend and mentor, the Auschwitz survivor Elie Wiesel, died at the age of 87 on July 2, 2016, his passing was emblematic of the fact that few Holocaust survivors remain and that the Holocaust itself recedes into the past even as other disasters and atrocities, real and probable, vie for attention, intervention, and relief. When this book first appeared, dates like 9/11 and acronyms like ISIS meant nothing. Ethnic cleansing in the former Yugoslavia, genocide in Rwanda and Darfur, the slaughter of Rohingya Muslims in Myanmar, and an ongoing twenty-first century refugee crisis of horrific proportions were unknown. Devastating terrorism, resurgent antisemitism and racism, upsurges of xenophobic nationalism and religious tribalism, and burgeoning threats of climate change and thermonuclear war were not on computer screens because the technology and communication revolution that dominates and complicates the world—including "tweets" and "hacking," "fake news" and "cyberwarfare"—had barely begun. But now these fraught realities and more are dreadfully upon us. In such currently volatile instability, why bother with the "old" words in these pages?

Voiced from Holocaust testimony and reflection, the writings found here are crucial for our treacherous times because they underscore what Wiesel called the right questions, the most real ones because they are so fundamental: Who are we? What is right and what is not? What is good and what is most important? Are we doing the best we can? What about God, or is that question absurd? How can we forestall despair and resist injustice? Where are we/should we be going, what are we/should we be doing? What must change to curb and heal the wasting of the world? Are our judgments true? Can our responses to such questions stand scrutiny, or do they require further inquiry and evidence to support them?

No event exceeds the Holocaust's power to provoke such right and real questions, to ground them in earth-shaking history, and to insist and convince that we ignore them at our peril. Wrestling with those questions will not be sufficient to resist further disasters, but that struggle may be a necessary condition for doing so.

Asking questions (who, what, where, when, how, and above all, *why*?) is one of the most significant features of human life. If we could not ask questions, if we do not pursue the right and real questions and follow where they lead, life will be impoverished and endangered. Curiosity and inquiry will be stunted, maybe absent altogether. Learning will be hampered, if it takes place at all. Critical thinking will be unthinkable; creativity will diminish. Error, lying, dogmatism, tyranny, injustice, and violence will gain traction they do not deserve.

Asking questions is more important than getting "answers," because often the "answers" we get are incomplete, short-sighted, limited and limiting, partisan, foolish and false, life-threatening and life-destroying. On the other hand, asking the right questions keeps inquiry going, encourages us look further and know better, urges us to think twice before plunging ahead recklessly, murderously. Asking the right questions seeks evidence to support or correct judgments, makes us wonder if we might be mistaken, and tests what we think and believe. Asking such questions can help us to make good choices, or at least to steer clear of bad ones. The right and real questions can help us to avoid taking good things for granted.

To a large degree, the Holocaust happened because too many people, especially but not only the perpetrators of that genocide, failed to ask the right and real questions long or well enough. Pursuing those questions, guided by them, *Holocaust: Religious and Philosophical Implications* offers warnings and insights to keep lethal threats at bay.

John K. Roth   Michael Berenbaum
Winthrop, Washington   Los Angeles, California

"And why do you pray, Moshe?" I asked him.
"I pray to the God within me that He will give me the strength to ask Him the right questions."
We talked like this nearly every evening.

ELIE WIESEL, Night

Prologue

Who, What, Where, When, How?

Who are you?
A number.
Your name?
*Gone. Blown away. Into the sky. Look up there. The sky
is black, black with names.*

ELIE WIESEL, "Dialogues I," *One Generation After*

The religious and philosophical implications of the Holocaust, the Nazi attempt to annihilate the Jews of Europe and to enslave and destroy millions of other people as well, take the form of questions. Those questions are grounded in history, but no human mind or book—perhaps not even God's—can fully comprehend how, let alone why, the Holocaust has scarred the earth. Such a claim owes nothing to a lack of knowledge. On the contrary, the history of the Holocaust is by now well documented. As Elie Wiesel's dialogue says, the findings reveal that "the sky is black, black with names." That outcome suggests how important it is to ask the right questions. It also suggests how much more there is to detail, for Holocaust history may have no end.

Prologues to the Holocaust abound. They exist, for example, in centuries of religious rivalry between Christians and Jews as well as in the cunning of socioeconomic history that ruled European politics on the eve of Adolf Hitler's ascent in January 1933. No prologue therefore can do justice to Holocaust history. And yet, if only to keep this book's inquiry rooted in the history from which it stems, the place to begin is with reflection on the historical questions—who, what, where, when, how?—that govern all the others.

Events do not undo themselves. They stay what they are. The same is not true for interpretation of them. However dispassionate and "value-free" historical scholarship may claim to be, it remains a swirl of controversy aimed at defending this-or-that, refuting this-or-that, with living interests at stake. Nowhere is this reality more apparent than in studies of the Holocaust; claims of complicity and resistance, guilt and innocence, delusion and insight, clash with emotional impact whenever the subject is broached. Since so much life and death are at stake—including senses of identity today, which depend on historical views much more than is sometimes realized—this outcome is natural. Indeed that result is as it should be, provided that new rounds of bitterness are not set loose by insistence that one view corners truth to the exclusion of every other.

In spite of—and, at the same time, because of—controversy, there is consensus on numerous facts. The Third Reich's system of concentration camps, ghettos, murder squadrons, and killing centers took more than twelve million defenseless human lives. Between five and six million of them were Jewish—more than a million of those were children not yet in their teens—and it bears remembering that the Jews were the only group explicitly targeted for extinction by the Nazis. Although not every Nazi victim was Jewish, the Nazi intent was to rid Europe, if not the world, of Jews. Hitler went far in fulfilling that goal. Two-thirds of the Jews in prewar Europe and the Soviet Union— and about one-third of the Jews worldwide—were dead by the end of World War II.

Such are the best-known and most widely accepted pieces of information about the Holocaust, but other data hold firm, too. The vast majority of the Jewish victims were from Eastern Europe, more than half from Poland where the Nazi annihilation effort was ninety percent successful. While judgments vary, even conservative calculations suggest that at Auschwitz alone (located in Poland and largest of the killing centers), more than one million Jews were gassed. More statistics—endless—could be piled up. But what of the forces that produced them?

In March 1933, Heinrich Himmler, head of the SS, established the first SS concentration camp. It was situated at Dachau, a town in southern Germany near Munich. Six years later, a network of these camps existed: Sachsenhausen, Esterwegen, Buchenwald, and Ravensbruck (for women) as well as Dachau and an Austrian camp at

Mauthausen. Part of a system that included book-burnings, control of education and industry, and state domination of everything from scientific research and technological development to literature and art, these camps terrorized and incarcerated people whom the state wished to eliminate, either temporarily or permanently, but who were not easily subjected to the normal workings of criminal law. Silencing all dissent against the Nazi regime was the goal. Thus, numerous Communists and clergymen, plus many Jehovah's Witnesses, were thrown together with other "undesirables."

Although far removed from the Auschwitz of 1943, the SS concentration camps in Germany in the 1930s also contained many Jews. They, too, were seen as a threat—albeit with a difference. Racism and antisemitism were at the heart of the matter, and the shock waves they produced still rupture the world. Their force started to build toward a crescendo on January 30, 1933, when Hitler took the chancellor's oath from Paul von Hindenberg, president of the Weimar Republic.

As the works of Brecht, Klee, Kandinsky, and the Bauhaus movement make clear, Weimar Germany provided a lively environment for the arts. For the future of democratic principles, however, it was another story. The elections of November 1932 showed that democracy in Germany was doomed by the divisions spawned in the aftermath of its World War I defeat. One disruptive factor was the economic instability produced initially by wartime destruction, reparation demands, and soaring inflation, and then by worldwide depression and massive unemployment. Another was the psychological tension throughout Germany linked to a failure to accept defeat due to the superior military power of the Allies, as well as a feeling that the loss had besmirched German honor, and in some circles the conviction that German power had been betrayed from within. There was also mistrust of republican government, especially among military leaders, old aristocratic families, and business concerns—small and large—many of which regarded the Weimer Republic as foisted on Germans from outside and unlikely to achieve desired stability.

Within this uneasy setting, the National Socialists (Nazis) garnered about one-third of the vote on November 6, 1932, a decline from an earlier showing but still more than any other party could muster. Shaky though it was, a coalition of right-wing nationalistic groups developed, and eventually Hitler emerged on top. Elections held on March 5, 1933—they followed a fire at the Reichstag on February 27, which Hitler conveniently blamed on his political opponents—failed to give him a clear majority, but his power was sufficient to obtain enactment of the so-called Enabling Act on March 23, 1933. It made Hitler's word as good as law. By July 14, 1933, his dictatorship was sufficiently secure for the Nazis to stand as the only legal political party in Germany.

Dissent against Nazi nationalism during the thirties found expression only in a relatively ineffective minority. For example, although a "Confessing Church" spoke out in its Barmen Declaration (May 1934)—and through individual leaders such as Dietrich Bonhoeffer, Karl Barth, Martin Niemöller, and Heinrich Grüber—a majority of Protestant pastors and laypersons went along with, and in numerous cases enthusiastically supported, domination of the church by the Nazi state. As for the Catholic side, individuals such as Bernard Lichtenberg and Cardinal Clemens von Galen took a stand; both were instrumental in stopping the "euthanasia program" (1939–41), although not before it destroyed thousands of mentally or physically handicapped Germans categorized by Nazi eugenics as *lebensunwertes Leben* ("life unworthy of life"). But Hitler's successful negotiation of a concordat with the Vatican (July 1933) stood as legitimacy of his rule and kept Catholic resistance under wraps. At the same time, neither a concordat nor Pope Pius XI's protesting encyclical, *Mit brennender Sorge* (1937), prevented Nazi interference in Catholic affairs. Incidentally, besides *Mit brennender Sorge*, which enraged the Nazis by condemning their "idolatrous cult of *Volk* and race," Pius XI had ordered preparation of an encyclical to attack racism, antisemitism, and the persecution of the Jews in Germany. The draft was completed as specified, but its transmission to Pius XI was intentionally delayed, and he died in February 1939 without being able to approve it. When his successor, Pius XII, read the document, he set it aside. As this episode helps to confirm, even where opposition against Hitler did emerge from Christian sources, concern for the plight of Jews was hardly the prevailing motive.

Meanwhile a major plank in the Nazi platform was racial purity. Based on principles of Social Darwinism, natural selection, and survival of the fittest, the aim was to make room for the so-called Nordic-Aryan race, especially as embodied in the German people, so it could achieve its rightful dominion on earth. Crucial corollaries linked with that program. For instance, Hitler's conviction and Nazi theory held that there were other racial strains, varying in their degree of inferiority but inferior to the Aryan nonetheless. Their very existence, however, set up a competitive situation that was an obstacle to Aryan supremacy and required a struggle (*Mein Kampf*) to subdue them.

The Jews were singled out as the most virulent threat, so that Hitler could portray them as instigating World War II. German propaganda described Jews as parasites, vermin, beasts of prey—in a word, subhuman. Other versions offered pictures of a race whose inferiority was deceptively masked behind a subversive cunning that was all too successful at destroying German political and economic life, and indeed bore responsibility for Germany's defeat a generation earlier. Although individual Germans could never see that such descriptions fitted all Jews ("Aren't there always exceptions?"), the net effect still fueled an antisemitism that had the "Final Solution" as its end.

That such attitudes could exist and reap their whirlwind should no longer elicit innocent astonishment, for racism and antisemitism continue to infest human experience. But still the question needs to be asked: Why were the Jews singled out by the Nazis? Ultimately the answers trail on to infinity, and yet some simple explanation is found: The Jews were different and available. However much they were assimilated into German society, the Jews remained an identifiable and largely compliant minority; thus they could be used as a scapegoat to provide the simple explanations craved by the mind where complexity reigns. This suggestion, however, is itself too simple; the German bureaucracy never obtained total satisfaction in defining who or what a Jew might be, a condition necessary for carrying out Nazi plans. Still, even if the Jews were neither identifiable nor available altogether, the process of tracking them down, first in Germany and then all over Europe, never relented until force from the outside prevented it. What could sustain such fervor?

It is well known that bureaucracies are self-sustaining, and it cannot be overemphasized that the Holocaust was a bureaucratic product. Propagandize racial hatred successfully, identify and mark millions of people, uproot and deport them, confiscate their property for the state, and finally annihilate them and make their corpses disappear—such jobs are not accomplished by random acts of violence and hooliganism. Organization must prevail. Decentralized though it may be, a network of offices and personnel involving every segment of society is indispensable. The Nazis produced it.

A destruction process of the kind the Nazis produced, moreover, has to be gradual. It takes time to complete the "checklist," especially when there is a war to be fought on several fronts simultaneously. Some steps cannot be taken until others have preceded them. Mass murder, replete with gas chambers and crematoria, comes far down the list, but all the more decisively when its time has arrived. Hitler and his closest associates may have envisioned the physical destruction of the Jews early on. Even so, there was no detailed master plan that timed and controlled every move in advance. The onslaught against the Jews had a structure and a logic of its own, but awareness of that structure and logic grew only as events unfolded blow by blow. Especially for the rank and file who carried out the measures, developments that led toward Auschwitz evolved step-by-step, more or less naturally out of day-to-day and month-to-month routine, as people went about doing their jobs.

But why *do* the jobs? Fear of reprisals, a long German tradition of obedience to authority, inability to see feasible alternatives, a sense that successful war efforts really did depend on eliminating a presumed conspiracy of Jews and Communists—all of those reasons played their part. Still, there is another reason without which the others form no sufficient account at all: a tradition of hatred for Jews strong enough in Germany to make it possible for many Germans to think that they were performing a service for the world by removing an undesirable and unwanted problem-population. And no matter how "understandable"—from expedience or ignorance—one finds the arguments that rationalized a policy of nonintervention against Nazi treatment of the Jews, or no matter how much one rightly warns that it is far easier to judge in retrospect than to act wisely and courageously in the present, still the record stands. Not only were Jewish refugees unwanted almost everywhere, Hitler could also take comfort from the fact that direct actions against his policies toward Jews, at whatever stage, were exceptions to prove the rule that most non-Jewish populations around the globe remained passive and indifferent, if not implicitly supportive, of Nazi aims to destroy European Jewry.

How those attitudes helped to propel German minds and Jewish bodies toward crematoria involves a history that took place long before the twentieth century. That history brings religion, in particular, to the fore. Christianity is carved out of Judaism. Furthermore, since religions deal with the ultimacies of life, and thus are highly charged with emotion, tension between them should come as no surprise. Add in the relationship of one faith being born out of the other—but in such a way that they can neither fully embrace nor reject each other, geographically as well as spiritually—and volatility ensues and escalates.

The Jewish establishment did not welcome early Christians with open arms. Animosities rooted in that experience lingered on to color relationships long after Christianity had moved from its status as a struggling Jewish sect, long after it achieved cultural dominance in the West. Likewise, even though the Christian New Testament stresses love for one's neighbor, it also contained ingredients to bolster a "teaching of contempt." That teaching caricatured the Judaism of Jesus' day as degenerate. It held, too, that the Jews were collectively responsible for killing Jesus and thus for rejecting God through deicide. And it also advanced belief that the dispersion of the Jews from Israel after the Judeo-Roman War (C. E. 66–70)—and perhaps all their subsequent difficulties—was God's punishment for the crucifixion.

Such attitudes do not exist with impunity, as a long history of religiously inspired persecutions, inquisitions, crusades, and pogroms testifies. The Jew had to *do* nothing to give offense. It was sufficient simply to *be*, although the gentile imagination had little trouble conjuring more specific pretexts for discrimination and violence. Thus, as if fated to be together, the Jewish diaspora and the spread of Christianity tracked each other, even as the Holy Land itself remained a home to both—and therefore, in a sense, to neither. When Matthew's gospel had Jesus say, "I have not come to bring peace, but a sword" (Matthew 10:34), the author wrote more than he knew. Uneasy tensions between Jews and Christians gnawed away for fifteen centuries, periods of peaceful coexistence mixing with pressures for Christian conversion and policies of isolation and expulsion.

The sixteenth-century Protestant Reformation brought many changes, but Christian attitudes toward Jews remained largely unconverted. If Martin Luther, for example, rightly stands as a hero on many counts, his position in *The Jews and Their Lies* (1543), as he entitled one of his writings, is not among them. His pronouncement that, next to the devil himself, a Christian has "no enemy more cruel, more venomous and violent than a true Jew" hardly represents a high point of Christian love. In addition, there is in Luther a logic that perpetually tempts the Christian mind: namely, that misfortune's falling on the Jews is corroborating evidence for the exclusive truth of the Christian faith. When a people rejects God's Messiah, who is also one of their own, no good can come of it. At the very least, so this reasoning goes, judgment and punishment will follow.

Four and a half centuries later, enlightenment may have occurred. Christian triumphalism is rightly found wanting. Interfaith dialogues are held. Prayer books, religious pronouncements, commentaries on Scripture, sermons have been revised to improve Christian images of Jewishness. The price for these steps, however, has been immense. The Nazis used religious history, including Luther's anti-Jewish teachings, to obtain precedents for many of the measures, killing among them, that they exacted against the Jews. If it was something else to find a credible mandate for *annihilation* in those sources, no matter— others were available. They could even intertwine successfully with religious precedents that did underwrite trouble for the Jews. Take, for example, anti-Jewish racism.

Christian antisemitism and anti-Jewish racism are closely linked but not identical. Anti-Jewish racism began to peak in Germany in the nineteenth century. And what supported it? The most crucial factors included: philosophical and political theories which held that cultural developments and social behavior—good or bad—are products of physical attributes (that is, of "blood"); a widespread yearning for national unity—"peoplehood"—fostered by political forces which argued that it was socially undesirable, if not biologically impossible, for Jews to be truly German; and suspicion that unsettling economic changes—ranging from periodic depressions to industrial advances that threatened old ways of doing business to urbanization that undermined traditional values—were the result of Jewish liberalism and Jewish capital.

The list could be extended, but clearly factors beyond religion combined in theory and practice to make way for Hitler's policies. Indeed they would have been sufficient in and of themselves to unleash mass death in ways that Christian antisemitism could scarcely have achieved alone. And yet their power in Germany was inseparable from the religious factor. When the two strands joined up, the required attitudes were ready and waiting. All that was needed was a little more sophistication in propaganda techniques, a little more chaos in the political-economic scene, and the right kind of leadership to mobilize the powers of will and bureaucracy. By 1933 the pieces were in place.

Apparently disparate forces had become a field that would destroy the European Jews.

As the Nazis entrenched their position and initiated a military build-up, their Jewish policy started its work. It involved: restriction of civil liberties and professional opportunities for Jews; boycotting of Jewish businesses; impoverishment through confiscation of property; outright expulsion of non-German Jews; arousal of public sentiment against Jews aimed at producing a climate so unpleasant as to make emigration the only option. Riots and violence against Jews broke out, too, as in the *Kristallnacht* of November 9–10, 1938, when synagogues were burned, Jewish shops looted, and thousands of German and Austrian Jews arrested and sent to concentration camps.

If *Kristallnacht* was the most volatile of the anti-Jewish events in prewar Nazi Germany, the devastations accomplished by legislative enactment and bureaucratic enforcement of the Nazi will were, if slower and less spectacular, more efficient and dependable in the long run. The "Nuremberg Laws," passed unanimously by the Reichstag on September 15, 1935, were a case in point. They contained two basic provisions. First, the "Reich Citizenship Law" stated that German citizenship could belong only to those of "German or related blood." Henceforth, Jews were to be subjects only. Even blood, moreover, was not a sufficient condition for citizenship. The state conferred it by granting a certificate. Receipt and retention of citizenship, then, depended less on an unalienable right and more on approved conduct. Second, a "Law for the Protection of German Blood and Honor" prohibited marriage and sexual intercourse between Jews and persons of "German or related blood." Also outlawed were employment in Jewish households of German females under 45 years of age and Jewish display of the Reich's flag.

Such decrees put Jews at the mercy of the German state, but of course the measures could not be fully enforced without a clear definition of what constituted being Jewish. The basic solution was to designate as Jewish anyone having at least three full Jewish grandparents. Also included were persons with two full Jewish grandparents and with any of the following features: belonging to the Jewish religious community as of September 15, 1935, or joining thereafter; being married to a Jew at that date or later; being born from a marriage contracted after September 15, 1935, in which at least one partner was a full or three-quarter Jew; or being born after July 31, 1936, as the illegitimate offspring of extramarital relations involving a full or three-quarter Jew. What to do with those who possessed lesser amounts of Jewish blood remained a problem and required still further categorization and definition. Suffice it to say that these German *Mischlinge* were discriminated against as non-Aryan, but for the most part they escaped death in the gas chambers.

Two footnotes are important. Designation as Jewish was for most people more a matter of fate than of choice; it had relatively little to do with anything one did. (A person could choose to identify as Jewish, but if one fit the definition of being Jewish, that fact was irreversible.) In addition, although blood was the issue, a religious test was decisive in determining the nature of one's blood. To know whether or not one's grandparents were Jewish entailed documentation of their religious identifications or of those of their ancestors. By providing records of births and baptisms, the Christian churches in Germany facilitated the definitional procedures of the Nazis and thereby were implicated in the destruction process early on. Though unaware of the "Final Solution" in 1935, the churches nevertheless contributed to that end.

Summer 1939: Hitler's power approached its zenith. His effort to make all German-controlled territory *Judenrein* (clean of Jews) was well under way. Ever alert to world opinion, Hitler detected no response to dissuade him from proceeding with his anti-Jewish policies. The situation was similar for his plans to obtain *Lebensraum* (living space) for Germans. Annexation of Austria in March 1938 was followed by the Munich Conference (September 29–30), which gave Hitler portions of Czechoslovakia in exchange for Neville Chamberlain's "peace in our time" pronouncements. On August 23, 1939, a pact of nonaggression temporarily neutralized the Soviets. Staging was set for the invasion of Poland on September 1, 1939.

Historians debate the turning points of war. Nevertheless it is safe to say that, with the notable exception of its failure to subdue England by air power, the German war machine had things its own way until reversals at El Alamein and Stalingrad in November 1942. The wasting of European Jews also forged ahead—although not quite apace. Indeed for a year after the war began, Nazi planning still envisioned forced emigration. There proved to be no satisfactory ways, however, to export Jews from soil under German control. One step carried to its conclusion, the next was always more drastic: Jews would have to be eliminated.

Auschwitz came into being as a concentration camp by Himmler's order on April 27, 1940. In the summer of 1941, its capacity was enlarged and modified. Within the next year—along with five other sites in Poland: Chelmno, Belzec, Sobibor, Treblinka, and Majdanek—Auschwitz became a full-fledged *Vernichtungslager* (extermination camp). Chelmno utilized gas-vans. Shooting was the method of choice at Majdanek, while Belzec, Sobibor, and Treblinka piped carbon monoxide into their gas chambers. Auschwitz "improved" the killing by employing fast-working hydrogen cyanide gas, which came in the form of a deodorized pesticide—Zyklon B. Efficiency at Auschwitz was still further improved in 1943 when new crematoria became available for corpse disposal. Optimum production in this largest death factory, however, was not achieved until the summer of 1944—well after the Germans began losing World War II—when ten thousand victims were dispatched per day.

Selective mass killing takes time. But the inference is not that the Nazis took their time. However plans for dealing with the Jews evolved, the officials in charge worked persistently and methodically to implement them. And once the first killing center, Chelmno, became operational in December 1941, Adolf Eichmann and his colleagues carried out extermination tasks as speedily as technology and circumstance permitted. It is arguable whether the Nazis were more interested in securing their gains of territory and resources against Allied opposition, or whether their top priority was elimination of Jews. Certainly the latter was no afterthought, and the Nazi war aims were never separable from their campaigns against the Jews. Jewish slave labor did provide energy for war industries, but transportation, materiel, and manpower were also diverted from military efforts against the Allies and used instead in the war against the Jews.

Timing and linking of events conspired ironically. Even as the Germans' eastern front crumbled—indeed as they were pushed back everywhere—their efforts to destroy the Jews were most successful. When Himmler ordered an end to the systematic killing at Auschwitz in late 1944, his reasoning was not based entirely on the Russian tanks nearby. For all practical purposes, he could argue, the "Final Solution" had answered the Jewish question.

Expulsion, extermination. If the movement from one policy to the other was gradual, what of the intervening steps? An important example occurred on January 20, 1942, at a conference of key Third Reich officials held in the Berlin suburb of Wannsee. Chaired by Reinhard Heydrich, who had been ordered to bring about "a complete solution of the Jewish question in the German sphere of influence in Europe," the conference legitimated a number of policies, many of which were already in practice. The conclusion of this gathering was that the European Jews should be evacuated to centers in occupied Eastern Europe, chiefly Poland. There the able-bodied would form labor gangs. Any survivors—and, by implication, any persons deemed unfit—would be "treated accordingly," the current euphemism for "killed." A massive deportation was soon under way, as trains and transports began to roll all over Europe. Converging on Poland, they fulfilled Hitler's long-standing belief that the only good Jew is a dead Jew.

Two other prologues to the death camps, both of which preceded the Wannsee Conference, also deserve attention. When the Nazis first gained control of Poland and other territories with large Jewish populations, one strategy was to rid entire areas of Jews by isolating them in ghettos. The largest of these ghettos was in Warsaw; at one time it contained a half-million Jews. Uprooted, tormented, overcrowded, starved, diseased, killed in one way or another, the suffering in the ghettos have been rarely paralleled. Although ghetto inhabitants were forced to work for the Nazis, the ghetto itself was never to be more than a temporary arrangement—initially, to be used as a way station for the expulsion effort. Later, and especially the spring of 1942, the ghetto became a staging area for deportations to the recently established killing centers.

Most of the ghettoized Jews, including members of the *Judenräte* (Jewish leadership councils formed at Nazi behest and ordered to facilitate Nazi policy toward the Jews) had little choice but to comply with the Nazis; they hoped that non-provocation would mitigate Nazi terror, or at least increase chances for survival. The first outcome resulted as infrequently as the second. Nonetheless many ghettoized Jews dedicated themselves unsparingly to keeping alive education, culture, and Jewish tradition in the miserable surroundings. There were also those who resisted violently, the most notable insurrection being the Warsaw ghetto uprising in April 1943.

Debates still ensue over the extent, effectiveness, and significance of Jewish resistance in Warsaw and elsewhere, including the death camps themselves. Some accounts stress Jewish passivity and trusting optimism, religiously motivated. They portray Jews as continual, if unwitting, accomplices in their own demise. Counter-interpretations see resistance as varied and widespread—including not only acts of outright violence, startling that they could occur at all under some of the circumstances in which they did appear, but also the determination of Jews to endure day-by-day against despair.

If the debates themselves suggest that the truth resides somewhere in the middle, at least this much is clear: heroic as it surely was, and symbolically important as it certainly remains, violent Jewish resistance—wherever it occurred—lacked the strength of numbers, resources, and especially outside support to be more than a minor roadblock to Nazi objectives. By mid-May 1943, the Warsaw ghetto was liquidated; and again and again, that outcome was repeated throughout the ghettos of Eastern Europe.

Although ghettoization was to kill a half-million Jews in Poland alone, apart from those deported to the killing centers, the Nazi decision to ghettoize the Jews was not yet a decision to annihilate them. Only with the *Einsatzgruppen* did that phase begin.

In the spring of 1941, as plans were laid for invasion of the Soviet Union, Hitler determined that special mobile killing units should be formed. Their task was to follow close on the heels of advancing German troops, round up Jews, and kill them. Four of these more-or-less autonomous teams accompanied the eastern thrust on June 22, 1941. Each team contained up to a thousand men; their leaders included Ph. Ds, lawyers, and other professionals. Operations followed a routine. Typically, having gathered a group of Jews together, the squads forced the victims to dig a large mass grave. After lining up along the edge, the Jews were mowed down with machine guns. At least 34,000 Jews were shot in two days at Babi Yar, near Kiev, in September 1941. Along the Russian front that year alone, about a million Jews lost their lives this way.

As the invasion and the work of the *Einsatzgruppen* proceeded, a die was cast: Hitler initiated the "final solution of the Jewish question" throughout the European continent. Although the Wannsee Conference was not held for nearly six months, plans unfolded. On July 31, 1941, Hermann Goering ordered Heydrich to ensure that the Jewish problem would never have to be solved again. All too soon, camps were prepared; they were ready when the transports delivered their freight. As the *Einsatzgruppen* moved killers toward their victims, a second prong of attack—bringing victims to their killers—became operational.

Words cannot fully describe, nor the mind completely grasp, what went on in the death camps. The magnitude and degree of brutality, suffering, and sorrow are beyond human understanding. And still we try to explain in mere words.

The horror of the death camps extended far down the railroad tracks that carried Jews to death. Jammed onto train cars, Jewish deportees faced long journeys in conditions so unbearable that many persons were dead on arrival. Those still living were routed from the cars at the destination. Thereafter the routine varied from place to place. In some camps—Treblinka, for example—entire transports were sent directly to the gas chambers. At Auschwitz, which was both a labor and a killing installation, a more elaborate procedure was followed.

Men and women were separated. Children, usually those under fourteen, remained with their mothers. Selection by a doctor sent to the right those fit for work; to the left the sick, aged, crippled, and the women with children. The group sent left, prodded by Nazi guards and inmate work crews, moved off to the gas chambers and crematoria of Birkenau, the killing-center section of Auschwitz. They were never seen alive again.

The others, momentary survivors, were left to work, always subject to further "selections" consigning them to gas and flame. What eventually developed was a slave society heretofore unseen in human history: work was performed quite literally by persons on their way to die, not merely due to sickness or weakness, but because more people were available than were needed. To be sure, the Nazis' efforts were at times counterproductive in that they killed specialists who could have been used to good advantage. But particularly in the killing centers themselves, the pattern of "slaves headed for death" was common. There were always substitute slaves readily available for most jobs; often the "reasonable" thing to do was simply to send a worn-out surplus to its death, if not by gas then by planned starvation aimed at getting the most labor for the least cost.

Required work was mainly hard physical labor: mining, road and armament construction, building the factories of I. G. Farben, or, most dismal of all, assignment to a *Sonderkommando* (units whose task it was to remove corpses from the gas chambers, extract gold from teeth, burn the bodies, and clean up the remains). As in all forms of enslavement, inmate status could vary with functions to be performed, and treatment could differ accordingly. At least for Jews, however, any respite from death was intended to be only temporary.

Housing and sanitation were abominable. Beatings, hangings, and shootings occurred at the slightest provocation or with none at all. Bizarre medical experiments performed on human guinea pigs, sexual abuse, disease, torture, and constant fear—every affliction of body and spirit was abundantly and continually present. Apart from infrequent acts of kindness from outsiders and the sharing that inmates could—and often did—provide each other, death was the only release.

Death stalked the barracks relentlessly. Every prisoner was vulnerable, but especially the Jews; and none more so than those forced to work in closest contact with the gas chambers and crematoria. Nazi intent was that there should be no Jewish witnesses. Their own camp personnel was also sworn to silence, and a vocabulary of euphemisms was used to mask murder. As the German armies retreated, the effort to transfer prisoners to camps farther west was matched by the time and energy expended to destroy the physical evidence of camps left behind.

Most people who entered the killing centers never returned. But there were survivors of the Holocaust—thousands of them—a fact both astonishing and yet not surprising. The manufacture of death by the Nazis was efficient. But their task was monumental, extremely complicated, and carried out in circumstances that often entailed chaos. Where any individual was concerned, however, the chances of survival were largely that: matters of *chance*. To be sure, individuals were sustained by family members who survived, by friends—both old and newly made in the camps—by relationships based on nationality, and even by the occasional kindness of a Polish townsperson or a German official. Hidden by farmers, villagers or even by some city dwellers, some Jews managed to avoid the ghettos and camps altogether. Degrees of individual ingenuity often determined survival; there were other factors: to stay alive so the dead would not be forgotten, or that the living would not be forsaken. Nevertheless, no matter how hard one tried, no matter how much hope, faith, or will power an individual possessed, most of the crucial factors in survival were beyond one's personal control: when a person was deported; whether he or she could ward off sickness; whether one might draw a work assignment that would reduce energy output or enable one to obtain better food; whether one could avoid the punishing whims of guards or the caprice of selection; whether there was help of any kind that one could count on.

By late 1944, the killing centers were mostly closed. European Jewry as it had existed before the Nazi era was virtually destroyed. Prisoners remained at Auschwitz, but it, too, was evacuated on January 17–18, 1945. With Hitler's suicide on April 30, and the subsequent surrender of Germany on May 7, a chapter ended. But there was no ending at all. If Europe was not the grave for every Jew who had lived there, most survivors found that it could be called home no more. A new exodus occurred, and Palestine was the frequent destination. Only after more hardship and bloodshed would Israeli independence be achieved in 1948. Meanwhile other people tried to recover, too— among them Germans who found their country wrecked by Hitler's determination that Germany would win the war or perish. As they rebuilt in the ruins, Germans joined British, French, Italians, Americans in facing or denying, remembering or forgetting as quickly as possible, the rise and fall of the Third Reich.

The Holocaust legacy has no end. It stretches from the prosecution of war criminals at Nuremberg in 1945–46 to the trial of Eichmann in Jerusalem in 1961 to a continuing series of Middle Eastern dilemmas whose roots are in the earth at Auschwitz. It is riddled with questions that move beyond this prologue to wonder about the Holocaust and its implications—religious and philosophical, concerning humankind and God. The voices that raise them in the following pages belong mostly to Jews. Many are survivors. Their words flesh out and humanize—try to reduce to scale—the incomprehensible figure of six million that so often stands for "Who?" In another sense, the words written here by those who were not "there" also belong to survivors. Everyone who lives after Auschwitz is affected by the Holocaust. To learn how, read on.

SUGGESTIONS FOR FURTHER READING

Bauer, Yehuda. A History of the Holocaust. New York: Franklin Watts, 1982.
Dawidowicz, Lucy S. The War against the Jews, 1933–1945. New York: Holt, Rinehart and Winston, 1975.

Gilbert, Martin. *The Holocaust: A History of the Jews of Europe during the Second World War.* New York: Holt, Rinehart and Winston, 1985.

Hilberg, Raul. *The Destruction of the European Jews.* 3 vols., rev. ed. New York: Holmes & Meier, 1985.

Kren, George, and Leon Rappoport. *The Holocaust and the Crisis of Human Behavior.* New York: Holmes & Meier, 1980.

Littell, Franklin H. *The Crucifixion of the Jews.* New York: Harper and Row, 1975.

Marrus, Michael R. *The Holocaust in History.* Hanover, N.H.: University Press of New England, 1987.

Mayer, Arno J. *Why Did the Heavens Not Darken? The "Final Solution" in History.* New York: Pantheon Books, 1989.

Oliner, Samuel P., and Pearl M. Oliner. *The Altruistic Personality: Rescuers of Jews in Nazi Europe.* New York: The Free Press, 1988.

Rubenstein, Richard L., and John K. Roth. *Approaches to Auschwitz: The Holocaust and Its Legacy.* Atlanta: John Knox Press, 1987.

Wyman, David S. *The Abandonment of the Jews: America and the Holocaust, 1941–1945.* New York: Pantheon Books, 1984.

Chronology

CRUCIAL HOLOCAUST-RELATED EVENTS
1933–1945

1933

January 30	Adolf Hitler becomes Reich Chancellor.
February 27	The Reichstag fire occurs.
March 9	Heinrich Himmler appointed chief of Munich police.
March 22	Himmler opens the first SS concentration camp at Dachau.
March 23	Reichstag passes the Enabling Act.
April 1	National boycott of Jewish business and professional people.
May 10	Public book-burnings in Germany target Jewish books and works by opponents of Nazism.
July 14	Nazi party established by law as the one and only legal political party in Germany.
July 20	Signing in Rome of a concordat between the Vatican and the Third Reich.
October 19	Germany leaves the League of Nations.

1934

January 26	Ten-year nonaggression pact signed by Germany and Poland.
April 20	Himmler appointed head of Gestapo.
June 30–July 2	Hitler's purge of Ernst Roehm and the SA.

July 20   SS becomes an independent organization and
                           is placed under Hitler with Himmler as
                           chief.

August 2   Death of President von Hindenburg. Hitler
                           becomes "Führer und Reichskanzler" of the
                           German state. Armed forces are required to
                           take a personal oath of loyalty to him.

1935

September 15   Sweeping anti-Jewish legislation passed at
                           Nuremberg.

1936

June 17   Himmler officially named Reichsführer SS and
                           Chief of German Police.

Summer   Germany hosts Summer Olympics: Jesse
                           Owens wins four gold medals.

1937

March 21   Pope Pius XI's encyclical *Mit brennender
                           Sorge* (With Deep Anxiety).

July 16   Buchenwald concentration camp established.

1938

March 12–13   *Anschluss:* Annexation of Austria to the Third
                           Reich.

September 29–30   Munich Conference parties agree to the Ger-
                           man annexation of part of Czechoslovakia.

October 27–28   Expulsion of 17,000 Polish Jews from Ger-
                           many.

November 7   Herschel Grynzspan shoots Ernst vom Rath in
                           Paris.

November 9–10   *Kristallnacht.*

1939

August 23	Soviet-German nonaggression pact signed in Moscow by Molotov and Ribbentrop.
September 1	Germany invades Poland.
September 3	Britain and France declare war on Germany.
September 17	Red Army invades eastern Poland.
September 21	Reinhard Heydrich decrees the establishment of Jewish ghettos and councils in occupied Poland.
November 23	Identity stars required to be worn by Jews in occupied Poland.

1940

Early January	First experimental gassing of mental patients, Jews, and others.
January–February	Jewish youth movements organize underground resistance in Poland.
February 12	Deportation of Jews from Germany to Poland gets under way.
April 27	Himmler orders the establishment of a concentration camp at Auschwitz.
May 1	Lodz ghetto is sealed.
May 20	Concentration camp opens at Auschwitz.
June 4	British evacuation from Dunkirk completed.
October 16	Order for the creation of the Warsaw ghetto.
November 15	Warsaw ghetto sealed off.

1941

May 14	More than 3,600 Jews arrested in Paris.
May 15	Marshal Pétain approves French collaboration with Germany.
June 22	Germany attacks the Soviet Union.

July   Construction of Majdanek concentration camp.
July 31   Goering appoints Heydrich to implement the
                        "Final Solution."
September 3   First experimental gassings with Zyklon B of
                        Soviet prisoners of war in Auschwitz.
September 29–30   Murder of 34,000 Jews at Babi Yar.
October 10   Ghetto established in Theresienstadt.
December 7   Japanese attack Pearl Harbor.
December 8   Chelmno death camp operational near Lodz.
December 11   Germany and Italy declare war on the United
                        States.

1942

January 20   Wannsee Conference members plan how to an-
                        nihilate the European Jews.
January 21   Jewish resistance and partisan groups orga-
                        nized in Vilna and Kovno.
February–March   Evacuation of Polish ghettos and deportation of
                        Jews to extermination camps.
March–July   Killing centers of Belzec, Sobibor, and Tre-
                        blinka made operational.
March 27   First transport of Jews from Paris to Auschwitz.
July 22   First large-scale deportation of Jews from War-
                        saw to Treblinka.
July 28   "Jewish Fighting Organization" established in
                        the Warsaw ghetto.
November 2   Germans defeated at El Alamein.
November 19–22   Red Army counterattacks at Stalingrad.
December 10   First transport of German Jews to Auschwitz.
December 17   Allies resolve to punish Nazis responsible for
                        the mass murder of Jews.

1943

January 18–21   Mordecai Anielewicz leads first armed re-
                        sistance in the Warsaw ghetto.

March 31	New crematorium opens at Auschwitz.
April 19–30	Bermuda Conference produces fruitless discussion about how to rescue Jewish victims of Nazism.
April 19	Liquidation of the Warsaw ghetto begins. Anielewicz leads the Warsaw ghetto revolt.
May 16	Liquidation of the Warsaw ghetto completed.
June 11	Himmler orders liquidation of all ghettos in Poland and the Soviet Union.
August 2	Treblinka prisoners revolt.
October 1–2	The Danes rescue Danish Jews from the Nazis.
October 14	Sobibor prisoners revolt.
October 18	First deportation of Jews from Rome to Auschwitz.

1944

January 22	President Roosevelt establishes the War Refugee Board.
March 19	Hungary occupied by the Germans.
April 2	Jews deported from Athens to Auschwitz.
May–July	Deportation of Hungarian Jews to Auschwitz.
June 6	D Day: Allies invade Normandy.
July 23	Majdanek liberated by Russian troops.
July 20	German officers attempt to assassinate Hitler.
October 7	*Sonderkommando* uprising in Auschwitz.
End of October	Last gassings in Auschwitz.
November 26	Himmler orders Auschwitz crematoria destroyed.

1945

January 17–18	Auschwitz evacuated. Prisoners' "death march" begins.
January 27	Soviet troops liberate Auschwitz.

April 11–May 4	The Allies liberate concentration camps at Buchenwald, Bergen-Belsen, Dachau, Mauthausen, and Theresienstadt.
April 30	Hitler commits suicide.
May 7	Nazi Germany surrenders unconditionally to the Allies.
May 8	V-E Day.
November 1945– October 1946	War crime trials held at Nuremberg.

THE CONCENTRATION CAMPS

Between 1939 and 1945, six million unarmed and innocent Jewish civilians—men, women, children and babies—were murdered in Nazi-controlled Europe, as part of a deliberate policy to destroy all traces of Jewish life and culture. As many as two million of these were killed in their own towns and villages, some confined in ghettos where death by slow starvation was a deliberate Nazi policy, others taken to be shot at mass-murder sites near where they lived. The remaining four million Jews were forced from their homes and taken by train to distant concentration camps, where they were murdered by being worked to death, starved to death, beaten to death, shot, or gassed.

North Sea

Vaivara

Klooga
ESTONIA

LATVIA

LITHUANIA

USSR

Stutthof

Neuengamme   Ravensbrück
Bergen-Belsen   Sachsenhausen
                              Chelmno   Treblinka
Mittelbau Dora   Gross   POLAND
Buchenwald   Rosen   Sobibor
GERMANY   Auschwitz   Majdanek
Flossenberg   Plaszow   Belzec
CZECHOSLOVAKIA
Natzweiler
FRANCE   Dachau
Mauthausen
AUSTRIA   HUNGARY
RUMANIA

Gospič   Jasenovac
YUGOSLAVIA
Sajmište

Adriatic Sea

ITALY

Among the hundreds of thousands of non-Jews sent by the Nazis to concentration camps were anti-Nazis, Jehovah's Witnesses, homosexuals, the mentally ill, and the chronically sick. In addition, more than 250,000 Gypsies were murdered, in a Nazi attempt to eliminate Gypsies as well as Jews from the map of Europe.

Auschwitz concentration camp in which more than 2 *million* people were murdered between 1941 and 1944, including Jews, Gypsies, and Soviet prisoners-of-war.

Camps set up solely for the murder of Jews.

Other camps in which Jews and non-Jews were put to forced labor, starved, tortured, and murdered in conditions of the worst imaginable cruelty. Most of these camps had "satellite" labor camps nearby.

In many of the camps shown here, so-called "medical" experiments were carried out, without anesthetics, solely to satisfy the curiosity and sadism of the doctors. Hundreds of otherwise healthy "patients" were tortured and murdered during these experiments.

0   100 miles
0   100 km

© Martin Gilbert 1978

"The Concentration Camps" map from *The Holocaust* by Martin Gilbert. Copyright (1978) by Martin Gilbert. Reprinted by permission of Hill and Wang, a division of Farrar, Straus and Giroux, Inc.

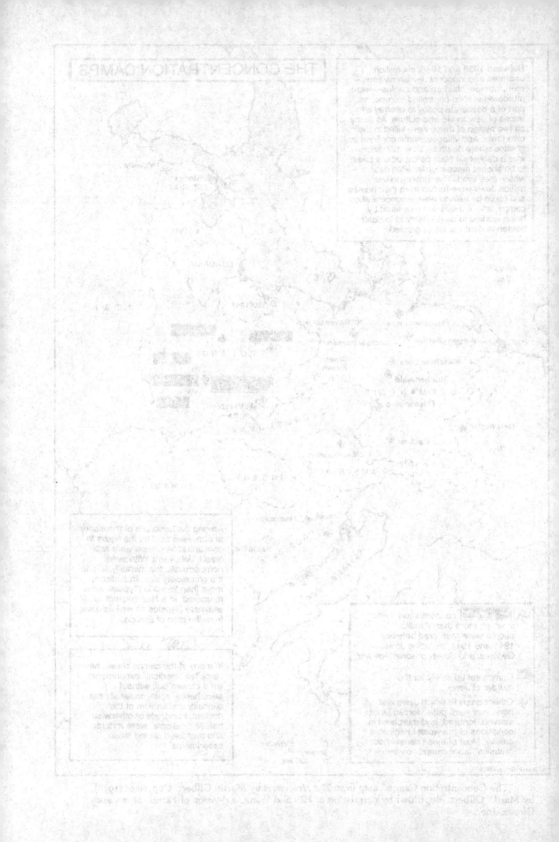

HOLOCAUST

PART ONE

"What If the Holocaust *Is* Unique?"

(EMIL FACKENHEIM, *To Mend the World*)

> How are you able to resist despair? How are you able to resist?
>
> *Easy. Whenever something pleasant happens, I close my eyes and see myself thirty years ago; and whatever seems good is not so good, after all. And whenever sadness and disappointment enter my life, I close my eyes and see myself thirty years ago; and what seems terrible is not so terrible after all.*
>
> ELIE WIESEL, "A Father and His Son," *A Jew Today*

In the introduction to his magnum opus, *To Mend the World: Foundations of Future Jewish Thought,* Emil Fackenheim writes of the "denial syndrome" that tempts intellectuals to doubt the uniqueness of the Holocaust. "It is hard to believe," Fackenheim admits, "that a unique event of catastrophic import should have happened in one's own lifetime." Especially so, when one is touched by the event directly, as was Fackenheim who was imprisoned in Sachenhausen concentration camp. Perhaps "the feeling of uniqueness is the mere result of one's own traumas," Fackenheim cautions. Furthermore, if the event is to be confronted in thought, "then an appropriate category—in philosophy, radical-evil-in-general, in theology, the demonic-in-general—seems sufficient to meet the case." If so, no new categories are needed; the event can be contained and explained by the previous categories of conventional thought. Finally, Fackenheim notes: "There is the well-known philosophical problem whether the unique—the unique of any kind—can be thought at all."

1

"But," he still wonders, "what if the Holocaust *is* unique?" While the arguments for its uniqueness are complex and subtle, he believes that the plain facts of the Holocaust—those which are beyond dispute—produce a configuration without parallel in history. However painful and difficult the conclusion may be, Fackenheim concludes that the Holocaust, undeniably, is a *novum* in history.

Fackenheim lists essential elements that he takes to distinguish the Holocaust from previous atrocities. First of all, the intention behind and the scope of the Holocaust were unprecedented. One-third of the Jewish people were murdered in the Holocaust, and Jewish survival itself was endangered. The Nazis' primary goal was total annihilation of the Jewish people (rather than conversion, persecution, the conquest of land, or political power). Moreover, the Nazis sought to eliminate an entire people—men, women, and children—solely because of their birth to Jewish grandparents and irrespective of their religious identity or faith. Jews were killed not for *what* they were but for *the fact* that they were. "Their 'crime,'" observes Fackenheim, "was Jewish existence." The destruction of the Jews was not a means to a goal but an *end in itself*. Among the perpetrators, the tone-setters were "idealists, except that their ideals were torture and murder."

Most of the scholars whose works are included in this book share Fackenheim's view that the Holocaust was an epoch-making event, an experience that demands a rethinking of traditional understandings of God and history. By reading their essays, you can ponder what constitutes the uniqueness of the Holocaust. None of these writers goes quite as far as Elie Wiesel, who rules out all comparisons to the Holocaust. He regards the Holocaust as entirely dissimilar to all other catastrophes. He considers all analogies to the Holocaust sacrilegious. Consider Wiesel's criticism of the widely successful 1978 television docudrama entitled *Holocaust*:

> The series treats the Holocaust as if it *were* just another event. . . . Whether culmination or aberration of history, the Holocaust transcends history. Everything about it inspires fear and leads to despair. The dead are in possession of a secret that we, the living, are neither worthy of nor capable of recovering.
>
> Art and Theresienstadt were perhaps compatible in Theresienstadt but not here—not in a television studio. The same is true of prayer

and Buchenwald, faith and Treblinka. A film about Sobibor is either not a picture or not about Sobibor. . . .

The Holocaust? The ultimate event, the ultimate mystery, never to be comprehended or transmitted.

While Wiesel and Fackenheim are widely respected, their views do not enjoy universal acceptance. A diverse group of Jewish thinkers strenuously dispute these positions; an equally diverse group of Christian and secular thinkers find their arguments parochial, evasive, or false. Since virtually all of the essays you will read consider the Holocaust unique, it is important that we explore together the contemporary debate. At a time when plans for a United States national memorial to the Holocaust go forward, and the subject of the Holocaust is taught in school systems and universities, the debate has political overtones. It creates ethnic tensions and is potentially the cause of acrimony.

No one can deny that the Holocaust was a catastrophe for the Jewish people. The slaughter of six million Jews, including more than one and a half million children, is simply too tragic an event to be dismissed as insignificant. Nevertheless, there are some Jewish thinkers who insist that the Holocaust is just another event in the long record of Jewish suffering—less consequential, some would argue, than the destruction of the first and second Temples; though surely more important than the 1492 expulsion of Jews from Spain, or the 1648 Chmielnicki massacres in the Ukraine. After all, these thinkers claim, martyrdom and misery have often been the lot of Jews throughout their long and painful history. After each catastrophe Jewish faith has confronted the suffering, and Jews have remained faithful to the covenant. Most Jews who minimize the uniqueness of the Holocaust are believers for whom too much is at stake, too much at risk, to allow a more radical reexamination of the assumptions of faith.

Other Jewish leaders deny the uniqueness of the Holocaust on purely political grounds; they are disturbed that the memory of the Holocaust is exploited to raise funds for Israel, justify Jewish particularism devoid of substantive content, or defend Jewish militarism.

The most serious Jewish critique on the emphasis of the Holocaust's uniqueness comes from those thinkers who fear that the recollection of destruction is inadequate to sustain the Jewish future. For example, Michael Wyschogrod, a philosopher at the City University of New York who fled from Germany shortly before the World War II, has repeatedly challenged Fackenheim's views. Wyschogrod writes: "Israel's faith has always centered on the saving acts of God: the election, the Exodus, the Temple, and the Messiah. However more prevalent destruction was in the history of Israel, the acts of destruction were enshrined in minor fast days while those of redemption became the joyous proclamation of Passover and Tabernacles. . . . The God of Israel is a redeeming God; this is the only message we are authorized to proclaim." Nevertheless, in Part Three of this anthology, survivors, theologians, and rabbis ask: How is it possible to speak of a redeeming God in a world of Auschwitz?

Jacob Neusner, Brown University's Ungeleider Distinguished Scholar of Judaica and University Professor, objects to the vacuous quality of Jewish consciousness that is rooted in the Holocaust. He regards the entire enterprise as theologically doomed to failure. Neusner writes: "The Judaic system of Holocaust and Redemption [the restoration of the Jews in the State of Israel] leaves unaffected the larger dimensions of human existence of Jewish Americans—and that is part of that system's power." As people look for answers to the various problems of their lives, the vicariousness of American Jewry's new theology will not serve them well.

Neusner also bemoans the demise of the intellect in American Jewish life. American Judaism that stresses the Holocaust-and-redemption theme works only with "the raw materials made available by contemporary experience—emotions on the one side, and politics on the other. Access to realms beyond require learning in literature, the only resource beyond the immediate." Neusner insists that a Judaism of Holocaust and redemption is not the product of intellectuals but bureaucrats—fundraisers, administrators, and public relations managers. "The correlation between mass murder and a culture of organizations," he argues, "proves exact: the war against the Jews called forth from the Jews people capable of building institutions to protect the collectivity of Israel, so far as anyone could be saved. Consequently much was saved. But much was lost."

In the end, however, even the most distinguished historian and empiricist must contend with the Holocaust's religious implications. For instance, Neusner writes: "The first century found its enduring memory in one man on a hill, on a cross; the twentieth, in six million men, women, and children making up a Golgotha, a hill of skulls of their own. No wonder that the Judaism of the age struggled heroically to frame a Judaic system appropriate to the issue of the age. No wonder they failed. Who would want to succeed in framing a world view congruent to such an age, a way of life to be lived in an age of death." In response, we must ask whether any theology can be authentic in the aftermath of Auschwitz and its accompanying nuclear age if it does not confront the overwhelming legacy and proximity of death.

Even those thinkers who agree that the Holocaust is unique differ in their understanding of *why* it is unique. They generally fall on one side or another of the functionalist/intentionalist debate. This debate is not to be confused with the functionalist/intentionalist debate currently rampant in Holocaust historiography, in which the intentionalists attribute the Holocaust to a deliberate ideology present in Nazism from the very beginning, and the functionalists see the Holocaust as an evolving policy that responded to new, unanticipated conditions. With respect to the uniqueness of the Holocaust, intentionalists speak of the unique ideology of the perpetrators; the Nazi aim was the elimination of an entire people in order to alter fundamentally the human community. The Nazis' pursuit of "the 'Final Solution' to the Jewish problem" was relentless from 1919 onward. Thus, Lucy Dawidowicz begins her important work, *The War Against the Jews*, with a chapter on Hitler's view of the Jews that directly links Hitler's genocidal fantasies of 1919 to the policies implemented by him and his followers two decades later. Furthermore, the intentionalists argue that Nazi Germany considered the elimination of Jews the prescription for national salvation.

In contrast, while the functionalists do not deny the role of ideology, they emphasize that the uniqueness of the Holocaust stemmed from the unprecedented institutions created gradually by the Nazis— institutions that eventually became devoted exclusively to the production of death. These theorists stress *l' univers concentrationnaire*, the world of extermination camps that grew and consumed millions of lives as it did so.

We will read further about the debate concerning the uniqueness of the Holocaust in Part Two when we consider life inside the camps, and once again in Part Three when we address the presence (or absence) of God in the Holocaust. But first the focus is on articles by scholars who maintain that the Holocaust is unique from both functionalist and intentionalist perspectives.

The question of the uniqueness of the Holocaust is not restricted to Jewish scholars. The most extreme critics of the uniqueness position are those people who feel that an emphasis on Jewish experience appears to overlook the death of millions of other people who suffered and perished alongside the Jews. Some object to claims that Jews were the primary victims. We will not consider the crudest form of this argument, such as the Russian omission of all mention of Jews at the Babi Yar memorial—erected on the site where the Jewish population of Kiev was murdered in 1941. The inscription on the monument recalls the slaughtered "citizens of the U.S.S.R.," deliberately obscuring the Jewish identity of the victims. Similarly, we reject the former Polish insistence that six million Poles were killed by the Nazis, a claim that failed to delineate the 3.1 million Jews who were annihilated as Jews and not as part of the German policy against Poles.

When Jews argue for uniqueness on historical grounds, some thinkers see evidence of unwarranted Jewish ethnocentricity. Professor Ian Hancock, a Romani [Gypsy] scholar, has asked: "What constitutes 'uniqueness'? Is it a matter of who was victimized earlier? Or the extent of the agonies endured? Or numbers lost? It seems quite tasteless to engage in one-upsmanship of suffering or in this case to quote numbers."

John Cuddihy has offered a sociological rather than a historical analysis of the problem of uniqueness. The "residual category" of non-Jews that continues to divide the world serves three critical functions for Jews. It preserves the sacred particularity of the Jews, freezing the presence of antisemitism in Jewish consciousness and thus eliminating the Sartresque question: "Why remain a Jew?" It continues to separate the Jew from the gentile not on the basis of Jewish free-choice but because of a decision imposed by Hitler. Finally, according to Cuddihy, uniqueness functions not so much to prevent historical fraud, denial, or dejudaization but as a continuing device for conferring status.

Cuddihy and Hancock ask penetrating questions: Why should the fate of the Jews be treated differently than the fate of the Gypsies or the Poles, the Jehovah's Witnesses or the gays, the Tartars or the Russian POWs, or millions of other civilian victims killed by the Nazis? Why, they ask, should the Holocaust be considered different than the Armenian genocide that preceded it, or the Cambodian genocide that followed it? Why not speak of the genocide of Native Americans or of black slaves? Why harp on the Holocaust?

The answer will be found in these essays. André Neher writes of multiple levels of silence that characterized the Holocaust—total si lence implicating humanity, history, and divinity. Gerd Korman relates the origins of the word "Holocaust," which denotes a unique event in history and suggests its most ultimate meaning. Yehuda Bauer argues that the Holocaust differs from genocide, from the experience of the Armenians and the Gypsies. Only by considering how the Holocaust differs can we confront history directly and face the scandal of its particularity. Lucy Dawidowicz compellingly presents the case that the Holocaust's uniqueness is found in its intent. In one essay, Michael Berenbaum disputes the view of Jewish thinkers, such as David W. Weiss, who deny that the Holocaust is unique in Jewish history and who blunt its radical religious implications. In another, Berenbaum maintains that the uniqueness of the Holocaust may begin with intent but is drastically different than other events in fact as well—that is, in form, scope, and quality. These dimensions can only be understood through informed historical comparisons. Berenbaum unites both the functionalist and intentionalist understanding of the Holocaust as a unique, seminal event in Western culture, a turning point that can only be ignored at our peril.

The tone of some discussions surrounding the question of the Holocaust's uniqueness demeans the memory of the victims and denigrates the seriousness of the intellectual issues at stake. Often these discussions degenerate into name calling and inter-ethnic strife. But in the essays presented in this anthology, the problem is probed with intellectual and moral rigor to match the insight contained in Elie Wiesel's dialogue between "A Father and His Son" with which Part One began. The survivor-son responds to the questions of a father who did not survive. What happened "then" gives every reason to despair now, but despair can and must be resisted so that "then" is neither forgotten nor allowed to have the last word. Life must be chosen, but it should be chosen with lucidity against the darkness of the Holocaust, which has changed everything before and after—even if that fact at times goes unrecognized.

These essays point to the uniqueness of the Holocaust as a fact and not as an article of faith alone. The systematic, bureaucratic extermination of an entire people—men, women, and children—solely because of the identity of their grandparents was an end in itself, a massive attempt to change the human species by eliminating one people. It resulted in the creation of major institutions of death, factories of murder staffed by the elite of one of Western society's most civilized nations. Death became an end and not a means; it was pursued with a fervor more intense than the war effort against the Allies. The Jews were the central target of the Nazi regime.

As we shall see, the Holocaust was unprecedented. Common to all these essays is the consensus that the term "unique" when applied to the Holocaust is in no way celebrative. Nor does it confer status. All these writers share the hope that the Holocaust will remain unique in human history, a warning against inhumanity and not a blueprint for future genocide.

ONE OF THE LEADING thinkers in contemporary Judaism, André Neher (1914–1988) was born in 1914 in Obernoi, France, and studied at the University of Strasbourg. During the Holocaust, he survived in southern France. Neher completed his Ph.D. dissertation on the prophet Amos and taught biblical and Jewish studies at the University of Strasbourg, where a chair was established for him.

Trained in philosophy and biblical literature, a joining of historical rigor and intellectual sophistication that reminds his readers of Martin Buber, Neher approaches philosophy with the passion of a prophet and the Bible with the critical stance of a philosopher. In 1967, he moved to Jerusalem. His books include *Moses and the Vocation of the Jewish People; The Prophetic Existence;* and *Biblical History of the People Israel* as well as *The Exile of the Word: From the Silence of the Bible to the Silence of Auschwitz,* which won the 1978 Remembrance Award in Jerusalem. The following selection is from that award-winning work.

Auschwitz is about silence. Therein lies an important element in the Holocaust's uniqueness. The victims often chose silence, and the survivors—even when they speak—evoke silence. The bystanders were silent. So were the perpetrators. "In our history, this is an unwritten and never-to-be-written page of glory"—that is how SS leader Heinrich Himmler described the "Final Solution." Apparently even God was silent. For Neher, that silence is more alarming than all the others.

Perhaps God's silence is more enduring, too.

André Neher

The Silence of Auschwitz

"After Auschwitz . . ."

Is philosophy yet ready for an evaluation of Auschwitz as an example of universal human suffering? If one is to judge from intellectual reactions during the past thirty years, one may doubt it, so superficial, timid, and often irresponsible have they been. Most recent studies of suffering have omitted any reference to Auschwitz, some preferring to substitute for the sufferings of Auschwitz those of Hiroshima or Dresden.* Few are the philosophic enquiries that have attempted a frontal interrogation of Auschwitz.†

Now Auschwitz is, above all, silence. This has been doubtless better understood by the poets than by the philosophers, for silence pervades them as soon as they say "Auschwitz." One of them, Uri Zvi Greenberg, seeking a single word to express the quality for which the martyrs of Auschwitz are distinguished in time and eternity, chose the word silence: the martyrs of Auschwitz are the "Martyrs of Silence."‡ And Elie Wiesel has built his entire work around silence; his books are like perpetual variations on that theme.

From André Neher, *The Exile of the Word: From the Silence of the Bible to the Silence of Auschwitz*, trans. David Maisel. Philadelphia: The Jewish Publication Society of America, 1981. This portion of the English translation from the French is reprinted by permission.

* In his large volume *Parousia* (subtitled *Hoffnung und Prophetie*, Heidelberg, 1960), the Protestant theologian Paul Schutz asks the burning question, "Has Christianity been unworthy of its Message of Hope?" He bases his reply on considerations arising out of the political and ideological conflict of East and West, but fails to mention Auschwitz as bearing witness to the failure of the West.

† We should call attention to the remarkable study by the Catholic thinker Gerd H. Theunissen, *Zwischen Golgotha und Auschwitz* (Cologne, 1959), and the inspiring works of the Jewish thinkers Emil Fackenheim and Eliezer Berkovits.

‡ Uri Zvi Greenberg, *Rehovot ha-nahar*, Jerusalem, 1956.

First, there is the silence of the "concentrational" city closed in upon itself, its victims, and its executioners, separated from the outside world by concentric circles of Night and Fog ("night and fog" was the term used by the Nazis to describe the policy of secrecy and concealment surrounding the concentration camps). This first form of silence, this gulf between Auschwitz and the world, as impenetrable as the deep, should never be forgotten when we mention Hiroshima, Dresden, or Coventry in the same phrase or in the same breath as Auschwitz. There is simply no comparison to be made; one cannot possibly compare Auschwitz to anything else. For at Hiroshima, Dresden, and Coventry events were clamorous, and the cry of suffering immediately reached out and gripped the entire world: war communiqués boasted or condemned; free witnesses were on the spot; assistance, effective or unavailing (no matter), at any rate came rushing up immediately. But at Auschwitz everything unfolded, was fulfilled and accomplished for weeks, months, and years on end in absolute silence, away from and out of the mainstream of history.

Then there is the silence of those few who finally understood, but who took refuge in an attitude of prudence, perplexity, and incredulity. This was the silence of the beholder, transgressing the iron law of Leviticus 5:1.

Lastly, there is the silence of God, which continues when the other rings of silence have been broken, and by that very fact is all the more serious and alarming. The approaches to this triple silence lead, if not to an impasse, then at least to a full-scale inversion of values, none of which can any longer claim to express reality as such, except through a total change of significance, forcing men to search where nothing can be found. It was this idea which was given prominence by Theodor W. Adorno, one of the first philosophers to use phrases such as "after Hegel and Auschwitz." The very title of his book, *Negative Dialectics*, is significant, relationships between things "after Auschwitz" being possible only in a vacant area, in a sort of philosophic no man's land.*

Auschwitz is like some perilous passage between the rocks where the millenial adventure of human thought met with absolute disaster. It went down in darkness, without even the ray of a lighthouse to indicate where it had been. It is a return to chaos, which we must first

* Theodor W. Adorno, *Negative Dialectics*, trans. E. B. Ashton, New York, 1973.

have the courage to enter if we wish to find our way out of it; otherwise there can be only false exits, spurious thought without any grasp of reality. Perhaps, moreover, entering into Auschwitz may encourage thought to make its dwelling there, and will spur it on to renew itself from within and to take, at last, the first step, which alone is absolutely free and which consists of self-creation out of nothingness. Did the world not spring up *ex nihilo*, out of such a creative act? The first step after Auschwitz then seems to be the one which would place us at the exact moment when nothing any longer exists but when all may be again. It is the moment of Silence, of that Silence which once, at the beginning of the world, held back the Word while also being its womb; of that Silence which at Auschwitz but a short while ago was identified with the history of the world.

A Total Collapse

For Auschwitz was a total collapse: quite simply the abandonment of men—of men, women, and children—who died an entirely mortal death whose disastrousness is demonstrated in its very limits.

That is why the Jewish experience at Auschwitz is so incapable of appraisal. Nothing, indeed, has been able to compensate for Auschwitz. The six million people who died at Auschwitz, at Treblinka, at Maidanek, at Bergen-Belsen died in the most inexorable reality of the term. The brutal, planned perfection of "concentrational" death instituted a new kind of death in the history of humanity. Death at Auschwitz bears comparison with no form of death known from the beginning of history until now. Until the twentieth century, such a death was unthinkable; it will forever be irrecompensable.

Auschwitz was a total collapse whose absolute starkness was further illustrated by its universal aspect. The meta-Jewish participation in the death of Auschwitz—the physical participation of the entire gypsy people, of so many non-Jews, Christians and Marxists, who died with the Jews, with the death of the Jews, the participation of the whole of humanity through the sheer enormity of all that was introduced into history through Auschwitz—this participation establishes the universal character of the disaster of Auschwitz.

And yet, from the disaster of Auschwitz there has sprung up hope, a hope which in Theunissen's fine expression is "fully human, stored up for the D-day of our distress"; and our astonishment before the uniqueness of the disaster of Auschwitz is only equaled by our amazement before the uniqueness of the hope which the Jews have extracted from Auschwitz like a springtime risen from the ruins. . . .

Improvisation Made Flesh and History

In creating man free, God introduced into the universe an element of extreme incertitude which no divine or divinatory wisdom, no mathematical calculation, no prayer even, could foresee or anticipate or incorporate into a predetermined design. Free man is improvisation made flesh and history; he is the absolutely unforeseeable; he is the limit which the directive forces of the creative plan encounter, and no one is able to foretell whether this limit may be crossed or whether, because of the mighty barrier it raises against them, it will compel these creative forces to retreat, by this shock of repercussion endangering the whole plan of the creation. Free man is God's dividing of the waters: those below, separated from those above, are henceforward to live from themselves.

According to Jewish tradition, the inception of this risk of God's is to be found in the curious statement *na'ase adam*, "let us make man," in Gen. 1:26. Whom is God addressing in this weighty moment of decision, when the plan of creating man hardly seems possible without the cooperation of some force other than the divine creative force? The angels? The world? Himself? Without dismissing prematurely any of these possibilities, the Sages finally suggest that God's call is addressed to man, to the potential Adam who is envisaged in God's plan but who can be brought into being only through a cooperation between man and God. "Let us make man," the two of us—you, man, and Me, God—and this Covenant establishes forever the liberty of man, whom it makes forever the partner of God.

Thus the initial phases in the unfolding drama of history are stages of apprenticeship in liberty. It is as though God were testing man, were forcing him to prove his liberty like a resistant steel, as though God had decided to try this creature He had endowed with freedom, and, having put him through the test, sought means of strengthening him further, of identifying him even more closely with his liberty.

There was a risk, however, that the point might be reached where man was completely unified with his liberty and that henceforth, with all the consequences it would inevitably entail, the angelic as well as the bestial condition would be definitely barred to man. There was a risk, as Maimonides* acutely observed, that liberty would become man's physical law not only potentially but in act, that this liberty which God had envisaged for man would invest him in a real and actual garment, that it would remain with him day by day, that it would accompany him in his thoughts, his history, and his sufferings, and that he would now be bound only by a single constraint, that, precisely, of being free. In the universe, where every creature has its law and cannot follow or acquire any other than its own, man's law is to be free. In the infinite landscape of the creation, he represents the special reserve of liberty. Inviolable, safe and secure from all other forces than its own, this reserve can dwell infinitely cloistered on itself, a peaceful enclosure.

But it can also at any moment overflow, burst the barriers, explode, and, up to the very end of days and the limits of space, threaten to invade, destroy, or sublimate the creation, to wrench it away from God with a brutal gesture or to restore it to Him in a completely new springtime, to offer it up to damnation or redemption. And it is this risk—this great risk of entrusting man, and him alone, with the formidable keys of choice—which God takes upon himself when He calls upon man, when from Adam to Abraham and down to Moses a tentative dialogue is joined, comes apart, and is joined again, when, in Ernst Bloch's vigorous expression, God expects men to be the "switchmen" of history.

---

* Moses Maimonides, *Mishneh Torah: The Book of Knowledge*, V, 5, 4.

OVER THE PAST two decades, Yehuda Bauer has established his reputation as the preeminent Israeli scholar of the Holocaust. Born in Prague, Czechoslovakia, in 1926, his family emigrated to Israel prior to World War II. A young *halutz* (pioneer), he became a member of *Hashomer Hatzair* (the young guardians), a socialist Zionist youth movement. To this day, despite his academic prominence as the Jonah M. Machover Professor of Holocaust Studies and the head of the International Center for the Study of Anti-Semitism at the Hebrew University in Jerusalem, Bauer continues to reside on Kibbutz Shoval in the Negev, a successful collective community in which all property and income are shared.

Editor of the journal *Holocaust and Genocide Studies*, Bauer is a distinguished historian whose books include *From Diplomacy to Resistance: A History of Jewish Palestine, 1939–45; They Chose Life: Jewish Resistance in the Holocaust; My Brother's Keeper: A History of the American Jewish Joint-Distribution Committee; The Holocaust in Historical Perspective; The Jewish Emergence From Powerlessness; American Jewry and the Holocaust;* and *A History of the Holocaust.* His work is detailed and precise. His conclusions are appropriately modest, the result of years of combing through archives and sifting through mountains of information.

Bauer dares to ask large questions. In the essay we have selected, Bauer brings his precision to bear on defining the uniqueness of the Holocaust. Bauer's answer is strictly empirical. As a Jewish nationalist and ardent humanist, he distinguishes between genocide and the Holocaust and views the uniqueness of the latter in the intentionality of the perpetrator, who sought to eliminate an entire people from the earth solely because they were the descendants of Jews. In doing so, the Nazis linked the elimination of Jews to the salvation of Germany. Even an empiricist like Bauer resorts to religious terminology when describing the Nazi passion for murder: "The Nazis viewed the destruction of the Jews as a quasi-apocalyptic redemptive event."

Bauer analyzes the differences between Nazi policy toward Slavs, political prisoners, homosexuals, and the infirm as well as Gypsies—who shared much of the Jews' fate without being, in Bauer's words, "victims of the Holocaust." He also probes the experience of the Armenians, who were victims of genocide a generation earlier, as well as the "auto-genocide" that he sees in Stalin's anti-kulak campaign of the 1930s and in the Cambodian debacle of the 1970s.

The distinctions Bauer ponders are not intended to create a calculus of calamity, to separate one victim from another, or to demean the suffering of any people. Rather, they are offered to focus our attention on the precise nature of the Nazi enterprise and the unprecedented dimensions of the Holocaust.

Genocide, suggests Bauer, refers most accurately to "the planned destruction . . . of a racial, national, or ethnic group as such" that stops short of "the planned physical annihilation, for ideological or pseudo-religious reasons, of all the members of a national, ethnic or racial group." The Holocaust differs precisely because it aimed at "the total extermination of a people."

The ideology of the killer may vary. For the Nazis, killing the Jews was a moral command of the German nation; for the Turks, killing Armenians was perceived as a practical necessity. For the victim, of course, there is cold comfort in the ideological differences that killers may exhibit. That point leads Bauer to warn that, "being general, as well as specific, the term holocaust carries with it the implication that, because it happened once, it may happen again—to any group if conditions are right."

As an objective historian, Bauer has described the conditions that lead to genocide and holocaust. As a moral man, he has spent much time over the past several years seeking to develop an early warning system to predict genocide and implement practical measures to prevent its occurrence.

Yehuda Bauer

The Place of the Holocaust in Contemporary History[1]

In recent discussions on the place of the Holocaust in the history of our century, there has been a clear tendency to find a way to reconcile the concept of its uniqueness with the idea of its universal importance. Most observers feel that both concepts are valid and indeed can hardly exist without each other. However, such attempts rarely link definitions with historical analyses of what the Holocaust actually was. It is therefore essential to devote attention first of all to questions of definition.

The Holocaust is the name now customarily used in English for the planned total annihilation of the Jewish people, and the actual murder of six million of them at the hands of the Nazis and their auxiliaries.[2] What sets the Holocaust apart from other crimes committed by Nazis, or by others, against many millions of other people, was neither the number of victims nor the way of their murder, nor the proportion of the murdered compared to the total number of the targeted victims. Many more Russians were murdered by the Nazis than Jews. In past history there have been cases in which a much higher proportion of a given community was annihilated than the thirty-five percent of the Jewish people that died in the Holocaust. And, while most of the victims of the gas chambers were Jews, some were not—Gypsies, Soviet POWs and others.

What made the Holocaust different from other cases of what is loosely termed "genocide" was the motivation behind it. It is perfectly clear that Nazi ideology saw in the Jew the non-human antithesis of

From Jonathan Frankel, ed., *Studies in Contemporary Judaism*, Vol. 1. Bloomington: Indiana University Press, 1984. This volume was published by Indiana University Press for the Institute of Contemporary Jewry, The Hebrew University of Jerusalem. Reprinted by permission.

what it considered to be the human ideal: the German Aryan. In the controversy regarding the problem of whether there was a Nazi ideology or not, it seems obvious that there were some tenets that were generally held by the Nazi elite, whether or not they constitute an ideology. Above all, there was the Manichean approach that saw in the world victory of the Germanic Aryans not only a geopolitical necessity for the survival of the Germanic race and its peoples, but a precondition for the continued existence of humankind. At the other pole stood the Jew, a Satanic element and a parasitic one, both weak and contemptible, and yet also immensely powerful and absolutely evil.

The Jew, though he looked human, was not. He controlled most of the world through his control of both capitalism and Russian Bolshevism; only Germany and, to an extent, England were still outside his grasp. His victory was imminent, and with it the destruction not only of Germany, but of all humanity. Germany's war against its enemies was therefore waged for two complementary reasons: the "positive" one of ensuring the victory of the Germanic peoples in Europe, and then in the entire world; and the "negative" one, of defeating the Jewish Satan and his world government. The former was unattainable except through the latter. [3]

An analysis of the events leading up to World War II and of the war itself shows that the expansionist policies of Nazi Germany were motivated primarily not by concrete German interests—political or strategic or economic—but rather by ideological considerations. These were expressed often enough in no unmistakable terms, but some historians tend to ignore documents that do not fit into their preconceived picture. Nazi Germany sought "Lebensraum" for the Germanic peoples (primarily, but by no means solely, for the Germans) so that they might control Europe and the world; in order to do so, war had to be waged against enemies, who were united by the arch-enemy that lurked behind all of them: the Jew. The anti-Jewish struggle was one of the two inextricably connected motivations which underlay the Nazi decision to wage World War II. The struggle against the Jews was a crucial part of the Nazi eschatology, an absolutely central pillar of their world-view, and not just one part of their program. The future of humanity depended on their "victory" over the Jew. This pseudo-religious motivation made their anti-Jewish actions unprecedented. There could be no exceptions to the murder of Jews, once that was decided upon, because Satan had to be extirpated completely, or else he would arise again. Anyone with three Jewish grandparents was sentenced to death, and the principle was that anyone with two Jewish grandparents should either be killed or sterilized. What was unique in the Holocaust was the totality of its ideology and of its translation of abstract thought into planned, logically implemented total murder. More than that—it became a central part of the rationale for a total war that caused some 35 million casualties[4] in the six-year long struggle. That is the uniqueness of the Holocaust.

What is the universality of that experience?

Mass murder of noncombatants in times of war or of quasi-peace has been with us since time immemorial. Massacres of civilian populations by conquering or marauding armies or police can be documented for most of human history. The very concept of mass murder, however, is highly problematical. When does murder become mass murder? With ten victims? Or a hundred? Or a thousand? When somebody causes mass starvation and epidemics—is that mass murder? When masses of prisoners are killed, is that on the same level as the murder of civilians? When, in the course of World War I, masses of soldiers were killed by gas, was that mass murder, or an acceptable taking of life in the course of armed action?

A detailed comparative analysis of such occurrences in past centuries is a task for the future. But, it may be argued, is not this all too scholastic? If a person was murdered at Verdun by German gas, at Dresden by British bombers, at Auschwitz by gassing, at Hiroshima by atomic fallout or at My Lai by an American bullet—or in the thirteenth century at Isfahan by a Mongol knife—it is all the same. Or is it? We do, after all, differentiate between different types of good. We know that there is a difference, however hard it may be to define, between helping an old lady across the street, and rescuing that same old lady from a burning building. We try to differentiate between different types of—in this case—socially commendable action which we call morally good, because we accept the Kantian approach which would see in such action an example to be, ideally, universally followed. In order that that may be so, we grade and differentiate. In effect, we usually do the same with actions that most of us would consider to be evil. In human history, judicial norms have clearly differentiated between crimes according to socially accepted criteria of what was seen as more serious or less so. The argument presented here is that the same consideration applies to different types of arbitrary life-taking. True, it makes, perhaps, no difference to the victim of My Lai or Auschwitz or Verdun, but it does make a great difference to the survivor.

Let us then try to differentiate. After a relatively civilized nine-teenth century, in the course of which "only" tens of thousands of soldiers died in the many wars that took place between 1815 and the American Civil War, methods of more efficient mass killing brought about an increase in what one might call the level of brutalization. This process reached its apogee in World War I, with its hecatombs of soldier-victims. But, one might argue, they died in the course of war, when ordinary social norms do not apply to the armies which butcher armed men. The murder of civilians in large numbers was the exception rather than the rule in 1914–1918. The most obvious such case was of course the destruction of the Armenian people in Anatolia, and we will return to this case later.

Whether one considers the murder of millions of soldiers, by more and more sophisticated means, mass murder or an unfortunate act of war—and it is suggested here that the former seems to be the more appropriate—it is clear that George Mosse's analysis of the First World War as a catalyst of aggressions manifesting themselves in a general brutalization of modern civilization is very convincing.[5] Surely the major point is that while mass murder was not the norm in a society which prided itself on its 'progress,' the First World War constituted a watershed event after which mass murder first becomes acceptable, or perhaps acceptable once again. One can point to the events of the Russian Civil War, including the murder of perhaps a hundred thou-sand Jews, as an example; or to the frightful wars that rocked China in the twenties, even prior to the Japanese invasion of 1931. The Holo-caust, surely, is unimaginable without this shift in attitudes to mass destruction of human life.

What, then, is the relation of mass murder to what we know as 'genocide'? Much has been written on the origin of the term and its meaning. The legal mind has, of course, no difficulty in defining a term that has received the sanction of the proposed United Nations Conven-tion on Genocide. As approved on 9 December 1948, it reads as follows: "In the present Convention, genocide means any of the follow-ing acts committed with intent to destroy, in *whole* or in *part* (our emphasis added), a national, ethnical or religious group, as such:

(a) Killing members of the group; (b) Causing serious bodily or mental harm to members of the group; (c) Deliberately inflicting on the group conditions of life calculated to bring about its physical destruction in whole or in part; (d) Imposing measures intended to prevent births within the group; (e) Forcibly transferring children of the group to another group". The wording seems to indicate that genocide is meant, in the extreme case, to be an act designed to destroy a group totally. However, a group can be totally destroyed without killing all of its members, so that the planned total physical annihilation of a group would appear not to be necessarily included in this definition.

These definitions followed those offered by the inventor of the term, Raphael Lemkin. Lemkin, in early 1943, under the influence of the information received from Europe on the Holocaust as well as on the persecution of other nationalities, formulated a contradictory definition. On the one hand, he defined genocide as the total "extermination" of a people; on the other hand, he defined it as extreme deprivation, destruction of educational institutions, interference in religious life, general denationalization and even moral poisoning by the introduction (for example) of pornography. In effect, we have here two definitions, which are obviously mutually exclusive: one cannot interfere in the religious life or destroy the educational institutions of a people who has been exterminated. Nor does it make sense to see in these actions steps necessarily leading to extermination, because in the case of many of the peoples under Nazi rule this did not happen. The first definition fits the case of the Jews during the war, while the other is suited to the fate of the Slav nations, for instance, under the Nazis.[6] It is here suggested that Lemkin's second definition be called 'genocide'—whatever the United Nations have to say about the matter; while the first be called, for want of a better term, Holocaust, or more accurately *Shoah* (Catastrophe), using the Hebrew term, which is more appropriate.

Lemkin's secondary definition of his term does indeed fit the fate of the Czechs, the Poles, the Serbs and others. Their institutions of self-government were destroyed; the social cohesion of these nations was disrupted; their intelligentsia largely killed; their churches harassed; the masses reduced to near-starvation. But only one people was sentenced to total and absolute annihilation: the Jews.

Some historians reject this description and maintain that the Nazi intention was to destroy all the members of certain Slav nations, such as the Czech and the Polish. This was simply not so. Because of the importance of this issue of differentiating between evil and evil, it is important to examine this problem more closely.

As far as the Slavic nations were concerned, documentary evidence makes it clear that the intention of the Nazis was to kill the leadership, to deport a part of these peoples, and to enslave the rest. There never was a plan for the physical mass annihilation of any one of these nations. To argue that Nazi policies would logically have led to such total annihilation policies has no basis in fact, and is a hypothesis at best. It is illogical, too, because the Third Reich needed millions of slave laborers, and a policy seems to have been evolving to turn the Slav peoples into a permanent population of Helots to serve their German masters.

Basic to the way the Nazis saw these things was the need to reconcile the racial, the economic and the political-strategic aims of a future Germanic world empire. In the writings of Nazi officials and ideologists alike, however, the racial-ideological element clearly dominates.

The Nazis viewed the Slavic peoples as Aryans, albeit of a lower racial order.[7] The Czechs, Poles, Ukrainians, Byelorussians and the Russians fell into this category. In addition, the Nazis had to contend with the three non-Slavic peoples in the Baltic states: the Lithuanians, the Latvians and the Estonians.[8]

"Nordic" elements among these populations were to be identified—a racial survey, based largely on external characteristics, was to be conducted—and those found racially akin to Germans would be germanized, voluntarily or by force. This meant, among other things, the kidnaping of racially "valuable" children, to be raised in Germany. Nordic leadership elements among the Poles, the Czechs and the Russians would be eliminated, because they might provide rallying points for anti-German resistance movements. The rest of the population was to be divided, part to be exiled to the East and part to form the slave labor force needed to make life bearable for the master race.

In the period before the Barbarossa Plan took shape (the plan to invade the USSR), Nazi planning for the future had to contend with the fact that one could not evict the existing Slav populations—the Czechs and the Poles—who were now living in territories controlled by the Germans. In a discussion that took place on 17 October 1939, Hitler declared that in the General-gouvernement the Nazi officials were to ensure "a low standard of living. We want only to get labor from there."[9] He repeated this view on 2 October 1940, when he said that he wanted to establish the General-gouvernement as "a Polish reservation, a big Polish labor camp."[10]

Prior to the German invasion of the USSR, therefore, we find the main lines of Nazi policy towards the Slav peoples clearly defined. It was indeed a program of genocide—slavery, removal of leadership groups by murder and intimidation, germanization and deportation—a program intended to destroy these nations as nations; it was not a program of holocaust: a planned, total physical annihilation.

After the decision to invade the USSR was taken, a new situation arose. In the time span between early 1941 and the end of 1942, we find the development of plans dealing with the future treatment of East European populations after a German victory. These plans revolved around the so-called Generalplan Ost, a first draft of which was submitted to Himmler at the end of 1941.[11] Meyer-Hetling dealt mainly with the problem of resettling the eastern areas that Himmler wanted cleared of the Slavic populations. Of the forty-five million "foreigners" (*Fremdvölkische*) who were in these areas, which included the Baltic states, Poland and most of the western part of European Russia, all of White Russia and the Ukraine, thirty-one million were to be deported and the rest germanized. It did not, however, go into the details, as its attention was focused on the resettlement of Germans and other "Teutonics" in the areas to be cleared. If we want to follow Nazi plans regarding the indigenous populations, we have to turn to two main sources: the comments on the "Generalplan" submitted to Himmler by Dr. Erhard Wetzel, and Heydrich's speeches on the "Czech question."[12]

Wetzel saw considerable difficulties in the plans for germanization (*Eindeutschung*), mainly because of the lack of German manpower to settle areas from which other populations would be removed. He also foresaw grave political difficulties in separating the populations, giving favorable treatment to one part and deporting the other.

Regarding the Baltic peoples, Wetzel opposed deportation by force, lest those whom the Germans hoped to germanize realize "that such a forcible evacuation would probably bring with it the demise (*Untergang*) of their brothers and sisters." Wetzel therefore proposed a program of more or less voluntary removal of the "Ungermanizables," the motivation to be the opportunity for the evacuees to become the middle class in eastern areas ruled, but not settled, by Germans. If, says Wetzel, we can use these racially unsuitable people to save German manpower in the East, we would have gained "a great advantage from both the 'racial-political' and also the political viewpoint."[13] In contrast to the plans for the Poles and the Czechs, this strategy envisaged the elimination of the Baltic nations as such and the use of their members for German power strategies.[14]

As for the Poles, he thought that most of them were not fit for germanization, and would have to be deported to western Siberia. Dispersed among the local population there, they would form an anti-Russian element. The transport of seven or eight hundred thousand people each year for the next thirty years would ensure the realization of this plan.

"It is obvious that the Polish question cannot be solved in such a way that one would liquidate the Poles in the same manner as the Jews. Such a solution of the Polish question would be a standing accusation against the German people into the far distant future and would deprive us of all sympathy, especially as the other neighboring nations would have to assume that they would be treated similarly when the time came."[15]

The Ukrainians would be concentrated in the northern and eastern parts of the Ukraine, and there be used for the Ukrainization of the considerable Russian minority. Wetzel opposed the deportation of the 'ungermanizable' (*nicht eindeutschungsfähige*) Ukrainians to Siberia. Those who were 'germanizable' would be treated in the same way as similar groups among the other peoples. As far as the Byelorussians were concerned, Wetzel believed they should mostly be left where they were, to be used as laborers. Many of the groups which were sound socially could be used as permanent slaves in Germany, and replace the South and Southeast Europeans who were then, in 1942, streaming to Germany and who were racially farther removed than the Slavs from the master race.

The main problem as he saw it was the Russian question. A leading German intellectual, Prof. Dr. Phil. Wolfgang Abel, of the Kaiser Wilhelm Institute for Anthropology at Berlin-Dahlem, had suggested that either the Russians be exterminated *in toto* (the term used was '*Ausrottung*'), or that the Nordic part of the Russian people be selected for germanization (I could not find out what the professor intended to do with the non-germanized Russians, but it is not very difficult to guess what he thought). Wetzel rejected Abel's proposal: "The policy proposed by Abel, to liquidate the Russian people, is impossible, not only because it is hardly possible to implement it, but also for political and economic reasons." In other words, it would be technically difficult, and then of course Germany needed the Russians for labor. The political difficulties would be the same as with the Poles. Instead, Wetzel proposed the subdivision of the Russian area into administrative units independent of each other in order to foster separatism. He also suggested giving Finnic and Turkic groups autonomy within these areas, and he joined a number of others in the Nazi hierarchy who advocated a policy of discouragement of population growth by various quasi-medical and political-hygienic measures. He mentioned that the racial experts of Nazi Germany had discovered among the Russians a so-called 'primitive europide' race, which had not been taken into account by Hans Günther. There were also many Nordics among the Russians. These should be germanizable and/or should be used in the Reich for labor.

Himmler's response to these ideas was generally positive.[16] They fitted well into the conception which he shared with Hitler of a future Pax Germanica in Eastern Europe—apart of course from the general injunction that anyone in the least opposed to the Germans should be immediately shot.[17]

For our purpose the above considerations seem to be sufficient. They show that there was an explicit rejection of ideas of total mass annihilation—not, of course for moral reasons—and instead the older ideas of a destruction of nations as such, their enslavement, forced germanization and deportation, in different proportions for the different nations, was to be adopted.

As far as the Czechs are concerned, we have Heydrich's speeches to tell us what the Nazi plans were. We must use the Czechs as Helots, Heydrich said on 2 October 1941.[18] On 2 February 1942, Heydrich further suggested that the removal of non-germanizable elements should be camouflaged as labor outside the country, with those sent for labor being granted the right to bring their families.[19]

What emerges quite clearly from Heydrich's speeches is the same line of policy as that favored by Wetzel towards the Poles and others: genocide, not holocaust. There was not only no plan for the physical annihilation of all or some of these nations, but there was an explicit rejection of such ideas by those who had the decision-making power.

However, the case of the Gypsies was different again. Nobody really knows the precise number of Romany people living in Europe in 1939. Some estimates put the number of Romanies murdered by the Nazis at 810,000[20] and their number today at 6 million in Europe, and 10 million in the entire world.[21] The first figure can hardly be proved, and both are probably considerably higher than the facts would indicate. However, in sheer demonic, cold-blooded brutality, the tragedy of the Romanies is one of the most terrible indictments of the Nazis. The fact that their fate is hardly ever mentioned, and that the mutilated Romany nation continues to be vilified and persecuted to this day should put all their European host nations to shame.

Branded and persecuted as thieves, sorcerers and child-kidnapers, the Romanies (Gypsies) in Germany largely belonged to the Sinti and to the Lalleri in Austria. Their numbers were given in Himmler's *Runderlass* of 7 August 1941, as 28,607 in Germany, and 11,000 in Austria.[22] Of those in Germany, 2,652 were "persons wandering about in Gypsy manner."[23] The figures for those murdered are unclear, but we know that 13,080 were deported to Auschwitz (this does not include non-German Romanies), and 5,007 Austrian Lalleri were deported to Lodz, and murdered at Chelmno. Three thousand more Austrian Romanies were put into concentration camps, and two and a half thousand deported to Poland, mostly into Jewish ghettoes. Most of these probably perished. When we add up all these victims, we arrive at 23,587, of the 39,607 total indicated above, most of whom died. We shall see that 14,017 Sinti and Lalleri were exempted by Himmler. The figures seem to tally.

What was the principle according to which the Gypsies were treated? Romanies (Gypsies) were considered *"artfremd"* (radically alien). The 1935 Nuremberg Laws really applied to them as well, as the two Nazi experts, Wilhelm Stuckart and Hans Globke made clear.[24] As they were considered to be asocial, their fate was affected by Himmler's order of 14 December 1937, to arrest 'asocials', defined as persons "who, without being criminals, endanger the community by their asocial behavior."[25] Further explications of that decree (4 April 1938) mentioned "e.g., beggars, vagabonds (Gypsies), prostitutes, etc." As this seemed to be a bit too extreme, Himmler issued a clarification on 1 June 1938, which included among the "asocials" "Gypsies and persons wandering about in Gypsy manner, when they do not show any desire for regular work or when they are the subject of criminal proceedings."[26]

Himmler's own attitude to the Romanies was ambivalent. In his *Runderlass* of 8 December 1938, he stated that in accordance with experience gathered in fighting the "Gypsy scourge" (*Zigeunerplage*) and with the results of racial-biological research, the Gypsy problem would be solved in the light of the "inner characteristic of that race" ("*aus dem Wesen dieser Rasse heraus*"). "For the final solution (*endgültige Lösung der Zigeunerfrage*) of the Gypsy problem it is therefore evidently essential to treat the racially pure Gypsies and the mixed breeds [*Mischlinge*] separately." In his explanation of the correct attitude to the Gypsy question, Himmler stated quite clearly the obvious dilemma of the racialist struggling between theoretical racialism, which would accord an equal status to all pure human races, and the variety adopted by the Nazis, which, of course, established a hierarchy led by the Nordic Aryans: "It must be established as a basic thesis in the fight against the Gypsy scourge that the German *Volk* also respects every race that is alien to its *völkish* essence . . . [and advocates] the racial separation of Gypsydom from the German *Volk*, and thus the prevention of race mixing and finally the ordering of the lives of racially pure and mixed-breed Gypsies [becomes necessary]."[27] Himmler did indeed try to solve the Gypsy problem in this way. His "Regelung" of 13 October 1942, separated the "racially pure" Sinti from the rest, and assimilated to them "good *Mischlinge* in the Gypsy sense" (*im zigeunerischen Sinne gute Mischlinge*) who should be again led towards Gypsydom (*sollen einzelnen reinrassigen Sinte-Zigeunersippen wieder zugefürt werden*). In line with Nazi policies, nine Romanies were appointed, who would be responsible for the organization of the segregated "pure" and "assimilated" Sinti and Lalleri and lead them in a Nazi-approved non-sedentary Gypsy life. This indeed appears to have happened, and 14,017 Romanies were exempted.

The fate of the others was eventually sealed, in close connection with the other racial policies of the Nazis. On 6 December 1942, an SS order established that the non-protected Gypsies should be sent to Auschwitz, except for ex-Wehrmacht soldiers, socially adapted Gypsies, and armament workers. For these, sterilization was to be provided. Prior to that, Gypsy soldiers were to have been dismissed from the army.

The execution of the December order was harsher than the order itself. In a "Schnellbrief" of 29 January 1943, the SS provided for the sending of Gypsy *Mischlinge*, Gypsies of the Rom tribes (presumably those in the Reich area) and "members of Gypsy clans of Balkan origin who are not of German blood" into concentration camps. [28]

In effect, we have limited knowledge as yet of what exactly happened, beyond the fact that two-thirds of the German Romanies were murdered, many of them (2,897) gassed in Auschwitz, on 2 August 1944. We do know that many of the survivors were put into German uniforms in the last period of the war and deployed in punitive battalions, on dangerous missions and the like. Others were sent to be slaves in armament factories. We have even less knowledge of what happened to the large Gypsy populations in the Balkans and in Eastern Europe. But it is known that Einsatzgruppe D under Otto Ohlendorf murdered all the Romanies it could find in its area of operations. Many Polish Gypsies were killed where they were—in forests, on the roads, etc. At least fifty (and possibly ninety) thousand Romanies were killed in Yugoslavia. But despite pioneer efforts by some writers, we are still in quest of a detailed description of the fate of the Romany people in Europe as a whole. [29]

And yet, what stands out very clearly are both the parallels and the differences in the Nazi treatment of the Gypsies and the Jews. These two peoples shared certain characteristics in the Nazi period: they both lacked a national territory and basic cultural differences separated them (each people in its own way) from their European host nations. The Nazi technique of dealing with both was similar, not only bureaucratically (they were handled by the same SS organizations) but also ideologically (Himmler applied the same racialist theories to them). The difference is indeed of great significance—Gypsies who were racially "pure" in Nazi eyes, or could be re-assimilated to "gypsydom" were spared. This could be done because the Nazis could live with another, albeit inferior, race, provided there was no 'mixed breeding'. Therefore the 'Mischlinge', but not the "pure" Gypsies, had to die. The murder even included 2,652 Germans who lived as Gypsies.

With the Jews, only quarter-Jews were relatively safe, because, contrary to the Gypsy case, Jews were not just another race, but the anti-race, Satan, bacteria, contaminators of culture, and mortal enemies of the Aryan peoples. Gypsies were just another inferior race, to be dealt with according to the rules of Nazi racial hygiene. The murder of innocent humans was the same; we are here interested in the motivation, and its implications, and these differed.

Let us now return to the discussion of genocide. The contradiction inherent in Lemkin's original definition became even clearer in the resolution passed by the U.N. General Assembly in December 1946. There, as we have seen, genocide is defined as "a denial of the right of existence of entire groups." There is an obvious difference between the denial of the right to exist and actual total murder.

In any case, the U.N. Convention is a purely arbitrary document, arrived at as a result of heated discussions between delegates of member states at the U.N.[30] There is actually no clear definition of genocide, because such a definition would have to emerge inductively, and not, as has in fact been the case, deductively—i.e., as a result of politically and ideologically motivated pressures. Lemkin did indeed try to define inductively: he was, naturally, affected and influenced by what he knew—in late 1942 and early 1943—of Nazi policies. He defined, as we have seen, what happened to Czechs, Poles and Serbs. When he came to discuss Jews, he seems to have been unable to comprehend fully what was happening to them. It seems that cognitively, he "knew" that they were being totally annihilated. But this was not something that could be accepted, or grasped. He therefore left his "first" definition—that of total "extermination"—in, and then went on to describe something else.

An argument evolved as to the correctness of including the destruction of political groups in the definition of genocide. One point to be remembered is, it seems, that political associations are voluntary, and the destruction of political groups is conditioned by the decision of the intended victims to stick to their convictions—with the exception, perhaps, of the leadership elites. Social Democrats and Communists were not killed in Germany, by and large. Millions of them recanted, or kept their views to themselves. Even leaders were—in the thirties—often arrested, and after a while, released from concentration camps. Many survived in the camps, having become part of the *Prominenz* in them. The other point is that in the destruction of political groups, the annihilation of their families is the exception rather than the rule. The destruction of political groups, whether by Nazis, Soviets, Chilean dictators, or Chinese Communists, while utterly to be condemned, is not genocide, though it is true that in their motivation, political and racial issues are at times intermingled. In some cases, such as that of the Communists in Indonesia—for the most part, ethnically Chinese—total mass murder, usually including the families, was aimed at.

Genocide should really be left where the etymology places it—the destruction of racial, tribal, national or ethnic groups. Even the destruction of religious groups poses problems, because there again, religious affiliation is a voluntary act. Admittedly, there are obvious cases where the element of choice is hardly there: the Druse are a religious community, but although they define themselves as ethnically Arab, persecution of the Druse has had a clearly religio-ethnic tinge about it. Persecution of the Jews in pre-modern times had that same quality about it. The mass murder of heretics in France in the Middle Ages was intended to be total, and included the total annihilation of whole towns (Beziers), without providing much choice to the hapless inhabitants whether or not to recant. But then, the concepts of ethnic, national or racial groups were much less clear in pre-modern times than they are today. Christians saw themselves as in some sense a "nation", as did the Muslims. In the industrial era, with the rise of nationalism, religion has become increasingly more voluntary, and the persecution of religious groups more and more parallels that of political ones. It would seem, therefore, that genocide ought to be defined so as to exclude religious persecution.

We thus arrive at a much narrower definition, and it seems that one ought to concentrate on the modern era, or the last one hundred years, because pre-modern genocide cannot really be subsumed under the same category as the modern variety. Bloody massacres there undoubtedly were. Entire cities were razed to the ground (Carthage by the Romans). But this was done for political power reasons. Those who ran away were not pursued, and there seems to have been little desire to eradicate ethnic groups or cultures as such, unless there were weighty power-political reasons to do so. Modern genocide, by contrast, has two decisive characteristics: it is ideological, and it is relentless, in that it desires the disappearance of a racial, national or ethnic group as such.

A limited, and therefore, it seems, more realistic definition of genocide would therefore run somewhat as follows: the planned destruction, since the mid-nineteenth century, of a racial, national, or ethnic group as such, by the following means: (a) selective mass murder of elites or parts of the population; (b) elimination of national (racial, ethnic) culture and religious life with the intent of "denationalization"; (c) enslavement, with the same intent; (d) destruction of national (racial, ethnic) economic life, with the same intent; (e) biological decimation through the kidnaping of children, or the prevention of normal family life, with the same intent.

Genocide, as thus defined, would include the Nazi policies towards Czechs, Poles, or Gypsies, for example, and Soviet policies towards the Chechens, Volga Germans, or Tatars. It would include the policies of American settlers towards many native American tribes (Seminoles, Blackfoot, Arapaho, Apache and others), though there are cases where policies went beyond what is here defined as genocide (Nez Percé, Lakotas): It would probably also include the cases of the Hutus, the Biharis and the Ibos.

Two cases are obviously outside the definition as offered here: one is that of so-called auto-genocide, when both the perpetrators and the victims of mass murder belong to the same national group—as in the case of Cambodia, or, earlier, Stalin's anti-kulak campaign. In all such cases, the mass murder is the result of tremendous internal upheavals, and should be seen as constituting a category of its own. Understanding such tragedies will not be made easier by lumping them together with cases of genocide as here defined. The other case is that of the use of nuclear weapons. Here warfare is escalated to the mass destruction of enemy populations, but there is no intention to "denationalize". In a sense, of course, the use of nuclear weapons indicates the danger of what might be called *urbicide*, i.e., the destruction of civilized life as such, going beyond both genocide and holocaust.

We are then left with a re-statement of Lemkin's "first" definition, namely, the planned physical annihilation, for ideological or pseudoreligious reasons, of all the members of a national, ethnic or racial group. That, indeed, seems to be the true meaning of holocaust. So defined, it becomes a general term, not limited to the Jewish experience in World War II, though that experience is the most thorough-going to date, the only case where "holocaust" (or "*Shoah*", as previously suggested) would appear fully applicable.

We then arrive at a kind of continuum of evil that would lead from mass murder' in recent times through 'genocide' to 'holocaust' ('*shoah*'). Such a continuum does not imply a value judgment as to the degree of moral condemnation, so that one could argue that 'mass murder' is in some way less reprehensible than 'genocide' or 'holocaust'. Whatever it is called in the context of our definition, any particular event of the sort we are describing will have to be put somewhere on the continuum, and may not fit precisely the three orientation points.

We would suggest that some of the most tragic events that have occurred in this century have to be placed between the terms 'genocide' and 'holocaust'. The two outstanding examples are those of the Romanies and the Armenians. The fate of the Romanies has been discussed above. Outside of Germany, there was wanton and near-total, but not very precisely organized, murder. The motivation was social rather than political; in Germany, racism operated almost the other way: it tended to save a remnant (one-third) of the Romany people. Escape from the general fate was made possible either by settled status, or by disappearance into the crowd of non-Romanies. We do not know of any special hunts for individual Romanies—it was the wandering groups that were the hardest hit. The massive destruction went beyond selective mass murder and therefore beyond our definition of genocide, but paradoxically, in Germany itself no attempt was made to destroy the life-style of the protected 'racially pure' remnant. This, at least, was the case in theory; in practice, things were different. We would therefore argue that what befell the European Romanies under Nazi rule has to be placed on our continuum between genocide and holocaust.

The case of the Armenians is grimmer still. There had been massacres of Armenians in 1894–1896, including the murder of three thousand Armenians burnt in the Armenian cathedral at Urfa on 28/29 December 1895. The total number of victims at that time has been estimated at three hundred thousand. Although the Armenian nationalists were welcomed among the Young Turks who gained control over Turkey in 1908, the triumvirate of Talaat, Enver and Djamal which gained control in 1913, finally broke with the Armenians. Massacres took place in 1909 (Adana) and 1912.

The Armenians in Turkey numbered, according to some sources, 1,850,000 in 1914. They were a Christian nationality, mostly peasants, but with a strong middle class and a significant stratum of intellectuals who played an important role in Ottoman society. Ostensibly, the Young Turks wanted to eliminate the Armenians in order to create a Pan-Turkic empire extending into Central Asia. The Armenians were an important element in the population of eastern Anatolia, which was regarded by the Turks as part of the Ottoman heartland. Frustration over the loss of the Ottoman Empire in Europe, and a resulting extreme nationalism played their part. The instigators and organizers of the murder were intellectuals who had seized the government. They utilized a war situation, and used primitive tribesmen and criminals, driven by sadistic instincts, greed and lust, to aid in mass murder. Religious factors may have been part of the general background, and appear from testimonies to have partially motivated the execution of government policy. However, the Young Turks themselves were not only secularist, but anti-religious. Post factum, Turkish apologists argued that the massacres were the result of an Armenian rebellion, or a threat of a rebellion. This is clearly incorrect.

Starting on 24/25 April 1915, with the arrest of two hundred and thirty five top Armenian intellectuals and leaders, the massacres spread in Anatolia, and lasted until early 1916. Armenian soldiers in the Turkish army were first disarmed, then used for slave labor, and then murdered. Women, children and the aged were "evacuated" from their villages and towns. En route, a high proportion were murdered, in part by Kurdish and Circassian tribesmen. The rest were brought to the Syrian desert, and there most of them died.[31]

It is very difficult to arrive at an agreed figure of the number of victims. The German expert on the Armenian question, Johannes Lepsius, says that 1.4 million Armenians were deported. Others put the number of the victims at between eight hundred thousand and over a million. The massacres were committed by central planning and the use of modern technology (the telegraph, the rail transportation of troops, modern propaganda and disinformation techniques, modern bureaucratic procedures). No contradiction appears to exist between that and the use of the most primitive methods—killing with clubs and knives, mass rapes, the denial of water and food.

The decisive document appears to be a cable of the ruling Turkish group to the provincial governors of 28 February 1915: "Jemiyet has decided to free the fatherland from the covetousness of this accursed race and to bear upon their shoulder the stigma that might malign the Ottoman history. Unable to forget the disgrace and bitterness of the past, filled with vengeful episodes, Jemiyet, hopeful about its future, has decided to exterminate all Armenians living in Turkey, without allowing a single one to remain alive."[32] At the trial of the killer of

Talaat in Berlin in 1921, another cable by Talaat to the prefect of Aleppo, of 9 September 1915, was quoted: "The right of the Armenians to live and work on Turkish territory is totally abrogated. The government, which assumes all responsibility in this respect, has ordered not to leave even children in their cribs. In several provinces the execution has been evidenced. Out of reasons unknown to us, exceptions were made with (sic) persons who were allowed to stay in Aleppo, instead of being sent to the place of exile, thus causing new difficulties for the government. Make women and children, whoever they may be, leave, without giving any reason, even those who cannot walk, and do not give the population any grounds for defending them . . . Wipe out every Armenian from the eastern province whom you can find on your territory" (text quoted as in the original). 33

The parallels with the Holocaust are too obvious to require elucidation. Due to the corrupt and disorderly nature of the Young Turkish regime, some Armenians survived: women were taken to Turkish harems or carried off by tribesmen; children were kidnaped and brought up as Turks; some people were left in villages, and there were small numbers who survived the death marches to the Syrian desert. In Istanbul and Izmir relatively large numbers of Armenians were spared, largely because of the proximity of foreign representatives. But, clearly, the intention was the planned, total annihilation of the Armenian nation in Turkey. This is the closest parallel to the Holocaust.

However, there are differences. They become evident in the above quote from Talaat Bey of 28 February 1915. The perpetrators announced that they had decided "to bear upon their shoulders the stigma that might malign Ottoman history." In other words, they were part of a moral world that rejected their deed, but for political-ideological reasons they decided to persist in it nevertheless. They saw themselves, no doubt, as Turkish patriots, and saw the murder of the Armenians as in line with the interests of the Turkish people; but they also knew that the murder could not be justified by appealing to national interest, and they took the responsibility on themselves for something they had difficulty in justifying. Compare this to Himmler's well-known speech at Posen on 4 October 1943: speaking of the "extermination of the Jewish people," he called it "an unwritten and never-to-be-written page of glory in our history." Himmler accepted petit-bourgeois morality (in the same speech he insisted that SS murderers must not take any Jewish property); he prided himself on the SS having "stayed decent" and "suffered no harm to our inner being, our soul, our character."[34] At the same time, he literally turned accepted morality upside-down: instead of 'thou shalt not kill', he decreed—'thou shalt kill'. Killing the Jewish enemy was a moral command, not as in the Armenian case, a practical "necessity" known to be in contrast to standards accepted even by the initiators of the murder.

This consideration is linked to another, perhaps more obvious one: the Nazis saw the Jews as *the* central problem of world history. Upon its solution depended the future of mankind. Unless International Jewry was defeated, human civilization would not survive. The attitude towards the Jews had in it important elements of pseudo-religion. There was no such motivation present in the Armenian case; Armenians were to be annihilated for power-political reasons, and in Turkey only. No anti-Armenian ideology developed in the writings of the Turkish leadership, and the Armenians were not seen as a universal threat. The motivation, in other words, was different in the two cases.

The differences between the holocaust and the Armenian massacres are less important than the similarities—and even if the Armenian case is not seen as a holocaust in the extreme form which it took towards the Jews, it is certainly the nearest thing to it. On the continuum, the two events stand next to each other.

The two definitions of holocaust indicate the dialectical tension between the universal and the particularistic aspects of that watershed event: holocaust has to be seen as a general category, as the outermost pole on a continuum of evil; yet at the same time, as an event which has (so far) overtaken Jews alone—for reasons which have to be explained in part by reference to the specific nature of Jewish history and to the inter-relationship of Jew and gentile throughout the ages. Being general, as well as specific, the term holocaust carries with it the implication that, because it happened once, it may happen again—to any group if the conditions are right.

Unless both parts of this duality are borne in mind, one runs the risk of making misleading and false comparisons between the Holocaust and other events. Any serious attempt to determine the contemporary significance of the Holocaust must start from the awareness that historical analogies usually distort and that history does not repeat itself.

Indeed, because political leaders, in particular, have recently indulged so frequently in the kind of nonsense that equates every act of war, every isolated terror attack, with Auschwitz, Belsen and Dachau,[35] it is not out of place here to point out that there has not been a holocaust since World War II. Such equations are certainly misleading, and often dangerous.

Moreover, Jews are no less vulnerable to the trap of false analogy. Two different kinds of historical error frequently recur in Jewish thought on the Holocaust.

A number of Jewish religious authorities have said that the Holocaust is not essentially new, and represents a continuation of the persecution which has plagued the Jews for two thousand years. The need to integrate the Holocaust into the tradition of Jewish martyrology is understandable from a religious point of view, but it is historically erroneous. For one thing, never before was there a plan to annihilate the Jewish people everywhere. Persecutions were limited in area—Jews usually had the possibility of escaping elsewhere. The attacks and expulsions were the result of local social, religious, economic or political tensions. And the Jews had, as a rule, the option of abjuring their faith—sometimes only temporarily—and if they chose to do so, their lives were usually spared. There was never a persecution that saw in the total annihilation of the Jewish people a panacea for the ills of humanity. In that sense, Nazi anti-Semitism represented a new departure, because while the elements on which it built were familiar, their combination was qualitatively unprecedented, total and murderous. From a Jewish historical perspective, therefore, the Holocaust, while containing many elements familiar from the long history of Jewish martyrdom, is unique.

The second type of false analogy increasingly common among Jews involves references to the Holocaust in the attempt to draw "lessons" for application to topical political situations. For example, it is absurd to compare (as some have done) the plea of a democratic French government that acts of anti-Semitic terror be regarded as an internal French problem which it will confront resolutely, with the Nazi claim in the thirties that the "Jewish problem" was an internal German one.[36] The context is entirely different—French society in the eighties is not Germany of the thirties.

When Israeli politicians thus invoke the Holocaust, accuse foreign statesmen of anti-Semitism reminiscent of the Nazi period, or engage in similar analogies, they often do so because they are under the influence of a collective (sometimes personal) trauma, with which they do not know how to deal. The Holocaust remains an unhealed psychic wound.

Collective traumatization has also produced a type of Jewish backlash. Jewish people and Jewish leadership, especially in Israel, seem to be developing a stance which assumes that anyone who is critical of actions by Jews anywhere, especially in Israel, is anti-Jewish and that therefore the only possible reaction of Jews must be to regard all non-Jews as potential or actual enemies, and to respond to any incipient danger with the threat of force. This attitude seems to be based on two misinterpretations of the events of the Holocaust.

On the one hand there is the assumption that all gentiles as individuals, and all nations (save for the Danes and sometimes the Bulgarians) somehow joined forces with the Nazis. And on the other, it is assumed that the Jewish reaction to the Nazi threat was almost wholly passive, and that therefore the lesson to be learned is that Jews must never again be caught in passivity.

Both these arguments are wrong. I have discussed them elsewhere[37] and will not repeat myself at length here. Belgians, Italians, Serbs and other nations, as well as individuals and groups elsewhere, proved ready by and large to help Jews. True, the picture is dark indeed, especially in Eastern Europe; but were it not for those who helped, not even the small remnant would have survived.

The charge of passivity is uniquely Jewish—no other people has similarly accused itself (though some of them would have had good reason to do so). Czechs and Hungarians glorify almost non-existent undergrounds, and no Soviet writer has yet asked the question why there were no major rebellions among the millions of Soviet POWs who were starved to death or were tortured and murdered by the Nazis. In reality, unarmed active resistance to Nazi policies permeated Jewish life under the Nazis. In Europe in general, armed resistance was marginal, except in Yugoslavia and, debatably, in the USSR (especially in Byelorussia); nevertheless, Jewish armed resistance was relatively widespread.

Peculiarly, the very uniqueness of the Holocaust on which so many Jewish leaders insist—rightly so—contradicts facile analogies. Nonetheless, because the Holocaust was certainly unique but also has its place on a continuum, room has to be found for carefully controlled historical comparisons. The fact that there are no facile "lessons" to be learned does not mean that nothing can be learned, or that this event should be beheld simply in mute horror.

First of all, and probably most important of all, there is the sense of the continuity of Jewish history, in which the Holocaust was a watershed event. The sense of continuity obliges us to know the 'why' and 'how' of the Holocaust, both because we are the heirs to the civilization of the victims and because we or our parents were intended to be the victims no less than those who actually were.

Behavior of the victims ranged from one extreme to the other. In part, this behavior was conditioned by the Jewish environment, by Jewish education, Jewish religion, culture and civilization, or specifically Jewish family and social structures. We can learn what these influences were, and whether they resulted in patterns of behavior that were different from those of non-Jews persecuted by the Nazis. We may be able to understand better who we are, as a Jewish society, by analyzing the history of those who were like us and whose heritage we share. We may be able to empathize with them through our learning, and empathy may lead to a deeper feeling of identification with them and their lives. All this need not be limited to an understanding of Jews only—though there is no possible way to understand universal problems unless we also approach them through the discrete, particular instances of particular people at a particular time.

Beyond these basic issues, more immediate historical and political problems emerge, because the context of the Holocaust is that of our century and our era, and we cannot escape from it. One problem is that of retaining a sense of moral values opposite to that espoused by Himmler, in an increasingly violent, increasingly cynical world.

An analysis of Jewish policies, Jewish leadership reactions in Europe and in the free countries during the Holocaust is called for: not in order to accuse and "draw lessons," but in order to see what the dynamics are that operate on the leadership of a largely dispersed people in times of stress; whether certain historic patterns of Jewish behavior tend to repeat themselves; and whether, in the extreme case of the Holocaust, there were not beginnings of behavior patterns that were different from the traditional ones and that might indicate new developments. By 'old' patterns, we mean attempts by Jewish philanthropic groups (JDC, HIAS, ICA) to come to the aid of victims of persecution within the legal framework of, and in complete loyalty to, the host societies; squabbles between individuals and groups as to primacy in leadership; attempts to influence governments by 'quiet diplomacy,' etc. The abandonment of strictly legalistic attitudes, even by JDC leaders (in Europe); the growing awareness of the need for publicity and of the efficacy of grass-roots organization and democratic procedure; the relatively quick adjustment to the new conditions by some Jewish groups both inside and outside Nazi-occupied Europe—all these appear to be new departures, or at least new emphases, influencing the post-Holocaust Jewish world.

Jewish contemporary consciousness of the Holocaust is troubled by the dialectical tension between the Holocaust as a traumatic caesura in Jewish history and the Holocaust as a part, albeit a tragic part, of the continuity of Jewish history. As such, the current argument about whether the Holocaust is over-emphasized, as some would have it, becomes rather irrelevant. It is a crucial, central event in general and Jewish history. It is set in this history. It has exerted and still exerts a vast impact on our objective situation and on our subjective reaction to events. It therefore has to be dealt with within the context of Jewish life in our era as the central event it is. Its interpretation is bound to have a vital influence, for good or for bad.

NOTES

1. This article is based on a very fruitful discussion that took place on 4 August 1977, at the Hebrew University in Jerusalem. The participants should not be surprised if some of their input is being used here, though of course, the sole responsibility for the views expressed lies with the author. Those who participated, and to whom I wish to extend my thanks, are: Moshe Davis, Emil Fackenheim, Israel Gutman, Dov Otto Kulka, Seymour M. Lipset, Deborah Lipstadt, Malcolm Lowe, Avraham Margaliot, Michael Meyer, George Mosse, Leni Yahil. The symposium, and the research on which this article is based was made possible by the Philip M. Klutznick Fund in Contemporary Jewry. I am grateful to Mr. Philip M. Klutznick for his constant encouragement and great personal interest in these topics.

2. Cf. Uriel Tal, "On the Study of the Holocaust and Genocide," *Yad Vashem Studies* XIII (1973) pp. 7–52.

3. Cf. *Hitler's Secret Book* (New York, 1961); Joshua Trachtenberg, *The Devil and the Jews* (New Haven, 1944); Norman Cohn, *Warrant for Genocide* (New York, 1967); Andreas Hillgruber, "Die Endlösung und das deutsche Ostimperium," *Vierteljahreshefte für Zeitgeschichte* 1972, no. 2, pp. 133–53; Jacob Talmon, in: *The European Jewish Catastrophe* (Jerusalem, 1974); Uriel Tal, "Anti-Christian Anti-Semitism," *ibid*. Alice L. and A. Roy Eckardt, "The Holocaust and the Enigma of Uniqueness," in:

Reflections on the Holocaust, The Annals of the American Academy of Political and Social Science (July 1980) pp. 165–78; Yehuda Bauer, "Genocide: Was It the Nazis' Original Plan?," *ibid.*, pp. 35–45.

4. Cf. Lucy S. Dawidowicz, *The Holocaust and the Historians* (Cambridge, Mass., 1981) pp. 5–11.

5. E.g., George L. Mosse, *Nazism: A Historical and Comparative Analysis of National Socialism* (New Brunswick, 1978) p. 55.

6. Raphael Lemkin, *Axis Rule in Occupied Europe* (New York, 1943) pp. xi–xii.

7. The Slavs were supposed to be a mixture of what the racial anthropologist Hans Günther had defined as "eastern" and "east Baltic" racial sub-groups, with additions from the Mongol and Finnic peoples, some Nordic influences, and even some Jewish influence.

8. In all the discussions on this matter there were two centers of power that had the most impact on policy-making: Alfred Rosenberg's *Ostministerium*, set up before the German invasion of the USSR to deal with the civilian administration of the territories to be conquered from the Soviets; and the various power structures controlled by Heinrich Himmler. Of these two, it was not the "Chaosministerium" (as it was known among Nazis in the know) but Himmler's empire that had the decisive voice. Himmler's general ideas on the subject were articulated in May 1940 in his memorandum on the treatment of foreign peoples, which he submitted to Hitler and which was approved by the Führer. (Printed in the original German in the *Vierteljahreshefte für Zeitgeschichte (VfZG)* 1957. no. 2, pp. 196–98; at Nüremberg this was Prosecutor's Exhibit 1314, NO-1880. For a partial English translation see my *A History of the Holocaust* [New York, 1982] p. 22).

9. PS-864; quoted in: Martin Broszat, *Nationalsozialistische Polenpolitik, 1939–1945* (Stuttgart, 1961) p. 22.

10. *Ibid.*, p. 24; USSR-172. It is hardly surprising to find the same basic attitude prevailing in the case of the Czechs. In a report on a speech of the state secretary to the German viceroy ('Protector') of Bohemia-Moravia, Karl H. Frank, of 9 October 1940, we read that Frank opposed "the most total solution, namely the deportation (*Aussiedlung*) of all the Czechs (*des Tschechentums*). He proposed the dissolution (*Aufsaugen*) of about one half of the Czech people in the German Folkdom, insofar as they are of any value from the point of view of their blood and anything else. This will occur through increased labor by Czechs in the Reich area (not in the Sudeten border areas), that is, through the dispersion of the concentrated Czech people. The other half of the Czech people must be made powerless, must be removed (*ausgeschaltet*) and deported . . . Elements opposed to the germanizing tendency must be dealt with harshly and must be removed . . . The Führer has approved the assimilation solution." (PS-867. Report of 15 October 1940 by Friderici, Wehrmacht plenipotentiary with the Reichsprotektor, on Frank's speech of 9 October.)

11. See Helmut Heiber, "Der Generalplan Ost," VfZG 1958, no. 2, pp. 281–325; also Josef Ackerman, *Himmler als Ideologe* (Göttingen, 1970) pp. 222–31.

The author of the plan's final version, Dr. Konrad Meyer-Hetling was not just another Nazi official. He was responsible for population matters in another of Himmler's offices, the *"Reichskommissariat zur Festigung des deutschen Volkstums"* (Reich Office for Strengthening the German Volkdom), in charge of the planning of racial and population policies. Closely allied with Heydrich's *"Reichssicherheitshauptamt"* (Reich Main Security Office), the RKF proposed its policies—and that included Meyer-Hetling's plan—with Heydrich's approval.

12. Dr. Erhard Wetzel (he survived the war) was not an old Nazi, but a latecomer: he joined the Party on 1 May 1933. A servile and intelligent bureaucrat, he became a leading light in the office of Racial Policy of the Nazi Party (*Rassenpolitisches Amt der Reichsleitung*) in 1939. He then became involved with the RSHA, especially with its section III B dealing with racial problems, and in 1941 received a post in Rosenberg's Ostministerium.

13. *VfZG* 1958, no. 2, pp. 302–03.

14. Before Wetzel dealt with the problem of the Slav nations, he had some interesting things to say about the Jews. Wetzel was not only informed of the mass murder by the Einzatsgruppen in the East, but actively supported it from his office. It was therefore very significant when he said this about the Jews: "A deportation (*Aussiedlung*) of the Jews as envisaged in the plan (i.e., Meyer-Hetling's plan—Y.B.) becomes redundant with the solution of the Jewish question. A possible removal (*Überführung*) after the end of this war of the still remaining Jews into forced labor camps in the area of northern Russia or Siberia is no 'removal.' " We have here a clear indication that the term '*Aussiedlung*' (removal, resettlement) as used towards the Jews has a different meaning in the language of German bureaucracy from the same term when used towards others. The context makes it clear that as far as the Jews are concerned, '*Aussiedlung*' means murder, rather than forcible deportation. (*VfZG* 1958, no. 2, p. 305)

15. *Ibid.*, p. 308.

16. *Ibid.*, p. 325.

17. *Ibid.*, p. 221–26.

18. Vaclav Kral, *Die Vergangenheit Warnt* (Praha, 1961) Doc. 19, pp. 122–23. "We have the following people: some are racially good and well disposed: this is very simple, we can germanize them. Then we have the others, that is, the other extreme: racially bad and ill-intentioned. These people I have to get out. There is plenty of room in the East. We then remain with the middle group, which I have to check out precisely. There are those who are racially bad but well-intentioned, and racially good but ill-intentioned. The racially bad and well-intentioned ones we will probably have to use for labor somewhere in the Reich and see to it that they do not have any more children . . . But we should not antagonize them . . . Then we are left with the racially good but ill-intentioned. Those are the most dangerous ones, because they are the racially good leadership group . . . only one thing will be left to do, namely . . . to settle them in the Reich, in a purely German environment, and educate them ideologically and germanize them, and if this does not work, to stand them up against the wall; because I cannot deport them, since they would form a leadership group over there in the East and would turn against us."

19. *Ibid.*, Doc. 22, pp. 145–48. For some of these people Heydrich foresaw the possibility of using them as labor stewards (*Vorarbeiter*) in the arctic area "where the concentration camps will, in the future, be the ideal homeland of the eleven million European Jews." Waxing enthusiastic about the possibilities of developing the arctic areas for utilization of their raw materials, Heydrich added that he did not want the

non-germanizable Czechs to go there as enemies of the Reich, but to give them certain material advantages, so that they could serve as guardians of European culture. (*Ibid.*, Doc. 22, p. 145–48.) Heydrich's speech took place about two weeks after the Wannsee conference (20 Jan. '42) the figure of eleven million Jews is that used by Heydrich at that conference. At Wannsee, the arctic concentration camps were not mentioned; but Wetzel alluded to them (see note 14).

20. Tilman Zülch (ed.), *In Auschwitz vergast, bis heute verfolgt* (Hamburg 1979) p. 382; Annegret Ehmann, "Gerechtigheit für Zigeuner," *Zeichen* no. 4 (Dec. 1970) p. 25; Ulrich Völklein, "Lästig ist das Zigeunerleben," *Die Zeit*, (7 March 1980) pp. 9ff.

21. *Ibid.*

22. *In Auschwitz vergast, bis heute verfolgt*, p. 315.

23. "Nach Zigeunerart umherziehende Personen."

24. *Kommentar zur Deutschen Rassengesetzgebung*, 1 (Munich, 1936).

25. *In Auschwitz vergast, bis heute verfolgt*, p. 76.

26. *Ibid.* In 1936, Dr. Robert Ritter was nominated to head a special research department for genetic science dealing specifically with Romanies (*"Erbwissenschaftliche Forschungsstelle"*). This became, in 1937, a research department on race hygiene and population biology (*"Rassenhygienische und bevölkerungsbiologische Forschungsstelle"*). Their researches into the racial purity of Gypsies resulted in a well-ordered card index, which was deposited with the health authorities. Just as those who decided on the murder of children and women in Auschwitz were medical doctors, so the fate of Gypsies was determined by pseudo-scientists attached to the Nazi health authorities. Does one have to mention that none of these Nazi women and men were ever punished?

27. Rd. Erl. des RFSS u ChdDtPol, 12/8/38, S-Kr. I., No. 557 VIII 38–2026–6; *In Auschwitz vergast, bis heute verfolgt*, p. 78.

28. The wording of the order is contradictory. Obviously, Gypsies were not of "German blood" so that what appears to have been meant is non-Sintis and non-Lalleri Romanies of Balkan origin. RSHA VA2 Nr. 59/43g; *In Auschwitz vergast, bis heute verfolgt*, pp. 327–28.

29. Cf. Donald Kenrich and Grattan Puxon, *The Destiny of Europe's Gypsies* (London, 1972); Siegfried Wölffling, "Zur Verfolgung und Vernichtung der Mitteldeutschen Zigeuner," *Wissensch. Zeitsch. der Martin-Luther Universität* 1965, H. 7.

30. Cf. Leo Kuper, *Genocide, Its Political Uses in the Twentieth Century* (New Haven, 1981) pp. 24–39.

31. The above has been culled from a number of sources: Richard G. Hovanissian, *Armenia on the Road to Independence* (Berkeley, 1967); Stanford J. Shaw and Ezel K. Shaw, *History of the Ottoman Empire and Modern Turkey* (Cambridge, Mass., 1976/77); Robert Melson, "A Theoretical Enquiry into the Armenian Massacres of 1894–1896," *Comparative Studies in Society and History* XXIV, no. 3 (1982) pp. 481–509; Johannes Lepsius, *Deutschland und Armenien, 1914–1918* (Potsdam, 1919); Tessa Hofmann, *Der Prozess Talaat Pascha* (Berlin, 1921/Göttingen, 1980); St. Stephanian, "Deutsche Armenien Politik," *Pogrom* X (1964) pp. 22–28.

32. Quoted from Helen Fein, *Accounting for Genocide* (New York, 1979) p. 15. Original document to be found in: *The Memoirs of Naim Bey* (Neuton Sq., Pa., 1966).

33. Stephanian, "Deutsche Armenien Politik;" cf. Hofmann, *Der Prozess*, p. 133ff.

34. *Documents on the Holocaust* (Jerusalem, 1981) pp. 344–45.

35. In an Israel TV interview on 8/20/82, Lebanese Christian leader Dany Chamoun referred to Bashir Jemayel's responsibility for the murder of men, women and children as tantamount to being responsible for Belsen and Dachau.

36. Prime Minister Menachem Begin made that comparison in a Knesset speech on 12 August 1982.

37. Yehuda Bauer, *The Holocaust in Historical Perspective* (Seattle, 1978) and *idem, The Jewish Emergence From Powerlessness* (Toronto, 1979).

Naming is an essential human activity. It is not only the way in which we identify reality but also a fundamental act by which we define the world we share. The unnamed can be frightening and unnerving. For example, a disease the physician cannot name evokes a sense of terror beyond that which can be clearly diagnosed. The ineffable has awesome power. Therefore, "I will be what I will be" was all God would reveal when Moses asked about God's name.

Much is at stake in deciding how to identify what Winston Churchill once called "a crime without a name." The Nazis spoke of *die Endlösung* (the "Final Solution"). Typically, we know the event today by another name: "the Holocaust." Or do we?

A contemporary dictionary will define "holocaust" as a great or complete devastation or destruction, especially by fire. The entry may indicate the word's derivation via the Latin *holocaustum* from the Greek *holokaustos*, which means "burnt whole." Biblical roots are important here. In the Septuagint, a Greek translation of Jewish Scripture dating from the third century B.C.E., variants of *holokaustos* are used for the Hebrew *olah*, which literally means "what is brought up." In context *olah* refers to a sacrifice, often specifically alluding to "an offering made by fire unto the Lord." Thus, for example, "holocaust" has been associated with the *Akedah*, the account in Genesis 22 where God orders Abraham to offer up his son, Isaac.

If such roots lend special religious significance to the Holocaust, not everyone regards the destruction of the European Jews that way. Some persons argue that to speak of "the Holocaust" conveys religious connotations that are repulsive. Walter Laqueur, for instance, is not alone when he finds the term "singularly inappropriate," arguing tersely that "it was not the intention of the Nazis to make a sacrifice of this kind, and the position of the Jews was not that of a ritual victim."

Other names are still being tried, the search provoked in part by a feeling that "holocaust" has been used to cover such a multitude of destructive acts that the term is no longer distinctive enough to identify the event's uniqueness. In Yiddish, the language spoken by millions of Eastern European Jews who were destroyed by the Nazis, the name given to the event has been *Khurbn,* a term used previously to designate the destruction of the first and second Temples in ancient Jerusalem. Growing in usage is the Hebrew name *Shoah*—which, like *Khurbn,* signifies catastrophic destruction. According to Uriel Tal, *Shoah* was used by Polish Jews as early as 1940 to speak of their plight under Hitler, but the roots of this word also go back much further. They, too, are biblical.

Shoah is found in the Psalms, in Isaiah's prophecies, and in Job's lamentations. Its meanings are multiple. Sometimes the word refers to dangers that threaten Israel from surrounding nations; at other times it refers to individual distress and desolation. If catastrophic destruction is signified in each case, Tal argues, "all Biblical meanings of the term *Shoah* clearly imply Divine judgment and retribution." Those ancient meanings, however, are called into question by the "Final Solution." In contemporary usage, *Shoah* conveys destruction but implies profound elements of doubt where religious tradition is concerned. Time will tell whether *Shoah* or some other term supplants Holocaust as the name of choice. In any case, it seems likely that no single name will do justice to the event in question.

The Israeli memorial day commemorating the victims of the Holocaust refers to *Shoah* and *Gevurah* (catastrophe and heroism), suggesting that the one must not be remembered without the other. Lucy Dawidowicz speaks of "the war against the Jews," while Raul Hilberg studies "the destruction of the European Jews." There has also been an evolution in the names applied to those who lived through the event. At first they were known as refugees, and later as survivors or witnesses. As for those who perished, some have designated them as martyrs or *kedoshim* (holy ones), while others have seen them simply as victims whose senseless death reveals the meaninglessness of creation.

Historians indicate that failure to name a crime while it is happening enables those in authority to ignore or even to advance it. The way in which a crime is later named, moreover, may affect future responses as well. Historian Gerd Korman, a professor at Cornell University, thoughtfully explores some of these dimensions in the selection that follows. Having previously published numerous writings about the Holocaust, including a 1973 anthology entitled *Hunter and Hunted: Human History of the Holocaust,* he is presently writing a book about preconditions for the Holocaust in the period from 1865 to 1921.

Gerd Korman

The Holocaust in American Historical Writing

I have used "Holocaust" in this article, but in 1949, there was no "Holocaust" in the English language in the sense that word is used today. Scholars and writers had used "permanent pogrom"—this term of Jacob Lestschinsky in 1941, meant that the pogrom had "no passing or limited political and economic aims but the extirpation, the physical elimination of its Jewish citizens"—or the "recent catastrophe," or the "recent Jewish catastrophe," or the "great catastrophe," or "disaster," or "the disaster." Sometimes writers spoke about annihilation and destruction without use of any of these terms. All of them, by intent or accident, translated accurately the Hebrew words *shoa* and *khurban* because like them they carried only secular freight. (Yiddish, the other language so profoundly involved with the disaster and with the literature about it, contributed besides *khurbn*, the word *umkummen*.)[1]

In 1953, the state of Israel formally injected itself into the study of the destruction of European Jewry, and so became involved in the transformation. In the anguish of mourning the dead of Europe and the dead who fell in Israel's lonely fight for nationhood, the Knesset gave post-humous citizenship to the 6,000,000 and established, in contro-

From *Societas* 2 (Summer 1972). Reprinted by permission.

[1] Jacob Lestschinsky, *Erev Churbn* (On the Eve of Destruction) (Buenos Aires, 1951); Samuel Gringanz, in *Jewish Social Studies*, XIV (October, 1952), 326–327; Leo Schwartz, *ibid.*, 378–379; Theodor Abel, *ibid.*, V (January, 1943), 79; Werner J. Cahnman, "A Regional Approach to German Jewish History," *ibid.*, (July, 1943), 211–224; Oscar Karbach, "The Founder of Political Antisemitism," *ibid.*, VII (January, 1945), 3–4; Adolf Kober, "Jewish Communities in Germany from the Age of Enlightenment to Their Destruction by the Nazis," *ibid.*, IX (July, 1947), 230–238; Lestschinsky, "The Anti-Jewish Program: Tsarist Russia, The Third Reich and Independent Poland," *ibid.*, III (April, 1941), 147–148; Yad Vashem, *Aims and Activities* (Jerusalem, 1955); Friedman, "Research and Literature," used most of these terms interchangeably. For examples of the use of *shoa* in Biblical writings see Ps. 35–8, 63–10, 35–17; Job, 30–3, 14, 38–27; Ez. 38–9.

versy, Yad Vashem as a "Martyrs' and Heroes' Remembrance Author-ity" in language not especially encouraging to the spirit of objective scholarship. "May every person in Israel, every Jew wherever he may be, know that our People has its own reckoning, the reckoning of the generations of the Eternal People—a reckoning of an Eternal People, whose entire history is proof and evidence of the prophetic promise: And I said unto you in your blood, 'Live' [Ezekiel, 16–6]." Two years later Yad Vashem translated *shoa* into "Disaster" and announced for itself and YIVO in New York that henceforth the study of the catastro-phe would be divided this way: "The approach of the Disaster, 1920–1933"; "The beginnings of the Disaster, 1933–1939"; and "The Disas-ter, 1939–1945."[2]

But then the change occurred quickly. When catastrophe had lived side by side with disaster the word holocaust had appeared now and then. In 1951, for example, Jacob Shatzky of YIVO spoke of "the Nazi holocaust," but apparently he did not mean to apply the phrase specifically to the destruction of European Jewry. Between 1957 and 1959, however, "Holocaust" took on such a specific meaning. It was used at the Second World Congress of Jewish Studies held in Jerusa-lem, and when Yad Vashem published its third yearbook, one of the articles dealt with "Problems Relating to a Questionnaire on the Holo-caust." Afterwards Yad Vashem switched from "Disaster" to "Holo-caust" although it retained the title of its yearbooks *Yad Vashem Studies of the Jewish Catastrophe and Resistance*.[3]

In other words, conversion of the destruction of European Jewry into "Holocaust" began before the publication of [Raul] Hilberg's book

[2] Yad Vashem, *Martyrs' and Heroes' Remembrance Authority* (Jerusalem, 1955), pp. 7, 9, 17, 19; *Jerusalem Post*, August 20, 1953. The Zionist Congress discussed such an authority in August, 1945. The *Va'ad Leumi* of Palestine Jewry kept the idea alive. After the establishment of Israel, Ben Zion Dinur, historian and Minister for Education and Culture, was instrumental in the Knesset's passage of the bill establishing Yad Vashem; Professor Dinur became its first head. Controversy in the Knesset involved the opposition of *Herut* to Moshe Sharet's government over the Reparations Agreement with Germany, and the Knesset's left-wing members, some of whom wanted to mention by name in the law specific groups of fighters.

[3] *Jewish Social Studies*, XIII (April, 1951), 175–176. Bernard Mark, "Problems Related to the Study of the Jewish Resistance Movement in the Second World War," *Yad Vashem Studies*, III (1959) 41–65; Zvi Bar-Or and Dov Levin, "Problems Relating to a Questionnaire on the Holo-caust," *ibid.*, 91–117. These papers and a number of others, such as Friedman's "Problems of Research on the European Jewish Catastrophe," pp. 25–40, published in this volume were read at the Second World Congress of Jewish Studies held in Jerusalem in 1957. The *Yad Vashem Bulletin* (April, 1957), p. 35, has a reference to "Research on the Holocaust Period." Of course, there had been writers who spoke of the Nazi holocaust even before 1951, but their use of the phrase was applied to the general destructive impact of Nazism. Morris Cohen used the phrase in that way as early as 1945. Cohen, *A Dreamer's Journey*, pp. 256–257.

[*The Destruction of the European Jews,* 1961] and before Eichmann's capture. There were those who refused to use the word so exclusively, preferring to apply it to the Civil War, World War II or III (a nuclear holocaust), but there appeared no formal effective opposition. Within the Jewish world the word became commonplace, in part because Elie Wiesel and other gifted writers and speakers, in public meetings or in articles for *Commentary* and journals such as *Judaism* and *Midstream* made it coin of the realm. By 1968, even the Library of Congress had no choice. As Jewish scholars in various parts of the world and in various languages revealed with Jewish sources the details of the suffering of the Jewish population and its struggle for spiritual and physical survival, the international serial and monographic literature using "Holocaust" became so significant, said the Library's Catalogue Division, committed to a policy of following usage, that it felt compelled to create a major entry card: "Holocaust—Jewish, 1939–1945."[4]

Thus it was that a word brought into the English language by Christian writers centuries ago—they took the Greek word used in the Septuagint exclusively for translating words in the *Torah* meaning sacrifices consumed by fire—came to be the noun symbolizing a new phenomenon in Western civilization: the destruction of European Jewry. It was also, I believe, that a change in word usage in the English language helped to shift concern from the particularity of the disaster within Jewish history to an emphasis on its uniqueness in modern history. In turn, that shift made it easier to level the charge of parochialism against Holocaust advocates, who, like myself, usually cannot conceive of Auschwitz without the Nazis' anti-Semitism. After all,

---

[4] Higham, *History,* pp. 200, 204: Robert E. Osgood, *Ideals and Self-Interest in America's Foreign Relations* (Chicago, 1964), p. 415, Louis L. Snyder, *The War: A Concise History 1939–1945* (New York, 1960), preface, and the caption underneath a picture of Hiroshima after the bomb—this picture is opposite a page showing "Ghastly scenes in a Nazi extermination camp." *Holocaust!* by Paul Benzaquin (New York, 1959) was a novel about the Coconut Grove fire, but increasingly the word was used in titles of anthologies, memoirs, and surveys of the destruction of European Jewry: Alexander Donat, *The Holocaust Kingdom: A Memoir* (New York, 1965); Sam E. Bloch (ed.), *Holocaust and Rebirth* (New York, 1965); Jack Kuper, *Child of the Holocaust* (London, 1967); Levin, *Holocaust;* Albert H. Friedlander, *Out of the Whirlwind: A Reader of Holocaust Literature* (New York, 1968); Jacob Glatstein, *Anthology of Holocaust Literature* (New York, 1969); Irving Halperin, *Messengers from the Dead: Literature of the Holocaust* (Philadelphia, 1970). My information about the Library of Congress comes from Charles Bead and Theodore Wiener via telephone on August 10, 1971. The Catalog Division has some correspondence form individuals who tried to find out why the new category was being used. Before 1968, the Library catalogued "Holocaust" books under various subcategories of World War II—Personal Narrative, Jewish, is one example—or under the history of Jews by communities.

Hannah Arendt had all along insisted that the uniqueness of Auschwitz lay elsewhere! "Antisemitism by itself," she declared, "has such a long and bloody history that the very fact that these death factories were chiefly fed with Jewish 'material' has somewhat obliterated the uniqueness of this operation. . . . Antisemitism only prepared the ground to make it easier to start the extermination with the Jewish people."

However, that difference between Holocaust advocates and those who share Miss Arendt's views on the place of anti-Semitism in the development of Nazi Germany's particular methods of domination and annihilation must not obscure the more fundamental agreement between them. In its totality, she also said in 1949, the German way "must cause social scientists and historical scholars to reconsider their hitherto unquestioned fundamental preconceptions regarding the course of the world and human behavior."[5]

5 Roland de Vaux, O.P., *Ancient Israel Its Life and Institutions* (New York, 1961), p. 415; Hannah Arendt, "Social Science Techniques and the Study of Concentration Camps," *Jewish Social Studies* 12 (January 1950): p. 49, p. 53; in the original these passages appear in a different sequence. Of course, from the very beginning, many people said or implied the sort of things Justice Robert H. Jackson declared in 1945: "History . . . does not record a crime ever perpetrated against so many victims or one ever carried out with such calculated cruelty. . . ." See Weinreich, *Hitler's Professors*, p. 6. See also Holborn, *War and Peace Aims*, II, 216–218, 266.

Lucy s. dawidowicz begins her important work on the Holocaust by describing the Jews' place in the mind of Adolph Hitler; she concludes her book as Jews enter the death camps, at the moment when Jewish history ended for the victims. Dawidowicz entitled her work *The War Against the Jews 1933–45* to signify that there were actually *two* wars that the Germans fought, a war for living space against enemies to the east and west, and a war of annihilation to eliminate one people from the face of the earth.

More than any other historian, Dawidowicz focuses on the intentionality of the perpetrator. The Jewish people were considered the biological—not religious—archenemy of the German nation; the physical existence of Jews was thought to threaten the purity of the Aryan race. Unlike the Slavs who, according to Nazi policy, were to be treated as subhumans and reduced to slaves, the Jews were considered unworthy of life and excluded from the family of nations.

The murder of six million Jews, Dawidowicz writes, was not a *by-product* of the war but an *end* in itself. The death of the Jews was *the* essential goal of Hitler's second war, which was made possible by the other war he was fighting. The extinction of the Jews was the ultimate goal of the National Socialist state.

Dawidowicz contemptuously dismisses those who write of the technological sophistication of the killing processes. "To talk of harnessing modern technology to mass murder is nonsense," she writes. "Jews were loaded on trucks or forced to march to some desolate area. . . . They were machine-gunned at the rim of the trench or pit into which their bodies toppled." Even the technology of the death camps, she contends, was barely more sophisticated than that of the *Einsatzgruppen*.

Yet Dawidowicz reserves her real contempt for those who speak of the Holocaust as a metaphor or as a symbol of universal evil. The scandal of its particularity is obliterated by pretenses to universality.

Dawidowicz was born in New York City. She has taught generations of students at Yeshiva University and has written many books including *The Golden Tradition: Jewish Life and Thought in Eastern Europe; The Jewish Presence: Essays on Identity and History; On Equal Terms; Jews in America 1881–1981;* as well as *The Holocaust and the Historians* from which the following selection is taken.

Lucy S. Dawidowicz

Thinking about the Six Million: Facts, Figures, Perspectives

> *A people dies intestate, its benediction lost. And the future succeeds, unfathered . . .*
>
> IRVING FELDMAN, "Psalm"

Rosa Luxemburg, a Jew who lived with a universal perspective, once upbraided a friend who lived with a Jewish perspective: "Why do you come with your special Jewish sorrows? I feel just as sorry for the wretched Indian victims in Putamayo, for the Negroes in Africa." In our time that kind of universalism has prompted questions about the particularity of the 6 million European Jews murdered during the Second World War by the Germans and their helpers. Why, it is sometimes asked, should the Jews be singled out from the statistics of the millions who were killed during the Second World War? Surely, it is argued, there is no hierarchy of suffering, for all peoples and nations suffered enormous losses of life. Surely, it is contended, to dwell only on the murder of the 6 million Jews is narrow and parochial, for that obscures the universal human condition of suffering and death.

In truth, the awesome statistics of the uncounted and unaccounted millions who lost their lives during the Second World War stun us into reverential silence for all the dead without distinction. The enormity of their numbers baffles the mind's comprehension and numbs the heart's feeling. How does one apprehend the vacancies left by millions who are missing and dead? The poet turns from the impersonal anonymity of statistics to grieve just for one person:

> We ask for no statistics of the killed . . . .
> However others calculate the cost,
> To us the final aggregate is *one*,
> One with a name, one transferred to the blest . . .[1]

Still, intellectual honesty demands a reckoning of the terrible statistics. The bottom line alone does not truly render the account. Statistical calculations may even quicken the historical imagination. By counting all the dead and recounting the manner of their deaths, we can better fathom the course of the entire war and the import of that single statistic of 6 million murdered Jews.

Statistics of Death: The War

It has been estimated that at least 35 million persons, perhaps even as many as 50 million, were killed during the Second World War in all theaters of operation in Europe, Africa, Asia, and the South Pacific, on land, on sea, and in the air. They were combatants and civilians, men, women, and children, killed on the battlefields and at home. Among some European peoples the statistics of the killed were so immense as to depress the statistics of those to be born in the next generation.

In Europe the scope of the war extended from the Atlantic to the Black Sea. The war began on September 1, 1939, when Germany invaded Poland and thereafter, in partnership with its then ally, the Soviet Union, occupied and despoiled Poland. Britain and France, committed to Poland's aid, declared war against Germany on September 3. The war engulfed Western Europe when Germany invaded and occupied Norway, Denmark, The Netherlands, Belgium, and France in April and May 1940, with Italy joining the hostilities as Germany's partner. By spring 1941, most countries of Southeast Europe fell under German rule or influence, by force or choice. In June 1941, when Germany launched the surprise invasion of its former ally, sweeping into Soviet territory, the war overwhelmed the whole European continent. Fighting the Russians on the Eastern front, the Germans conducted mainly a motorized, mechanized ground warfare. In the West, they engaged mainly in air warfare, at first offensive but increasingly defensive. After the Allied landings in Italy in 1943 and in Normandy in 1944, Germany was compelled to fight land and air warfare on two fronts. Early in 1945, the Allied armies and Soviet forces began to converge on Germany and by May forced Germany's unconditional surrender.

Of all European countries, the USSR suffered the greatest loss of life in the war. According to the *Great Soviet Encyclopedia*, Soviet military and civilian losses amounted to some 20 million. Other sources estimate Soviet losses at about 11 million combatants and 7 million civilians. (Polish sources put Soviet losses at barely 7 million, the lowest of any estimate, suggesting that statistics can serve political ends, as a weapon of the weak against the strong.) The civilian losses included those killed in air raids and bombardments, those who died of starvation and disease, the millions deported to Germany for forced labor who are counted among the missing, and about 1.5 million murdered Soviet Jews.[2]

Most of the military losses were combat casualties, but about 3.5 million Soviet prisoners of war are believed to have been murdered by the Germans, gassed at Auschwitz, machine-gunned en masse, or shot in military-style executions. A month before the Germans invaded the Soviet Union, Hitler had issued a decree guaranteeing his armed forces immunity from subsequent prosecution for shooting enemy civilians, "even if the action is also a military crime or misdemeanor." On June 6, 1941, the German High Command, implementing Hitler's decree, issued the infamous *Kommissarbefehl* (Commissar Order), which authorized combat troops to single out from their captured prisoners "political commissars of all kinds" and to kill them. Thus, millions of Soviet prisoners of war were removed from the rights and protection of international law and murdered.[3]

Poland ranks second in the number of war losses. The Bureau of War Indemnities of the Polish People's Republic issued official figures of Poland's wartime losses, estimating a total of 6,028,000 deaths, about 22 percent of the prewar population.[4] (If the Jewish losses are computed separately, the number is about 3 million, or 12.5 percent of the Polish population.) The wartime deaths are categorized in four odd and unsystematic rubrics, without any subdivisions. The first, classified as "direct military action," gives the number of deaths as 644,000, presumably military personnel killed in combat and civilians killed in air raids and artillery fire. The second category, "victims of death camps, raids, executions, annihilation of ghettos, etc.," gives a total of 3,577,000 deaths, of whom 3 million were Jews, though the statistical table does not specify that. The third category, "deaths in prison and other places of confinement, due to epidemics, emaciation, ill treatment etc.," gives 1,286,000 deaths, without any further clarification as to how this estimate was derived. The fourth category, classified as "deaths outside prisons and camps, caused by wounds, mutilation, excessive work etc.," lists 521,000 deaths.

Even if these figures are high, as several Polish scholars acknowledge privately, the Poles did suffer great losses, for the German military and civilian occupation authorities dealt ruthlessly with the Polish population. In the first months of the German invasion, the SS's armed security forces rounded up and murdered thousands of Poland's leadership elite: political and military leaders, church authorities, and top educators. Their murder was intended to leave the Poles leaderless and thus less likely to resist their German despoilers. About 10,000 Poles were killed in the first year of German occupation. In the later years, about 25,000 Poles were killed in mass executions, many in reprisal for resistance activities.[5] No one can say with any exactness how many thousands, or perhaps tens of thousands, of Poles died in concentration and labor camps.

Yugoslavia sustained great wartime losses. Some 1.5 million Yugoslavs, about 9 percent of the population, were killed or disappeared. About 1.2 million of these were civilian casualties, mainly victims of German reprisals for the continuing guerrilla warfare that the Yugoslavs conducted during the German occupation. In Greece, where similar conditions prevailed, the loss of life has been estimated at about 250,000, some 3 to 4 percent of the population.

In Western Europe, in contrast, losses were fewer.* In France, for example, the number of persons killed or missing has been put at 600,000, about 1.5 percent of the population. Of these, some 200,000 were combat casualties, and 400,000 were civilians (including about 90,000 Jews) who were killed in air raids, executed, or deported.[6] Belgium's losses are put at 50,000, out of a population just under 10

---

* The Germans, who launched the war that brought these unprecedented statistics of death and destruction and who had to fight on both Eastern and Western fronts, suffered about 3.5 million combat casualties and 430,000 civilian casualties (mostly victims of air raids), about 8 percent of the German population in 1939.

million. In Great Britain, deaths were estimated at about 360,000, comprising both military combat losses and civilians killed in air raids, amounting to less than 1 percent of the population. The English and French probably lost more men in the Battle of Verdun in the First World War than in all of the Second World War.

All over Europe, wherever the Germans had the power, they enforced their total rule by arresting masses of the civilian population whom they regarded as politically dangerous, socially harmful, or economically expendable. The categories were diverse: Communists, socialists, and other political opponents; outspoken members of the clergy and especially Jehovah's Witnesses, who refused to recognize the secular sovereignty of National Socialism; prostitutes, homosexuals, perverts, and professional criminals. To make room for all these prisoners, the National Socialist regime constructed a vast network of concentration camps. In time, to exploit the available human resources under their control, the Germans developed a system of forced labor in the camps, and in the later years of the war, when German manpower needs were desperate, the slave labor of these prisoners from all over Europe became a staple of the German war economy. It has been estimated that over the years about 1,650,000 persons were incarcerated in these camps. Over a million of them died or were killed. Some died of "natural" causes: hunger, exhaustion, disease. Those who lingered, the ailing, the sick, and the dying, no longer able to work and consequently, in the Nazi view, no longer worth keeping alive, were sent to the gas chambers that nearly every camp maintained to dispose of what Hitler called the "useless eaters."[7]

Statistics of Death: Mass Murder

While planning and conducting the military war to gain *Lebensraum*—"living space" for the German people—and mastery over the whole European continent, Germany simultaneously planned and carried out a systematic program of mass murder. The National Socialists regarded this mass murder as nothing less than an ideological war and its prosecution was synergized with the conventional military war. The High Command of the German Armed Forces conducted the military war, while the SS, the dreaded armed police force of the National Socialist movement, conducted the ideological war.

Both wars were concurrent undertakings, strategically and operationally meshed. The success of the mass-murder offensive was made possible by the SS's parasitic dependence upon Germany's military establishment and its national wartime resources, and the operations of the military war provided the cover for the mass murder.

The mass murder represented itself as a holy war to annihilate Germany's "mortal enemy." The mortal enemy—*Todfeind* was Hitler's word—consisted of the Jews, who were, according to the doctrines of National Socialism, the chief antagonists to the German "Aryans." In Nazi ideology the Jew was the primal adversary, the biological archenemy of the German people, whose physical presence, it was alleged, threatened the purity and even the very existence of the "Aryan" race.[8] No other people, nation, or "race" held that status.

Racial purity was a Nazi obsession and embraced every aspect of life in the German dictatorship. Racial eugenics became a matter of state policy. "Positive" racial eugenics encouraged "pure" Aryan Germans to have children. "Negative" eugenics discouraged—to the point of murder and mass murder—the procreation of life that the racists regarded as "valueless." Hitler himself had initiated a racially motivated program of murder, euphemistically called "euthanasia." Its purpose was to kill mentally ill "Aryan" adults, because their abnormalities were believed to infect the "Aryan" race and defile its national health. Within Germany itself, the euthanasia program claimed about 100,000 lives. During the war, convoys of patients from mental institutions from various countries arriving at Auschwitz were sent straight to the gas chambers. No records were kept of their arrival or their murder; their numbers were estimated to be in the thousands.[9]

In the hierarchy of Nazi racism, the "Aryans" were the superior race, destined to rule the world after the destruction of their racial archfoe, the Jews. The lesser races over whom the Germans would rule included the Slavs—Poles, Russians, Ukrainians.

It has been said that the Germans also planned to exterminate the Poles and the Russians on racial grounds since, according to Hitler's racial doctrine, Slavs were believed to be subhumans (*Untermenschen*). But no evidence exists that a plan to murder the Slavs was ever contemplated or developed. The German racists assigned the Slavs to the lowest rank of human life, from which the Jews were altogether excluded. The Germans thus looked upon Slavs as people not fit to be educated, not able to govern themselves, worthy only as slaves whose existence would be justified because they served their German masters. Hitler's racial policy with regard to the Slavs, to the extent that it was formulated, was "depopulation." The Slavs were to be prevented from procreating, except to provide the necessary continuing supply of slave laborers. Whether the Russians—or other "non-Aryan" peoples—lived or died was, as Himmler once put it to his top SS officers, "a matter of indifference." In contrast, he justified and even extolled the murder of the Jews as "an unwritten and never-to-be-written page of glory" in German history.[10]

The European Gypsies, too, suffered enormous losses at the hands of the Germans, yet the National Socialist state had no clear-cut racial policy with regard to them. Hitler appears to have overlooked them in his racial thinking. The Germans regarded the Gypsies primarily as an antisocial element, consisting of thieves and vagrants, rather than as an alien racial group. When the National Socialist regime began to incorporate its racial ideas in legislation, the Ministry of Interior ordered investigations to be made as to whether Gypsies were racially fit to be educated. (The answer was no.) But not until August 1941 did the German bureaucracy make any systematic attempt to classify the Gypsies racially. At that time Nazi officials established two basic categories, dividing the native Gypsy tribes from the foreign ones. The native tribes were defined as those who had settled in Germany since the fifteenth century, and hence were entitled to citizenship and the protection of German law. Distinctions also began to be made between "pure" Gypsies and "part" Gypsies (offspring of marriages between Gypsies and Germans), classifications that were patterned on the Nuremberg Laws promulgated in 1935 and frequently refined and implemented. When the Nazis began in 1941 to formulate a racial policy with regard to the Gypsies, no agreement on the matter had been reached by the top Nazi leaders. Late in 1943, the German occupying authorities in the Eastern areas ruled, with Himmler's approval, that sedentary Gypsies and their offspring were to be treated as citizens of the country, whereas nomadic Gypsies and their offspring were to be treated as Jews (that is, murdered). This distinction between two kinds of Gypsies blunted their classification as a racial group and strengthened the idea that nomadic Gypsies were antisocial. SS security forces, "cleansing" the occupied countryside of "dangerous elements," murdered many Gypsies on grounds that they were unreliable, unemployable, and criminal. Only in the last year of the war did the Nazi ideologues begin to regard the Gypsies not only as an undesirable social element, but also as an undesirable racial element.

During the war, tens of thousands of Gypsies living in Germany, Austria, and other German-occupied countries were deported to camps in Poland, including Auschwitz. The statistics of the murdered Gypsies are gross estimates: of about 1 million Gypsies in the countries that fell under German control, nearly a quarter of them were murdered—machine-gunned or gassed. [11]

The Jews: A Special Case

The fate of the Jews under National Socialism was unique. They obsessed Hitler all his life and their presence in Germany, their very existence, preoccupied the policymakers of the German dictatorship. The *Judenfrage*—the question of the Jews—riveted all Germany. The age-old heritage of anti-Semitism, compounded of Christian prejudices, economic rivalries, and social envy, was fanned by Nazi racism. Every German city, town, and village applied itself to the Jews and the Jewish question with rampant violence and meticulous legalism.

Once the National Socialists came to power, they incorporated their racist beliefs into law, in a short time enacting a major corpus of anti-Jewish legislation. The laws established legal definitions of the Jews and then, step by step, deprived the Jews of their rights, their property, and their livelihoods. In time, the Jews became segregated and ostracized from German society and were deprived of the protection of the law—even such as it was in Nazi Germany.

But National Socialist Germany had a still more radical objective with regard to the Jews: total ar.nihilation. The war which Hitler unleashed in September 1939 was intended to achieve that objective while the Germans also pursued their aggressive expansionism against the nations of Europe.

The German dictatorship devised two strategies to conduct its war of annihilation against the Jews: mass shooting and mass gassing. Special-duty troops of the SS's Security Service and Security Police, called *Einsatzgruppen,* were assigned to each of the German armies invading the Soviet Union. Following hard upon the armed forces and dependent upon them for basic services, the Einsatzgruppen were given the task of rounding up the Jews and killing them. The procedures used everywhere behind the Russian front were crude and primitive. (To talk of harnessing modern technology to mass murder is nonsense.) The Jews were loaded on trucks or forced to march to some desolate area with antitank trenches already dug or natural ravines. Otherwise, the Jews were ordered to dig what would become their own mass graves. Then they were machine-gunned at the rim of the trench or pit into which their bodies toppled. The International Military Tribunal at Nuremberg estimated that the Einsatzgruppen murdered about 2 million Jews.

To systematize the murder of the rest of the European Jews the National Socialist state built six installations with large-scale gassing facilities and with crematoria for the disposal of the bodies. These were all located on Polish territory: Oświęcim (better known by its German name, Auschwitz), Belzec, Chelmno, Majdanek, Sobibór, and Treblinka. The technology applied here—discharging poison gas through shower-head vents in sealed chambers—was barely more sophisticated than the brute violence of the Einsatzgruppen. The logistics, however, were impressive, and in the three years during which these killing installations operated, about 3.5 million Jews from every country of Europe were murdered there.* (Approximately 1.5 million non-Jews were gassed in these camps most at Auschwitz.)

Of the 9 million Jews who lived in the countries of Europe that fell under German rule during the war, about 6 million—that is, two-thirds of all European Jews—were murdered.[12] Their numbers and concentration in Eastern Europe and their uninterrupted cultural traditions there for a thousand years had rendered them the most vital Jewish community, whose creativity sustained Jews throughout the world. Though the Soviet Union suffered greater losses than the Jews in absolute figures, no other people anywhere lost the main body of its population and the fountainhead of its cultural resources. No other people was chosen for total extinction.

The deaths of the 6 million European Jews were not a by-product of the war. The Jews did not die as a consequence of the indiscriminate reach of bombs or gunfire or of the unselective fallout of deadly

---

* In computing the statistics of the 6 million murdered Jews, it is estimated that in addition to the 2 million killed by the Einsatzgruppen and the 3.5 million in the gas chambers, about 500,000 died in the ghettos of Eastern Europe of hunger, disease, and exhaustion, and as victims of random terror and reprisals.

weapons. Nor were they the victims of the cruel and brutal expediency that actuated the Nazis to kill the Soviet prisoners of war and the Polish elite. Those murders were intended as means to practical ends: they were meant to protect and to consolidate the position of the Germans as undisputed masters over Europe. The murder of the Jews and the destruction of Jewish communal existence were, in contrast, ends in themselves, ultimate goals to which the National Socialist state had dedicated itself.

To refer to the murder of the 6 million Jews as distinctive, as unique, is not an attempt to magnify the catastrophe that befell them nor to beg tears and pity for them. It is not intended to minimize the deaths of the millions of non-Jews that the Germans brought about, or to underplay the immeasurable and unendurable suffering of Russians, Poles, Gypsies, and other victims of the German murder machine. To speak of the singularity of the murder of the 6 million European Jews is not to deny the incontestable fact that the gas chambers extinguished without discrimination all human life.[13] The murder of the 6 million Jews stands apart from the deaths of the other millions, not because of any distinctive fate that the individual victims endured, but because of the differentiative intent of the murderers and the unique effect of the murders.

The intent on the part of the German dictatorship to annihilate the Jews was based on their judgment that the Jews had no right to live, a judgment that no one has the right to make. Karl Jaspers, German philosopher, explained the uniqueness of the murder of the 6 million Jews: "Anyone who on the basis of such a judgment plans the organized slaughter of a people and participates in it, does something that is fundamentally different from all crimes that have existed in the past."[14]

The effect of the murder of the 6 million Jews is still to be evaluated. From the Jewish point of view, we know one thing now for certain. The immensity of the Jewish losses destroyed the biological basis for the continued communal existence of Jews in Europe. Every country and people ravaged by the war and by the German occupation eventually returned to a normal existence. All the nations, the victims now become victors, the aggressors now defeated, once again assumed their positions in the political order. Having mourned their dead, commemorated their martyrs and heroes, all the peoples of Europe, including the Germans, recovered from their wounds, rebuilt their shattered cities. London, Warsaw, and Rotterdam, as well as Berlin and Dresden, were reconstructed. They restored their factories and their marketplaces. They resuscitated their institutions of learning and culture. They reestablished their armed forces. But the annihilation of the 6 million European Jews brought an end with irrevocable finality to the thousand-year-old culture and civilization of Ashkenazic Jewry, destroying the continuity of Jewish history.* This is the special Jewish sorrow. This is why the surviving Jews grieve, mourning the loss of their past and the imperilment of their future.

The Holocaust Universalized: Metaphor and Analogy

The murder of the 6 million Jews, in its unparalleled scope, devastating effect, and incomprehensible intent, overtook the capacity of man's imagination to conceive of evil. The killing camps, an empire of death with their bulging gas chambers and smoke-belching crematoria operated by the SS Death's Head Division, eclipsed man's visions of hell. The names of these death factories—and especially the name of Auschwitz—replaced Dante's Nine Circles of Hell as the quintessential epitome of evil, for they were located not in the literary reaches of the medieval religious imagination, but in the political reality of twentieth-century Europe.

It was to be anticipated that Auschwitz would become a metaphor and a paradigm for evil. How could it be otherwise? But what was unexpected was the occasional attempt to turn Auschwitz into a metaphor for the "ecumenical nature" of the evil that was committed there or to render the murder of the Jews as mere atrocity, sheer blood lust. What was unexpected was the failure to understand—or to acknowledge—that the evil was not ecumenical, that the killing was not blood lust for its own sake, but that the evil and killing were specifically directed against particular victims. To make Auschwitz serve as the paradigm for universal evil is in effect to deny the histori-

---

* The Jewish community in Israel, a state whose political existence was legitimated as a recompense for the murder of the European Jews, is producing a radically different Jewish culture from that of European Jewry. It is not yet evident whether Israel can develop the creative cultural energy that will succeed in binding Jews of the world together, while conserving the traditions of the past and evolving new ones.

cal reality that the German dictatorship had a specific intent in murdering the Jews.*

Auschwitz was a social and political reality. It was neither conceived nor constructed as a theater of atrocity to play out Everyman's capacity for evil, to satisfy a universal lust for killing. Auschwitz was the direct consequence of a specific and particular history of racist anti-Semitism. It was invented and assembled by National Socialist Germany to kill its mortal enemy, the Jews. Once its killing facilities were devised and installed, once Auschwitz became an operational enterprise for mass-murdering the Jews, it became convenient for the Germans to use that equipment also to murder those non-Jews who had, for one reason or another, become expendable.

What underlies the attempt to deprive the Jews, as it were, of their terrible unique experience as a people marked for annihilation? Does it derive from a form of contempt for the Jews, from some personal resentment against Jews, or out of professional rivalry with Jews and envy of them, out of some barely conscious stirrings of anti-Jewish hostility? By subsuming the Jewish losses under a universal or ecumenical classification of human suffering, one can blur the distinctiveness of Jewish fate and consequently one can disclaim the presence of anti-Semitism, whether it smolders in the dark recesses of one's own mind or whether it operates in the pitiless light of history. Therefore, one can feel free to reject political or moral responsibility for the consequences of that anti-Semitism.

In denying the uniqueness of the fate the Jews experienced as the chosen victims of mass murder, the universalizers of Auschwitz do not necessarily deny the uniqueness of the mass murderers. At least they understand that the mass murder which the National Socialist state perpetrated stands alone in the annals of human murderousness, that something new in human history happened when Hitler's Germany arrogated to itself the right to decide who was entitled to live in the world and who was not. But all too often the necessary and essential distinction between the murder of the 6 million Jews and the accelerat-

---

* I am not here referring to those who altogether deny that the European Jews were annihilated, like Arthur R. Butz, author of an overtly anti-Semitic work called *The Hoax of the Twentieth Century.* Those people are outright Nazis or Nazi apologists. I find it difficult to believe that any person of good will, however ignorant of the recent past, can give credence to such notions. For more about the neo-Nazi attempt to deny the historicity of the murder of the European Jews see Lucy S. Dawidowicz, "Lies About the Holocaust," *Commentary,* 70, 6 (December 1980), 31–37.

ing violence and terror of our time is blurred, sometimes erased, whether mindlessly or with political intent.*

How commonplace nowadays the glib equation of the murder of the Jews with any disaster or atrocity, with any state of affairs one abhors or even merely dislikes. Extremist blacks, with careless disregard for linguistic precision or conceptual clarity, have abused words like "genocide," "Auschwitz," "holocaust," exploiting them in excesses of rhetorical overkill to describe conditions in urban slums. Some American antiabortionists, with the fanaticism of zealots, have compared advocates of population control to Nazis who murdered the Jews. Vladimir Nabokov characterized this as *poshlost*, a Russian word whose many nuanced meanings he summarized as "corny trash, vulgar cliches, Philistinism in all its phases, imitations of imitations, bogus profundities." *Poshlost*, he said, "speaks in such concepts as 'America is no better than Russia' or 'We all share in Germany's guilt' . . . Listing in one breath Auschwitz, Hiroshima, and Vietnam is seditious *poshlost*."15

The extravagances that equate any offensiveness in contemporary life with the murder of the 6 million European Jews are not just the mouthings of imperceptive innocents or literary vulgarians. For one, they camouflage an underlying contempt for the Jews. By denying the particularity of the Jewish experience under the German dictatorship and, still more, the enormity of Jewish losses, by equating the destruction of the European Jews with other events, they succeed in obscuring the role of anti-Semitism in accomplishing that murder. All atrocities are reduced to the same rubble. For another, when they equate National Socialist Germany with the United States, they bespeak a vicious anti-Americanism. Their purpose is to depict America as Amerika, a Nazified United States, heir as it were of the unredeemed evil which the Nazis represented.

Thus, Hiroshima, the Japanese city upon which the Americans dropped the first atomic bomb in August 1945, becomes an accusatory byword against America. How valid is the equation? As for numbers, the A-bomb left 130,000 casualties in dead, injured, and missing. (At

* Those guilty of muddleheaded indiscriminateness include also Jews who are overwhelmed by anxiety for Israel's existence. For decades some have, with the intemperance of hysteria, equated Arab leaders with Hitler. Jewish poets and politicians alike often compare Auschwitz with Ma'alot, an Israeli settlement where in 1974 Arab terrorists killed 20 children and wounded 70 more.

Nagasaki, where the second A-bomb was dropped, about 75,000 persons were killed or injured.) But numbers are not the only factor. America's decision to use the atomic bomb against Japan was not motivated by a wish to wipe out the Japanese people. The purpose of the bombing was to demonstrate America's superior military power and thus convince the Japanese that they had to capitulate, thereby ending the war and further killing. Merely to set down the bare outlines of what Hiroshima was intended to accomplish, and did in fact accomplish, is to expose the discongruity between the A-bombing of Hiroshima and the mass murder of the Jews, a discongruity not only with regard to extent, but more important, with regard to intent. (To say this is in no way to minimize Hiroshima's terrible cost of life and the fearful consequences of atomic radiation on the survivors.)

The ugly incident of My Lai, during the last years of United States involvement in the war in Vietnam, provided another spurious parallel with Auschwitz to fuel anti-American rhetoric. My Lai was a Vietnamese village where an American army unit in the course of combat operations against the Viet Cong in 1968 shot to death 347 unarmed civilians—men, women, and children. The army had covered up the incident, but when the story came to light a year later, public indignation prompted investigations and subsequently the responsible officer was brought to trial. Anti-Americanists, trying to justify their parallel between the Americans at My Lai and the Nazis, charged that the officer's decision ordering his men to kill the Vietnamese had been motivated by racism. (The more persuasive evidence indicated that the killings were prompted by fear that the civilians were in fact members of the Viet Cong.)

Furthermore, the argument that America committed crimes as monumental as those of the Nazis can justify a reverse claim: since the United States committed crimes as evil as those of Nazi Germany, then Nazi Germany committed no worse crimes than other states and was not unique among nations as a perpetrator of evil deeds. Thus, all states and all forms of government are reduced to a simplistic uniformity: differences between democracy and totalitarianism become unimportant. No distinction is made between a just war and an unjust war, between murdering 6 million Jews and, for instance, bombing Dresden. Thus Kurt Vonnegut in *Slaughterhouse-Five* baldly asserts that "the greatest massacre in European history" was the firebombing of Dresden.[16] Dresden, the historic German city, was bombed by

British and American planes in February 1945, in retaliation for the launching of German V-2 rockets against London. The estimate of lives lost in the Dresden bombing is 35,000; the damage to the city was extensive. Though Vonnegut was himself held prisoner of war by the Germans in Dresden during the bombing, he leaned heavily for an account of that event and even for moral judgment on a shamelessly fanciful anti-Allied version of the Dresden bombing by David Irving, an English journalist who has achieved a measure of notoriety as a German apologist and even as a Hitler apologist.[17]

The Lesson of National Socialism

Jacob Burckhardt, the nineteenth-century Swiss historian, observed that "history is the record of what one age finds worthy of note in another." The mountainous accumulation of histories about World War II and especially about the event-laden twelve-year National Socialist era testifies to the consensus among historians and consumers of history alike that the period was worthy of record. The rise and fall of the German dictatorship, and especially the rise and fall of its dictator, continue to fascinate scholars and the public at large.

Why should this be so? The National Socialist regime effected no abiding transformations of society within Germany's borders or beyond and left no lasting monuments to its once overmastering presence on the European continent. To be sure, when Hitler came to power, a revolution of political and social magnitude erupted, but unlike other revolutions—political, industrial, scientific—the National Socialist revolution left no enduring heritage. The Russian Revolution, in contrast, set in motion political upheavals and economic convulsions whose effects still reverberate around the world. The Communist revolution in China has already radically altered the social and political face of Asia itself. In the wake of the Second World War the Third World nations emerged to transform the international arena and the struggle for world power. As for science and technology, their development in the last three decades has challenged the foundations of our past knowledge as well as of our future existence. The terrifying capacity of the scientific mind to destroy life may soon be outstripped by its still more terrifying capacity to fabricate life.

National Socialist Germany achieved no comparable far-reaching or fundamental impact on society. Yet even as the events of its short reign and its still briefer dominion over Europe recede into the past, its ghostly ghastly presence continues to hover over us, to inhabit our political and moral universe. For Nazism, as we have seen, has come to represent the essence of evil, the daemon let loose in society, Cain in a corporate embodiment. The accomplishment of the National Socialist state was nothing less than the consummation of mass murder in the service of fanatic racism whose unconditional imperative was: destroy the Jews. Obsessed by its passion to kill the Jews, the Nazi state harnessed the energies of its people and of its institutions of govern- ment; of industry, technology, and science; of education, art, and religion. It succeeded in consolidating and systematizing them for that mission of monumental mass murder. Never before had the principles and methods of rational organization been employed on behalf of the irrational, the demonic. Never before had mass murder been so regu- lated and regularized, organized on scientific principles of industrial management, its standardized procedures for killing developed by a system of empirical testing and designed to achieve a maximum effi- ciency of operation. Never before in human history had a state and a political movement dedicated itself to the destruction of a whole people.

The destruction of the European Jews was and remains a special Jewish sorrow. But the National Socialist state and its capacity to organize mass murder on grounds of racist anti-Semitism was and remains a universal concern because it represents a terrifying juncture in human history. Things once unthinkable are now not only possible, but have actually happened. In 1897, when the Dreyfus Affair was tearing France apart, Bernard Lazare, a French Jew active in Dreyfus's defense, addressed a group of Jewish students in Paris on the subject of anti-Semitism. "For the Christian peoples," he remarked, "an Arme- nian solution" to their Jew-hatred was available. He was referring to the Turkish massacres of Armenians, which in their extent and horror most closely approximated the murder of the European Jews. But, Lazare went on, "their sensibilities cannot allow them to envisage that."[18] The once unthinkable "Armenian solution" became, in our time, the achievable "Final Solution," the Nazi code name for the annihilation of the European Jews.

What men do today, Karl Jaspers said, becomes the source of their future actions. Nothing but the most lucid consciousness of the horror that happened can help avoid it for the future:

> That which has happened is a warning. To forget it is guilt. It must be continually remembered. It was possible for this to happen, and it remains possible for it to happen again at any minute. Only in knowledge can it be prevented.[19]

NOTES

1. Karl Shapiro, "Elegy for a Dead Soldier," *Selected Poems* (New York: Vintage, 1973), p. 105.

2. No sources cite the same statistics; discrepancies exist among all figures. Cf. "Great Patriotic War of the Soviet Union of 1941–45," *Great Soviet Encyclopedia: A Translation of the Third Edition* (New York: Macmillan, 1974), vol. 4; "World Wars," *Encyclopedia Britannica*.

3. Szymon Datner, *Crimes Against POWS: Responsibility of the Wehrmacht* (Warsaw: Zachodnia Agencja Prasowa, 1964), esp. pp. 218–227; Hans-Adolf Jacobsen, "The Kommissarbefehl and the Mass Executions of Soviet Russian Prisoners of War," in Helmut Krausnick et al., *Anatomy of the SS State* (New York: Walker, 1968), p. 531.

4. Jan Szafranski, "Poland's Losses in World War II," *1939–1945: War Losses in Poland*, Studies and Monographs (Poznań: Zachodnia Agencja Prasowa, 1960), esp. pp. 44–49.

5. Central Commission for the Investigation of German Crimes in Poland, *German Crimes in Poland*, 2 (Warsaw, 1947), 49–50.

6. Henri Michel, *The Second World War* (New York: Praeger, 1975), pp. 781–782.

7. Central Commission for the Investigation of German Crimes in Poland, *German Crimes in Poland*, 1 (Warsaw, 1946), esp. 45. For the variety of reasons that brought people to Auschwitz see Bernd Naumann, *Auschwitz: A Report on the Proceedings Against Robert Karl Ludwig Mulka and Others Before the Court at Frankfurt* (London: Pall Mall, 1966). For an excellent critical analysis of available statistics on concentration camp population, turnover, and mortality see Joseph Billig, *Les Camps de Concentration dans L'Economie du Reich Hitlérien* (Paris: Presses Universitaires de France, 1973), pp. 68–99.

8. For an exposition of racial anti-Semitism in National Socialist ideology and practice see Lucy S. Dawidowicz, *The War Against the Jews, 1933–1945* (New York: Holt, Rinehart & Winston, 1975), esp. pp. 3–22, 56–60, 63–69, 130–166.

9. Ota Kraus and Erich Kulka, *The Death Factory: Document on Auschwitz* (Oxford: Pergamon Press, 1966), pp. 205–206.

10. H[elmut] Kr[ausnick], "Denkschrift Himmlers über die Behandlung der Fremdvölkischen im Osten," *Vierteljahrshefte für Zeitgeschichte*, 5 (1957), 197. For Himmler's speech, October 4, 1943, see Lucy S. Dawidowicz, ed., A Holocaust Reader (New York: Behrman House, 1976), pp. 131–132.

11. The most reliable source about the fate of the Gypsies under the Nazis is Donald Kenrick and Grattan Puxon, *The Destiny of Europe's Gypsies* (London: Chatto Heineman for Sussex University Press, 1972), esp. pp. 83–99, 144–149, and the statistics on pp. 183–184.

12. For statistics on the European Jews killed see Dawidowicz, *The War Against the Jews*, pp. 402–403.

13. See William Styron, "Auschwitz's Message," *New York Times*, June 25, 1974, and his essay "Hell Reconsidered," *New York Review of Books*, June 29, 1978, which appeared, in somewhat different form, as an introduction to the paperback edition of Richard L. Rubenstein, *The Cunning of History* (New York: Harper Torchbook, 1978). See also Kurt Vonnegut, Jr., *Slaughterhouse-Five* (New York: Dell, 1971), p. 96, where he provides an indiscriminate list of victims of the Nazi state: "Jews and Gypsies, and fairies and communists, and other enemies of the State."

14. Karl Jaspers and Rudolf Augstein, "The Criminal State and German Responsibility: A Dialogue," *Commentary*, 41 (February 1966), 35.

15. Vladimir Nabokov, interviewed by Herbert Gold, in George Plimpton, ed., *Writers at Work: The Paris Review Interviews*, 4th ser. (New York: Penguin, 1977), pp. 101–102. I am indebted to Norma Rosen for this reference.

16. Vonnegut, *Slaughterhouse-Five*, p. 101 et passim. See also Gabriel Habib, "A Statement," in Eva Fleischner, ed., *Auschwitz: Beginning of a New Era? Reflections on the Holocaust* (New York: Ktav, 1977): "The drama of Auschwitz should not be separated from the drama of World War II. Decisions such as those to bomb Dresden, or the annihilation of Hiroshima, along with the more recent massacre of the Vietnamese, can only be characterized as the same madness on the part of the industrialized nations" (p. 417).

Everyone has his favorite disaster. Thus Louis Morton, a specialist in American military and diplomatic history, wrote on the siege of Leningrad: "No incident of World War II, with the possible exception of the gas chambers of Auschwitz and Belsen, can compare in human suffering to the epic defense of Leningrad." "World War II: A Survey of Recent Writings," *American Historical Review*, 75 (December 1970), 1993.

17. See Chapter 2 for a discussion of Irving's *Hitler's War.*

Vonnegut's choice of historical sources may be more deliberate than would appear, for he chose to flaunt his own German ancestry in *Slaughterhouse-Five*, describing himself on the title page as "a fourth-generation German-American." That statement of identity in that book assumes the defiance of a political statement. Even in World War II, Vonnegut appears to be saying, to have been a German was no worse morally than to have been an American, for in his view, it was more reprehensible to have bombed Dresden than to have murdered 6 million European Jews.

18. Bernard Lazare, *Job's Dungheap* (New York: Schocken Books, 1948), p. 68.

19. Karl Jaspers, *The Origin and Goal of History* (New Haven: Yale University Press, 1953), p. 149.

JEWISH THINKERS DISAGREE about the place of the Holocaust in Jewish history. Most of the scholars whose works are in this book share the view that the Holocaust was an epoch-making event, an experience that demands a rethinking of Jewish tradition and conventional understandings of God and history. Yet for others, too much is at stake, too much at risk, to allow for such a fundamental reexamination of the assumptions of faith.

The following dialogue between David Weiss and Michael Berenbaum concerns the importance of the Holocaust as an event within the covenantal history of Israel. Weiss—a Viennese-born, American-trained, Israeli scientist and rabbi—is the chairman of the Lautenberg Center for General and Tumor Immunology at the Hebrew University Hadassah Hospital in Jerusalem. Weiss maintains that, from the perspective of faith, the Holocaust is not a singular event unprecedented in history but a continuation of similar atrocities that can be understood within the context of faith like other catastrophes in the past. The covenant remains unchanged for Weiss, untouched by the epoch-making events of our era.

Weiss's views are shared by many believers who speak about the God of mercy and the God of history as if the events of 1933–45 never happened. In some quarters, such as among the followers of Rabbi Joel Teitelbaum (the late master of Satmar Hasidim) or of Ignaz Maybaum (a Reform rabbi), faith is affirmed by speaking of God as punishing the Jewish people for their sins. In other Orthodox traditions, stories are retold that convey the miraculous experience of individual Jews who were saved in the Holocaust. Yaffa Eliach, a child survivor of the Holocaust and now a distinguished professor of Judaic Studies at Brooklyn College, collected some of these stories in her aesthetically crafted work, *Hasidic Tales of the Holocaust*.

Michael Berenbaum, co-editor of this anthology, dissents. Born after the Holocaust and educated both in the United States and Israel, he belongs to a generation for whom the Holocaust is history but not personal experience. A student of Richard Rubenstein, Berenbaum has written a book on Elie Wiesel and devoted the past few years to the creation of an American national memorial to the Holocaust. Born in 1945, he was reared in a traditional Jewish home and attended Orthodox schools. His early religious teachers were survivors in the process of adjusting to America. Contra Weiss, he argues that the Holocaust was a transformative event with dramatic implications for Jewish faith and fate. Conventional categories are inadequate to deal with the implications of the Holocaust; the covenant itself has been shattered, and the next generation must find new ways of wrestling with tradition and with the memory of God.

The dialogue between Weiss and Berenbaum echoes the many dialogues that have taken place among those whose belief is untouched by the momentous events of this century and those whose faith has been broken and who seek a new resolution. The former enjoy the fullness of eternal belief; the latter have entered a dialectical world of paradox and contradiction. They are guided by the words of Rabbi Nachman of Bratzlav: "Nothing is as whole as a heart that has been broken."

David W. Weiss and Michael Berenbaum

The Holocaust and the Covenant

I. Weiss: After the Holocaust, Another Covenant?

The incumbency of a radically new Judaic theology has been argued with growing insistence during the past thirty years. Pivotal to the claim is the imputed uniqueness of the European holocaust of 1939–1945. The horror visited on the Jewish people during these years has been, it is claimed, a wholly singular experience, and one that signals the beginning of a new era. The classic Judaic delineation of the relationship between God and the House of Israel is no longer tenable, perhaps, indeed, has not been since the destruction of the Second Temple and Jewish commonwealth. The covenant that was, or the illusion of this covenant, has been abrogated in the German death camps. What is demanded of the survivors is a new covenant, a unilateral, voluntary assertion by the House of Israel of the will to continue Jewish existence in the face of an indifferent, changeable, or non-existent deity.

I address myself not to the terrifying implications of the proposed new theology, nor make any attempt to analyze the diverse motivations of its proponents. I ask: Is the contention valid?

It is not, and I am at a loss to comprehend the reasoning of serious thinkers who posit the view. Perhaps I do not have the privilege of saying this. I have not experienced in my body the suffering of European Jewry—although I lived for nearly a year in Austria after the

From Sh'ma 14 (April 13, 1984). Reprinted by permission.

Anschluss until escaping, and lost all but my immediate family in the period that followed—and I may therefore lack a certain right, or authority, to speak. But then, perhaps the obligation to speak has now devolved on those not so seared, who still have speech.

The Holocaust of 1939–1945 Was Not Unique

It may be that what transpired was unprecedented in scope, setting, and expectation. One would not have thought it possible that this could take place in mid-twentieth century, at the hands of a cultured nation, and to the apathy of the rest of the civilized world. But the uniqueness of even these aspects of the holocaust is debatable. A more sober estimation of the behavior of technologically advanced peoples before, during, and after the destruction of European Jewry, and in other regards, leaves less room for astonishment. Man has always given evidence of the potential for humanity and compassion, but the dominant theme of his record to the present is not undeserving of the epitomization *hominis lupus est*. The Jewish people have accepted, as part of their ancient covenant, the challenge of witness to greater possibilities.

For this we have suffered, horribly, uniquely, and repeatedly throughout post-biblical history. Whole regions have been devastated of their Jewish communities in recurrent, earlier holocausts; I employ that denotation advisedly. I doubt that the impact on individual Jew, or community, or a land of communities of devastation in the reaches all about was very different in the past than the impact now on world Jewry of ruin on a larger geographic and numerical scale. It is uncertain, too, whether the German attrition was in fact of a vastly different order proportionately than earlier desolation; there are data that suggest otherwise.

Theologically, religiously, it seems to be absurd to hold that the extirpation of Judean, Rhineland, or South-Eastern European Jewry was a more acceptable experience than what transpired between 1939 and 1945. Is the vision of an infinite God who is Guardian of Israel less shaken by the annihilation of *only* a million Jews at the hands of the Romans, of *only* several hundred thousand each by crusaders, cossacks, haidamuks, than by the six million dead in German Europe? A god who plays these odds is not the God of Judaism. And Judaism has survived until 1939, as it shall now, without denying its God and the covenant with Him.

Individuals Choose; The People May Not

Certainly, this last havoc demands a searching, penetrating reaffirmation of faith and commitment, as there have been urgent gropings for renewed meaning in the wake of earlier holocausts. The striving for new perspectives and new apperceptions is indeed constant demand of the spirit on every Jew, at all times. But a "new *covenant*," a "new *epoch*"—that is a closing of the book of Judaism. Whatever their sincerity, their love of Israel, their loyalties to Jewish practice, the prophets of the new covenant call not to a revitalization but to denial of the God of Israel and annulment of the Jew's *raison d'etre* in the world. That, too, is not unique. Not all the gropings after preceding desolation remained anchored in the covenant that is. Those that were not, led into apostate movements and disappearance.

The endeavor for new covenants today too shall fail, to be remembered as a tragic aberration. The *individual* Jew has choice before him. He can opt for the prototype antipodes of hasidism and of Sabbatean-Frankist oblivion, to add new dimensions and nuance to the mainstream of Judaism or to cut himself off. The House of Israel has no such choice. Once initiated with the Patriarchs and reconfirmed by the assembled multitudes at Sinai, the covenant is irrevocable. This is a principle of the faith of Judaism. It is put eloquently in *Midrash Rabba* on Exodus 3:14: " 'I Shall Be As I Shall Be.' R. Johanan said: 'I Shall Be As I Shall Be' to individuals, but for the community of Israel, I rule over them even if against their desire and will, even though they break their teeth, as it is said: 'As I live, saith the Lord God, surely with a mighty hand and with an outstretched arm, and with fury poured out, will I be King over you' (Ezekiel 20:33)." The commentary on the Midrash, *Matnat Kehunah*, amplifies: "The individual who desires and chooses me, to him I shall be God; and if he does not so desire, it is given him to cast off the yoke; but to the community of Israel I do not give the option of casting off the yoke of heaven."

The advocates of new covenants will not halt the salvational history of the Jewish people, but they can add to the century's attritions.

They must not go unchallenged, therefore. It must be told unequivocally: They are advocates not of a reaffirmed Judaism, but of something other than the religion eternal of a God eternal.

A Perspective of Holocausts

The Jew must struggle to come to grips with ravage and loss on two distinct levels, that of the People collectively and that of the individual.

For the People, the covenant is indissoluble, and its conditions have been spelled out: "See, I have set before thee this day life and good, and death and evil . . . I command thee this day to love the Lord thy God, to walk in his ways, and to keep his commandments . . . Then thou shalt live and the Lord thy God shall bless thee in the land into which thou goest . . . But if thy heart turn away . . . and shalt worship other gods . . . I announce to you this day, that thou shalt surely perish, and that thou shalt not prolong your days upon the land . . . I call heaven and earth to witness this day against you, that I have set before thee life and death, blessing and cursing. Therefore choose life . . . And the Lord said to Moses, Behold, thou shalt sleep with thy fathers; and this people will . . . go astray after the gods of the . . . land into which they go . . . and break my covenant which I have made with them. Then . . . I will forsake them, and I will hide my face from them, and they shall be devoured . . . so that they will say on that day, are these evils not come upon us, because our God is not among us? And I will surely hide my face on that day for all the evils which they shall have perpetrated." (Deuteronomy 30:15-20; 31:16-18).

This is a clear blueprint of Jewish history, in promise and realization. The terms of the covenant are repeated, again and again, throughout Scripture and Rabbinic literature, and their fulfillment is historical record. The People that chose and was chosen to bear witness to the God who is revealed in the affairs of mankind cannot survive at ease the betrayal of that God and the forcing him to turn his face. We are given the choice to make God's presence large in the world of man or to banish the *Shechinah*, but we cannot avoid the consequences of then being alone in a godless world. God's banishment paves the way to holocausts. In Jewish mysticism, every Jew is held to be an organic member of the corpus of the *Shechinah*. No people has flourished intact for very long in the eclipse of the divine; we Jews are left especially vulnerable—but we survive, and in our pain remain incandescent.

The Covenant's Truth Remains Eternal

There is an additional stipulation in the covenant with the Jewish people: "And it shall come to pass, when all these things are come upon thee . . . and thou shalt return to the Lord thy God and shalt obey his voice . . . with all thy heart and with all thy soul; that then the Lord thy God will turn thy captivity, and have compassion upon thee, and will return, and gather thee from all the nations among whom the Lord thy God has scattered thee . . ." (Deuteronomy 30:1-3).

That promise, too, echoes throughout the chronicles of God's dialogue with the Jewish people. The covenant is not for review, neither is the eternity of Jewish existence. God is in exile with his people, and when they permit him, He returns from exile and with him once more the people. With Jewish justice and righteousness lies Jewish redemption. Until then, the door remains closed and the lights darkened.

The privilege of *being* a covenantal people is transcendent. The consequences of violation are agonizing. Many Jews have individually reasserted their allegiance to the collective covenant, even in bitter experience of its terms. I ask myself whether I should have the strength for such personal reassertion, had I endured them fully in my being. But I do know this: The covenant has unfolded for the people, and continues to unfold, in panlucid verity. It has not been broken by God, nor has he permitted the People to shake it off.

For the individual, the question of theodicy—the innocent who suffer, the evildoers who flourish—is ultimately the same whether suffering is in the midst of an inclusive catastrophe or in aloneness. The question to God, Why?, is the same for the first child struck down in human history and for the last to perish in Auschwitz. That is the eternal confrontation of all men with God.

R. Johanan, the *amorah* who lost his children, would visit mourners and show a bone of his tenth, last son. A mute rendering of comfort in a sharing of faith: R. Johanan remained the sage. Elishah b.

Abuyah did not. Countless human beings, Jews and non-Jews, have found it possible, somehow, to take the way of Johanan, Jews even after the German visitation. That is the challenge to the individual always. For the individual Jew to whom the evidence for the being of God as Judaism has known him is too persuasive to elude, for all the suffering experienced, the seeking of new covenants is a search in the wrong dimension, a delusion.

II. Berenbaum: Our Ancient Covenant Has Been Shattered

The Hofetz Chaim once said: "For the believer there are no questions and the unbeliever there are no answers." David Weiss has sidestepped the questions posed by the Holocaust.

He has restated the eternity of the covenant that binds God and Israel, but he has not wrestled with the fundamental question. What can we say of that covenant in the wake of Auschwitz? Need we alter our understanding? Need we rely less upon God and more upon our fellow Jews in the struggle for survival? And finally, how can we talk of God's attributes of compassion and mercy in a world of death camps?

Weiss' conclusions are expected. *Bitachon* (trust), as Zwi Werblowsky so beautifully demonstrated, is central to the religious Jew's perception of the world. I concur that there are dangers in a Godless world. There is also a sense of emptiness and aloneness, a void. Jewish salvational history is jeopardized: most Jews do not live salvational history (except in its most secularized form of Israel and Zionism), and many devout Jews have politicized salvational history, identifying it with settlement of Judea and Samaria.

But in order to avoid the existential problem posed by the Holocaust, Professor Weiss is forced to deny its historical uniqueness and theological singularity. He also questions the religious integrity of unnamed thinkers who wrestle with the question of covenant after Auschwitz.

Space will not permit me to argue for the uniqueness of the Holocaust. I am uncomfortable with the term "Holocaust"—an *olah* (a sacrificial offering burnt whole unto the Lord)—for I believe that the term softens and falsifies the impact of the event by imparting a religious meaning to the destruction. Yet the case for uniqueness is overwhelming. Divergent thinkers who disagree on many issues agree that the Holocaust was a singular and unprecedented event.

Its Uniqueness Should Not Be Denied

For Yehuda Bauer two historical elements mark the Holocaust as unique: the total planned annihilation of a people and its quasi religious-apocalyptic meaning. Forever an empiricist, Bauer argues that "to date, this has only happened to Jews." Scholars such as Uri Tal, Lucy Dawidowicz, Emil Fackenheim, and George Mosse essentially agree with his judgment. Other thinkers maintain that the inner experience of the victim and the survivor or the mechanisms and processes of destruction mark the Holocaust as unique. (Raul Hilberg, Joseph Borkin, Hannah Arendt, Lawrence Langer, and Richard Rubenstein share this perspective to various degrees.)

Suffice it to say that there is credible evidence advanced by distinguished scholars to suggest that the Holocaust was unprecedented not only in scope, setting, expectation, and proportion but in intention, intensity, duration, methodology, and consequences.

Professor Weiss' reasons for denying the uniqueness and offending many by using the plural, small "h" (holocausts) is religious rather than scholarly. He is not alone. Many who object to aesthetics or politics of Holocaust commemorations or the disproportionate role the Holocaust assumes in contemporary Jewish identity strike out at the concept of uniqueness instead of tackling the troubling issue more directly.

Now to the heart of the matter. One good Midrash deserves another. Moses said: "The great, powerful, and awesome God." Jeremiah came along and said: "Aliens are rampaging His Temple. Where is His awesomeness?" He no longer spoke (of God as) awesome. Daniel came along and said "His children are slaves to foreigners. Where is His power?" He no longer spoke of God as powerful.

The men of the Great Synod restored the crown to God's attributes by reinterpreting the power and the awesomeness of God. This change took time. And although the words were the same, their meaning had changed.

The Covenant Has Been Reevaluated Before

Jewish history testifies to a reinterpretation of the covenant after every transformative historical experience: the Exodus, Sinai, the destruction of the first and second Temples, the defeat of 135 C.E. and the Spanish Inquisition. While the covenant may be eternal, our understanding of the covenant and hence our relationship to the God of history was changed by each of these events.

When the poet said: "The Torah was given at Sinai and returned at Lublin" or when the novelist proclaims "For the first time in Jewish history the covenant was broken . . . We must begin all over again . . ." they are reshaping the language of tradition in order to bear witness to their historical experience. Perhaps until the next Great Synod we will be unable to speak of God's power or His mercy except in the most muted of voices.

If we judge by the behavior of Jews as a people, our understanding of the covenant has changed. From Gush Emunim to Hashomer Hatzair, Jews have reentered history and are struggling for their survival by military and political means. They are no longer relying upon the promise of God's salvation, nor content to await the Messiah. Even those who profess their faith in the eternal covenant have altered the way they behave in history.

Professor Weiss does not refer to new convental thinkers by name. Nor can I recognize their thought from his characterizations. The men, whose writings I have read, share three essential convictions. The Holocaust has shattered the Jewish people and made it difficult to use religious language in a traditional way. Irving Greenberg's principle of truth sums it up best. "No statement, theological or otherwise, should be made that can not be said in the presence of the burning bodies of Jewish children."

Secondly, they maintain that the Holocaust has imposed new responsibilities on the Jewish people. While I do not concur with Fackenheim's "commanding Voice of Auschwitz", he has captured the sense of obligation that the Holocaust has imposed upon the Jewish people. Thirdly, they are not closing the door on Judaism or on the Jewish witness "to something better."

With the notable exception of my teacher Richard Rubenstein, most post-Holocaust theologians believe that the reality of despair must energize us to hope. In a world of evil, we must create good. In a world without God, we must restore His image. This is neither an aberration nor a tragic path to assimilation. Rather it is the essence of the contemporary Jewish challenge; the core of our witness.

For Weiss there are no questions. Many theologians of the Holocaust have chosen to wrestle with serious questions and not to avoid them or argue that they just don't exist.

SOME ARTICLES ARE prompted by purely intellectual concerns. A scholar may confront a problem in research and explore the perplexing issue in writing. Other articles are not purely the product of contemplative thought but of political and organizational strife. A problem cannot be dealt with until some new intellectual ground is broken. Such were the circumstances under which Michael Berenbaum first wrote on the uniqueness and universality of the Holocaust.

In 1979, Berenbaum was invited to serve as Deputy Director of the President's Commission on the Holocaust. He worked directly with the chairman of the commission, Elie Wiesel (whose writings we will read and whose questions frame this anthology), and with Irving Greenberg, the Holocaust Commission's director. Their combined task was to recommend to the president an appropriate United States national memorial to the Holocaust.

The commission was soon wrestling with a serious problem that threatened to undermine its efforts. It was assumed that the Holocaust was an event that happened to Jews; they were the victims to be memorialized. For the first time, the federal government—not the Jewish community or an individual church—would be wrestling with the question of the Holocaust.

Because the memorial would be national in scope, all ethnic groups that felt themselves victimized by the Holocaust sought to be included in the memorial; while Jewish survivors feared that such an inclusion would misrepresent the nature of the Holocaust and dejudaize the event.

Elie Wiesel, in his characteristic style, suggested a poetic solution. "While not all the victims were Jews," he told President Jimmy Carter, "all Jews were victims." Yet the problem still remained; how could one speak of Jewish uniqueness in the Holocaust while also including a mosaic of victims killed by the Nazis?

By the time Berenbaum wrote his essay on "The Uniqueness and Universality of the Holocaust," he was no longer involved with the President's Commission or its successor body, the United States Holocaust Memorial Council. Therefore he could probe the issue without political pressure.

Berenbaum argues that the uniqueness of the Jewish experience is a matter of historical fact, not metaphysical faith, yet only by including all the victims of Nazism in the memorial can the uniqueness of the Jewish experience be established.

Now serving as Project Director for the United States Holocaust Memorial Museum, Berenbaum has been given the opportunity to demonstrate that his writings can solve a thorny problem of political constituencies and survivor sensibilities by simply resorting to truth.

Michael Berenbaum

The Uniqueness and Universality of the Holocaust

The question of the uniqueness and universality of the Holocaust is being considered with increasing frequency not only in scholarly quarters with a focus on historiography but also in communities throughout the United States where Holocaust Memorials and commemorative services raise a consciousness of the Holocaust, which then enters the mainstream of American culture. In the process the word *Holocaust*, shorn of its particular reference along with its article, threatens to become a symbolic word connoting mass murder and destruction, whatever the magnitude. The debate over the place of the Holocaust in human history is being conducted within the academy, in the streets among political activists and community leaders, in schools by educators developing curricula, among a cultural elite in literature and the arts, and in religious and philosophical circles.

Perhaps it is as much the force of personality as of circumstance that has brought the definition of the Holocaust to the fore. The chief protagonists for alternate conceptions, Elie Wiesel and Simon Wiesenthal, are both survivors, both European Jews, both men of towering stature and magnificent accomplishment in bringing the Holocaust to the attention of the world. Yet these two men differ markedly not only in their achievements but in their personal histories, their legacy and destiny. For Simon Wiesenthal, the word Holocaust refers to the systematic murder of eleven million people, six million of whom were Jews killed because of their Jewishness and five million non-Jews killed for a variety of reasons in an apparatus of death and destruction designed for mass extermination: the *Einzatsgruppen*, the concentration

From *American Journal of Theology & Philosophy* 2 (September 1981). Reprinted by permission.

camp, and the extermination camp. Wiesenthal maintains that although all Jews were victims, the Holocaust transcended the confines of the Jewish community. Other people shared the tragic fate of victimhood.

As a person Wiesenthal personifies two self-characterizations of the Jewish people, *din* (justice) and *am kisheh oref* (a stiff-necked people); he has been tenacious in his pursuit of law, demanding that the European nations bring their Nazi war criminals to trial. He has stubbornly refused to abandon the quest for justice after some thirty-five years, when its meaning may have been tarnished by international disinterest and by the absence of appropriately severe sentences. (One war criminal was recently sentenced to the equivalent of 1.5 minutes in jail for every person he killed.) He has also declined to resort to revenge as a swifter, more primitive form of punishment. Wiesenthal hounds both the criminal and the state to remember and reaffirm the value of justice in a world that would prefer to forget.

Wiesenthal's perception of the Holocaust may reflect his most basic post-Holocaust commitment, the prosecution of Nazi war criminals. When apathetic governments are reminded that their non-Jewish citizens were also killed, a greater measure of their cooperation can be enlisted. By more broadly defining the Holocaust, Wiesenthal can intensify the political pressure he can exert. Wiesenthal's more universal predilection may also reflect his present status as a European Jew, namely, that of belonging to a demoralized community that may be psychologically incapable of taking a Judeocentric perspective in the public domain—preferring instead the aphorism of Gordon, "be a Jew in your own home and a man in the street," even if in this instance the choice of a wider definition is most efficacious. Yet lest we lose perspective here, we should remember that in over 200 panels in the museum of the Simon Wiesenthal Center for Holocaust Studies in Los Angeles, less than 7 percent mention the five million non-Jews, and half of those displays center on the righteous among the nations who lived with the Jews, fought beside them, helped rescue Jews, and eventually died with them. Those who would contend that there is a major dilution of the Jewish meaning of the Holocaust in the work of the Wiesenthal Center had better look elsewhere for the substantiation of their accusations. [1]

1. Oral Communication, the Simon Wiesenthal Center for Holocaust Studies, Los Angeles, California.

Wiesenthal himself, it should be added, is not the only person who has included non-Jews among those killed in the Holocaust; nor has he become an active participant in the debate over definition. Rather, his general position and his stance in the past have led to his being seen by others as the representative of a "universalist" posture that some interpret as an affront to the unique experience of the Jews in the Holocaust.

By contrast, Elie Wiesel is the poet laureate of the Holocaust, a man who has become, in the words of Steven Schwarzschild, "the de facto high priest of our generation," the one who speaks most tellingly in our time of our hopes and fears, our tragedy and our protest.[2] If Wiesenthal represents justice and the tenacity of the Jewish soul, Wiesel stands as the embodiment of *shirah* (poetry) and *Rachamim* (compassion). Wiesel relates to the Holocaust as the *mysterium tremendum* (sacred mystery) that can be approached but never understood, the *PARDES*, a world that one can only apprehend at great peril and that should not be approached without preparation and extreme caution. Elsewhere I have written at great length of Wiesel's abiding significance as a thinker and his impact on contemporary Jewish consciousness.[3] Wiesel's contribution as a writer and story-teller toward keeping the memory of the Holocaust alive and transmitting it to my generation and beyond should not be underestimated. Wiesel fears that Wiesenthal's definition of the Holocaust may set in motion an irreversible process by which the memory of the six million Jews will be erased. First, he argues, people will speak of eleven million people, six million of whom were Jews, then of eleven million people some of whom were Jews, and finally of eleven million people without any reference to Jews.

Wiesel is the only American Jewish author of renown who writes solely from a Jewish perspective and for whom the process of Americanization was never central to his tale or to his literary contribution. Even though Wiesel has been an American citizen for close to two decades, he continues to write in French and, unlike other of his literary contemporaries, he has not reflected upon the American Jewish experience in any significant way. His novels are primarily set in

2. Steven Schwarzschild, "Jewish Values in the Post-Holocaust Future," *Judaism*, Vol. 16, No. 3 (Summer, 1967), p. 157.

3. Michael Berenbaum, *The Vision of the Void* (Middletown: Wesleyan University Press, 1979).

Europe or Israel, and few American characters ever appear. (*The Accident*, a lone exception, is set in New York but deals with the psychological scars left by the Holocaust on a survivor, and in that sense the American setting is irrelevant.) Nevertheless, it was as an American figure that Elie Wiesel was appointed Chairman of the President's Commission on the Holocaust and its successor body, the United States Holocaust Memorial Council, which is charged to create a national museum to tell the story of the Holocaust, to transmit the legacy of Jewish suffering to a general American audience. In my opinion, the task of the Holocaust Memorial Council involves the Americanization of the Holocaust; that is, the story must be told in such a way that it resonates not only with the survivor in New York, his son in Houston or his daughter in San Francisco, but with the Black leader from Atlanta and his child, the farmer from the Midwest, the Industrialist from the Northeast, and the millions of other Americans who each year make a pilgrimage to Washington to visit their nation's capital. The Americanization of the Holocaust is an honorable task provided that the story told is truthful, faithfully representing the historical event in a way that can be grasped by an American audience. Each culture inevitably leaves its stamp on the past it remembers. Israel, for example, has retold the story of the Holocaust as *Shoah ve Gevurah* (Holocaust and Resistance), emphasizing the pockets of armed rebellion along with the victimization that was in fact more prevalent. The intersection of the historical event and societal need, what happened and what can be understood, leaves neither history nor society unchanged. Indeed, this process is integral to the formation of what sociologists have termed the civil religion of a given society. Through the Holocaust/Resistance tale, Israelis have linked their origins to the heroic warriors who defied the mighty powers of the world in order to affirm the honor and dignity of the Jewish people. Charles Leibman, who has written eloquently of the civil role of the Holocaust in the Israeli consensus, has shown the degree to which the Holocaust tale has been shaped by societal need.

The task of the National Memorial Council in America in designing a museum is far more difficult than was Israel's endeavor at Yad Vashem (the Israeli Holocaust memorial museum), for the council must address itself to an audience that finds the tale itself alien and not directly a part of the American experience. The council also runs the risk of creating a magnet for antisemitism if others who perceive themselves, rightly or wrongly, as victims of the Holocaust feel excluded from the memorial and/or sense that their suffering has been trivialized or denied. The museum must grapple intelligently and painfully with the problem of complicity with the Nazis in the destruction of the Jews by people who were themselves the victims of Nazism, and it must struggle with the dilemma of the bystander in a way that makes sense of the few successes and many failures of American policy toward the Holocaust during and following the war.

Enter the historians—Yehuda Bauer, the prominent historian and head of the Institute of Contemporary Jewry at the Hebrew University in Jerusalem, distinguished between two definitions of the Holocaust offered in speeches by the then President of the United States, Jimmy Carter. Carter twice defined the Holocaust, once speaking of the memorial to "six million Jews and millions of other victims of Nazism during World War II" and on another occasion decrying the "systematic and state-sponsored extermination of six million Jews and five million non-Jews." Bauer comments:

> The memorial as seen by the president [not the commission] should commemorate all the victims of Nazism, *Jews and non-Jews* alike and should *submerge* the specific Jewish tragedy in the general sea of atrocities committed by the Nazi regime [emphasis added].[4]

Bauer attributed what he perceived as a submersion of the specific Jewish tragedy to pressure from ethnic groups within America and warned that an Americanized, non-Jewish memorial would misrepresent the Holocaust. Professor Bauer marshals three highly emotional arguments to foster his claim. He invokes the Russian attempt to deny the Jewishness of the Holocaust, which resulted in the abomination of the memorial at Babi Yar, where no mention of Jews is made either in the content of the sculpture or in an inscription on the memorial. Secondly, Bauer refers to the Western denial of the particular "War Against the Jews," which led to the failure to rescue. Thirdly, Bauer alludes to the international antisemitism that seeks to deny the Holocaust altogether.

We must separate the emotional elements of these arguments from their substantive components. It is ironic that Bauer should focus

4. Yehuda Bauer, "Whose Holocaust?" *Midstream*, Vol. XXVI, No. 9 (November 1980), p. 42.

on the president's words when Carter had delegated responsibility for designing and implementing the museum to the Holocaust Memorial Council, which consistently and conspicuously chose over and over again to emphasize the uniqueness of the Jewish experience and the centrality of Jewish suffering. For Bauer, displaying an almost mythical regard for the power of a president, Carter's words on a ceremonial occasion or in a message to Congress were viewed as all-important, while the deliberations of the commission, its *Report to the President*, which is the central document of the legislative history of the Holocaust Memorial Bill, and indeed the work of the council in implementing its recommendations were seen as secondary. Notice also that *inclusion* of others (non-Jews) is transformed in Bauer's logic to *submergence* in the general sea of atrocities. Why, indeed, must inclusion become submergence if, as was argued in the commission report and in what follows, the uniqueness of the Jewish experience can only be detailed and documented by comparing it with the Nazi treatment of other subservient populations persecuted by the Nazis? Only by understanding the fate of others who suffered, where it paralleled the Jewish experience and more importantly where it differed, can we demonstrate the distinctive character of the Jewish fate as a matter of historical fact.

With respect to Bauer's fear of Americanization, the question of audience should not be confused with content. The Holocaust is only "Americanized" in so far as it is explained to Americans and related to their history with ramifications for future policy. Insights can be gained from the study of the Holocaust that have a universal import for the destiny of all humanity. A presidential commission funded at taxpayers' expense to design a *national* memorial does not have the liberty of creating an exclusively Jewish one in the restricted sense of the term, and most specifically with regard to audience. Such is the task of the American Jewish Community operating with private funding and without government subvention. In the final analysis, private Jewish memorials and the national Holocaust museum (along with work of scholarship, art, and media productions) will speak a message that will endure in America far longer than the words of an American president.

There is a fundamental paradox that reflects itself in an ambivalence expressed by many survivors and shared by other Jews about bequeathing the story of the Holocaust. For the Holocaust to have any sustained impact it must enter the mainstream of international consciousness as a symbolic word denoting a particular, extraordinary event with manifest moral, political, and social implications. The moment it does enter the mainstream, however, it becomes "fair game" for writers, novelists, historians, theologians, and philosophers from all backgrounds and with unequal skill. Some lesser minds or insensitive talents are bound to disappoint, dilute, and misrepresent. Transmitting the Holocaust entails a degree of uncontrolled dissemination. We cannot simultaneously maintain the Holocaust as a horribly sanctified topic untrespassed and inviolate while complaining that the world is ignorant of its occurrence. Even for Wiesel, the decision to run the risks of exposure began the day *Night* was published in French rather than remaining in its Yiddish original, which was printed five years earlier. Nonetheless, Bauer does provide his readers with a valuable definition of the uniqueness of the Holocaust, which he sees as containing two central elements: the planned, total annihilation of an entire community and a quasi-apocalyptic, religious component whereby the death of the victim becomes an integral ingredient in the drama of salvation. Bauer adds that "to date such an act has only been directed against the Jews." As we shall see, Bauer presents us with two necessary but perhaps not exhaustive conditions for the uniqueness of the Holocaust.

Bauer displays no discomfort with the word *Holocaust* even though the term itself is not without its problems. Holocaust is a theological term in origin rather than a historical one. It is an English derivative from the Greek translation of the Hebrew word *olah* meaning a sacrificial offering burnt whole before the Lord. Some serious students of the Holocaust have maintained that the word itself softens and falsifies its impact by imparting religious meaning to the events.[5] The Yiddish word *churban*, meaning destruction, is far more stark and refers to the results of the event itself. The Hebrew word *Shoah* shares much in common with its Yiddish antecedent. Bauer's views are essentially supported with minor modifications by scholars such as Lucy Dawidowicz, Uriel Tal, and George Mosse. Their work centers on intent and ideology. There is another argument for the uniqueness of the Holocaust that focuses not on its purposes or ideology but on the mechanisms of destruction and the creation of concentration and extermination camps. This argument is culled from the work of Raul Hilberg

---

5. Walter Laqueur, *The Terrible Secret* (Boston: Little Brown and Company, 1980), p. 7.

who centers his research not on the philosophy that underscored the destruction but on the processes by which Jews were executed. In fragmented form, Hannah Arendt, Lawrence Langer, Richard Rubenstein, and Joseph Borkin also examine this dimension of the Holocaust. Its importance should not be overlooked, for its implications are far too critical.

Joseph Borkin has argued that Auschwitz represented the perverse perfection of slavery. In almost all previous manifestations of human slavery, including the particularly cruel form practiced in North America, the slave was considered a capital investment to be protected, fed, and sheltered by the master and generally permitted the opportunity to reproduce and hence increase his master's wealth. In contrast, under Nazism the human being was reduced to a consumable raw material, expended in the process of manufacture, from which all material life was systematically drained before the bodies were recycled into the Nazi war economy, gold teeth for the treasury, hair for mattresses, ashes for fertilizer. At I. G. Auschwitz the average slave lived for ninety days, at Buna, thirty. As one survivor put it, "they oiled the machines, but they didn't feel the need to feed the people." These corporate decisions, Borkin hastens to remind us, were made in Frankfurt and *not* in the field, made for "sound" economic reasons and not under the exigencies of battlefield conditions.

Yet it was not only slavery that reached its most demonic, absolute expression at Auschwitz. The need to eliminate surplus population, as Rubenstein explains, was also carried to its logical conclusion. Bureaucracy was perfected to tackle ever more difficult problems in the machinery of destruction. The coexistence of demonic evil with banal evil in a bureaucratic mechanism points to another unique dimension of the Holocaust.

The camps themselves represent a society of total domination, one which Langer has called the universe of choiceless choices. Langer has explained that Auschwitz was a world apart, shattering our conceptions of language and meaning and remaining with us, now some three-and-a-half decades later, for it eludes the inner space or time in which to bury it:

> The fault lies not in our own deficient vision but in the nature of the experience, which challenges our imagination with a nearly impossible task. Confrontation with the springs of conduct in the death

camps represents less a recollection of times past (with the observer imposing a Proustian order on chaotic material) than a collection of past moments, whose intrinsic chaos urges us to invent a new moral and temporal dimension for its victims to inhabit.[6]

No theory of the uniqueness of the Holocaust that refuses to probe the inner dimensions of the mechanisms of destruction will suffice, for it is in the inner world of how the terrible crime was committed, as much as in the conception of the deed or its importance, that an understanding of the unparalleled world of the Holocaust must be sought.

In response to Bauer, the prominent Jewish historian and Dean of Graduate Studies at the Jewish Theological Seminary, Professor Ismar Schorsch, entered the dialogue. Schorsch joined with those advocating a limited role to the Holocaust in the civil religion of American Jews, fearing a lachrymose theory of Jewish history.[7] The history of Jew as victim threatens to dominate Jewish consciousness, to diminish the totality of Jewish history in which the Jews were the authors of their own destiny, and to overwhelm the vital, energizing celebration of life or the hope for redemption. Moreover, Schorsch argues, the consequence of an overemphasis on the Holocaust has been an "obsession with the uniqueness of the event as if to forgo the claim would be to diminish the horror of the crime."[8]

The truth, Schorsch argues, is that Jews were the only victims of genocide in World War II. "To insist on more is to imply or overindulge in invidious comparisons" either of which evokes earlier or later genocide. When used indiscriminately the argument for the uniqueness of the Holocaust is a "throwback to an age of religious polemics, a secular version of chosenness."[9] This argument is seen most clearly in the writings of the orthodox Jewish theologian Eliezer Berkovits in which he writes:

> The metaphysical quality of the Nazi-German hatred of the Jews as well as the truly diabolical, superhuman quality of the Nazi-German criminality against the Jews are themselves testimonies to

6. Lawrence Langer, "The Dilemma of Choice in the Deathcamps," a presentation to Zachor: Holocaust Resource Center's Faculty Seminar, January 1979 (unpublished manuscript), p. 19.

7. Ismar Schorsch, "The Holocaust and Jewish Survival," *Midstream*, Vol. XXVII, No. 1 (January 1981) pp. 38–42.

8. Ibid., p. 39.

9. Ibid.

the dark knowledge with which a nazified Germany sensed the presence in history of the hiding God.[10]

For Schorsch the claim of uniqueness is both historically unproductive and politically counterproductive, for it "impedes dialogue and introduces issues that alienate potential allies from among other victims of organized depravity," i.e. other victims of Nazism, Armenians, Gypsies, Blacks, etc. Schorsch recommends that Jews translate their experience into existential and political symbols meaningful to non-Jews without "submerging our credibility." What for Schorsch is the process of translation appears to Bauer as Americanization and dejudaization. When the Holocaust is properly communicated to Americans, it can assume its rightful place as a symbolic orienting event within human history, pregnant with meaning and implications for our common destiny.

While I find Bauer's characterization of the uniqueness of the Holocaust inadequate and Schorsch's resistance inappropriate, both Bauer's assertions and Schorsch's reticence could be informed by a more comparative approach to understanding the Holocaust. The fruits of such consideration are amply apparent in important works such as Irving Horowitz's study of the Holocaust and the Armenian Genocide, *Taking Lives,* Helen Fein's *Accounting for Genocide,* and the literary analysis of Terrence Des Pres. A search for uniqueness need not alienate potential allies for it might properly sharpen our insights into areas in need of greater research and additional scholarship. Nevertheless, Schorsch's inhibiting cautions, like Bauer's misplaced fears, should be taken as warning signals of what must be avoided in order to secure serious scholarship and responsible application.

Professor John Cuddihy of Hunter College is an informed, brilliant, yet eccentric critic of contemporary American Jewry. His insights often glisten even if they do not long endure deep introspection—his information is wide-ranging and his comparative understanding of modernity and the Jewish condition original and innovative, exciting even if not entirely accurate or friendly. Cuddihy probes critically not the history of the Holocaust but its historiography. To his credit, Cuddihy had the courage to present the original version of some of his work to a faculty seminar of Holocaust scholars from the Northeast to

10. Eliezer Berkovits, *Faith after the Holocaust,* (New York: Ktav, 1973), p. 118.

sharpen his thoughts through dialogue and open exchange.[11] He first cites a number of scholars, all of whom are making similar points regarding the Holocaust as unique in its character, in its systematic, senseless, and non-instrumental organization, in its totality and its focus on death. For Henry Feingold, perhaps the most important historian of the Roosevelt Administration in relationship to the Jews, the danger is that we may rob the Holocaust of its horrendous particularity. We may generalize and modulate Nazism by treating it not as a uniquely demonic force but as the dark side of the human spirit that lurks in all of us. For A. Roy Eckardt, a Christian theologian of the Holocaust, the event is "uniquely unique," a category apart from even those historical events one would classify as unique. In his critical work *The Cunning of History*, Richard Rubenstein projects the precedent of the Holocaust toward its present and future ramifications, as noted by William Styron both in his introduction to Rubenstein's work and in his novel *Sophie's Choice*. For both Rubenstein and Styron the Holocaust looms as the extreme technological nightmare, the manifestation extraordinaire of the potentialities of Western civilization. Emil Fackenheim, by contrast, believes that the uniqueness of the Holocaust is found in the uniqueness of its victims. The Holocaust was directed against Jews who were "not the *waste products* of Nazi society but its *end product*"[12] (italics added). In reviewing these claims of uniqueness, Professor Cuddihy has remarked that the distinction between Jews and non-Jews is the key element that unites Fackenheim and Feingold, Bauer, and Wiesel. The "residual category" of non-Jews that continues to divide the world serves three critical functions for the Jews. It preserves the sacred particularity of the Jews, freezing the presence of antisemitism in the consciousness of the Jew and thus eliminating the Sartresque question: "Why remain a Jew?" It continues to separate the Jew from the gentile not as the free choice of the Jews but the imposed decision of Hitler who divided Jews from non-Jews and caused the ultimate separation of their fates. Thirdly, according to Cuddihy, uniqueness functions not so much for preventing historical fraud, denials, or dejudaization, but as a continuing device for conferring status.

11. John Cuddihy, "The Holocaust: The Latent issue in the Uniqueness Debate," a presentation to Zachor: the Holocaust Resource Center's Faculty Seminar, January 1980 (unpublished manuscript).

12. Emil Fackenheim, *The Jewish Return into History: Reflections in the Age of Auschwitz and a New Jerusalem* (New York: Schocken Books, 1978), p. 93.

In fairness to Cuddihy, one must stress that his concern is not history but sociology, and he is writing something of a cryptosociology of historiography. Often one can dissent from his views with much ease, especially when his statements are flip and inaccurate. Yet one must examine his claim that inherent in the desire to affirm the uniqueness of the Holocaust, apart from the issue of its factual validity, may be a secular translation of Jewish chosenness wherein the special-ness of the people, once formulated in terms of spiritual descent from the recipients of the divine revelation at Sinai, is now recast as the inheritance of those wronged by the most demonic, the anti-God, so to speak, which acted at Auschwitz.

In response to the arguments of Cuddihy and others, it is incum-bent upon us to consider the factual arguments for the uniqueness of the Holocaust and the resistance to the centrality of the Holocaust in contemporary Jewish consciousness that is currently surfacing in dis-cussions among Jewish historians and theologians. Questions about the uniqueness and universality of the Holocaust in world history are accompanied by queries regarding the place of the Holocaust in Jewish history. The current discussion centers on three major questions: whether the Holocaust is indeed unprecedented within Jewish his-tory; whether it occupies an all too prominent position in contempo-rary Jewish consciousness, threatening to obscure and perhaps even exclude the promise of Sinai, the triumph of Israel, and the totality of previous Jewish history; and whether the Holocaust has normative implications for Jewish history and theology. To rehearse the parame-ters of the dialogue and summarize the discussions between Jacob Neusner and Irving Greenberg, *The New York Times* article by Paula Hyman, the theology of Michael Wyschogrod, the writing of Robert Alter, and both the public and printed debates between Arnold Wolfe and myself would sidetrack us at this juncture.[13] Suffice it to say that essential to the general argument for the uniqueness of the Holocaust is the more specific conclusion that the Holocaust is not only quan-titatively but qualitatively different from other episodes of persecution in Jewish history, a point not universally accepted by some scholars in the field, whose objections are often motivated by the politics and

13. Robert Alter, "Deformations of the Holocaust," *Commentary* (February 1981). Arnold Jacob Wolfe and Michael Berenbaum, "The Centrality of the Holocaust: An Overemphasis?" *The National Jewish Monthly* (October 1980).

aesthetics of Holocaust commemoration rather than by specific historical data.

Elsewhere I have indicated my own conviction that the Holocaust
is unprecedented in Jewish history; it was not simply a continuation of
traditional antisemitism for four fundamental reasons. The Holocaust
differs from previous manifestations of antisemitism in that the earlier
expressions were episodic, non-sustained, illegal (they took place outside the law), and religiously rather than biologically based. (That is,
Jews were killed for what they believed or practiced; conversion or
emigration were possible alternatives.) By contrast, Nazism was unre-
lenting; for twelve years the destruction of the Jewish people was a
German priority. Trains that could have been used to bring soldiers to
the front or transport injured personnel to the rear were diverted to
bring Jews to their death. The persecution of Jews was geographically
widespread throughout Europe from Central Russia to the Spanish
border. Furthermore, it was legally conducted, the legal system serving as an instrument of oppression. The persecution of Jews and their
annihilation was a policy of state, utilizing all facets of the government.
Most importantly, Jews were killed not for *what* they were, for what
they practiced or believed, but for the *fact* that they were—all Jews
were to be exterminated, not merely the Jewish soul. Jews were no
longer considered, as they were in Christian theology, the symbol of
evil; rather, they had become its embodiment and as such were to be
eliminated.

Even the traditional category of Jewish martyrdom was denied to
the victims of the Holocaust, for they lacked the essential element of
choice in their deaths. Since they did not die because of their beliefs
but due to the accident of their biological birth as Jews (or the children
or grandchildren of Jews), a new category of martyrdom, a new language, had to be invented.

The Jewish uniqueness of the Holocaust can also be considered a
matter of historical fact, not of theological faith, the case for which
becomes even more apparent when the fates of other victims of Nazism, such as the Poles, are included. Undoubtedly, the Nazis planned
to destroy the Polish intelligentsia and to Germanize the elite Polish
youth by arranging for their adoption and assimilation into the dominant culture. This plan for destruction and assimilation was part of the
overall effort to make the Poles a subservient yet useful population for
Germany. For the Jews subservience was insufficient; the aim was

annihilation, the killing of every Jew regardless of his or her potential usefulness to the Germans (as Mordecai Chaim Rumkowski, the leader of the Lodz Judenrat who predicated the survival of his ghetto on its undeniable utility and absolute subservience to the Nazis, learned to his ultimate dismay). The Nazis wished to eradicate all Jews from the face of the earth.

When we consider the fate of the Gypsies, who share with the Jews the unfortunate distinction of being targeted for destruction, we discover more differences between the fate of the Jews and others in the Holocaust. While the Gypsies were killed in some countries, they remained relatively untouched in others. The fate of rural Gypsies often differed. By contrast, the murder of Jews was a priority in every country the Nazis invaded. In country after country the Nazis pressed the bureaucracy to process the Jews for the complete implementation of their "final solution." While the Gypsies were murdered as asocials, the destruction of the Jews had an apocalyptic, religious character to it that made it psychologically central to the Nazi drama of salvation for the German people. Even though Gypsies were also subject to gassing and other forms of extermination, the number of Gypsies killed was not as vast, and individual death by gassing was far less certain than it was for Jews. I stress these comparisons not to diminish the loss to these communities or the significance of each death. Jewish tradition teaches that every death shatters creation. However, the distinctness of the Jewish fate cannot be understood except in contrast with and relationship to the fate of the other victims of Nazism.

Like Gypsies, homosexuals were arrested and incarcerated, and many Ukrainians were sent to concentration camps where they were jailed as prisoners of war, yet a Ukrainian or a gay could hope to outlive the Nazis merely by surviving. In contrast, all Jews lived under the sentence of death. The ovens and the chambers were primarily restricted to Jews. An apparatus originally designed for the retarded and the mentally disturbed consumed the Jews, though in all likelihood it would not have ceased its operation had the Nazis won both the World War and the War Against the Jews.

Bohdan Wytwycky, a young philosopher from Columbia, has offered a compelling image for describing the Holocaust when he refers to the many circles of hell in Dante's inferno. The Jews occupy the center of hell with the concentric rings extending outward to incorporate many other victims much as the waves of water spread outward with diminishing intensity from a stone tossed into a quiet lake. In order to comprehend the Jewish center, we must fully probe the ripple effects as well as the indisputable core.

In arming themselves to protect the uniqueness of the Holocaust, many defenders of the faith (rather than the fact) have shied away from comparisons with other instances of subjugation or mass murder. Such comparisons do not innately obscure the uniqueness of the Holocaust; they clarify it. Inclusion of the Armenian experience, for example, in commemorating the Holocaust does not detract from the uniqueness of the Holocaust but deepens our moral sensitivity while sharpening our perception. Additionally, such inclusion may intensify our moral worth since it displays a generosity of spirit and an ethical integrity. We let our sufferings, however incommensurate, unite us in our condemnation of inhumanity rather than deride us in a calculus of calamity.

The exploration of the analogies between the Armenian Genocide and the Holocaust establishes several themes that are central to the moral lessons of the Holocaust. For example, Hitler used the excuse of the world's indifference to Armenian suffering to silence his Cabinet opposition and as a license to proceed at will with the destruction of the Jews without the fear of permanent negative consequences. If our aim is to teach that remembrance of the Holocaust might prevent future catastrophe not only to Jews but to other people as well, then what better example is there than the Armenian one? Similarly, one can probe with fruitful results the influence of Henry Morgenthau, Sr., the American Ambassador to Turkey during the Armenian massacres, on his son and namesake, the courageous Secretary of the Treasury, who confronted President Roosevelt with undeniable evidence of American inaction, if not complicity, with the extermination of European Jewry. The Jewish resistance fighters at Bialystok invoked the memory of Mesudah, the Armenian uprising, in fighting for freedom and honor.

Common to all these examples are three principles for dealing with events analogous but not equivalent to the Holocaust. The analogies must flow from history, they must illuminate other dimensions of the Holocaust and/or the analogous event, and finally, they must be authentic. If these three principles are followed, then we need not fear engaging in analogies that illumine our scholarship and our memory. They will not trivialize nor dejudaize the Holocaust.

SUGGESTIONS FOR FURTHER READING

Bauer, Yehuda. *The Holocaust in Historical Perspective*. Seattle: University of Washington Press, 1978.

Browning, Christopher. *Fateful Months: Essays on the Emergence of the Final Solution*. New York: Holmes & Meier, 1985.

Fein, Helen. *Accounting for Genocide: National Responses and Jewish Victimization during the Holocaust*. New York: The Free Press, 1979.

Garber, Zev, with Alan L. Berger and Richard Libowitz, eds. *Methodology in the Academic Teaching of the Holocaust*. Lanham, Md.: University Press of America, 1988.

Lemkin, Raphael. *Axis Rule in Occupied Europe*. Washington, D.C.: Carnegie Endowment for International Peace, 1944.

Marrus, Michael R. *The Unwanted: European Refugees in the Twentieth Century*. New York: Oxford University Press, 1985.

Rosenberg, Alan, and Gerald E. Myers, eds. *Echoes from the Holocaust: Philosophical Reflections on a Dark Time*. Philadelphia: Temple University Press, 1988.

Rubenstein, Richard L. *The Age of Triage: Fear and Hope in an Overcrowded World*. Boston: Beacon Press, 1983.

Wallimann, Isidor, and Michael N. Dobkowski, eds. *Genocide and the Modern Age: Etiology and Case Studies of Mass Death*. Westport, Conn.: Greenwood Press, 1987.

Wytwycky, Bohdan. *The Other Holocaust: Many Circles of Hell*. Washington, D.C.:

PART TWO

"Is It True What One Hears of Selections, of Gas, of Crematoriums?"

(PRIMO LEVI, *Survival in Auschwitz*)

You don't look well, you really don't.
Oh, I'll be all right.
Are you sad?
Could be. Nothing serious.
You should see yourself.
I believe you.
You can't go on like this.
What do you want me to do?
How should I know? Look around you. The trees in bloom.
The shop windows. The pretty girls. What the hell, let your-
self go. I promise you that after . . .
After? Did you say: after? Meaning what?

ELIE WIESEL, "Dialogues II," *One Generation After*

Primo Levi asked the question that forms the title for this book's Part
Two. It pressed itself upon him not long after his arrival at Monowitz-
Buna, a satellite of Auschwitz, where he was sent to do slave labor after
being deported from Italy in the winter of 1944. When Levi first
learned that Auschwitz was his destination, the name of that place was
"without significance" to him. Soon enough, this Jewish chemist would
learn about selections, gas, and crematoriums, but, for those who had
just arrived, the nature of Auschwitz was less than clear. Even for those
who were there, it took time—even if tragically little—to learn how
significant Auschwitz really was.

Too soon Levi no longer had to ask, "Is it true what one hears of selections, of gas, of crematoriums?" He knew because Auschwitz was his "home" until he was liberated in January 1945. His book, *Survival in Auschwitz*, from which the query comes, describes life and death in that place. Levi wrote it to respond to the question he had asked before learning the truth. For it was still being asked after Auschwitz, though not by him, and what raised the issue was the disconcerting voice of disbelief.

Before the Holocaust, too many people disbelieved such a thing could happen. During the Holocaust, too many people disbelieved that such a thing was happening. After the Holocaust, too many people disbelieved what had happened and that repetitions of it are possible. True, some people were ignorant about Auschwitz—how it arose and what it produced. There are those who remain ignorant about those realities even now. But disbelief and ignorance are not the same, and ignorance was not at the heart of disbelief about the Holocaust. The testimony of Jan Karski, gathered from a July 1988 interview by Ken Adelman in the *Washingtonian* magazine, helps to make the case.

Kozielewski was his real name, but this Polish Catholic, who is honored as a "righteous gentile" at the Yad Vashem memorial in Jerusalem, became Jan Karski and resisted the German occupation of his homeland during World War II. As this book goes to press, he is a semiretired professor at Georgetown University, where he has taught for more than thirty-five years. Only in his mid-twenties at the time, Karski served from 1939 to 1943 as a courier for the Polish underground and government-in-exile. Captured and tortured by the Gestapo, he managed to escape and continued to carry out one dangerous mission after another.

Toward the end of September 1942, Karski was headed for London. There he would convey important messages to the Polish government-in-exile. Shortly before his departure, two Jewish underground organizations inquired whether he would be their courier, too. Specifically, they asked Karski to make known that the Nazis were implementing their intention to destroy all Jews and to stress that only direct intervention by the Allies could stop the "final solution." Although Karski agreed to spread this word abroad, one of the Jewish leaders, fearing that Karski might not be believed, pressed on. It would help to disarm disbelief, he argued, if Karski saw firsthand what was happening to European Jewry. Thus it was that Jan Karski found himself smuggled inside the death camp at Belzec and, not once but twice, into the Warsaw ghetto as well.

Although Karski might prefer not to speak about those explicit experiences, he confesses that "I saw horrible, horrible things." He is much more outspoken, however, about the disbelief he encountered when trying to convince the Allies to acknowledge the Holocaust's reality and to take direct action to alleviate Jewish plight. He met with President Franklin D. Roosevelt and British Foreign Minister Anthony Eden. He testified to leading American Jews as well. Rabbi Stephen Wise and Justice Felix Frankfurter were among them. But *futile*—that is one of the words Karski would use to sum up his private diplomacy on behalf of the Jewish people.

It was not primarily ignorance, contends Karski, that produced the heartless abandonment of the Jews and thereby made the Nazis' genocidal aims all the easier to achieve. Self-imposing disbelief to dismiss inconvenient evidence, too many Allied leaders knew what was happening and yet were unconvinced and unmoved. They acted—or failed to act—accordingly. Granted, Allied might eventually crushed the Third Reich, and in that process the Holocaust was brought to an end. The ending was not complete, however, because Karski—and he is far from alone—remains haunted by the fact that "six million Jews perished. Six million totally helpless, abandoned by all. No country, no government, nobody, nothing."

Not all of the disbelief encountered by Jan Karski had the same texture. He recalls, for example, his meeting with Felix Frankfurter. Asked by Frankfurter to describe what was going on in Poland, Karski obliged in detail. Frankfurter listened intently until Karski had no more to say. When the Justice broke the silence that followed, he said, "Mr. Karski, a man like me talking to a man like you must be totally frank. So I say I am unable to believe you."

Clarifying his point, Frankfurter underscored that he did not think Karski was lying. "I am unable to believe him," the Justice insisted. "There is a difference." Then and even now, Karski reports, that difference has remained less than completely clear to him, and thus Karski adds, "My conscience is telling me that I should speak so that the postwar generation—Jews and non-Jews—realize where lack of tolerance, anti-Semitism, racism, and hatred lead."

Even if Jan Karski and Primo Levi never met, they are brothers who have worked to battle the multiple forms of disbelief lurking in the question, "Is it true what one hears of selections, of gas, of cremato-riums?" With words as their weapons, they have fought against disbelief and the illusion, indifference, and injustice it can spawn. They have not been alone. But words have their limitations, especially where disbelief and the Holocaust are concerned, as anyone who has tried to testify about that event with sensitivity and power comes to know.

Words may be insufficient to disarm disbelief about the Holo-caust, but without them—carefully chosen—disbelief gains an advan-tage it does not deserve and that humankind can ill afford. The writings in Part Two are all from persons who have devoted their lives to dispell such disbelief. These writers use words differently. Some record his-tory's detail meticulously. Others tell stories. Still others testify about their personal experiences, and some interpret and reflect upon these histories, tales, and autobiographies.

Just as written testimony about the Holocaust includes diverse genres, its authors represent different nationalities and write in differ-ent languages. Most, though by no means all, are Jewish, but even that shared identity promotes a broad stylistic spectrum. Permeating the diversity, however, are issues that these writers confront in common. They invite their readers to wrestle with them, too. These writers, for example, feel a profound ambivalence. It is impossible to write ade-quately about the Holocaust; yet that task must be attempted. They regard themselves as unequipped to do such work; yet they are com-pelled to try. The corresponding tension for a reader, at least for one who was not "there," is between an effort to understand and an aware-ness that the Holocaust eludes full comprehension. These dilemmas have multiple dimensions. The Holocaust, for instance, outstrips imag-ination. It is one thing to be creative when the possibilities open to imagination exceed what has become real. It is quite another to find that reality has already given birth to persons, places, and events that defy imagining. As David Rousset, one of the authors represented in the selections that follow, has put the point: "Normal men do not know that everything is possible."

Perhaps history prepares post-Holocaust minds to be more ac-cepting of the idea that "everything is possible." Nonetheless how is one to comprehend that the Nazi way included "idealism" that did not merely permit torture and murder but commanded that they continue day and night? So a problem remains: Can words help one to know what happened and to cope with its impact? There are no metaphors or adequate analogies for the Holocaust. Nor can Auschwitz be a metaphor or an analogy for anything else. If those realizations inform the ambivalence of those who write about the Holocaust, still they must feel that their expressions are at least potentially capable of communicating something urgent that can be said in no other way. But that conviction makes their task no easier, and when a reader works to grasp what the best of the Holocaust writers say, he or she will sense how the Holocaust makes those writers struggle with words. How can words tell the truth convincingly, describe what must be portrayed honestly, convey and yet control emotion so that clear insights will emerge and move people to make good decisions? Every serious author faces such questions, but they become unusually demanding when one encounters the Holocaust. Now words must be used against themselves, since they are unable to say all that is required and yet no comparable resources are available.

When writers emphasize the impossibility of communicating completely the realities of the Holocaust via words, they are sometimes accused of mystifying that event. They either make the Holocaust so exceptional that it loses contact with the rest of human history, the argument contends, or they obscure and becloud it in rhetoric that invests Auschwitz with a mythical aura that opposes lucid, rational analysis. Such mystifications may exist, but we trust that the contents of this book are not among them. Far from culling the Holocaust out of worldly reality, far from obscuring or beclouding the past, they complement, and are complemented by, all sound historical analysis. They are rooted both in the enormity of human loss brought about by the Holocaust and in the need to retrieve whatever can be left of a human future after Auschwitz has exposed the illusory quality of so many cherished assumptions.

In addition to David Rousset and his warning that "normal men do not know that everything is possible," a selection from Primo Levi probes further "the enormity and therefore the noncredibility of what took place in the Lagers." Historian Raul Hilberg provides a similar service by concentrating on the Jewish ghetto as a form of government aimed at the destruction of the European Jews. Acknowledging with Hilberg that "the basic situation of Jews during the Hitler period was one of political powerlessness," Yehuda Bauer, another eminent historian, explores the chances for and characteristics of Jewish resistance during the Holocaust, a task that glimpses more moments of heroism than might be expected in the Holocaust's unexpected times and places.

The short story is Tadeusz Borowski's way of recording what he experienced as a Polish gentile in Auschwitz. Helping one to see the invisible dimensions of the Holocaust, his tales bring to life, for example, how at one-and-the-same time some men could be playing soccer in Auschwitz while others were being gassed. Jean Améry survived Auschwitz, too. But this Jew endured the Gestapo's torture before he got there. How that experience marked him forever, and perhaps all of us as well, is what governs the essay by Améry that is reprinted here.

Robert Jay Lifton, a physician and psychiatrist, was not "there." Nevertheless his study of the medical profession's role in the Holocaust shows how important scholarship about the event, as well as eyewitness testimony, can be. For Lifton and others provide essential perspectives that were probably unavailable to anyone, save God, when the Holocaust was actually under way. Lifton's work is supplemented here by the contributions of literary scholars Terrence Des Pres and Lawrence Langer. They explore, respectively, the realities of "excremental assault" and "choiceless choice," two concepts that have proved invaluable in attempts to comprehend the Holocaust's significance. If those realities validate David Rousset's claim that "normal men do not know that everything is possible," they also tend to support Jean Améry's that the Holocaust has damaged, perhaps beyond repair, what he calls "trust in the world." In Part Two's final essay, philosopher John Roth assesses that damage and wonders whether there may still be ways to mend it. All of these contributions strive to dislodge disbelief and to encourage the conviction necessary to check the wasting of human life.

Like the other parts of this book, we began this one with a dialogue by Elie Wiesel. It, too, struggles against disbelief and for encouragement. The scene is unidentified. So are the speakers—or the speaker, for the conversation might be one that an individual carries on internally. But both the scene and the voices invite you to believe that they are—in their special way—about the Holocaust.

The voice asking, "After? Did you say: after? Meaning what?" could belong to one who survived. Survivors know—better than anyone—that "after" implies "before." They also know that "after" cannot mean "put 'before' behind you." Nor can "after" mean simply to look ahead, to get on with your life and let yourself go. Too much has happened, including too much disbelief, for that.

Most of those who read Wiesel's dialogue will not be survivors. One day none will be. But the questions—"After? . . . Meaning what?"—that close his dialogue remain vital and open-ended. Anyone who wrestles with their meanings will be challenged to search out the truth about "what one hears of selections, of gas, of crematoriums." Such discovery requires, and can inspire, courage to bear witness against disbelief.

PRIMO LEVI (1919–1987), born in Turin, Italy, took his degree in chemistry from the university there in 1941. On December 13, 1943, he was arrested for resisting fascism. Deported from Italy, he entered Auschwitz about a month later. His skill as a chemist, which the Germans wanted, probably saved his life. Liberated in late January 1945, Levi eventually found his way back to Italy, where he resumed his career as a chemist and also became an acclaimed author.

His major works include *The Reawakening; The Periodic Table; If Not Now, When?; Moments of Reprieve;* and *The Monkey's Wrench.* The best-known of his books, however, is his first, *Survival in Auschwitz: The Nazi Assault on Humanity* (originally published as *If This Is a Man*). This classic memoir about his year in Auschwitz describes what Levi called "a journey toward nothingness." Understated, naturalistic, ironic—Levi's language drives home how survival in Auschwitz required learning to unlearn patterns of behavior taken for granted before Auschwitz.

Utterly honest, Levi documents how this coping often required prisoners to dwell in "the gray zone," a realm of genuine moral ambiguity. This theme achieves special prominence in his last book, *The Drowned and the Saved*, whose preface is the selection that follows. Having survived Auschwitz for forty years, Levi wonders in this final book whether many of the Holocaust's lessons have been learned. Levi was a life-affirming author, and yet darkness shadows his last words. On April 11, 1987, he died from a fall down a stairwell in an apparent suicide attempt.

Primo Levi

The Drowned and the Saved

The first news about the Nazi annihilation camps began to spread in the crucial year of 1942. They were vague pieces of information, yet in agreement with each other: they delineated a massacre of such vast proportions, of such extreme cruelty and such intricate motivation that the public was inclined to reject them because of their very enormity. It is significant that the culprits themselves foresaw this rejection well in advance: many survivors (among others, Simon Wiesenthal in the last pages of *The Murderers Are Among Us*) remember that the SS militiamen enjoyed cynically admonishing the prisoners:

> However this war may end, we have won the war against you; none of you will be left to bear witness, but even if someone were to survive, the world will not believe him. There will perhaps be suspicions, discussions, research by historians, but there will be no certainties, because we will destroy the evidence together with you. And even if some proof should remain and some of you survive, people will say that the events you describe are too monstrous to be believed: they will say that they are the exaggerations of Allied propaganda and will believe us, who will deny everything, and not you. We will be the ones to dictate the history of the Lagers.

Strangely enough, this same thought ("even if we were to tell it, we would not be believed") arose in the form of nocturnal dreams produced by the prisoners' despair. Almost all the survivors, orally or

From Primo Levi, *The Drowned and the Saved*, trans. Raymond Rosenthal. New York: Summit Books, 1988. Copyright © 1986 by Giulio Einaudi editore s.p.a. Torino. Translation copyright © 1988 by Simon & Schuster, Inc. Reprinted by permission of Summit Books, a division of Simon & Schuster, Inc.

in their written memoirs, remember a dream which frequently re-curred during the nights of imprisonment, varied in its detail but uniform in its substance: they had returned home and with passion and relief were describing their past sufferings, addressing themselves to a loved one, and were not believed, indeed were not even listened to. In the most typical and cruelest form, the interlocutor turned and left in silence. This is a theme to which we shall return, but at this point it is important to emphasize how both parties, victims and oppressors, had a keen awareness of the enormity and therefore the noncredibility of what took place in the Lagers—and, we may add here, not only in the Lagers, but in the ghettos, in the rear areas of the Eastern front, in the police stations, and in the asylums for the mentally handicapped.

Fortunately, things did not go as the victims feared and the Nazis hoped. Even the most perfect of organizations has its flaws, and Hitler's Germany, especially during the last months before the col-lapse, was far from being a perfect machine. Much material evidence of the mass exterminations was suppressed, or a more or less dextrous attempt was made to suppress it: in the autumn of 1944 the Nazis blew up the gas chambers and crematoria at Auschwitz, but the ruins are still there, and despite the contortions of epigones it is difficult to justify their function by having recourse to fanciful hypotheses. The Warsaw ghetto, after the famous insurrection in the spring of 1943, was razed to the ground, but thanks to the superhuman concern of a number of fighter-historians (historians of themselves!), in the rubble, often many meters deep, or smuggled beyond the wall, other histo-rians would later rediscover the testimony of how the ghetto lived and died day by day. All the archives in the Lagers were burned during the final days of the war, truly an irremediable loss, so that even today there is discussion as to whether the victims were four, six, or eight million—although one still talks of millions. Before the Nazis had recourse to the gigantic multiple crematoria, the innumerable corpses of the victims, deliberately killed or worn down by hardship and illness, could have constituted evidence and somehow had to be made to disappear. The first solution, macabre to the point of making one hesitate to speak of it, had been simply to pile up the bodies, hundreds of thousands of bodies, in huge common graves, and this was done, in particular at Treblinka and other minor Lagers, and in the wake of the German army in Russia. This was a temporary solution decided upon with bestial insouciance when the German armies were winning on all fronts and final victory appeared certain: they would decide afterward what should be done, and in any case the victor is the master even of truth, can manipulate it as he pleases. Somehow the common graves would be justified, or made to disappear, or attributed to the Soviets (who, for that matter, proved at Katyn not to be lagging too far behind). But after Stalingrad there were second thoughts: best to erase everything immediately. The prisoners themselves were forced to exhume those pitiful remains and burn them on pyres in the open, as if so unusual an operation of such proportions could go completely unnoticed.

The SS command posts and the security services then took the greatest care to ensure that no witness survived. This is the meaning (it would be difficult to excogitate another) of the murderous and apparently insane transfers with which the history of the Nazi camps came to an end during the first months of 1945: the survivors of Maidanek to Auschwitz, those of Auschwitz to Buchenwald and Mauthausen, those of Buchenwald to Bergen-Belsen, the women of Ravensbrück to Schwerin. In short, everyone had to be snatched away from liberation, deported again to the heart of a Germany that was being invaded from the west and east. It did not matter that they might die along the way; what really mattered was that they should not tell their story. In fact, after having functioned as centers of political terror, then as death factories, and subsequently (or simultaneously) as immense, ever renewed reservoirs of slave labor, the Lagers had become dangerous for a moribund Germany because they contained the secret of the Lagers themselves, the greatest crime in the history of humanity. The army of ghosts that still vegetated in them was composed of *Geheimnisfräger*, the bearers of secrets who must be disposed of; the extermination plants, also very eloquent, having been destroyed, had to be moved to the interior, it was decided, in the absurd hope of still being able to lock those ghosts up in Lagers less threatened by the advancing fronts and to exploit their final ability to work, and in the other, less absurd hope that the torment of those Biblical marches would reduce their number. And in fact their number was appallingly reduced, yet some nevertheless had the luck or the strength to survive and remained to bear witness.

Less well known and less studied is the fact that many bearers of secrets were also on the other side, although many knew little and few knew everything. No one will ever be able to establish with precision how many, in the Nazi apparatus, could not not know about the frightful atrocities being committed, how many knew something but were in a position to pretend that they did not know, and, further, how many had the possibility of knowing everything but chose the more prudent path of keeping their eyes and ears (and above all their mouths) well shut. Whatever the case, since one cannot suppose that the majority of Germans lightheartedly accepted the slaughter, it is certain that the failure to divulge the truth about the Lagers represents one of the major collective crimes of the German people and the most obvious demonstration of the cowardice to which Hitlerian terror had reduced them: a cowardice which became an integral part of mores and so profound as to prevent husbands from telling their wives, parents their children. Without this cowardice the greatest excesses would not have been carried out, and Europe and the world would be different today.

Without a doubt those who knew the horrible truth because they were (or had been) responsible had compelling reasons to remain silent; but inasmuch as they were depositories of the secret, even by keeping silent they could not always be sure of remaining alive, witness the case of Stangl and the other Treblinka butchers, who after the insurrection there and the dismantling of that Lager were transferred to one of the most dangerous Partisan areas.

Willed ignorance and fear also led many potential "civilian" witnesses of the infamies of the Lagers to remain silent. Especially during the last years of the war, the Lagers constituted an extensive and complex system which profoundly compentrated the daily life of the country; one has with good reason spoken of the *univers concentrationnaire*, but it was not a closed universe. Small and large industrial companies, agricultural combines, agencies, and arms factories drew profits from the practically free labor supplied by the camps. Some exploited the prisoners pitilessly, accepting the inhuman (and also stupid) principle of the SS according to which one prisoner was worth another, and if the work killed him he could immediately be replaced; others, a few, cautiously tried to alleviate their sufferings. Still other industries—or perhaps the same ones—made money by supplying the Lagers themselves: lumber, building materials, cloth for the prisoners' striped uniforms, dehydrated vegetables for the soup, etc. The crematoria ovens themselves were designed, built, assembled, and tested by a German company, Topf of Wiesbaden (it was still in operation in

1975, building crematoria for civilian use, and had not considered the advisability of changing its name). It is hard to believe that the personnel of these companies did not realize the significance of the quality or quantity of the merchandise and installations being commissioned by the SS command units. The same can be, and has been, said with regard to the supplies of the poison employed in the gas chambers at Auschwitz: the product, substantially hydrocyanic acid, had already been used for many years for pest control in the holds of boats, but the abrupt increase in orders beginning with 1942 could scarcely go unnoticed. It must have aroused doubts, and certainly did, but they were stifled by fear, the desire for profit, the blindness and willed stupidity that we have mentioned, and in some cases (probably few) by fanatical Nazi obedience.

It is natural and obvious that the most substantial material for the reconstruction of truth about the camps is the memories of the survivors. Beyond the pity and indignation these recollections provoke, they should also be read with a critical eye. For knowledge of the Lagers, the Lagers themselves were not always a good observation post: in the inhuman conditions to which they were subjected, the prisoners could barely acquire an overall vision of their universe. The prisoners, above all those who did not understand German, might not even know where in Europe their Lager was situated, having arrived after a slaughterous and tortuous journey in sealed boxcars. They did not know about the existence of other Lagers, even those only a few kilometers away. They did not know for whom they worked. They did not understand the significance of certain sudden changes in conditions, or of the mass transfers. Surrounded by death, the deportee was often in no position to evaluate the extent of the slaughter unfolding before his eyes. The companion who worked beside him today was gone by the morrow: he might be in the hut next door, or erased from the world; there was no way to know. In short, the prisoner felt overwhelmed by a massive edifice of violence and menace but could not form for himself a representation of it because his eyes were fixed to the ground by every single minute's needs.

This deficiency conditioned the oral or written testimonies of the "normal" prisoners, those not privileged, who represented the core of the camps and who escaped death only by a combination of improbable events. They were the majority in the Lager, but an exiguous minority among the survivors: among them, those who during their imprisonment enjoyed some sort of privilege are much more numerous. At a distance of years one can today definitely affirm that the history of the Lagers has been written almost exclusively by those who, like myself, never fathomed them to the bottom. Those who did so did not return, or their capacity for observation was paralyzed by suffering and incomprehension.

On the other hand, the "privileged" witnesses could avail themselves of a certainly better observatory, if only because it was higher up and hence took in a more extensive horizon; but it was to a greater or lesser degree also falsified by the privilege itself. The discussion concerning privilege (not only in the Lager) is delicate, and I shall try to go into it later with the greatest possible objectivity. Here I will only mention the fact that the privileged par excellence, that is, those who acquired privilege for themselves by becoming subservient to the camp authority, did not bear witness at all, for obvious reasons, or left incomplete or distorted or totally false testimony. Therefore the best historians of the Lagers emerged from among the very few who had the ability and luck to attain a privileged observatory without bowing to compromises, and the skill to tell what they saw, suffered, and did with the humility of a good chronicler, that is, taking into account the complexity of the Lager phenomenon and the variety of human destinies being played out in it. It was in the logic of things that these historians should almost all be political prisoners: because the Lagers were a political phenomenon; because the political prisoners, much more than the Jews and the criminals (as we know, the three principal categories of prisoners), disposed of a cultural background which allowed them to interpret the events they saw; and because, precisely inasmuch as they were ex-combatants or antifascist combatants even now, they realized that testimony was an act of war against fascism; because they had easier access to statistical data; and lastly, because often, besides holding important positions in the Lager, they were members of the secret defense organization. At least during the final years, their living conditions were tolerable, which permitted them, for example, to write and preserve notes, an unthinkable luxury for the Jews and a possibility of no interest to the criminals.

For all the reasons touched on here, the truth about the Lagers has come to light down a long road and through a narrow door, and many aspects of the *univers concentrationnaire* have yet to be explored in depth. By now more than forty years have passed since the liberation of the Nazi Lagers; this considerable interval has, for the purposes of clarification, led to conflicting results, which I will try to enumerate.

In the first place, there has been the decanting, a desirable and normal process, thanks to which historical events acquire their chiaroscuro and perspective only some decades after their conclusion. At the end of World War II, quantitative data on the Nazi deportations and massacres, in the Lagers and elsewhere, had not been acquired, nor was it easy to understand their import and specificity. For only a few years now has one begun to understand that the Nazi slaughter was dreadfully "exemplary" and that, if nothing worse happens in the coming years, it will be remembered as the central event, the scourge, of this century.

By contrast, the passage of time has as a consequence other historically negative results. The greater part of the witnesses, for the defense and the prosecution, have by now disappeared, and those who remain, and who (overcoming their remorse or, alternately, their wounds) still agree to testify, have ever more blurred and stylized memories, often, unbeknownst to them, influenced by information gained from later readings or the stories of others. In some cases, naturally, the lack of memory is simulated, but the many years that have gone by make it credible. Also, the "I don't know" or "I did not know" spoken today by many Germans no longer shocks us, as it did or should have when events were recent.

Of another or further stylization we are ourselves responsible, we survivors, or, more precisely, those among us who have decided to live our condition as survivors in the simplest and least critical way. This does not mean that ceremonies and celebrations, monuments and flags are always and everywhere to be deplored. A certain dose of rhetoric is perhaps indispensable for the memory to persist. That sepulchres, "the urns of the strong," kindle souls to perform lofty deeds, or at least preserve the memory of accomplished deeds, was true in Foscolo's time and is still true today; but one must beware of oversimplifications. Every victim is to be mourned, and every survivor is to be helped and pitied, but not all their acts should be set forth as examples. The inside of the Lager was an intricate and stratified microcosm; the "gray zone" of which I shall speak later, that of the prisoners who in some measure, perhaps with good intentions, collaborated with the authority, was not negligible. Indeed, it constituted a phenomenon of fundamental importance for the historian, the psychologist, and the sociologist. There is not a prisoner who does not remember this and who does not remember his amazement at the time: the first threats, the first insults, the first blows came not from the SS but from other prisoners, from "colleagues," from those mysterious personages who nevertheless wore the same striped tunic that they, the new arrivals, had just put on. This book means to contribute to the clarification of some aspects of the Lager phenomenon which still appear obscure. It also sets itself a more ambitious goal, to try to answer the most urgent question, the question which torments all those who have happened to read our accounts: How much of the concentration camp world is dead and will not return, like slavery and the dueling code? How much is back or is coming back? What can each of us do so that in this world pregnant with threats at least this threat will be nullified?

I did not intend, nor would I have been able, to do a historian's work, that is, exhaustively examine the sources. I have almost exclusively confined myself to the National Socialist Lagers because I had direct experience only of these; I also have had copious indirect experience of them, through books read, stories listened to, and encounters with the readers of my first two books. Besides, up to the moment of this writing, and notwithstanding the horror of Hiroshima and Nagasaki, the shame of the Gulags, the useless and bloody Vietnam War, the Cambodian self-genocide, the *desaparecidos* of Argentina, and the many atrocious and stupid wars we have seen since, the Nazi concentration camp system still remains a *unicum*, both in its extent and its quality. At no other place or time has one seen a phenomenon so unexpected and so complex: never have so many human lives been extinguished in so short a time, and with so lucid a combination of technological ingenuity, fanaticism, and cruelty. No one wants to absolve the Spanish conquistadors of the massacres perpetrated in the Americas throughout the sixteenth century. It seems they brought about the death of at least sixty million Indios; but they acted on their own, without or against the directives of their government, and they diluted their misdeeds—not very "planned" to tell the truth—over an arc of more than one hundred years, and they were also helped by the epidemics that they inadvertently brought with them. And, finally, have we not tried to dispose of them by declaring that they were "things of another time"?

RAUL HILBERG, whose magisterial three-volume work, *The Destruction of the European Jews*, is arguably the single most important book about the Holocaust, was born in Vienna, Austria, in 1926. There he saw the rise of the Third Reich, emigrated to the United States in 1939, became a naturalized citizen in 1944, and witnessed the fall of Germany as an American soldier. Working as a member of the War Documentation Project, he studied German records in detail. His expertise in such work is evident in *The Destruction of the European Jews*, which Hilberg started in 1948. Unrivaled, it is a meticulous, carefully documented analysis of what Hilberg shows to be a "bureaucratic destruction process."

Since 1956, Hilberg has taught at the University of Vermont, where he is the John G. McCullough Professor of Political Science. A member of the United States Holocaust Memorial Council, he also testifies frequently for the Department of Justice in Holocaust-related cases. Hilberg's philosophy as a scholar is evident in the essay that follows. He says: "In all of my work I have never begun by asking the big questions, because I was always afraid that I would come up with small answers; and I have preferred to address these things which are minutiae or details in order that I might then be able to put together in a gestalt a picture which, if not an explanation, is at least a description, a more full description, of what transpired."

Raul Hilberg

The Ghetto as a Form of Goverment

In 1972, more than a quarter century after the end of the Holocaust, Isaiah Trunk published his pathbreaking book, *Judenrat*, the first major attempt to portray systematically the institutions and conditions of Jewish life in the ghettos of Nazi Eastern Europe.[1] It is a big volume, some 700 pages long, but it is also, despite its size, an understated work; for Trunk is one of those uncommon authors who promise less than they deliver. His preface deals with limits and limitations, giving an outline of Nazi administration in the East and a recital of sources at his disposal. The introduction, which was written not by Trunk but by Jacob Robinson, is partly philosophical, partly polemic, and in no event foreshadows the dimensions of the contents. The substantive account is presented by Trunk in ordinary matter-of-fact language without buildup or climax. As he traverses his terrain, from schools to synagogues, from labor to deportations, his tone remains constant. In this evenness, Trunk has managed to submerge everything: his range, his depth, and his findings.

The title of the book is *Judenrat*, meaning the "Jewish Council" or rather hundreds of them in various Eastern European ghettos. Trunk wanted to "achieve an objective history of the Councils," and thereby "find the key to internal Jewish history under Nazi rule."[2] But his book is not merely a depiction of that key; it deals with the whole house, for

From Yehuda Bauer and Nathan Rotenstreich, eds., *The Holocaust as Historical Experience: Essays and a Discussion.* New York: Holmes & Meier, 1981. Originally Hilberg's essay was printed under the title "The Ghetto as a Form of Government," *The Annals of the American Academy of Political and Social Science* 450 (July 1980). Copyright © 1980 by the American Academy of Political and Social Science. All rights reserved. Reprinted by permission.

it is a full-scale political, economic, and social history of the ghetto as
such. The various headings of chapters and subchapters indicate the
scope of the discussion, which comprises a whole gamut of topics:
organizational developments in the ghetto bureaucracy, commissions
and police; the problem areas of finances, taxes, production and pur-
chases; and programs involving bathhouses, kitchens, welfare or medical aid.

There is a similar richness of documentation. Although Trunk calls
special attention in the preface to a survey that netted replies from 927
respondents concerning 740 former Council members and 112 ghetto
police, the questionnaire material constitutes only about 5 percent of
the 2,000 citations in the notes, which are filled with references to
orders issued by German supervisory agencies, reports of Jewish
Councils to the Germans, minutes of Council meetings, newspapers,
diaries, memoirs, and memorial books. Text and sources reveal the
extent of Trunk's effort, while intricate facts on every page reflect the
author's long preoccupation with numerous aspects of ghetto life.[3]

Trunk cautions against over-generalization. At the outset he
stresses the importance of local conditions and the individuality of
leaders in the Jewish communities.[4] Yet he does not present the
Warsaw Ghetto in one chapter, Lodz in another, and additional ghettos
down the line. The fragmentary nature of the source material would
not have allowed for an approach of that kind. Instead, he addresses
himself to the essence of the ghettos; that is, the mode of their operations with regard to such all-pervasive problems as crowding, hunger,
or the demands of the Germans; and he does so implicitly by using
almost any item of information about a particular ghetto as illustrative
of the situation in all of them. In this manner, he builds a mosaic that is
generalization *par excellence*.

More than that, his whole book is a demonstration (rather than the
mere assertion) that, notwithstanding the different internal structures
of the Jewish communities or the diversity of personalities in the
Jewish Councils, the story of all ghettos must be read as one history.
Jewish perceptions and reactions were remarkably similar across the
occupied territories, despite the relative isolation of the communities
and their Councils from each other. In the final analysis, the variation
among ghettos is not as crucial as their commonality, nor is it primarily
the classification of ghettos in terms of demographic or economic
factors that counts, but the singularity of meaning in the very phrase

"Jewish ghetto" as compared with everything else that has transpired in recent times throughout the world.

If Trunk had done no more than organize a compendium of facts in subject-matter categories, he would have furnished us with significant additions to our knowledge; but beyond any compilation he also set forth a series of propositions about the nature of the ghettos and the Councils governing them. One cannot find these propositions in some final chapter; Trunk eschews discoveries and there is no recapitulation at the end. His summation is confined to five pages and there he considers solely an issue raised by Jacob Robinson in the introduction: the question of the Councils' "collaboration" with the Germans. Thus, an entire set of observations and conclusions is left buried in the text, some in lengthy passages, others in single sentences, still others in recurring themes and characterizations. For a review of *Judenrat*, nothing is more important than a consolidation of these points in analytic form. Here they are, under four headings, partly condensed from his account, partly developed from it, but mainly rooted in his evidence.[5]

The Ghetto as a Political Entity

The principal characteristic of the ghetto was the segregation of its inhabitants from the surrounding population. The Jewish ghetto was a closed-off society, its gates permanently shut to free traffic, so much so that Trunk labels as relatively "open" those of the ghetto communities (in smaller cities) that dispatched labor columns daily to projects outside the ghetto limits.[6] This is not to imply the total absence of contacts with Germans or Poles. There were electrical, telephone, gas and water connections, removals of human waste, exports of manufactured goods, imports of coal, food or raw materials, mail and parcel shipments through ghetto post offices, loans from banks, payments of rents, etc. In examining these links one must, however, always differentiate between institutional transactions that had to be maintained if the ghetto was to function and private bonds, across the boundaries, that could no longer be tolerated because they were incompatible with the function of the ghetto.

Even the official correspondence of Jewish ghetto authorities with neighboring German or Polish agencies or firms was largely severed, and the flow of orders and reports confined as much as possible, though never completely, to a channel running from the German supervisors to the Jewish Council. The horizontal relationships that are built into so much of modern life were consequently replaced by an almost all-embracing vertical regime, sometimes complex as in the cases of Warsaw and Lodz, often simple as in outlying localities, but always standardized in a dictatorial manner.[7]

The hierarchical system of German supervision was designed for the purpose of absolutism. German orders were unqualified and Council members were required to carry them out promptly and fully. Trunk underscores the fact that the members of the Councils were not Nazi sympathizers: that although some were ambitious and many deluded, they were not, and could not be regarded as a German institution.[8] They were, in short, Jews and they could not fail to perceive the fate of Jewry as their fate as well.[9] All the more bitter then was their task of receiving and implementing German decrees. Yet the directives of the Germans were only half of their problem. Less stark, but equally burdensome, was the necessity of asking for authorization to carry out every function of government, including duties expected of them. The Councils had to obtain clearance for a variety of revenue measures; they had to "borrow" Jewish funds previously sequestered or confiscated under occupation ordinances; they even had to request permission to post German orders.

If the Councils were thus rendered totally subordinate and dependent in their relations with the Germans, a corresponding status was fashioned for the Jewish population subjected to Council rule. German sentiment in this matter was expressed unambiguously by one official when he asserted: "It lies in the interest of the difficult administration of the Jewish district that the authority of the Jewish Council be upheld and strengthened under all circumstances."[10]

Jewish executives, like the Germans in charge, could make use of coercion and take advantage of helplessness. Compliance and acquiescence were ensured by the Jewish police, which had the power to make arrests and guard prisoners.[11] Relief could be dispensed in that the Councils controlled food and space: German shipments of flour, sugar, or coal were doled out under conditions of constantly increasing privation.[12]

Throughout the system power was exercised in levels of dominance, and each level was reinforced in every way. An illustration of such reinforcement was the principle of limiting correspondence and conversations to immediate superiors and inferiors. The Jewish Council could make appeals only to the German supervisory authorities in its locality; it could conceivably urge the city commander or ghetto commissioner to submit a plea to higher officials, [13] but it could not carry messages directly to regional governors or their staffs. The ghetto inhabitants, in turn, might stand in line to see the "Elder" of the Council, but they had no ordinary access to German agencies. In fact, there is reason to suppose that the Councils acquired a stake in establishing themselves as the sole representatives of the Jewish population vis-à-vis German officialdom. They certainly felt themselves empowered to govern the Jews and, in some ghettos, announced that persons who had failed to pay taxes or report for labor would be handed over to a German organ because of their recalcitrance. [14] For Jewish bureaucrats, no less than German, there was no substitute for authority.

The physical and administrative constrictions of Jewry reduced its space and narrowed its horizon, but at the same time intensified its organizational activity. While the Germans outside became invisible, [15] the Jewish community machinery within evolved into the government of a captive city-state. Trunk explains the transformation as clearly stemming from two causes: one was the need to supply those regular municipal and economic services from which the community was now cut off and without which it could not have survived; the other was the burden thrust upon the Councils by the Germans, who used them to fulfill German needs. [16] The multiplication of tasks inherent in this dual evolution, coupled with continuing unemployment and periodic fears of disaster, led also to swollen ghetto bureaucracies that were filled with minor functionaries and clerks, both paid and unpaid. In ghettos featuring public enterprise (particularly Lodz and Vilna), the Council payrolls at the beginning of 1942 encompassed as much as a fifth of the employable population. [17]

Although ghetto office personnel often did very little, some officials wielded power—at times almost undisturbed power—in specialized spheres of jurisdiction. One area in particular lent itself to what Trunk calls, albeit between quotation marks, ghetto self-government. This island of Jewish freedom was located in the courts, where disputes between Jewish litigants were settled by Jewish judges without German interference. [18]

The ghettos were consequently political entities with governmental attributes much larger and fuller than the social, cultural, or religious functions carried out by the prewar communities. Soon, however, Jewish Councils everywhere came face to face with the basic paradox inherent in their role as preservers of Jewish life in a framework of German destruction. They could not serve the Jews indefinitely while simultaneously obeying the Germans. A good deal of what Trunk calls the "strategy and tactics" of the Councils[19] involved their futile attempt to resolve this contradiction. The Jewish leadership was completely non-provocative: it did not fight the Germans, it seldom fought the orders, but in its distress it made numerous offerings. From time to time the Councils offered words, money, labor, and finally lives.

Appeals were probably the most frequently used device. They were often generated by upheaval, especially at the beginning of the German occupation during the formation of ghettos and at the onset of deportations; but the content of the appeals was broad-ranging. The Councils asked for permission to turn on the lights after 8 p.m. (Lublin), for reductions of confiscations (Bialystok), or for the return of hostages (Warsaw). "Seldom did Jewish petitions have any success," states Trunk; yet one has the feeling from such documents as the Czerniakow diary that an occasional or partial German concession, even if only for the mitigation or postponement of some harsh measure, fueled the pleadings time and again. They remained, throughout, the strategy of first resort.

Trunk devotes considerable space to bribes, which he believes to have been widespread, but which obviously could have been used only under special conditions. They must have been more successful than intercessions, but the objects attained by bribery are likely to have been limited and the results short-lived. Typical were payments to effect the transfer of a particularly troublesome official or policeman, the ransom of young girls from forced prostitution (a practice which under German "race-pollution" law was in any case prohibited), or the tender of money to avert "resettlement."

Most extensive is Trunk's discussion of the "rescue-through-work" strategy[20] that reflected German dependence on products of Jewish manufacture, especially war material, but also simple things such as brushes, which in labor-hungry Axis Europe could not be turned out in quantity with ease. In Lodz, Vilna, and Czestochowa, such dependence led to the construction by the Councils themselves of fairly large-scale industries. The factories bought time for tens of thousands, but the Jews were playing a determined game in which the outcome was always under German control.[21]

Mass deportations forced the Jews to the extreme ends in the spectrum of alternatives. There was no longer any middle ground between open opposition and total compliance: the Jewish communities were bound to choose the one or the other. Trunk gives some examples of Councils with a "positive attitude" toward resistance. However, most manifestations of that inclination turn out to have been actions of individual Council members in aiding escapes or establishing contacts with partisans.[22] The predominant pattern was the active implementation of German directives.

Thus, the Councils themselves organized confiscations and forced labor. In most ghettos, they themselves delivered the victims for the death transports. Of course, the Germans would frequently ask for only a certain number of deportees. It was such requests that ignited internal Jewish arguments to the effect that if 1,000 Jews were given up, 10,000 would be saved, but if none were sacrificed, all would be lost. In delivering a part of the community, the Councils could also choose the less worthy.[23] Trunk quotes Zalman Shazar, the President of Israel, as having pointed out in 1964 that the negative selections in the ghettos had been preceded by similar behavior in Tsarist times, when the Jewish community leaders were forced to designate youngsters for 25 years of service in the Russian imperial army. Then, too, Jewish leaders chose the simpletons.[24]

Because of its compliance strategy, the *Judenrat* could be a dangerous organization precisely when it functioned most smoothly. Impersonality, as in the recruitment of the strong and the weak or the healthy and the sick for heavy labor, could become brutality. Order, as shown in Lodz where smuggling was curbed, could intensify deprivation. Efficiency, in the collection of taxes or furs, could bring about more suffering. Thus, many of the virtues of Jewish ghetto government became vices; responsibility was turned into unresponsiveness and salvage into loss.

The Ghetto as a Socio-Economic Organization

The Jewish ghettos mark an interim phase between prewar freedom and wartime annihilation. These last moments of organized existence in the Jewish community were endured in a vise of progressively diminished space and gradually increasing hunger. If social and economic policies in normal societies can have long-range effects on large groups of people seeking comforts, security, or some pleasure in life, the internal measures and practices of ghetto Councils were bound to have an immediate and massive impact on a population hovering between survival and death.

We may safely assume that many times the meager resources at the disposal of the Councils were strained for the benefit of the community. There were occupational training programs, workshops, rationing systems, housing authorities, hospitals, ambulances, and other services in a large number of ghettos. Their very existence demonstrates what Jewish bureaucrats and technocrats could accomplish even under these conditions. At the same time, Trunk leaves little doubt that the ghettos as a whole were no triumphs of social equality and economic justice. The ghetto was the scene of all forms of corruption including bribery, favoritism, and nepotism. Moreover, in the critical areas of labor, food, and taxes, prevailing regulations were particularly harsh for the most destitute families.

Instances of dishonesty are difficult to document, but Trunk cites relevant testimony of survivors from several ghettos. Council members accepted personal bribes for exemptions from labor duty (Zamosc) and deportation (Horodenka and other ghettos).[25] Bribes were said to have been taken for appointments to the ghetto police (Warsaw, etc.).[26] Patronage in the award of jobs to inexperienced applicants, sometimes resulting in the employment of entire families, was apparently widespread in Warsaw, Lodz, Bialystok, Lublin, and elsewhere.[27] Friendships were also important in the soup kitchens of Lodz, where the chairman, Rumkowski, is reported to have issued supplementary food ration stamps "at whim," favoring particularly Orthodox groups and rabbis.[28]

While abuses for private ends may be regarded as transgressions of individuals, a regime of exploitation through official routines can only be described as systemic. The difference is important; for the concealed bribes and favors were intrinsically unjustifiable, whereas the open decrees and decisions, which so often took advantage of the most helpless portion of the population, were defended by Jewish Councils as the best they could do under the circumstances. Nowhere is this posture more clearly expressed than in the pronouncements, correspondence, and diary of Adam Czerniakow, Chairman of the Jewish Council in the laissez-faire ghetto of Warsaw. During the early days, Czerniakow excused the well-to-do from forced labor for a fee to finance the compensation of poor families whose men were digging ditches for the Germans.[29] Later, as he struggled with the Council's unbalanced budget, he proposed as his principal revenue source a monthly tax on bread.[30] Still later, when the Council was threatened with declining German food shipments, cash reserves were created as a precautionary measure by increasing the surcharges on the bread and sugar rations.[31]

One of the effects of ghetto class structure was the emergence of what Trunk calls a "food pyramid." Quite simply, the social ladder became more and more conspicuous in the number of calories consumed. Thus, a survey in the Warsaw Ghetto during December 1941 revealed that Council employees were receiving 1,665 calories, artisans 1,407, shopworkers 1,225, and the "general" population 1,125.[32] A similar picture of relative starvation may be observed in the Lodz Ghetto, where differential rationing, by type of employment, was official policy.[33] This is how status became instrumental in the prolongation of basic survival. Czerniakow himself made the point obliquely at the end of 1941 when he observed that the intelligentsia were dying now.[34]

In retrospect, the tiers of privilege in ghetto society should not surprise us that much. Ghetto life rewarded special talents such as smuggling or wheeling and dealing. It accommodated the more usual skills of the doctors and artisans, or of people who could speak German. The ghetto protected its rabbis as well, for the Jews clung to the past and also approached their most extraordinary problems with all traditional means. Finally, the Jewish bureaucrat who ran the ghetto during its formation and who presided at its dissolution was granted his temporary reprieve. In the vast majority of instances, however, the last occurrence of even the most shielded existence was violent death.

The Ghetto as a Mirage

Adam Czerniakow was the sort of man who did not want to draw a salary so long as there was not enough money to pay his staff.[35] In the midst of starvation, he shunned elaborate meals, eating soup for lunch in his office.[36] During a contraction of the ghetto boundaries, he refused a German offer that would have allowed him to keep his apartment on a street from which the Jews were being expelled.[37] In July 1942, when he realized that the Jews were going to be deported *en masse*, he took his own life. Yet in February 1942, just about six months before that fateful day, Czerniakow had decided to have stained glass windows installed in the Council chambers.[38] Czerniakow, as well as most of the other Jewish leaders, acted on the premise that there was a future. From the outset, Council members at their desks and crowds in the streets bore their crushing burdens as temporary inflictions to be suffered until liberation. To the end, Jewish hospitals tried to heal the sick, schools continued to train the young, and kitchens fed the starving. There was no alternative.

Many ghetto activities, especially in education and culture, bordered on illusionary behavior—the Vilna Ghetto, for example, established a music school in the summer of 1942.[39] Readers in the Warsaw Ghetto fantasized in the pages of Tolstoy's *War and Peace* that a German collapse was imminent.[40] In the upper echelons of ghetto leadership, a kind of unreality surfaced in "power struggles" in and around the Council headquarters.

Jurisdictional questions were a major preoccupation of the ghetto managers. One of these contests was waged between the Councils and a centralized Jewish Welfare Service (JSS), which reported to the German Population and Welfare Division of the Generalgouvernement in Krakow and which maintained local committees in the ghettos.[41] A complex federal structure with built-in frictions evolved in the Warsaw Ghetto, where more than a thousand "House Committees" began to perform all sorts of voluntary and assigned functions, including the provision of shelter for refugees, the staging of one-act plays, emergency assistance, reports of illnesses, and collections of taxes.[42] In the same ghetto, the Council was challenged by an organization known as the "Control Office for Combatting the Black Market and Profiteering in the Jewish District" under Abraham Gancwajch. Czerniakow won that battle when the Gancwajch apparatus was dissolved, with provision for the incorporation of its members into the regular Jewish "order service" (police).[43] Again, the following story, told by Czerniakow in his diary, illustrates the manner and extent to which administrators in the Warsaw Ghetto were absorbed by problems of entitlement. A Provisioning Authority had been formed as a quasi-independent agency in Summer 1941 to deal with the approaching food crisis. In the Council's own labor department, an official wanted the local German labor office to approve applicants for positions in the Authority. Incensed, Czerniakow wrote on February 15, 1942: "This clearly amounts to undermining the authority of the Council and diminishing its prerogatives. According to the [Council's] legal department, there is no basis for this position in law."[44]

Ghetto government at times became a distorted facsimile of a viable political system. The politics in the administrative processes of the ghettos may strike us as a caricature, because so many of the functionaries had come to think of life in the German enclosure as a stabilized condition of existence; they claimed not only some of the food, space, or medical services for themselves and their families, they fought also for a share of power in this "weird, crippled structure." Yes, even in this run-down machine, which could no longer cope with its narrowest tasks, they wanted a piece of the action.

Trunk speaks at some length of "The German Policy of Fraud and Deceit."[45] The Germans, he says, kept the Jews in the dark about their intentions. Indeed, the German perpetrators did not install a warning system in the ghetto. They did not practice chivalry toward their victims. On the other hand, the Jewish leaders did not attempt to acquire information about the Germans systematically and they did not come to grips with disturbing news in time.

At the start, the Polish Jews viewed ghettoization as the culmination of German plans. They failed to think in terms of a further, more drastic stage in the destruction process. The diary of Adam Czerniakow, leader of the largest ghetto in Europe, is the most detailed record of that characteristic train of thought in the face of peril.

Anyone with a deep interest in the Warsaw Ghetto might well approach the diary with the direct question: what were Czerniakow's predictions? What were his plans? What did he think the Germans would do eventually and what did he see as his alternatives? Nothing, almost nothing of this kind will be found in these notes. Czerniakow does not make forecasts. He does not draw up options. He does not refer to the Germans as foes. From October 1941 to Spring 1942 he expresses himself only in subdued tones, very briefly in passing, about ominous reports. As early as October 4, 1941, he quotes an ambiguous and enigmatic statement of a German official: "Bischof disclosed yesterday that Warsaw is merely a temporary haven for the Jews."[46] The entry for October 27 states: "Alarming rumors about the fate of the Jews in Warsaw next spring." On January 17, he asks whether Lithuanian guards were coming. More rumors on February 16. Disturbing news reached him on March 18 from Lvov (30,000 resettled) and from Mielec and Lublin. As of April 1, he hears that 90 percent of the Jews of Lublin were to leave their ghetto within the next few days. All this was written in entries of a sentence or two, in the middle of paragraphs containing other sentences on other subjects.

Czerniakow viewed himself as having taken over an impossible task to be pursued from morning to night against increasingly unfavorable odds. He lived through daily nightmares of blocked funds, labor columns, apartment allocations, bricks for the wall, furs for the Germans, soup for the poor. There was hardly anything that could be put off—everything was urgent. This is why, when the Germans accepted his revenue statute imposing a tax on bread, he felt that he had accomplished something and that he could face the next day. This is also why a modest collection of money for children was entered as a notable success. And this is the reason that in February 1942, when most of the Warsaw Ghetto had not yet starved to death, he could feel a sense of vindication. He and hundreds more on Jewish Councils all over Eastern Europe, had fallen into a cadence that did not allow for prolonged reflection about the real meaning of the ghettos in the Nazi scheme of things. In fact, any German laxity or inefficiency only served to reinforce the pace and intensify the activities of the Jewish officials who worked in tandem with their German supervisors, reporting to them, seeking clarifications, and requesting authorizations. Thus, administrative-economic dependence increasingly became psychological as well. It was a trap into which the Jewish leadership slipped and from which it could not extricate itself.

On July 20, 1942, the deportations in Warsaw were imminent. Trunk cites an excerpt from Czerniakow's diary describing that day.[47] At this moment of panic in the Warsaw Ghetto, Czerniakow went from Gestapo man to Gestapo man in desperation to ask whether the rumors of a "resettlement" were true. The Germans assured him that they did not know anything and that the reports were all nonsense (*Quatsch und Unsinn*). The passage is a fairly good example of how crude the Germans could be in their policy of "fraud and deceit." One has the feeling that their simple denials were almost lame. Not so simple are Czerniakow's frantic requests for reassurances. He was not a naive man. At the beginning of the paragraph, he himself states that he left the office of the Gestapo man Mende "unconvinced," and later in the day he was to ask for permission to transmit German denials to the Jewish population. The Germans could see no harm in that and, by evening, in Commissioner Auerswald's office, promised an "investigation" of the rumors. Three days after that meeting, all the camouflage was gone and Czerniakow killed himself with poison. We do not know how long he had kept that pill in his drawer.

The Jewish communities were lulled by the continuation of sheer routines, including the endless rebuilding of walls and fences, the periodic exactions, confiscations, and arrests, and even the desultory firing by German guards into the ghettos. Yet, they did not lack indices of danger. The whole economic system of the ghettos was not geared to long-term survival. There was large-scale, chronic unemployment and, as Trunk points out in one of his important findings, a finite supply of personal belongings was mobilized to supplement the insufficiency of production in an effort to pay for legally and illegally imported food.[48] The clock was running down, and soon there were signs of massive German violence. As German armies crossed the Bug and San rivers in June 1941 to assault the USSR, mobile units of the SS and Police began to kill Jews by the hundreds of thousands in Eastern Poland, the Baltic states, Belorussia, and the Ukraine. By the Spring of 1942, deportations to death camps commenced in the heart of Poland. The deported Jews were not heard from again.

In the remnant ghettos of 1943, the issue of life and death could no longer be avoided. The alternatives were brought forth and discussed: one could plan escape, prepare resistance, or redouble efforts to produce goods for the Germans. Even in this drastic situation, there was a tendency to veer away from methodical dispersal or organized battle; for while it was not feasible for the entire population to participate in acts of defiance, it was possible for everyone to suffer the consequences.[49]

This is how the doctrine of "rescue through work" became paramount from Upper Silesia to Vilna. It was, in more ways than one, the strategy of least resistance, and it was founded on the assumption that Germans were rational and would not obliterate a work force that was engaged in so much war production for them. The thought was, of course, a misconception. The Jews had once placed their trust in rules and regulations for protection against the ravages of totalitarianism;

now they clung to contracts and deliveries for safety from destruction. Thus, the Jews in Czestochowa were bewildered by the report that in the Warsaw Ghetto workers had been dragged from their shops.[50] Still, the rationale of work salvation was not dispelled. If the unskilled were lost, it was hoped that the skilled would remain; and when some of those were removed, it was reasoned that the raids would occur only once in a while. In this manner, Jewry sacrificed more and more for less and less until it was annihilated.

The Ghetto as a Self-Destructive Machine

We have seen now that the Jewish ghetto was a provider of administrative services, a social and economic laboratory, and a state of mind. It was also a form of organized self-destruction.

Once more, it should be emphasized that the Jewish Councils were not the willful accomplices of the Germans. Within the German superstructure, however, they were its indispensable operatives. Even when their activities were benign, as in the case of housing refugees or promoting sanitary conditions, they could contribute to the overall purposes and ultimate goals of their German supervisors. The very institution of an orderly ghetto was, after all, an essential link in the chain of destructive steps. In building this order and preserving it, the Councils could not help serving their enemy.

We know, of course, that the Germans expected much more than general government from their Jewish deputies. It was German policy to transfer to Jewish middlemen a large part of the physical and psychological burdens of destroying millions of men, women, and children. One aspect of that assignment was financial, another entailed selection, and the third enforcement; we shall examine these in turn.

The destruction of Jewry generated administrative costs and, throughout Europe, German agencies attempted to obtain some of the necessary resources from the Jews themselves. So far as possible, the destruction process was to be self-financing. In Poland, too, an effort was made to balance the books without drawing from the budget of the German Reich. Trunk cites the fact that the German administration of the Lodz Ghetto (the *Gettoverwaltung*) covered expenses by taxing deliveries to the Ghetto.[51] In Warsaw there was wall-building. The Jewish engineer Marek Lichtenbojm (who was to succeed Czerniakow as chairman of the Council) and a large crew of Jewish laborers were engaged at the site, and financial responsibility for the wall was passed to the Jewish community.[52]

Indirectly, the Warsaw Jews may have subsidized Treblinka. From a letter written to the Warsaw Ghetto Commissioner Auerswald by the first Treblinka commander Dr. Eberl, it appears that the Commissioner was to supply various materials to the camp where shortly afterwards the ghetto inhabitants were to be gassed.[53] (This is not to say that the Jewish leadership was able to decipher the nature of Treblinka while it was under construction.)[54] There may also have been remote funding of death transports from Jewish sources. We know, for example, that the German railways in Lodz billed the Gestapo in the city for the one-way fares. The Gestapo passed the bill to the Lodz *Gettoverwaltung* for payment.[55] We can only surmise how it was ultimately paid.

First the Jewish Councils handed over money; then they delivered human beings. Let us remember, though, that the process of selecting victims began with the social structuring of the ghetto population. We have seen that from the moment of their incarceration, the Jews were discernably divided according to their advantages and privileges in life. To be sure, few individuals had any inkling then that these stratifications would acquire a special meaning during the "Final Solution." However, growing suspicions and forebodings had the effect of accentuating the differentiations. Everyone was now concerned with his position all of the time, and soon the passes and identification cards made out by the Councils became more varied and colorful.[56] The papers spelled out a rank order of protection and, by the same token, vulnerability. Ultimately, separation was bound to be selection per se, since in the course of a roundup quotas were often filled with readily available old people, hospitalized patients, or children.[57] In the final analysis, the Councils only had to save some to doom all the others.

Jewry became at least passively a participant in its own undoing, by thus underwriting German operations through financial mechanisms and involvements, and arraying its own people on an axis defining degrees of safety or danger. But Jews were engaged also in a more active and virulent mode of self-destruction when their police were employed in the enforcement of German designs. Trunk devotes an entire chapter to the "order service."[58] Much attention has always been riveted on the Jewish police, because of the role that these semi-uniformed auxiliaries of annihilation performed in the pivotal occurrences of 1941 and 1942.

The "order service" exercised all the expected functions of a regular police department such as traffic control and the pursuit of petty thieves. Furthermore, it carried out tasks that were normal only in an abnormal society, from the collection of ghetto taxes, to the enforcement of compulsory labor, to the seizure of families for deportation, including the penetration of their hiding places. In some of the large ghettos the organization of the Jewish police revealed distinctly German features (particularly a division into ordinary and security police components), but even more visible was the adoption of German methods such as the arrest of parents whose sons did not report for labor duty,[59] or the sealing of houses in which individual tenants had not paid taxes.[60] The Jewish police arrested people in the middle of the night and beat up smugglers or reluctant volunteers for death transports. They ate well and frequently filled their pockets with the bribes and ransom payments of frightened fellow-Jews. So many were the instances of sheer brutality and corruption that Trunk patiently recites case after case of exceptions.

Yet the very composition of the "order service" deepens the paradox of Jews acting against Jew. Whereas some of the recruits may well have been drawn from the underworld (and Ringelblum complains that also a hundred baptized Jews were serving in ranking positions of the Warsaw Ghetto force),[61] some were included for their prior military experience, a large number were fairly well educated, and many were idealistic.[62] Here then was a concentration of healthy young men, uniquely capable of conducting intelligence operations or psychological warfare against the Germans, or of aiding in escapes or even engaging in physical resistance. On isolated occasions, Jewish police may have done just that, but most of the time they were the most conspicuous Jewish instrument in the German destructive machine.

Ringelblum wrote in his notes on February 19, 1941, that the Jewish population had an understanding of the difficulties of being a Jewish policeman. It was hard for Jews to take a Jewish policeman seriously and often, in those days, the "order service" would refrain from ordering people around and "discuss" things with them instead. At one point it was therefore said: "You would have minded a Polish policeman, so why don't you mind a Jewish one!"[63] However, this very trust in the Jewish police was to result in one of the greatest moral disappointments of the Holocaust, an experience from which Jewry has not recovered to this day. Irving Louis Horowitz, in reviewing Trunk's *Judenrat*, concludes: "Jewish policemen of Lodz, Vilna, and Warsaw were, after all, still policemen."[64]

The Jewish ghetto has just been opened and we see it now with all of its institutions and processes. This is Trunk's lasting achievement. On the other hand, the moral questions raised over so many years have not been closed; they have only become more complicated. We know that the ghetto leaders themselves were fully aware of their dilemma, that for some it was always on their minds. A small, sensitive book by Leonard Tushnet has illuminated the lives of just three of them: Rumkowski of Lodz, Czerniakow of Warsaw, and Gens of Vilna.[65] They were different men in background and ideas, but in the end all three declined to save themselves after they had failed to save their people.

NOTES

1. Isaiah Trunk, *Judenrat: The Jewish Councils in Eastern Europe under Nazi Occupation* (New York: Macmillan, 1972 and Scarborogh, 1977). Subsequent page references, where not otherwise specified, are to Trunk's book.

2. P. xviii.

3. Trunk does concentrate his attention on ghettos that were located within the prewar boundaries of Poland and Lithuania. There are a few details about Riga in Latvia and Minsk in White Russia, but the ghettos farther east as well as the Jewish communities under Romanian administration between the Dniester and the Bug are almost entirely, if understandably, omitted.

4. Pp. xvii, xviii.

5. To allow for deeper treatment of some of the problems, illustrations in this discussion will be drawn mainly from the Warsaw Ghetto.

6. P. 104.

7. Trunk discusses at some length intra-German rivalries for control of the ghettos (pp. 264–76). The police in particular wanted power over the Jews. See, for example, the letter by the SS and Police Leader in Warsaw (Wigand), November 11, 1941, claiming jurisdiction of his "protective police" (Schupo) over the Warsaw Ghetto's "order service." Yad Vashem microfilm JM 1112 (YIVO microfilm MKY 76).

8. Pp. 572–74.

9. In statistical terms, membership in Jewish Councils was in fact hazardous. Trunk reports on the basis of his questionnaires that the incidence of violent death among Council members in the period before the deportations was somewhat high. In his group of 720, about one in four was killed in the ghettos, most were deported, and

one in nine survived (pp. 326–28). However, the 99 councils covered in his survey must cumulatively have contained several times as many members as the number of recollected names. If the forgotten members died in the gas chambers, the ratios would be less striking.

10. Mohns (Deputy Chief of the Resettlement Division in the office of the Governor of the Warsaw District) to Leist (Plenipotentiary of the Governor for the City of Warsaw), January 11, 1941, Yad Vashem microfilm JM 1113 (YIVO microfil MKY77).

11. Trunk, pp. 82–83.

12. P. 99.

13. For an example of such a request, see the diary of Adam Czerniakow, Chairman of the Jewish Council in the Warsaw Ghetto, entry for January 7, 1942, in *The Warsaw Diary of Adam Czerniakow*, eds. Raul Hilberg, Stanislaw Staron and Josef Kermisz. (New York: Stein and Day, 1979), pp. 312–13 (hereafter cited as *Diary of Czerniakow*).

14. See Trunk on Lublin, Bedzin, Zamosc, Vilna, p. 484.

15. See Trunk, pp. 528–29, on the psychological implications of this shift.

16. P. 44.

17. Pp. 50–51. Also Trunk's "The Organizational Structure of the Jewish Councils in Eastern Europe," *Yad Vashem Studies* 7 (1968), 147–64.

18. Pp. 180–81, 185. Other areas of autonomy were Saturday as a day of rest and the use of Hebrew or Yiddish in schools, etc. (pp. 189, 196–215).

19. Pp. 390–95.

20. Pp. 400–420.

21. Trunk indulges in the thought that if, in August 1944, the Red Army had not stopped about 75 miles outside Lodz, some 70,000 Jews in its ghetto might have been saved (p. 413). The same speculation is offered by Robinson in his introduction (p. xxix) and was reiterated on another occasion by Yehuda Bauer (Holocaust Conference at the Hebrew College, Boston, 1973). The question, however, is counterfactual. Red Army offenses, though broad, were conducted for limited territorial gain to allow for resupply and regroupment. The halting of the Russian drive so many miles from Lodz was in no sense an "accident." The chance event would have been its opposite—a rapid German collapse.

22. In the Minsk Ghetto, the entire Jewish Council appears to have favored a liaison with partisans (p. 466). Also of interest are the Councils in Bialystok and Vilna, which had "ambiguous" attitudes (pp. 467–71).

23. See Trunk on the Lodz resettlement commission (p. 52).

24. Pp. 435–36.

25. Pp. 385–87.

26. *Ibid.*

27. P. 354.

28. P. 385.

29. Czerniakow to the Plenipotentiary of the Warsaw District for the City of Warsaw, May 21, 1940: Yad Vashem microfilm JM 1113 (YIVO Institute microfilm MKY 77). The Warsaw District Chief was Gouverneur Fischer, his City Plenipotentiary Leist. For examples of similar labor recruitment in other ghettos, see Trunk, pp. 379–80.

30. Czerniakow to the Warsaw District Chief/Resettlement Division/Exchange, January 8, 1941: JM 1113. (Schön was in charge of the Resettlement Division.) Krakow also instituted a head tax (Trunk, p. 381). Levies on earnings were considered problematical, because in ghettos like Warsaw smuggling accounted for considerable income.

31. Proclamation of the Warsaw Ghetto Provisioning Authority, signed by Czerniakow, August 31, 1941; *Diary of Czerniakow*, pp. 273–74. On February 2, 1942, Czerniakow noted in his diary that the reserve had made possible free distributions of bread and sugar.

32. Trunk, pp. 356, 382. For a detailed discussion of the medical aspects of food deprivation in the Warsaw Ghetto, see Leonard Tushnet, *The Uses of Adversity* (New York, 1966). See also Trunk, pp. 146–48.

33. Trunk, p. 383. In several ghettos (Kutno, Kolomea, Chelm, etc.) the social pyramid was particularly visible in housing (pp. 374–77).

34. *Diary of Czerniakow*, entry for December 4, 1941, p. 305.

35. Entry for May 24, 1941.

36. Entry for June 23, 1941.

37. Entry for October 6, 1941.

38. Entries for February 4 and 10, 1942.

39. P. 227.

40. Emmanuel Ringelblum, *Notes from the Warsaw Ghetto* (New York, 1958), p. 300.

41. Pp. 332–42.

42. Pp. 343–45. Czerniakow diary, entries for June 27 and December 3, 1941, pp. 252–53, 304–5. Trunk mentions House Committees also in Bialystok (pp. 515–16).

43. Pp. 505, 644. The text of the agreement between the council and the "Control Office," dated August 5, 1941, appears in the *Diary of Czerniakow*, pp. 265–67.

44. *Diary of Czerniakow*, pp. 325–26.

45. Pp. 413–36.

46. The remark is cited in another connection by Trunk, p. 292.

47. P. 414.

48. Pp. 101–2.

49. See pp. 451–74.

50. P. 404.

51. Pp. 282–83. See also requisitions of furnishings, etc., pp. 66–67, 296. Also *Diary of Czerniakow*, entries for July 22 and November 28, 1941, pp. 260 and 302.

52. Documents in Yad Vashem microfilm JM 1112 (YIVO film MKY 76). Czerniakow letter of January 8, 1941. Czerniakow diary, entries for July 5 and December 30, 1941. In Warsaw, Lodz and Kovno, the councils had to build bridges to connect ghetto sections divided by Aryan streets (Trunk, p. 110).

53. Eberl to Auerswald, June 26, 1942. Facsimile in Jüdisches Historisches Institut Warschau, *Faschismus-Getto-Massenmord* (2nd ed., Berlin, 1961), p. 304.

54. While Czerniakow became aware of "resettlement" and was told about Treblinka, he did not connect the two. On January 17, 1942, he asked whether Lithuanian guards were coming and was assured that the rumor was false. That same day, he talked to Auerswald who informed him of a conversation with Generalgouverneur Frank as a result of which Jewish prisoners held in Warsaw's Pawiak prison would, if fit

for labor, be sent to Treblinka to work. Two days thereafter, Czerniakow noted that Auerswald was going to Berlin. In this entry, Czerniakow also expressed fear of mass resettlement. (In fact, a conference of bureaucrats on the "Final Solution" was held in Berlin on January 20, 1942. Trunk comments on Auerswald's deception on pp. 295–96.) On February 19, 1942, Czerniakow complained that German prosecutors had failed to produce the appropriate papers for the "release" of prisoners at Treblinka. A day later, the prisoners left. On March 10, he recorded the departure of five Jewish clerks to the camp, and in April some 160 young German Jews, recently arrived from the Reich, were sent there. *Diary of Czerniakow*, pp. 316–17, 323–24, 333, 344.

55. Both items of correspondence, dated May 19 and 27, 1942, on a single sheet of paper. Facsimile, *Getto-Faschismus-Massenmord* (op. cit.), p. 214.

56. Trunk, pp. 175–77. The crass illustration is Vilna.

57. Pp. 507–8, 514.

58. Pp. 475–527; also passages in other chapters.

59. Bedzin, Sosnowiec, Zawiercie, Bialystok (p. 584). In Warsaw, members of House Committees were taken hostage if a tenant did not present himself for labor. Ringelblum, *Notes* (op. cit., note 40 above), p. 176.

60. Czerniakow, Radom, etc. (Trunk, p. 483).

61. Ringelblum, *Notes*, p. 138.

62. Trunk, pp. 489–98. Interesting is the finding that Jewish militants (Betar, etc.) were well represented in the police.

63. Ringelblum, *Notes*, pp. 125–26.

64. Horowitz, *Israeli Ecstasies/Jewish Agonies* (New York, 1974), p. 197.

65. Tushnet, *The Pavement of Hell* (New York, 1972).

YEHUDA BAUER has been introduced already in Part One. Like Raul Hilberg, he has the historian's penchant for detail. But while Hilberg aims at the perpetrators, Bauer focuses more on their victims. His scholarly outlook also tends to resist generalization and concentrates instead on the differences that manifest themselves when one examines closely the particularities of times and places. That philosophy prods Bauer to debunk stereotypes about the Holocaust and about Jewish behavior in particular. None of those stereotypes is more common than the one that regards Jews as passive, non-resisting victims who went like "sheep to the slaughter." In his careful study of resistance, *The Jewish Emergence from Powerlessness*—from which the following selection is taken—Bauer shows how misleading that stereotype can be.

Yehuda Bauer

Forms of Jewish Resistance During the Holocaust

We have already seen that the basic situation of Jews during the Hitler period was one of political powerlessness. Negotiations to save them, if conducted at all, would have to have been supported by one or more of the major powers; without that there would be little chance of success. Jews could appeal to the powers, they could try to impress public opinion in the Western democracies, but in the end they were perilously dependent upon the mercy of others. In the free world, Jews could appeal or beg for help; behind the barbed wire of Hitler's hell they could cry out in the hope that muted echoes would reach the outside. Was there anything more that the trapped Jews of Europe could do? If so, did they do it? What was the reaction of the victims to the most terrible terror any regime had yet exercised?

Jewish reaction to Nazi rule is of tremendous importance to Jews and non-Jews alike. The Jew wants to know the tradition to which he is heir. How did that tradition, that whole range of historically developed values, stand up to the supreme test of Hitler's death sentence on the Jewish people? Did Jewish civilization, demoralized under the blows of the brutal enemy, surrounded in the East by largely indifferent or hostile populations, simply collapse?

These questions are equally significant for non-Jews. Nothing like the Holocaust had happened before, but there are no guarantees against its recurrence. Jews are not the only possible victims of genocide. It is urgent to know how people react in such extreme circum-

From Yehuda Bauer, *The Jewish Emergence from Powerlessness*. Toronto: University of Toronto Press, 1979. Reprinted by permission of University of Toronto Press. © University of Toronto Press 1979.

stances; to find out how people, who were Jews, reacted when it happened to them.

What do we mean by resistance? What, more specifically, do we mean by that term in the context of World War II? What, when we apply it to Jews? Henri Michel, perhaps the most important contemporary historian of anti-Nazi resistance, defines the term negatively: resistance was the maintenance of self-respect. He writes that "acceptance of defeat whilst still capable of fighting, was to lose one's self-respect; self-respect dictated that one should not yield to the blandishments of collaboration."[1] But it is practically useless to analyse Jewish resistance with such categories—the Nazis certainly did not use the blandishments of collaboration on the Jews.

Professor Raul Hilberg, on the other hand, seems to regard armed resistance as the only, or nearly only, legitimate form of real resistance. In his monumental book, *The Destruction of the European Jews* (Chicago, 1961), he stated categorically and, to my mind, mistakenly, that the lack of Jewish armed resistance to the Holocaust was a consequence of the fact that Jews during their long diaspora had not had occasion to learn the art of self-defense.[2]

Let me start off with a definition of my own and we shall then subject it to the test of known facts. I would define Jewish resistance during the Holocaust as any *group* action consciously taken in opposition to known or surmised laws, actions, or intentions directed against the Jews by the Germans and their supporters. I cannot accept Michel's definition because there were in fact very few Jews who consciously collaborated with the Germans, or who were willing to help Germany achieve victory in the hope that they would help themselves or the Jewish people. There were, of course, paid Jewish Gestapo agents and others who helped the Germans having been promised their lives—quite a number of these. But I know of only one clear and one marginal case of collaboration as defined here: I am referring to the group known as the 13 (*Dos Dreizentl*) of Avraham Gancwajch, in Warsaw, and to Moshe Mietek Merin's Judenrat in Zagłębie.

I cannot accept Hilberg's definition or description for two reasons. In the first place, I do not think he is being historically accurate. Jews did defend themselves throughout the ages by force of arms when this was feasible or when they had no other choice—in Polish towns against Chmielnicki's hordes in 1648; in Palestine against the Crusaders; in medieval York. One could cite many such instances. In pre-1939

Poland, moreover, the socialist Bund party had special defence groups that fought street battles with antisemitic hooligans. Early in this century, Jewish students in Prague, Vienna, and Berlin established fraternities that fought duels against antisemites, and so on.

The second and more important point is surely that armed resistance during the Holocaust was possible only under conditions that most Jews did not enjoy. You either have arms or you do not; for the most part, the Jews did not. Still, the nature of Jewish armed resistance was much more complicated than one might expect.

In the Generalgouvernement (the central area of Poland ruled by the Nazis) there were, according to exhaustive historical accounts,[3] about 5,000 Jewish fighters. Of these about 1,000 fought in the Warsaw ghetto rebellion, 1,000 in the Warsaw Polish uprising in 1944, and the rest as partisans in forests and in a number of ghetto and camp uprisings. There were some 1.5 million Jews in the area in 1939, so one gets a ratio of resisters of 0.33 percent—not a very high figure—and concludes that Jewish armed resistance was marginal at best. In eastern Poland, where there were about one million Jews before the war, 15,000 armed Jews came out of the forests at liberation—a ratio of 1.5 percent—which will still not cause one to change the verdict. But during the time Jews were organizing to fight, that is in 1942 and 1943, they accounted for one half of all the partisans in the Polish forests. The other half, about 2500, were Poles. There were more than 20 million Poles in the Generalgouvernement, so one arrives at a resistance ratio of 0.0125 percent. The same game can be played regarding other nations in Nazi Europe. One begins to appreciate Mark Twain's adage that there are lies, damned lies, and statistics.

Let us then disregard such futile exercises and examine the real facts concerning Jewish armed resistance in Poland and, subsequently, elsewhere. It is generally accepted that large-scale operations were mainly dependent on two ingredients: the availability of weapons, and the support of a civilian population capable of aiding underground fighters. Neither of these preconditions existed for the Jews. Jews did not have access to the arms buried by the collapsing Polish army in 1939. There were very few Jewish officers in that army, fewer of them holding high ranks (e.g., one general), and the secrets of the buried arms were kept by right-wing officers who went into hiding.

The Polish government underground, the Armia Krajowa (AK), did not buy any arms from deserting German soldiers until very late in the war. No partisan detachments of any importance were established by it before 1943, and, anyway, not only were Jews not accepted in AK ranks, but a number of AK detachments were actively engaged in hunting down and murdering them. Thus when the Jews realized that they were being threatened with mass murder in 1942, there were no AK detachments for them to join. When these did come into existence, most Jews had already been murdered, and the detachments, in any case, would still not accept the survivors.

The Communist Gwardia Ludowa, later the Armia Ludowa (AL), was founded in the spring of 1942. It was then very weak, had very few arms, and about half its partisan forces were in fact the Jewish detachments in the forests of the Lublin area and elsewhere. By the time the AL grew stronger (in 1943) large numbers of Jews were no longer alive, but survivors did join the AL. Its weapons were bought or captured from peasants or, in most cases, parachuted by Soviet aircraft.

Jews locked in ghettos generally had no way to procure arms. The AK would not provide them; the Communists still did not have them. Controls at the gates were so strict that it was virtually impossible to bring any arms that could be obtained into the ghetto. The best known exception to the rule was in Vilna where Jews worked in German armouries. There, despite very stringent security measures, arms were smuggled into the ghetto from the city. The same general conditions applied in Czestochowa, which explains why the underground there had secured arms despite the obstacles.

Let us now turn to the three basic scenes of armed resistance in the east—the ghettos, the forests, and the camps. In the ghettos, the Jewish population was starved and decimated by disease and forced labour. They were, moreover, surrounded by a gentile population whose reaction to Jewish suffering varied between indifference, mostly hostile, and open enmity toward the victims. As applied to the ghettos Hilberg's thesis seems correct, that so long as the Jews thought they would survive the Nazi rule and the war they could see an incentive to re-enact the modes of passive conduct that in the past had tended to ensure the survival of the community, and they were accordingly reluctant to engage in armed resistance.

Resistance would have met with the disapproval, not only of the Polish population, but even of the Polish underground, the AK. Stefan Rowecki, commander in chief of the AK, issued an order (No. 71) as late as 10 November 1942 which bluntly stated that 'the time of our uprising has not come.' He mentioned the fact that the 'occupant is exterminating the Jews,' and warned his people not to be drawn into a 'premature' (!) action against the Germans.4

An examination of ghetto armed underground organizations shows quite clearly that, indeed, the Jews entered into the phase of practical preparations for armed action only *after* the first so-called *Aktion*, i.e., mass murder operation by the Nazis. Ghetto rebellions never took place when a hope of survival could be entertained—only when the realization finally struck that all Jews were going to be killed anyway. All other armed rebellions during World War II were predicated on the assumption that there was some chance of success. In the ghettos, no such success could be contemplated; the only result of ghetto rebellion would be the annihilation of all Jewish residents and the subsequent plundering of the empty Jewish houses by the surrounding population—that is, when the Germans did not plunder the houses themselves. This plunder, by the way, ensured the cooperation of the local population in the murder of the Jews and also prevented the escape of survivors: the local population had a strong incentive to ensure that no witnesses survived.

By the time of the first major waves of Nazi murder in 1942, only a small remnant (some 15 to 20 percent) of the Jewish population still lived in the ghettos. This remnant then had to form an organization which might either be opposed by the Judenrat or, if the Judenrat supported a rebellion, would have to coordinate its plans with the latter in some way, and would have to secure arms in the face of supreme difficulties. In the western and central part of Poland, moreover, there were no forests where partisans could hide, so that escape was impossible. During the summer of 1942 the Warsaw underground did send Jewish groups into forests some distance from the capital, but the hostility of the Poles, the murderous actions of the AK, and German patrols quickly put an end to these attempts.

The situation was different in the eastern parts of Poland, western Byelorussia, and the eastern parts of Lithuania. Here the forests were thick, but in 1942 and early 1943 very few Soviet partisan groups were operating. In Minsk, where there was a ghetto of 84,000 Jews, the Judenrat led by Eliahu Mishkin was part of an underground movement which tried to smuggle Jews out to the forests. Some arms were obtained, luckily, for the few Soviet partisans in the area would not accept Jews without them. But only a small number of persons could be suitably equipped from among the many who were sent out. In the city itself no effective non-Jewish underground was organized for a long time and no help was obtained from the Byelorussians; on the contrary, the ghetto had to hide anti-Nazis who could not hold out in the city. We do not yet know how many Jews were smuggled out to the forests from Minsk; we are working on a list, and it will take a long time yet before the job is finished. But I would guess the number to be between 6,000 and 10,000. About 5,000 survived the war in the forests—which shielded only those bent on escape and capable of bearing arms.

I should now like to address another problem: collective responsibility. The Nazis murdered a great many persons in retribution for the rebellious acts or suspected sedition of the few. In Dolhynov, near Vilna for instance, two young men who were about to leave the ghetto for the forest were caught, but managed to escape and hide. The Germans told the Judenrat that if these men did not return and surrender, the ghetto would be annihilated immediately. The two men refused to return, knowing that they were endangering the lives of hundreds of others. On the morrow the inhabitants of the ghetto were shot. What would we have done in the place of the youngsters?[5]

Yet the main internal problem for the Jews was not that of the collective responsibility imposed upon them by Nazi reprisals so much as the more fundamental problem of family responsibility. To belong to a resistance group one had to abandon one's family to death—not just leave it at some risk, as with the non-Jewish resister. The young Jewish man had to make the clearcut decision to leave his parents, brothers, sisters, relatives, and sweethearts, and watch them being transported to death while he stood helpless, albeit wearing the mantle of the resistance fighter. Abba Kovner, the great Israeli poet and former head of the FPO (Farainikte Partisaner Organizacje), the resistance movement in the Vilna ghetto, has told how he gave the order to his people to assemble at an appointed hour: they were to leave the ghetto through the sewers in order to continue the battle in the forests. When the time came, and he stood at the entrance to the sewer, his old mother appeared and asked him for guidance. He had to answer her that he did not know. And, said Kovner, from that time on he did not know whether he deserved the prestige of a partisan fighting the Nazis or the stigma of a faithless son.[6]

Let us then recount, in the face of these facts, what the armed resistance of Jews in the East amounted to. In the Generalgouvernement there were three armed rebellions, at Warsaw, Czestochowa, and Tarnów; four attempted rebellions, at Kielce, Opatów, Pilica, and Tomaszów Lubelski; and seventeen places from which armed groups left for the forests, Chmielnik, Cracow, Iwanska, Józefów, Kalwaria, Markuszew, Miedzyrzec Podlaski, Opoczno, Radom, Radzyn, Rzeszów, Sokolów Podlaski, Sosnowiec, Tomaszów Lubelski, Tarnów, Wlodawa, and Zelechów.

There were moreover rebellions in six concentration and death camps—Kruszyna, Krychów, Minsk Mazowiecki ('Kopernik'), Sobibor, and Treblinka, together with the famous Jewish rebellion in the gas chambers at Auschwitz in late 1944. These were the only rebellions that ever did take place in any Nazi camps, except for that of Soviet prisoners of war at Ebensee at the end of the war. There were armed international undergrounds, in Buchenwald and Auschwitz for instance, but they never acted. (In Buchenwald they took over the camp after the ss withdrew.)

We know also of 30 Jewish partisan detachments in the Generalgouvernement, and a further list of 21 detachments where Jews formed over 30 percent of the partisans. These latter groups were all part of the AL, because as I have explained, the AK wouldn't accept them. Individual Jews fulfilled important functions in the AK, but they had to hide their Jewishness and appear under assumed names. A further 1,000 Jews participated in the Polish Warsaw uprising of August 1944. The total number of these fighters was about 5,000, of whom over 4,000 were killed.

The situation in Lithuania, eastern Poland, and Byelorussia is much more complicated, and I cannot render a complete picture. At least sixty ghettos had armed rebellions (such as those in Tuczyn, Lachwa, and Mir), attempted rebellions (as in Vilna), or armed underground movements which sent people to the forests (as in Kovno, Zetl, and so on). In some ghettos resistance took more than one form, as in Nieswiez, where an armed rebellion was followed by an escape to the forests.[7] An estimate of Jewish partisans in this area is most difficult to make, though, again, we are currently working on a list. We know that there were some 15,000 Jewish partisans in the area towards the end of the war, and many more must have died before that. Some 2,000

Jewish partisans in the Tatra mountains of Slovakia must be added to any account dealing with eastern Europe.

Two further points. First, the problem of defining a "Jewish partisan" is no simple matter. Do we include in that category only Jews who fought in Jewish groups? Or may we include Jews who fought as individuals in non-Jewish groups, such as Soviet partisan units? Moreover, what about Jews who denied their Jewishness and fought as Poles, or Russians? There were, after all, a number of communists (such as Yurgis-Zimanas, the commander of the Lithuanian partisans) who emphatically defined themselves as Soviet or Polish citizens, specifically denying their Jewish backgrounds. This is also true of a few Jews in the AK, and of some of the central figures in the AL command. But these cases were generally few and far between, for Jews were required to identify as such, irrespective of their particular political ideology. Indeed, the attitude toward Jews who refused to identify as anything but Poles or Soviets was often negative in character, so that one is left to wonder whether there is any justification for excluding even communist leaders and assimilationists from an analysis of Jewish resistance. Were not their individual idiosyncrasies overwhelmed by the intruding fate of the Jewish community to which they perceived themselves to belong only by birth?

Second, we cannot ignore antisemitism even in the Soviet partisan detachments, especially those in which Ukrainian partisans had great influence. A large number of such cases have been documented, as have the fatal consequences for a number of Jewish fighters. This hatred was directed not only against Jewish units—which the Soviet partisan command disbanded—but also against individual Jews in general units. Where there were large numbers of Jews in some unit, a struggle against antisemitism was likely; but in smaller detachments with relatively few Jews, defiance was much more difficult.

Let us also deal, albeit summarily, with western Europe. Here the story is less dramatic, first, because the total number of Jews in France, Belgium, and Holland was less than one-sixth of the Jewish population of prewar Poland and, second, because armed resistance movements of a serious kind did not become active until well into 1943. By that time there were not many Jews left to fight. In the west, of course, the same hostility towards the Jews did not exist as in the east, but there were notable exceptions. In France, for instance, the French police effected most of the anti-Jewish measures.

There were Jewish armed groups in the OJC (Organisation juive de combat) and the MOI (a communist group) in France, two groups in Belgium, and two communist groups of Jews in Germany. By and large, however, Jews participated as individuals in non-Jewish organizations because no ghettos were set up in western Europe. Should we consider them as Jewish resisters, or as Belgian and French resisters?

I think the answer depends on the way these Jews acted. Was their behaviour more likely the result of specifically Jewish concerns or not? The answer is important because it would help us to measure the depths of Jewish identification among western Jews. It would also help to reveal the extent of integration among Jews and non-Jews. We are still in the middle of these researches, but I would venture the general conclusion that these Jews were usually fighting for "Jewish" reasons.

How many Jews fought? In France there were thousands rather than hundreds and there were probably close to a thousand in Belgium. Moreover, the Jews were usually the first to act—for example, the first urban guerillas fighting against the Nazis in Paris during the spring of 1942 were members of a Jewish unit of the pro-communist MOI. The Guttfreund group in Belgium took up arms as early as September 1941, killing a Jewish Gestapo agent, robbing a factory producing for the Germans, and later burning a card index of Jews at the Judenrat offices in Brussels. Finally, thousands of Jews fought in northern Italy in 1943–4, and thousands more fought with Tito's army in Yugoslavia.

Let me summarize: Jewish armed resistance was considerably more widespread than has been subsequently assumed. In eastern Europe, a high proportion of those who survived the first wave of murders participated in armed activities. Jewish rebellions in Warsaw and elsewhere were the first urban struggles against the Germans anywhere in Europe, and the Jewish rebellions in the camps were the only ones of their kind. Michel's conclusion that Jewish armed resistance was proportionately higher than that of other people, with few exceptions, is probably true. This is remarkable in light of the greater difficulties Jews encountered and of their lack of modern military tradition. Surely the radical nature of the Nazi threat to Jewish communities is pertinent here. But persecution does not explain resistance, especially when the former is attended by elaborate forms of control and coercion. At any rate, it seems easier to explore the ways Jews in Palestine and then Israel met their military challenges in the light of the above analysis than to believe, with Hilberg, that there was little struggle in Europe and then a sudden inexplicable upsurge of martial skills that enabled the Jews of Israel to fight for their existence.

I have dealt with armed resistance first because unarmed active resistance is best explained against the background of armed struggle. Let us now therefore consider the problem of resistance without weapons.

Unarmed struggle took place largely before the murder actions began. In such situations, when Jews were unaware of any Nazi intentions to murder them, Jewish behaviour was at least in some measure comparable to the behaviour of non-Jewish populations under Nazi rule. Such comparisons are important as measuring-rods for the behaviour of populations subject to the rule of terror. On the other hand, differences between Jewish and non-Jewish situations will stand out clearly as time moves on, and we cannot avoid approaching both comparable and noncomparable situations with the knowledge that the Jews were later subjected to Holocaust, whereas other nationalities were not.

What, then, did these other subject nationalities in Europe do? Did they obey German law, even those laws forbidding education in Poland and Russia? Yes, they did. Did they resist the shipment of slave labour to Germany? No, they did not.

By and large the Jews, on the other hand, proved recalcitrant. History had taught them the art of evasion, and they showed themselves to be highly skilled practitioners. In the first place, contrary to conventional wisdom, most German and Austrian Jews, some 410,000 out of 700,000, did manage to leave the Third Reich. (Some of these, tragically, were caught again as the German armies advanced.)

In Poland, after the war had begun, German rules were so brutal that, had the Jews passively acquiesced—even though every infringement of Nazi law was punishable by death—they would have died out in no time at all. Let me give a few examples. Official German food allocations distributed by the Warsaw Judenrat came to 336 calories daily in 1941. It is unlikely that the Warsaw Jews could have survived longer than a few months on such rations. But smuggling, illicit production on a considerable scale, and great inventiveness produced an average of 1125 calories daily. Unfortunately, a large population of unemployed Jewish refugees who had been expelled by the Germans from their homes in the provinces into Warsaw slowly died because their food supplies fell below that average. Many others managed to survive on these rations nevertheless.[8] I would consider this stubbornness, this determination to survive in defiance of Nazi authority, to be an act of resistance under the definition I offered at the beginning of this essay. In Kovno, similar smuggling was organized by groups that were controlled by the Judenrat and the Jewish police—the police here were the very heart of the armed resistance organization. It was thus an organized act, under public supervision of sorts, and the aim was very definitely to subvert German laws.

Consider the question of education. Until the late autumn of 1941, education of any kind was forbidden in Jewish Warsaw. But it took place clandestinely, in so-called *complets* where small groups of pupils would meet either in the soup kitchen or in the home of the teacher. We find evidence for this, in fact, in a large number of places in Poland. There were also clandestine high schools in Warsaw which received some funds from illegal JDC (American Jewish Joint Distribution Committee) sources. The activities of such schools are documented. Their older students passed official matriculation exams under conditions which were, to put it mildly, unusual.

Also, according to Ringelblum, there were in Warsaw alone some 600 illegal *minyanim*, groups of Jews praying together throughout the period when all public religious observance was forbidden.[9] Political parties were of course proscribed, as were newspapers or printing of any description. But we now know of more than fifty titles of underground newspapers in Warsaw alone, and most of the political parties continued their clandestine existence.

There is, one is inclined to think, something typically Jewish or—more profoundly—*traditionally* Jewish, in the importance that cultural institutions achieved in such a time. There was, for instance, YIVO, the Yiddish Scientific Institute in Vilna, where Kovner and the poet Abraham Sutzkever were active in preserving materials, establishing a library system, and encouraging literary output in a conscious effort to maintain morale. It was no accident that the YIVO group was a recruiting ground for FPO, the resistance movement in Vilna. The most famous of these cultural institutions was the Oneg Shabbat group in Warsaw. Founded and headed by Dr. Emmanuel Ringelblum, the historian and public figure, it methodically assembled reports and diaries and initiated research in order to preserve documentary evidence of the life of the Jews in the Warsaw ghetto. Among its studies were the famous medical investigations into the effects of hunger on the human body under the direction of Dr. Milejkowski, which were published after the war in 1946 in Poland.

Oneg Shabbat did not know of the speech in Poznan in 1943 in which Himmler boasted that nothing would ever become known of the Final Solution. But the basic idea of Oneg Shabbat was that knowledge and documentation were forms of defiance of Nazi intent. In this the group succeeded. Despite the fact that only two-thirds of the Oneg Shabbat archives were found after the war, they are our main source of knowledge regarding Jewish life in Poland during the Holocaust.

Of all active unarmed resistance, most intriguing, I believe, were the activities of the "Joint" (the Joint Distribution Committee), the American-based social welfare agency. The Joint was actually just an office which, in Poland, distributed American funds to local Jewish agencies such as TOZ, a health agency, Centos, a society for the care of orphans, Cekabe, a network of free-loan banks, and Toporol, a society for agricultural vocational training. On the face of it, nothing more tame could be devised. But when war came the Joint offices in Warsaw happened to be headed by a group of men with leftist political convictions, among whom Dr. Ringelblum is perhaps the best known today. They very early on realized that it would be their job to fight against Nazi-imposed starvation, humiliation, and gratuitous cruelty.

Until the end of 1941, certain sums still arrived from America through a complicated transfer system; although no dollars were actually sent to Nazi-controlled territory, German marks left behind by Jewish emigrants were sent to Warsaw from Berlin and Vienna. This stopped in December 1941, and the Joint became an illegal institution. But even before this, additional funds were being obtained by illegal means. In 1941, the Joint fed 260,000 Jews in the Generalgouverne-ment, including some 42,000 children. [10] Centos and TOZ, which had themselves been declared illegal, still maintained their operations under the cover of an official welfare organization. Kitchens and children's homes became the centres of illegal political activities, including party meetings, clandestine presses, and illegal schooling. All this was consciously activated by the Joint.

Parallel to this was Joint support for so-called house committees, of which over 1,000 existed in the ghetto of Warsaw. Residences in eastern Europe were usually built around a courtyard, so that in each instance the 'house' included four apartment buildings, about 200 or

300 families. These groups of people organized spontaneously, outside any Judenrat groupings, to institute mutual aid, schooling for children, cultural activities, and so on. (Unfortunately these groups included Warsaw Jews only; the refugees, crammed in their shelters, were dependent on the woefully insufficient feeding of Joint soup kitchens which were meant to provide only supplementary nourishment.) The house committees sprang up from below, but the Joint quickly realized their potential and Ringelblum set up a roof organization called Zetos. This body tried to create a central fund through which more affluent house committees would help the poorer ones, and encouraged activity essentially opposed to the Judenrat. The steering committee of Zetos became the political base for the resistance movement. The Joint was also behind the preparations for the Warsaw ghetto rebellion, and financed the uprising to a large degree. Giterman, the Joint's chief director, also helped to finance resistance movements in Bialystok and elsewhere by sending them money explicitly for this purpose.

The Joint's was a mass activity which embraced hundreds of thousands of Jews. Still, it obviously could not stand up to the forces of mass murder. Giterman was killed on 19 January 1943 in Warsaw, and Ringelblum was murdered in March 1944 when the Germans finally found his hiding place. They shared the fate of the millions whom they had tried to feed, encourage, and lead. But we cannot be concerned here with their ultimate fate; we are concerned rather with their behaviour prior to their murder. We want to know how widespread was unarmed active opposition to Nazi rule among the Jews; and we discover that owing to the work of men like Ringelblum and Giterman the range of such resistance was considerable.

Let us now very briefly touch upon the question of the Judenraete, the Jewish Councils nominated or approved by the Germans. It must be stated at the outset that their behaviour cannot be subsumed under any generalization. Minsk, which I have mentioned, was not the sole example of Judenrat defiance. Other councils tried to stand up to the Germans and their members were murdered as a result. Still others tried to find a way round German regulations, and managed to survive for a time: the Judenraete of Kovno, Siauliai, Siedlce, Kosow, Piotrkow Tribunalski, France, Slovakia, and other locations belong to this category. Some Judenraete obeyed German commands, but within that framework tried to help their communities. A typical example of this was the Warsaw Judenrat under Adam Czerniakow, who in the end committed suicide rather than be responsible for handing Jews over to the Germans for killing.

A final group consisted, I would submit, of those who saw no alternative but complete submission to the Germans, including the handing over of Jews to the Nazis for deportation, even after there were no illusions about the consequences. Such were the Judenraete of Lodz or Vilna or Lublin. But in the case of Lodz and Vilna submission resulted from the conviction that the only way for a *part* of a community to survive was by doing the Germans' bidding and performing slave labor for them. In the case of Lublin, no policy at all was followed—only terror and frightened submission. There was in fact no Judenrat whose policies, attitudes, and actions quite equalled those of another. However, we find resisters among Judenraete as groups and among Judenrat members as individuals in a fairly large variety of cases.

I have dealt with eastern Europe; but it would be wrong to disregard the 500,000 Jews of western Europe, or indeed the Jews of Germany, Austria, and Czechoslovakia. The Joint, Zetos, and various cultural institutions could be classified as self-governing institutions interposed between the Judenrat and the Jewish masses. Similar groups and organizations existed in western and central Europe as well.

Take for example the OSE.[11] This was a general Jewish health organization which had a rather modest branch in prewar France. During the Holocaust, OSE became the main child-care organization in the Jewish sector. In France, of course, the gentile population had a much more positive attitude toward Jews than that which prevailed in Poland. German rule was comparatively less oppressive; Nazi police and SS were less numerous, while German Army interests, which did not always parallel those of the SS, were more important. In this climate OSE and some other groups managed to hide about 7,000 Jewish children, some in Catholic and Protestant institutions but mostly among peasants, and we do not know of one single case where children were betrayed by those undertaking to hide them. OSE, the Jewish Scout movement, and some other groups managed to smuggle some 2,000 people into Switzerland and a smaller number into Spain. In Belgium, the Comité de défense des juifs, headed by a Jewish member of the Belgian underground, hid thousands of Jews as well.

Let us now turn, very briefly, to what is probably the most important, but also the most diffuse, form of resistance: that of popular, mass reaction. Here we are on uncertain ground, because this form barely comes within our own definition. Can one speak of an unorganized, spontaneous action of Jews as expressing true resistance to Nazi enactments?

Well, up to a point it seems one can. Let us cite a few examples. In Holland, which had a Judenrat of the Lodz type, the Jewish proletariat of Amsterdam reacted forcefully in February 1941 to provocations by Dutch Nazis. A Dutch Nazi died in the scuffle, and Jewish and non-Jewish inhabitants of the Jewish quarter chased the Nazis out. This was the immediate cause for the famous strike of Dutch workers in support of the Jews. It failed, largely because of the intervention of the Jewish leaders who were told by the Nazis that, if the strike did not stop, large numbers of Jews would be taken to concentration camps and killed. The Dutch desisted, and the same Jewish leaders became the nucleus of the Dutch Judenrat. But what should concern us here is the popular Jewish reaction, especially since the story of the anti-Nazi acts in Amsterdam had further instalments.

Nazi documents record that after the first deportations from Holland in July 1942, the Jews ceased to appear at the appointed time and place when called. From the summer of 1942 on the Nazi and the Dutch police had to ferret the Jews out. This was popular unarmed resistance. We know, of course, that this tactic did not succeed; but the measure of resistance is not its success but its incidence. Was the moral backbone of the Dutch-Jewish population broken? It appears, rather, that their desire to live as free human beings was maintained.

Turning to the east, let us inspect another example. The so-called Slovak National Uprising broke out in the hills of Slovakia in August 1944. The Jews from some Slovak towns and camps fled there in large numbers. Those who could, fought; those who could not tried to hide. As the German troops advanced into the Slovak mountains suppressing the uprising, the Jews refused to obey Nazi orders and certainly avoided concentrating in places where they could be picked up by the Germans. This was typical unarmed resistance.

Some of the popular mood of this kind of resistance is captured in diaries which have survived: the young boy who believes that his father is being taken away and will not come back but writes that he believes his own place is with his father; the young man who jumps out the window of the deportation train only when he is already separated from his mother, whom he had not dreamed of leaving to face her fate alone; Chaim A. Kaplan, in Warsaw, who is sorry he will not see the Nazis' downfall which he is sure will come. Such acts and sentiments are beyond our definition of resistance, to be sure; but they form the background to those acts of unarmed circumspect defiance which I have tried to relate.

Let us not exaggerate. There were communities that collapsed. One cannot even find the dignity of quiet defiance in some Jewish responses. In Copenhagen, for example, the whole Jewish community was saved without its lifting a finger to help itself; in Vienna, but for a few hundred people in hiding, nothing but abject submission was the rule. Unfortunately it is impossible to explore here the reasons behind this apparent lethargy.

The range of Jewish resistance was broad, as I have shown: armed, unarmed but organized, semi-organized or semi-spontaneous. Let me conclude with a form of resistance which I have saved to the last because it is the most poignant. My example is from Auschwitz, and I am relating it on the authority of the late Yossel Rosensaft, head of the Bergen-Belsen Survivors' Association. Yossel was also a 'graduate' of Auschwitz, and he testified that in December 1944 he and a group of inmates calculated when Hanukka would occur. They went out of their block and found a piece of wood lying in the snow. With their spoons, they carved out eight holes and put pieces of carton in them. Then they lit these and sang the Hanukka song, 'Ma Oz Tsur Yeshuati.'

None of the people who did this were religious. But on the threshhold of death, and in the hell of Auschwitz, they demonstrated. They asserted several principles: that contrary to Nazi lore, they were human; that Jewish tradition, history, and values had a meaning for them in the face of Auschwitz; and that they wanted to assert their humanity in a Jewish way. We find a large number of such instances in concentration and death camps. Of course, there were uncounted instances of dehumanization in a stark fight for survival: bread was stolen from starving inmates by their comrades, violent struggles broke out over soup, over blankets, over work details—struggles which only too often ended with death. In the conditions of the camps, incidents of this kind are not surprising or unusual, but examples such as the one mentioned are. The few Jews who did survive could not have done so without the companionship and cooperation of friends. And friendship under such conditions is itself a remarkable achievement.

I think the story of Kosów is also appropriate. It exemplifies most vividly the refusal of so many Jewish victims to yield their humanity in the face of impending murder. Kosów is a small town in eastern Galicia, and it had a Judenrat which was not very different from others. On Passover 1942, the Gestapo announced it would come into the ghetto. The Judenrat believed that this was the signal for the liquidation of the ghetto, and told all the Jews to hide or flee. Of the twenty-four Judenrat members, four decided to meet the Germans and offer themselves as sacrificial victims—to deflect the wrath of the enemy. With the ghetto empty and silent, the four men sat and waited for their executioners. While they were waiting one of them faltered. The others told him to go and hide. [12] The three men of Kosów prepared to meet the Nazis on Passover of 1942. Was their act less than firing a gun?

NOTES

1. Henri Michel, *The Shadow War*, London 1965, p. 247.

2. For other definitions of "resistance" see *Jewish Resistance During the Holocaust*, Jerusalem 1971, especially the contributions of Yahil, Blumenthal, and Zuckermann.

3. Shmuel Krakowsky, *Jewish Resistance in Poland*, Jerusalem 1977.

4. Ireneusz Caban and Zygmunt Mankowski, *Zwiazek Walki Zbrojnej i Armia Krajowa w okregu Lubelskim, 1939–1944*, vol. 2, Lublin 1968, pp. 504–5.

5. Moreshet Archive, D. 331.

6. Abba Kovner, in a paper to the conference, "Holocaust—A Generation After," March 1975, New York.

7. Shalom Cholawski, *Ir Vaya'ar Bamatzor*, Tel-Aviv 1974, and "Armed Jewish Resistance in West Byelorussian Ghettoes," PHD thesis, Hebrew University 1978.

8. Artur Eisenbach, *Hitlerowska Politika Zaglady Zydow*, Warsaw 1961, pp. 228–9.

9. Jacob Sloan, ed., *Notes From the Warsaw Ghetto: the Journal of Emmanuel Ringelblum*, New York 1958, p. 47.

10. Yad Vashem, AJDC Krakow, 345–145, Bericht fuer's erste Halbjahr 1942.

11. Nili Keren Patkin, *OSE Rescue Operations in France, 1939–1944*, unpublished MA thesis, Institute of Contemporary Jewry, Jerusalem 1975.

12. Aharon Weiss, "Ledarkam shel Ha'Judenratim bidrom-mizrach Polin," in *Yalkut Moreshet*, no. 15, 1972, p. 98.

TADEUSZ BOROWSKI (1922–1951), the masterful Polish short story writer, poet, essayist, historian, and journalist, was imprisoned in Auschwitz and Dachau from 1943 to 1945. After the Germans occupied Poland in 1939, education for Poles was banned. Borowski finished his secondary education in the Warsaw underground and then attended secret lectures at Warsaw University. In addition to poetry, Borowski wrote for the underground press, an activity punishable by the concentration camp, if not by death.

The Gestapo caught up with Borowski. His prison for two months was near the Warsaw ghetto. From his cell window, he witnessed the uprising there in April 1943; but toward the end of that month he was sent to Auschwitz, where he became prisoner 119198. Three weeks earlier, the gassing of non-Jews had been halted. So Borowski was put to work as a hospital orderly. If this work saved his life, it also haunted him. Long after his liberation, Borowski harbored the feeling that he himself was implicated in the system that had destroyed so many defenseless persons.

Liberated from Dachau in 1945, Borowski returned to Poland the following year and took up writing again. The Polish edition of his most famous book, a collection of short stories entitled *This Way for the Gas, Ladies and Gentlemen*, appeared in 1948. Subverting neat distinctions between criminals and victims, indeed between good and evil, Borowski shows—unrelentingly and bitingly—how Auschwitz calls into question traditional categories such as "hero" or even "tragedy."

Like other stories in this collection, "The People Who Walked On," which follows, is narrated by Vorarbeiter Tadeusz, a deputy kapo. This man, like Borowski himself, inhabits what Primo Levi called "the gray zone." Though a prisoner, he is also a cog that keeps the camp's infrastructure operational. Vorarbeiter Tadeusz is not there by choice, but he is there; and Borowski shows, often with icy detachment to match the brutality of Auschwitz, what that involves.

That includes an ultimate irony. Scarred by the Holocaust and apparently disillusioned by the communism he had chosen to support after World War II, Borowski opened a gas valve on July 1, 1951, and took his own life.

Tadeusz Borowski

The People Who Walked On

It was early spring when we began building a soccer field on the broad clearing behind the hospital barracks. The location was excellent: the gypsies to the left, with their roaming children, their lovely, trim nurses, and their women sitting by the hour in the latrines; to the rear—a barbed-wire fence, and behind it the loading ramp with the wide railway tracks and the endless coming and going of trains; and beyond the ramp, the women's camp—*Frauen Konzentration Lager.* No one, of course, ever called it by its full name. We simply said F.K.L.—that was enough. To the right of the field were the crematoria, some of them at the back of the ramp, next to the F.K.L., others even closer, right by the fence. Sturdy buildings that sat solidly on the ground. And in front of the crematoria, a small wood which had to be crossed on the way to the gas.

We worked on the soccer field throughout the spring, and before it was finished we started planting flowers under the barracks windows and decorating the blocks with intricate zigzag designs made of crushed red brick. We planted spinach and lettuce, sunflowers and garlic. We laid little green lawns with grass transplanted from the edges of the soccer field, and sprinkled them daily with water brought in barrels from the lavatories.

Just when the flowers were about to bloom, we finished the soccer field.

From then on, the flowers were abandoned, the sick lay by

themselves in the hospital beds, and we played soccer. Every day, as soon as the evening meal was over, anybody who felt like it came to the field and kicked the ball around. Others stood in clusters by the fence and talked across the entire length of the camp with the girls from the F.K.L.

One day I was goalkeeper. As always on Sundays, a sizeable crowd of hospital orderlies and convalescent patients had gathered to watch the game. Keeping goal, I had my back to the ramp. The ball went out and rolled all the way to the fence. I ran after it, and as I reached to pick it up, I happened to glance at the ramp.

A train had just arrived. People were emerging from the cattle cars and walking in the direction of the little wood. All I could see from where I stood were bright splashes of colour. The women, it seemed, were already wearing summer dresses; it was the first time that season. The men had taken off their coats, and their white shirts stood out sharply against the green of the trees. The procession moved along slowly, growing in size as more and more people poured from the freight cars. And then it stopped. The people sat down on the grass and gazed in our direction. I returned with the ball and kicked it back inside the field. It travelled from one foot to another and, in a wide arc, returned to the goal. I kicked it towards a corner. Again it rolled out into the grass. Once more I ran to retrieve it. But as I reached down, I stopped in amazement—the ramp was empty. Out of the whole colorful summer procession, not one person remained. The train too was gone. Again the F.K.L. blocks were in unobstructed view, and again the orderlies and the patients stood along the barbed-wire fence calling to the girls, and the girls answered them across the ramp.

Between two throw-ins in a soccer game, right behind my back, three thousand people had been put to death.

In the following months, the processions to the little wood moved along two roads: one leading straight from the ramp, the other past the hospital wall. Both led to the crematoria, but some of the people had the good fortune to walk beyond them, all the way to the Zauna, and this meant more than just a bath and a delousing, a barber's shop and a new prison suit. It meant staying alive. In a concentration camp, true, but—alive.

Each day, as I got up in the morning to scrub the hospital floors, the people were walking—along both roads. Women, men, children. They carried their bundles.

When I sat down to dinner—and not a bad one, either—the people were walking. Our block was bathed in sunlight; we threw the doors and the windows wide open and sprinkled the floors with water to keep the dust down. In the afternoons I delivered packages which had been brought that morning from the Auschwitz post office. The clerk distributed mail. The doctors dressed wounds and gave injections. There was, as a matter of fact, only one hypodermic needle for the entire block. On warm evenings I sat at the barracks door reading *Mon frère Yves* by Pierre Loti—while the procession continued on and on, along both roads.

Often, in the middle of the night, I walked outside; the lamps glowed in the darkness above the barbed-wire fences. The roads were completely black, but I could distinctly hear the far-away hum of a thousand voices—the procession moved on and on. And then the entire sky would light up; there would be a burst of flame above the wood . . . and terrible human screams.

I stared into the night, numb, speechless, frozen with horror. My entire body trembled and rebelled, somehow even without my participation. I no longer controlled my body, although I could feel its every tremor. My mind was completely calm, only the body seemed to revolt.

Soon afterwards, I left the hospital. The days were filled with important events. The Allied Armies had landed on the shores of France. The Russian front, we heard, had started to move west towards Warsaw.

But in Birkenau, day and night long lines of trains loaded with people waited at the station. The doors were unsealed, the people started walking—along both roads.

Located next to the camp's labor sector was the deserted, unfinished Sector C. Here, only the barracks and the high voltage fence around them had been completed. The roofs, however, were not yet covered with tar sheets, and some of the blocks still had no bunks. An average Birkenau block, furnished with three tiers of bunks, could hold up to five hundred people. But every block in Sector C was now being packed with a thousand or more young women picked from among the people on the ramp . . . Twenty-eight blocks—over thirty thousand women. Their heads were shaved and they were issued little sleeveless summer dresses. But they were not given underwear. Nor spoons, nor bowls, nor even a rag to clean themselves with. Birkenau was situated on marshes, at the foot of a mountain range. During the day, the air was warm and so transparent that the mountains were in clear view, but in the morning they lay shrouded in a thick, icy mist. The mornings were cold and penetrating. For us, this meant merely a refreshing pause before a hot summer day, but the women, who only twenty yards to our right had been standing at rollcall since five in the morning, turned blue from the cold and huddled together like a flock of partridges.

We named the camp—Persian Market. On sunny, warm days the women would emerge from the barracks and mill around in the wide aisles between the blocks. Their bright summer dresses and the gay kerchiefs on their shaved heads created the atmosphere of a busy, colourful market—a Persian Market because of its exotic character.

From afar, the women were faceless and ageless. Nothing more than white blotches and pastel figures.

The Persian Market was not yet completed. The Wagner Kommando began building a road through the sector, packing it down with a heavy roller. Others fiddled around with the plumbing and worked on the washrooms that were to be installed throughout all the sectors of Birkenau. Still others were busy stocking up the Persian Market with the camp's basic equipment—supplies of blankets, metal cups and spoons—which they arranged carefully in the warehouses under the direction of the chief supervisor, the assigned S.S. officer. Naturally, much of the stuff evaporated immediately, expertly "organized" by the men working on the job.

My comrades and I laid a roof over the shack of every Block Elder in the Persian Market. It was not done on official order, nor did we work out of charity. Neither did we do it out of a feeling of solidarity with the old serial numbers, the F.K.L. women who had been placed there in all the responsible posts. In fact, we used "organized" tar-boards and melted "organized" tar, and for every roll of tar-board, every bucket of tar, an Elder had to pay. She had to pay the Kapo, the Kommandoführer, the Kommando "bigwigs." She could pay in various ways: with gold, food, the women of her block, or with her own body. It depended.

On a similar basis, the electricians installed electricity, the carpenters built and furnished the shacks, using "organized" lumber, the masons provided metal stoves and cemented them in place.

It was at that time that I came to know the anatomy of this strange camp. We would arrive there in the morning, pushing a cart loaded with tar-sheets and tar. At the gate stood the S.S. women-guards, hippy blondes in black leather boots. They searched us and let us in. Then they themselves went to inspect the blocks. Not infrequently they had lovers among the masons and carpenters. They slept with them in the unfinished washrooms or the Block Elders' shacks.

We would push our cart into the camp, between the barracks, and there, on some little square, would light a fire and melt the tar. A crowd of women would immediately surround us. They begged us to give them anything, a penknife, a handkerchief, a spoon, a pencil, a piece of paper, a shoe string, or bread.

"Listen, you can always manage somehow," they would say. "You've been in the camp a long time and you've survived. Surely you have all you need. Why won't you share it with us?"

At first we gave them everything we happened to have with us, and then turned our pockets inside out to show we had nothing more. We took off our shirts and handed them over. But gradually we began coming with empty pockets and gave them nothing.

These women were not so much alike as it had seemed when we looked at them from another sector, from a distance of twenty metres.

Among them were small girls, whose hair had not been shaved, stray little cherubs from a painting of the Last Judgment. There were young girls who gazed with surprise at the women crowding around us, and who looked at us, coarse, brutal men, with contempt. Then there were married women, who desperately begged for news of their lost husbands, and mothers trying to find a trace of their children.

"We are so miserable, so cold, so hungry," they cried. "Tell us, are they at least a little bit better off?"

"They are, if God is just," we would answer solemnly, without the usual mocking and teasing.

"Surely they're not dead?" the women asked, looking searchingly into our faces.

We would walk away without a word, eager to get back to work.

The majority of the Block Elders at the Persian Market were Slovak girls who managed to communicate in the language of the new inmates. Every one of these girls had behind her several years of concentration camp. Every one of them remembered the early days of the F.K.L., when female corpses piled up along the barracks walls and rotted, unremoved, in hospital beds—and when human excrement grew into monstrous heaps inside the blocks.

Despite their rough manner, they had retained their femininity and human kindness. Probably they too had their lovers, and probably they too stole margarine and tins of food in order to pay for blankets and dresses, but . . .

. . . but I remember Mirka, a short, stocky "pink" girl. Her shack was all done up in pink too, with pink ruffled curtains across the window that faced the block. The pink light inside the shack set a pink glow over the girl's face, making her look as if she were wrapped in a delicate misty veil. There was a Jew in our Kommando with very bad teeth who was in love with Mirka. He was always running around the camp trying to buy fresh eggs for her, and then throwing them, protected in soft wrapping, over the barbed-wire fence. He would spend many long hours with her, paying little attention to the S.S. women inspecting the barracks or to our chief who made his rounds with a tremendous revolver hanging from his white summer uniform.

One day Mirka came running over to where several of us were laying a roof. She signalled frantically to the Jew and called, turning to me:

"Please come down! Maybe you can help too!"

We slid off the roof and down the barracks door. Mirka grabbed us by the hands and pulled us in the direction of her shack. There she led us between the cots and pointing to a mass of colorful quilts and blankets on top of which lay a child, she said breathlessly:

"Look, it's dying! Tell me, what can I do? What could have made it so sick so suddenly?"

The child was asleep, but very restless. It looked like a rose in a golden frame—its burning cheeks were surrounded by a halo of blond hair.

"What a pretty child," I whispered.

"Pretty!" cried Mirka. "All you know is that it's pretty! But it can die any moment! I've had to hide it so they wouldn't take it to the gas! What if an S.S. woman finds it? Help me!"

The Jew put his arm around her shoulders. She pushed him away and suddenly burst into sobs. I shrugged, turned around, and left the barracks.

In the distance, I could see trains moving along the ramp. They were bringing new people who would walk in the direction of the little wood. One Canada group was just returning from the ramp, and along the wide camp road passed another Canada group going to take its place. Smoke was rising above the treetops. I seated myself next to the boiling bucket of tar and, stirring it slowly, sat thinking for a long time. At one point a wild thought suddenly shot across my mind: I too would like to have a child with rose-colored cheeks and light blond hair. I laughed aloud at such a ridiculous notion and climbed up on the roof to lay the hot tar.

And I remember another Block Elder, a big redhead with broad feet and chapped hands. She did not have a separate shack, only a few blankets spread over the bed and instead of walls a few other blankets thrown across a piece of rope.

"I mustn't make them feel," she would say, pointing to the women packed tightly in the bunks, "that I want to cut myself off from them. Maybe I can't give them anything, but I won't take anything away from them either."

"Do you believe in life after death?" she asked me once in the middle of some lighthearted conversation.

"Sometimes," I answered cautiously. "Once I believed in it when I was in jail, and again once when I came close to dying here in the camp."

"But if a man does evil, he'll be punished, won't he?"

"I suppose so, unless there are some criteria of justice other than the man-made criteria. You know . . . the kind that explain causes and motivations, and erase guilt by making it appear insignificant in the light of the overall harmony of the universe. Can a crime committed on one level be punishable on a different one?"

"But I mean in a normal, human sense!" she exclaimed.

"It ought to be punished. No question about it."

"And you, would you do good if you were able to?"

"I seek no rewards. I build roofs and want to survive the concentration camp."

"But do you think that they," she pointed with her chin in an indefinite direction, "can go unpunished?"

"I think that for those who have suffered unjustly, justice alone is not enough. They want the guilty to suffer unjustly too. Only this will they understand as justice."

"You're a pretty smart fellow! But you wouldn't have the slightest idea how to divide bread justly, without giving more to your own mistress!" she said bitterly and walked into the block. The women were lying in the rows of bunks, head to head. Their faces were still, only the eyes seemed alive, large and shining. Hunger had already started in this part of the camp. The redheaded Elder moved from bunk to bunk, talking to the women to distract them from their thoughts. She pulled out the singers and told them to sing, the dancers—and told them to dance, the poets—and made them recite poetry.

"All the time, endlessly, they ask me about their mothers, their fathers. They beg me to write to them."

"They've asked me too. It's just too bad."

"Ah, you! You come and then you go, but me? I plead with them, I beg them—if anyone is pregnant, don't report to the doctor, if anyone is sick, stay in the barracks! But do you think they believe me? It's no good, no matter how hard you try to protect them. What can you do if they fall all over themselves to get to the gas?"

One of the girls was standing on top of a table singing a popular tune. When she finished, the women in the bunks began to applaud. The girl bowed, smiling. The red-headed Elder covered her face with her rough hands.

"I can't stand it any longer! It's too disgusting!" she whispered. And suddenly she jumped up and rushed over to the table. "Get down!" she screamed at the singer.

The women fell silent. She raised her arm.

"Quiet!" she shouted, though nobody spoke a word. "You've been asking me about your parents and your children. I haven't told you, I felt sorry for you. But now I'll tell you, so that you know, because they'll do the same with you if you get sick! Your children, your husbands and your parents are not in another camp at all. They've been stuffed into a room and gassed! Gassed, do you understand? Like millions of others, like my own mother and father. They're burning in deep pits and in ovens . . . The smoke which you see above the rooftops doesn't come from the brick plant at all, as you're being told. It's smoke from your children! Now go on and sing," she finished calmly, pointing her finger at the terrified singer. Then she turned around and walked out of the barracks.

It was undeniable that the conditions in both Auschwitz and Birkenau were steadily improving. At the beginning, beating and killing were the rule, but later this became only sporadic. At first, you had to sleep on the floor lying on your side because of the lack of space, and could turn over only on command; later you slept in bunks, or wherever you wished, sometimes even in bed. Originally, you had to stand at roll-call for as long as two days at a time, later—only until the second gong, until nine o'clock. In the early years, packages were forbidden, later you could receive 500 grams, and finally as much as you wanted. Pockets of any kind were at first strictly taboo, but eventually even civilian clothes could sometimes be seen around Birkenau. Life in the camp became "better and better" all the time—after the first three or four years. We felt certain that the horrors could never again be repeated, and we were proud that we had survived. The worse the Germans fared at the battle front, the better off we were. And since they fared worse and worse . . .

At the Persian Market, time seemed to move in reverse. Again we saw the Auschwitz of 1940. The women greedily gulped down the soup which nobody in our blocks would even think of touching. They stank of sweat and female blood. They stood at roll-call from five in the morning. When they were at last counted, it was almost nine. Then they were given cold coffee. At three in the afternoon the evening roll-call began and they were given dinner: bread with some spread. Since they did not work, they did not rate the *Zulage*, the extra work ration.

Sometimes they were driven out of the barracks in the middle of the day for an additional roll-call. They would line up in tight rows and march along the road, one behind the other. The big, blonde S.S. women in leather boots plucked from among them all the skinny ones, the ugly ones, the big-bellied ones—and threw them inside the Eye. The so-called Eye was a closed circle formed by the joined hands of the barracks guards. Filled out with women, the circle moved like a macabre dance to the camp gate, there to become absorbed by the great, camp-wide Eye. Five hundred, six hundred, a thousand selected women. Then all of them started on their walk—along the two roads.

Sometimes an S.S. woman dropped in at one of the barracks. She cased the bunks, a woman looking at other women. She asked if anyone cared to see a doctor, if anyone was pregnant. At the hospital, she said, they would get milk and white bread.

They scrambled out of the bunks and, swept up into the Eye, walked to the gate—towards the little wood.

Just to pass the time of day—for there was little for us to do at the camp—we used to spend long hours at the Persian Market, either with the Block Elders, or sitting under the barracks walls, or in the latrines. At the Elders' shacks you drank tea or dozed off for an hour or two in their beds. Sitting under the barracks wall you chatted with the carpenters and the bricklayers. A few women were usually hanging around, dressed in pretty little pullovers and wearing sheer stockings. Any one of them could be had for a piece of bright silk or a shiny trinket. Since time began, never has there been such an easy market for female flesh!

The latrines were built for the men and the women jointly, and were separated only by wooden boards. On the women's side, it was crowded and noisy, on ours, quiet and pleasantly cool inside the concrete enclosure. You sat there by the hour conducting love dialogues with Katia, the pretty little latrine girl. No one felt any embarrassment or thought the set-up uncomfortable. After all, one had already seen so much . . .

That was June. Day and night the people walked—along the two roads. From dawn until late at night the entire Persian Market stood at roll-call. The days were warm and sunny and the tar melted on the roofs. Then came the rains, and with them icy winds. The mornings would dawn cold and penetrating. Then the fair weather returned once again. Without interruption, the trains pulled up to the ramp and the people walked on . . . Often we had to stand and wait, unable to leave for work, because they were blocking the roads. They walked slowly, in loose groups, sometimes hand in hand. Women, old men, children. As they passed just outside the barbed-wire fence they would turn their silent faces in our direction. Their eyes would fill with tears of pity and they threw bread over the fence for us to eat.

The women took the watches off their wrists and flung them at our feet, gesturing to us to take them.

At the gate, a band was playing foxtrots and tangos. The camp gazed at the passing procession. A man has only a limited number of ways in which he can express strong emotions or violent passions. He uses the same gestures as when what he feels is only petty and unimportant. He utters the same ordinary words.

"How many have gone by so far? It's been almost two months since mid-May. Counting twenty thousand per day . . . around one million!"

"Eh, they couldn't have gassed that many every day. Though . . . who the hell knows, with four ovens and scores of deep pits . . ."

"Then count it this way: from Koszyce and Munkacz, almost 600,000. They got 'em all, no doubt about it. And from Budapest? 300,000, easily."

"What's the difference?"

"*Ja*, but anyway, it's got to be over soon. They'll have slaughtered every single one of them."

"There's more, don't worry."

You shrug your shoulders and look at the road. Slowly, behind the crowd of people, walk the S.S. men, urging them with kindly smiles to move along. They explain that it is not much farther and they pat on the back a little old man who runs over to a ditch, rapidly pulls down his trousers, and wobbling in a funny way squats down. An S.S. man calls to him and points to the people disappearing round the bend. The little old man nods quickly, pulls up his trousers and, wobbling in a funny way, runs at a trot to catch up.

You snicker, amused at the sight of a man in such a big hurry to get to the gas chamber.

Later, we started working at the warehouses, spreading tar over their dripping roofs. The warehouses contained mountains of clothing, junk, and not-yet-disembowelled bundles. The treasures taken from the gassed people were piled up at random, exposed to the sun and the rain.

Every day, after lighting a fire under the bucket of tar, we went to "organize" a snack. One of us would bring a pail of water, another a sack of dry cherries or prunes, a third some sugar. We stewed the fruit and then carried it up on the roof for those who took care of the work itself. Others fried bacon and onions and ate it with corn bread. We stole anything we could get our hands on and took it to the camp.

From the warehouse roofs you could see very clearly the flaming pits and the crematoria operating at full speed. You could see the people walk inside, undress. Then the S.S. men would quickly shut the windows and firmly tighten the screws. After a few minutes, in which we did not even have time to tar a piece of roofing board properly, they opened the windows and the side doors and aired the place out. Then came the *Sonderkommando** to drag the corpses to the burning pits. And so it went on, from morning till night—every single day.

---

* The *Sonderkommando*, a labor gang composed mostly of Jews and assigned specifically to crematorium duties.

Sometimes, after a transport had already been gassed, some late-arriving cars drove around filled with the sick. It was wasteful to gas them. They were undressed and Oberscharführer Moll either shot them with his rifle or pushed them live into a flaming trench.

Once, a car brought a young woman who had refused to part from her mother. Both were forced to undress, the mother led the way. The man who was to guide the daughter stopped, struck by the perfect beauty of her body, and in his awe and admiration he scratched his head. The woman, noticing this coarse, human gesture, relaxed. Blushing, she clutched the man's arm.

"Tell me, what will they do to me?"

"Be brave," said the man, not withdrawing his arm.

"I am brave! Can't you see, I'm not even ashamed of you! Tell me!"

"Remember, be brave, come. I shall lead you. Just don't look."

He took her by the hand and led her on, his other hand covering her eyes. The sizzling and the stench of the burning fat and the heat gushing out of the pit terrified her. She jerked back. But he gently bent her head forward, uncovering her back. At that moment the Oberscharführer fired, almost without aiming. The man pushed the woman into the flaming pit, and as she fell he heard her terrible, broken scream.

When the Persian Market, the gypsy camp and the F.K.L. became completely filled with the women selected from among the people from the ramp, a new camp was opened up across from the Persian Market. We called it Mexico. It, too, was not yet completed, and there also they began to install shacks for the Block Elders, electricity, and windows.

Each day was just like another. People emerged from the freight cars and walked on—along both roads.

The camp inmates had problems of their own: they waited for packages and letters from home, they "organized" for their friends and mistresses, they speculated, they schemed. Nights followed days, rains came after the dry spells.

Towards the end of the summer, the trains stopped coming. Fewer and fewer people went to the crematoria. At first, the camp seemed somehow empty and incomplete. Then everybody got used to it. Anyway, other important events were taking place: the Russian offensive, the uprising and burning of Warsaw, the transports leaving the camp every day, going West towards the unknown, towards new sickness and death; the revolt at the crematoria and the escape of a *Sonderkommando* that ended with the execution of all the escapees.

And afterwards, you were shoved from camp to camp, without a spoon, or a plate, or a piece of rag to clean yourself with.

Your memory retains only images. Today, as I think back on that last summer in Auschwitz, I can still see the endless, colorful procession of people solemnly walking—along both roads; the woman, her head bent forward, standing over the flaming pit; the big redheaded girl in the dark interior of the barracks, shouting impatiently:

"Will evil be punished? I mean in human, normal terms!"

And I can still see the Jew with bad teeth, standing beneath my high bunk every evening, lifting his face to me, asking insistently:

"Any packages today? Couldn't you sell me some eggs for Mirka? I'll pay in marks. She is so fond of eggs . . ."

JEAN AMÉRY (1912–1978), the only child of a Catholic mother and a Jewish father, was born Hans Maier in Vienna, Austria. The Holocaust changed more than his name, and how it did so is Améry's topic in *At the Mind's Limits: Contemplations by a Survivor on Auschwitz and Its Realities*, which first appeared in Germany in 1966. Subsequently he wrote *Über das Altern* (*On Aging*) and *Hand an sich legen: Diskurs über den Freitod*, a work on suicide. The latter foreshadowed Améry's own death. Like that of his fellow Holocaust interpreters, Primo Levi and Tadeusz Borowski, it came by his own hand.

Nazi intentions, Améry realized early on, meant that the Jews' "sole right, our sole duty was to disappear from the face of the earth." Understanding that he had become "a dead man on leave, someone to be murdered, who only by chance was not yet where he properly belonged," this Jewish thinker fled to Belgium and joined the Resistance when the Germans occupied that country. Eventually put under arrest, he was sent to Auschwitz. He survived, changed his name from Hans Maier to Jean Améry in 1955, and became an exceptional essayist who protested eloquently and poignantly against the conditions that had forced him to lose what he called "trust in the world."

As shown by the following reflection on "Torture," Améry took *At the Mind's Limits* to be "a personal confession refracted through meditation." Fearing that Hitler would gain "a posthumous triumph" if the Holocaust were eventually relegated to a few paragraphs in the world's history, Améry was often discouraged that he could "do no more than give testimony." In part, such disillusionment may have driven him to suicide as his final act of protest. Jean Améry's protest lives on. The Holocaust has not been reduced to a footnote in history—at least not yet.

Jean Améry

Torture

Whoever visits Belgium as a tourist may perhaps chance upon Fort Breendonk, which lies halfway between Brussels and Antwerp. The compound is a fortress from the First World War, and what its fate was at that time I don't know. In the Second World War, during the short eighteen days of resistance by the Belgian army in May 1940, Breendonk was the last headquarters of King Leopold. Then, under German occupation, it became a kind of small concentration camp, a "reception camp," as it was called in the cant of the Third Reich. Today it is a Belgian National Museum.

At first glance, the fortress Breendonk makes a very old, almost historic impression. As it lies there under the eternally rain-gray sky of Flanders, with its grass-covered domes and black-gray walls, it gives the feeling of a melancholy engraving from the 1870s war. One thinks of Gravelotte and Sedan and is convinced that the defeated Emperor Napoleon III, with kepi in hand, will immediately appear in one of the massive, low gates. One must step closer, in order that the fleeting picture from past times be replaced by another, which is more familiar to us. Watchtowers arise along the moat that rings the castle. Barbed-wire fences wrap around them. The copperplate of 1870 is abruptly obscured by horror photos from the world that David Rousset has called "l'Univers Concentrationnaire." The creators of the National Museum have left everything the way it was between 1940 and 1944. Yellowed wall cards: "Whoever goes beyond this point will be shot." The pathetic monument to the resistance movement that was erected

From Jean Améry, *At the Mind's Limits: Contemplations by a Survivor on Auschwitz and Its Realities*, trans. Sidney Rosenfeld and Stella P. Rosenfeld. New York: Schocken Books, 1986. Copyright © 1980 by Indiana University Press. All rights reserved. Reprinted by permission.

in front of the fortress shows a man forced to his knees, but defiantly raising his head with its oddly Slavic lines. This monument would not at all have been necessary to make clear to the visitor *where* he is and *what* is recollected there.

One steps through the main gate and soon finds oneself in a room that in those days was mysteriously called the "business room." A picture of Heinrich Himmler on the wall, a swastika flag spread as a cloth over a long table, a few bare chairs. The business room. Everyone went about his business, and theirs was murder. Then the damp, cellarlike corridors, dimly lit by the same thin and reddishly glowing bulbs as the ones that used to hang there. Prison cells, sealed by inch-thick wooden doors. Again and again one must pass through heavy barred gates before one finally stands in a windowless vault in which various iron implements lie about. From there no scream penetrated to the outside. There I experienced it: torture.

If one speaks about torture, one must take care not to exaggerate. What was inflicted on me in the unspeakable vault in Breendonk was by far not the worst form of torture. No red-hot needles were shoved under my fingernails, nor were any lit cigars extinguished on my bare chest. What did happen to me there I will have to tell about later; it was relatively harmless and it left no conspicuous scars on my body. And yet, twenty-two years after it occurred, on the basis of an experience that in no way probed the entire range of possibilities, I dare to assert that torture is the most horrible event a human being can retain within himself.

But very many people have preserved such things, and the horrible can make no claim to singularity. In most Western countries torture was eliminated as an institution and method at the end of the eighteenth century. And yet, today, two hundred years later, there are still men and women—no one knows how many—who can tell of the torture they underwent. As I am preparing this article, I come across a newspaper page with photos that show members of the South Vietnamese army torturing captured Vietcong rebels. The English novelist Graham Greene wrote a letter about it to the London *Daily Telegraph*, saying:

> The strange new feature about the photographs of torture now appearing in the British and American press is that they have been taken with the approval of the torturers and are published over

captions that contain no hint of condemnation. They might have come out of a book on insect life. . . . Does this mean that the American authorities sanction torture as a means of interrogation? The photographs certainly are a mark of honesty, a sign that the authorities do not shut their eyes to what is going on, but I wonder if this kind of honesty without conscience is really to be preferred to the old hypocrisy.

Every one of us will ask himself Graham Greene's question. The admission of torture, the boldness—but is it still that?—of coming forward with such photos is explicable only if it is assumed that a revolt of public conscience is no longer to be feared. One could think that this conscience has accustomed itself to the practice of torture. After all, torture was, and is, by no means being practiced only in Vietnam during these decades. I would not like to know what goes on in South African, Angolese, and Congolese prisons. But I do know, and the reader probably has also heard, what went on between 1956 and 1963 in the jails of French Algeria. There is a frighteningly exact and sober book on it, *La question* by Henri Alleg, a work whose circulation was prohibited, the report of an eyewitness who was also personally tortured and who gave evidence of the horror, sparingly and without making a fuss about himself. Around 1960 numerous other books and pamphlets on the subject appeared: the learned criminological treatise by the famous lawyer Alec Mellor, the protest of the publicist Pierre-Henri Simon, the ethical-philosophic investigation of a theologian named Vialatoux. Half the French nation rose up against the torture in Algeria. One cannot say often and emphatically enough that by this the French did honor to themselves. Leftist intellectuals protested. Catholic trade unionists and other Christian laymen warned against the torture, and at the risk of their safety and lives took action against it. Prelates raised their voices, although to our feeling much too gently.

But that was the great and freedom-loving France, which even in those dark days was not entirely robbed of its liberty. From other places the screams penetrated as little into the world as did once my own strange and uncanny howls from the vault of Breendonk. In Hungary there presides a Party First Secretary, of whom it is said that under the regime of one of his predecessors torturers ripped out his fingernails. And where and who are all the others about whom one learned nothing at all, and of whom one will probably never hear anything? Peoples, governments, authorities, names that are known, but which no one says aloud. Somewhere, someone is crying out under torture. Perhaps in this hour, this second.

And how do I come to speak of torture solely in connection with the Third Reich? Because I myself suffered it under the outspread wings of this very bird of prey, of course. But *not only* for that reason; rather, I am convinced, beyond all personal experiences, that torture was not an accidental quality of this Third Reich, but its essence. Now I hear violent objection being raised, and I know that this assertion puts me on dangerous ground. I will try to substantiate it later. First, however, I suppose I must tell what the content of my experiences actually was and what happened in the cellar-damp air of the fortress Breendonk.

In July 1943 I was arrested by the Gestapo. It was a matter of fliers. The group to which I belonged, a small German-speaking organization within the Belgian resistance movement, was spreading anti-Nazi propaganda among the members of the German occupation forces. We produced rather primitive agitation material, with which we imagined we could convince the German soldiers of the terrible madness of Hitler and his war. Today I know, or at least believe to know, that we were aiming our feeble message at deaf ears. I have much reason to assume that the soldiers in field-gray uniform who found our mimeographed papers in front of their barracks clicked their heels and passed them straight on to their superiors, who then, with the same official readiness, in turn notified the security agency. And so the latter rather quickly got onto our trail and raided us. One of the fliers that I was carrying at the time of my arrest bore the message, which was just as succinct as it was propagandistically ineffectual, "Death to the SS bandits and Gestapo hangmen!" Whoever was stopped with such material by the men in leather coats and with drawn pistols could have no illusions of any kind. I also did not allow myself any for a single moment. For, God knows, I regarded myself—wrongly, as I see today—as an old, hardened expert on the system, its men, and its methods. A reader of the *Neue Weltbühne* and the *Neues Tagebuch* in times past, well up on the KZ literature of the German emigration from 1933 on, I believed to anticipate what was in store for me. Already in the first days of the Third Reich I had heard of the cellars of the SA barracks on Berlin's General Pape Street. Soon thereafter I had read what to my knowledge was the first German KZ

document, the little book *Oranienburg* by Gerhart Segers. Since that
time so many reports by former Gestapo prisoners had reached my
ears that I thought there could be nothing new for me in this area.
What would take place would then have to be incorporated into the
relevant literature, as it were. Prison, interrogation, blows, torture; in
the end, most probably death. Thus it was written and thus it would
happen. When, after my arrest, a Gestapo man ordered me to step
away from the window—for he knew the trick, he said, with your
chained hands you tear open the window and leap onto a nearby
ledge—I was certainly flattered that he credited me with so much
determination and dexterity, but, obeying the order, I politely ges-
tured that it did not come into question. I gave him to understand that
I had neither the physical prerequisites nor at all the intention to
escape my fate in such an adventurous way. I knew what was coming
and they could count on my consent to it. But does one really know?
Only in part. "Rien n'arrive ni comme on l'espère, ni comme on le
craint," Proust writes somewhere. Nothing really happens as we hope
it will, nor as we fear it will. But not because the occurrence, as one
says, perhaps "goes beyond the imagination" (it is not a quantitative
question), but because it is reality and not phantasy. One can devote an
entire life to comparing the imagined and the real, and still never
accomplish anything by it. Many things do indeed happen approximately the way they were anticipated in the imagination: Gestapo
men in leather coats, pistol pointed at their victim—that is correct, all
right. But then, almost amazingly, it dawns on one that the fellows not
only have leather coats and pistols, but also faces: not "Gestapo faces"
with twisted noses, hypertrophied chins, pockmarks, and knife scars,
as might appear in a book, but rather faces like anyone else's. Plain,
ordinary faces. And the enormous perception at a later stage, one that
destroys all abstractive imagination, makes clear to us how the plain,
ordinary faces finally become Gestapo faces after all, and how evil
overlays and exceeds banality. For there is no "banality of evil," and
Hannah Arendt, who wrote about it in her Eichmann book, knew the
enemy of mankind only from hearsay, saw him only through the glass
cage.

When an event places the most extreme demands on us, one
ought not to speak of banality. For at this point there is no longer any
abstraction and never an imaginative power that could even approach
its reality. That someone is carried away shackled in an auto is "self-

evident" only when you read about it in the newspaper and you rationally tell yourself, just at the moment when you are packing fliers: well of course, and what more? It can and it will happen like that to me someday, too. But the auto is different, and the pressure of the shackles was not felt in advance, and the streets are strange, and although you may previously have walked by the gate of the Gestapo headquarters countless times, it has other perspectives, other ornaments, other ashlars when you cross its threshold as a prisoner. Everything is self-evident, and nothing is self-evident as soon as we are thrust into a reality whose light blinds us and burns us to the bone. What one tends to call "normal life" may coincide with anticipatory imagination and trivial statement. I buy a newspaper and am "a man who buys a newspaper." The act does not differ from the image through which I anticipated it, and I hardly differentiate myself personally from the millions who performed it before me. Because my imagination did not suffice to entirely capture such an event? No, rather because even in direct experience everyday reality is nothing but codified abstraction. Only in rare moments of life do we truly stand face to face with the event and, with it, reality.

It does not have to be something as extreme as torture. Arrest is enough and, if need be, the first blow one receives. "If you talk," the men with the plain, ordinary faces said to me, "then you will be put in the military police prison. If you don't confess, then it's off to Breendonk, and you know what that means." I knew, and I didn't know. In any case, I acted roughly like the man who buys a newspaper, and spoke as planned. I would be most pleased to avoid Breendonk, with which I was quite familiar, and give the evidence desired of me. Except that I unfortunately knew nothing, or almost nothing. Accomplices? I could name only their aliases. Hiding places? But one was led to them only at night, and the exact addresses were never entrusted to us. For these men, however, that was far too familiar twaddle, and it didn't pay them to go into it. They laughed contemptuously. And suddenly I felt—*the first blow.*

In an interrogation, blows have only scant criminological significance. They are tacitly practiced and accepted, a normal measure employed against recalcitrant prisoners who are unwilling to confess. If we are to believe the above-cited lawyer, Alec Mellor, and his book *La Torture*, then blows are applied in more or less heavy doses by almost all police authorities, including those of the Western-democratic countries, with the exception of England and Belgium. In America one speaks of the "third degree" of a police investigation, which supposedly entails something worse than a few punches. France has even found an argot word that nicely plays down a beating by the police. One speaks of the prisoner's "passage à tabac." After the Second World War a high French criminal investigator, in a book intended for his subordinates, still explained in extravagant detail that it would not be possible to forgo physical compulsion at interrogations, "within the bounds of legality."

Mostly, the public does not prove to be finicky when such occurrences in police stations are revealed now and then in the press. At best, there may be an interpellation in Parliament by some leftist-oriented deputy. But then the stories fizzle out; I have never yet heard of a police official who had beaten a prisoner and was not energetically covered by his superior officers. Simple blows, which really are entirely incommensurable with actual torture, may almost never create a far-reaching echo among the public, but for the person who suffers them they are still experiences that leave deep marks—if one wishes not to use up the high-sounding words already and clearly say: enormities. The first blow brings home to the prisoner that he is *helpless*, and thus it already contains in the bud everything that is to come. One may have known about torture and death in the cell, without such knowledge having possessed the hue of life; but upon the first blow they are anticipated as real possibilities, yes, as certainties. They are permitted to punch me in the face, the victim feels in numb surprise and concludes in just as numb certainty: they will do with me what they want. Whoever would rush to the prisoner's aid—a wife, a mother, a brother, or friend—he won't get this far.

Not much is said when someone who has never been beaten makes the ethical and pathetic statement that upon the first blow the prisoner loses his human dignity. I must confess that I don't know exactly what that is: human dignity. One person thinks he loses it when he finds himself in circumstances that make it impossible for him to take a daily bath. Another believes he loses it when he must speak to an official in something other than his native language. In one instance human dignity is bound to a certain physical convenience, in the other to the right of free speech, in still another perhaps to the availability of erotic partners of the same sex. I don't know if the person who is beaten by the police loses human dignity. Yet I am certain that with the very first blow that descends on him he loses something we will perhaps temporarily call "trust in the world." Trust in the world includes all sorts of things: the irrational and logically unjustifiable belief in absolute causality perhaps, or the likewise blind belief in the validity of the inductive inference. But more important as an element of trust in the world, and in our context what is solely relevant, is the certainty that by reason of written or unwritten social contracts the other person will spare me—more precisely stated, that he will respect my physical, and with it also my metaphysical, being. The boundaries of my body are also the boundaries of my self. My skin surface shields me against the external world. If I am to have trust, I must feel on it only what I *want* to feel.

At the first blow, however, this trust in the world breaks down. The other person, *opposite* whom I exist physically in the world and *with* whom I can exist only as long as he does not touch my skin surface as border, forces his own corporeality on me with the first blow. He is on me and thereby destroys me. It is like a rape, a sexual act without the consent of one of the two partners. Certainly, if there is even a minimal prospect of successful resistance, a mechanism is set in motion that enables me to rectify the border violation by the other person. For my part, I can expand in urgent self-defense, objectify my own corporeality, restore the trust in my continued existence. The social contract then has another text and other clauses: an eye for an eye and a tooth for a tooth. You can also regulate your life according to that. You *cannot* do it when it is the other one who knocks out the tooth, sinks the eye into a swollen mass, and you yourself suffer on your body the counter-man that your fellow man became. If no help can be expected, this physical overwhelming by the other then becomes an existential consummation of destruction altogether.

The expectation of help, the certainty of help, is indeed one of the fundamental experiences of human beings, and probably also of animals. This was quite convincingly presented decades ago by old Kropotkin, who spoke of "mutual aid in nature," and by the modern animal behaviorist Lorenz. The expectation of help is as much a constitutional psychic element as is the struggle for existence. Just a moment, the mother says to her child who is moaning from pain, a hot-water bottle, a cup of tea is coming right away, we won't let you suffer so! I'll prescribe you a medicine, the doctor assures, it will help you. Even on the battlefield, the Red Cross ambulances find their way to the wounded man. In almost all situations in life where there is bodily injury there is also the expectation of help; the former is compensated by the latter. But with the first blow from a policeman's fist, against which there can be no defense and which no helping hand will ward off, a part of our life ends and it can never again be revived.

Here it must be added, of course, that the reality of the police blows must first of all be accepted, because the existential fright from the first blow quickly fades and there is still room in the psyche for a number of practical considerations. Even a sudden joyful surprise is felt; for the physical pain is not at all unbearable. The blows that descend on us have above all a subjective spatial and acoustical quality: spatial, insofar as the prisoner who is being struck in the face and on the head has the impression that the room and all the visible objects in it are shifting position by jolts; acoustical, because he believes to hear a dull thundering, which finally submerges in a general roaring. The blow acts as its own anesthetic. A feeling of pain that would be comparable to a violent toothache or the pulsating burning of a festering wound does not emerge. For that reason, the beaten person thinks roughly this: well now, that can be put up with; hit me as much as you want, it will get you nowhere.

It got them nowhere, and they became tired of hitting me. I kept repeating only that I knew nothing, and therefore, as they had threatened, I was presently off, not to the army-administered Brussels prison, but to the "Reception Camp Breendonk," which was controlled by the SS. It would be tempting to pause here and to tell of the auto ride from Brussels to Breendonk through twenty-five kilometers of Flemish countryside, of the wind-bent poplars, which one saw with pleasure, even if the shackles hurt one's wrists. But that would sidetrack us, and we must quickly come to the point. Let me mention only the ceremony of driving through the first gate over the drawbridge. There even the Gestapo men had to present their identification papers to the SS guards, and if, despite all, the prisoner had doubted the seriousness of the situation, here, below the watchtowers and at the sight of the submachine guns, in view of the entrance ritual, which did not lack a certain dark solemnity, he had to recognize that he had arrived at the end of the world.

Very quickly one was taken into the "business room," of which I have already spoken. The business that was conducted here obviously was a flourishing one. Under the picture of Himmler, with his cold eyes behind the pince-nez, men who wore the woven initials SD on the black lapels of their uniforms went in and out, slamming doors and making a racket with their boots. They did not condescend to speak with the arrivals, either the Gestapo men or the prisoners. Very efficiently they merely recorded the information contained on my false identity card and speedily relieved me of my rather inconsiderable possessions. A wallet, cuff links, and my tie were confiscated. A thin gold bracelet aroused derisive attention, and a Flemish SS man, who wanted to appear important, explained to his German comrades that this was the sign of the partisans. Everything was recorded in writing, with the precision befitting the occurrences in a business room. Father Himmler gazed down contentedly onto the flag that covered the rough wooden table, and onto his people. They were dependable.

The moment has come to make good a promise I gave. I must substantiate why, according to my firm conviction, torture was the essence of National Socialism—more accurately stated, why it was precisely in torture that the Third Reich materialized in all the density of its being. That torture was, and is, practiced elsewhere has already been dealt with. Certainly. In Vietnam since 1964, Algeria 1957. Russia probably between 1919 and 1953. In Hungary in 1919 the Whites and the Reds tortured. There was torture in Spanish prisons by the Falangists as well as the Republicans. Torturers were at work in the semifascist Eastern European states of the period between the two World Wars, in Poland, Romania, Yugoslavia. Torture was no invention of National Socialism. But it was its apotheosis. The Hitler vassal did not yet achieve his full identity if he was merely as quick as a weasel, tough as leather, hard as Krupp steel. No Golden Party Badge made of him a fully valid representative of the Führer and his ideology, nor did any Blood Order or Iron Cross. He had to *torture*, destroy, in order to be great in bearing the suffering of others. He had to be capable of handling torture instruments, so that Himmler would assure him his Certificate of Maturity in History; later generations would admire him for having obliterated his feelings of mercy.

Again I hear indignant objection being raised, hear it said that not Hitler embodied torture, but rather something unclear, "totalitarianism." I hear especially the example of Communism being shouted at me. And didn't I myself just say that in the Soviet Union torture was practiced for thirty-four years? And did not already Arthur Koestler . . . ? Oh yes, I know, I know. It is impossible to discuss here in detail the political "Operation Bewilderment" of the postwar period, which defined Communism and National Socialism for us as two not even very different manifestations of one and the same thing. Until it came out of our ears, Hitler and Stalin, Auschwitz, Siberia, the Warsaw Ghetto Wall and the Berlin Ulbricht-Wall were named together, like Goethe and Schiller, Klopstock and Wieland. As a hint, allow me to repeat here in my own name and at the risk of being denounced what Thomas Mann once said in a much attacked interview: namely, that no matter how terrible Communism may at times appear, it still symbolizes an idea of man, whereas Hitler-Fascism was not an idea at all, but depravity. Finally, it is undeniable that Communism could de-Stalinize itself and that today in the Soviet sphere of influence, if we can place trust in concurring reports, torture is no longer practiced. In Hungary a Party First Secretary can preside who was himself once the victim of Stalinist torture. But who is really able to imagine a de-Hitlerized National Socialism and, as a leading politician of a newly ordered Europe, a Röhm follower who in those days had been dragged through torture? No one can imagine it. It would have been impossible. For National Socialism—which, to be sure, could not claim a single idea, but did possess a whole arsenal of confused, crackbrained notions—was the only political system of this century that up to this point had not only practiced the rule of the antiman, as had other Red and White terror regimes also, but had expressly established it as a principle. It hated the word "humanity" like the pious man hates sin, and that is why it spoke of "sentimental humanitarianism." It exterminated and enslaved. This is evidenced not only by the corpora delicti, but also by a sufficient number of theoretical confirmations. The Nazis tortured, as did others, because by means of torture they wanted to obtain information important for national policy. But in addition they tortured with the good conscience of depravity. They martyred their prisoners for definite purposes, which in each instance were exactly specified. Above all, however, they tortured because they were torturers. They placed torture in their service. But even more fervently they were its servants.

When I recall those past events, I still see before me the man who suddenly stepped into the business room and who seemed to count in Breendonk. On his field-gray uniform he wore the black lapels of the SS, but he was addressed as "Herr Leutnant." He was small, of stocky figure, and had that fleshy, sanguine face that in terms of popular

physiognomy would be called "gruffly good-natured." His voice crack-
led hoarsely, the accent was colored by Berlin dialect. From his wrist
there hung in a leather loop a horsewhip of about a meter in length.
But why, really, should I withhold his name, which later became so
familiar to me? Perhaps at this very hour he is faring well and feels
content with his healthy sunburned self as he drives home from his
Sunday excursion. I have no reason not to name him. The Herr
Leutnant, who played the role of a torture specialist here, was named
Praust. P-R-A-U-S-T. "Now it's coming," he said to me in a rattling and
easygoing way. And then he led me through the corridors, which were
dimly lit by reddish bulbs and in which barred gates kept opening and
slamming shut, to the previously described vault, the bunker. With us
were the Gestapo men who had arrested me.

If I finally want to get to the analysis of torture, then unfortunately
I cannot spare the reader the objective description of what now took
place; I can only try to make it brief. In the bunker there hung from the
vaulted ceiling a chain that above ran into a roll. At its bottom end it
bore a heavy, broadly curved iron hook. I was led to the instrument.
The hook gripped into the shackle that held my hands together behind
my back. Then I was raised with the chain until I hung about a meter
over the floor. In such a position, or rather, when hanging this way,
with your hands behind your back, for a short time you can hold at a
half-oblique through muscular force. During these few minutes, when
you are already expending your utmost strength, when sweat has
already appeared on your forehead and lips, and you are breathing in
gasps, you will not answer any questions. Accomplices? Addresses?
Meeting places? You hardly hear it. All your life is gathered in a single,
limited area of the body, the shoulder joints, and it does not react; for it
exhausts itself completely in the expenditure of energy. But this cannot
last long, even with people who have a strong physical constitution. As
for me, I had to give up rather quickly. And now there was a crackling
and splintering in my shoulders that my body has not forgotten until
this hour. The balls sprang from their sockets. My own body weight
caused luxation; I fell into a void and now hung by my dislocated arms,
which had been torn high from behind and were now twisted over my
head. Torture, from Latin *torquere*, to twist. What visual instruction in
etymology! At the same time, the blows from the horsewhip showered
down on my body, and some of them sliced cleanly through the light
summer trousers that I was wearing on this twenty-third of July 1943.

It would be totally senseless to try and describe here the pain that was inflicted on me. Was it "like a red-hot iron in my shoulders," and was another "like a dull wooden stake that had been driven into the back of my head"? One comparison would only stand for the other, and in the end we would be hoaxed by turn on the hopeless merry-go-round of figurative speech. The pain was what it was. Beyond that there is nothing to say. Qualities of feeling are as incomparable as they are indescribable. They mark the limit of the capacity of language to communicate. If someone wanted to impart his physical pain, he would be forced to inflict it and thereby become a torturer himself.

Since the *how* of pain defies communication through language, perhaps I can at least approximately state *what* it was. It contained everything that we already ascertained earlier in regard to a beating by the police: the border violation of my self by the other, which can be neither neutralized by the expectation of help nor rectified through resistance. Torture is all that, but in addition very much more. Whoever is overcome by pain through torture experiences his body as never before. In self-negation, his flesh becomes a total reality. Partially, torture is one of those life experiences that in a milder form present themselves also to the consciousness of the patient who is awaiting help, and the popular saying according to which we feel well as long as we do not feel our body does indeed express an undeniable truth. But only in torture does the transformation of the person into flesh become complete. Frail in the face of violence, yelling out in pain, awaiting no help, capable of no resistance, the tortured person is only a body, and nothing else beside that. If what Thomas Mann described years ago in *The Magic Mountain* is true, namely, that the more hopelessly man's body is subjected to suffering, the more physical he is, then of all physical celebrations torture is the most terrible. In the case of Mann's consumptives, they still took place in a state of euphoria; for the martyred they are death rituals.

It is tempting to speculate further. Pain, we said, is the most extreme intensification imaginable of our bodily being. But maybe it is even more, that is: death. No road that can be travelled by logic leads us to death, but perhaps the thought is permissible that through pain a path of feeling and premonition can be paved to it for us. In the end, we would be faced with the equation: Body = Pain = Death, and in our case this could be reduced to the hypothesis that torture, through which we are turned into body by the other, blots out the contradiction of death and allows us to experience it personally. But this is an evasion of the question. We have for it only the excuse of our own experience and must add in explanation that torture has an indelible character. Whoever was tortured, stays tortured. Torture is ineradicably burned into him, even when no clinically objective traces can be detected. The permanence of torture gives the one who underwent it the right to speculative flights, which need not be lofty ones and still may claim a certain validity.

I speak of the martyred. But it is time to say something about the tormentors also. No bridge leads from the former to the latter. Modern police torture is without the theological complicity that, no doubt, in the Inquisition joined both sides; faith united them even in the delight of tormenting and the pain of being tormented. The torturer believed he was exercising God's justice, since he was, after all, purifying the offender's soul; the tortured heretic or witch did not at all deny him this right. There was a horrible and perverted togetherness. In present-day torture not a bit of this remains. For the tortured, the torturer is solely the other, and here he will be regarded as such.

Who were the others, who pulled me up by my dislocated arms and punished my dangling body with the horsewhip? As a start, one can take the view that they were merely brutalized petty bourgeois and subordinate bureaucrats of torture. But it is necessary to abandon this point of view immediately if one wishes to arrive at an insight into evil that is more than just banal. Were they sadists, then? According to my well-founded conviction, they were not sadists in the narrow sexual-pathologic sense. In general, I don't believe that I encountered a single genuine sadist of this sort during my two years of imprisonment by the Gestapo and in concentration camps. But probably they *were* sadists if we leave sexual pathology aside and attempt to judge the torturers according to the categories of, well, the *philosophy* of the Marquis de Sade. Sadism as the dis-ordered view of the world is something other than the sadism of the usual psychology handbooks, also other than the sadism interpretation of Freudian analysis. For this reason, the French anthropologist Georges Bataille will be cited here, who has reflected very thoroughly on the odd Marquis. We will then perhaps see not only that my tormentors lived on the border of a sadistic philosophy but that National Socialism in its totality was stamped less with the seal of a hardly definable "totalitarianism" than with that of *sadism*.

For Georges Bataille, sadism is to be understood not in the light of sexual pathology but rather in that of existential psychology, in which it appears as the radical negation of the other, as the denial of the social principle as well as the reality principle. A world in which torture, destruction, and death triumph obviously cannot exist. But the sadist does not care about the continued existence of the world. On the contrary: he wants to nullify this world, and by negating his fellow man, who also in an entirely specific sense is "hell" for him, he wants to realize his own total sovereignty. The fellow man is transformed into flesh, and in this transformation he is already brought to the edge of death; if worst comes to worst, he is driven beyond the border of death into Nothingness. With that the torturer and murderer realizes his own destructive being, without having to lose himself in it entirely, like his martyred victim. He can, after all, cease the torture when it suits him. He has control of the other's scream of pain and death; he is master over flesh and spirit, life and death. In this way, torture becomes the total inversion of the social world, in which we can live only if we grant our fellow man life, ease his suffering, bridle the desire of our ego to expand. But in the world of torture man exists only by ruining the other person who stands before him. A slight pressure by the tool-wielding hand is enough to turn the other—along with his head, in which are perhaps stored Kant and Hegel, and all nine symphonies, and the World as Will and Representation—into a shrilly squealing piglet at slaughter. When it has happened and the torturer has expanded into the body of his fellow man and extinguished what was his spirit, he himself can then smoke a cigarette or sit down to breakfast or, if he has the desire, have a look in at the World as Will and Representation.

My boys at Breendonk contented themselves with the cigarette and, as soon as they were tired of torturing, doubtlessly let old Schopenhauer be. But this still does not mean that the evil they inflicted on me was banal. If one insists on it, they were bureaucrats of torture. And yet, they were also much more. I saw it in their serious, tense faces, which were not swelling, let us say, with sexual-sadistic delight, but concentrated in murderous self-realization. With heart and soul they went about their business, and the name of it was power, dominion over spirit and flesh, orgy of unchecked self-expansion. I also have not forgotten that there were moments when I felt a kind of wretched admiration for the agonizing sovereignty they exercised over me. For is not the one who can reduce a person so entirely to a body and a whimpering prey of death a god or, at least, a demigod?

But the concentrated effort of torture naturally did not make these people forget their profession. They were "cops," that was métier and routine. And so they continued asking me questions, constantly the same ones: accomplices, addresses, meeting places. To come right out with it: I had nothing but luck, because especially in regard to the extorting of information our group was rather well organized. What they wanted to hear from me in Breendonk, I simply did not know myself. If instead of the aliases I had been able to name the real names, perhaps, or probably, a calamity would have occurred, and I would be standing here now as the weakling I most likely am, and as the traitor I potentially already was. Yet it was not at all that I opposed them with the heroically maintained silence that befits a real man in such a situation and about which one may read (almost always, incidentally, in reports by people who were not there themselves). I talked. I accused myself of invented absurd political crimes, and even now I don't know at all how they could have occurred to me, dangling bundle that I was. Apparently I had the hope that, after such incriminating disclosures, a well-aimed blow to the head would put an end to my misery and quickly bring on my death, or at least unconsciousness. Finally, I actually did become unconscious, and with that it was over for a while—for the "cops" abstained from awakening their battered victim, since the nonsense I had foisted on them was busying their stupid heads.

It was over for a while. It still is not over. Twenty-two years later I am still dangling over the ground by dislocated arms, panting, and accusing myself. In such an instance there is no "repression." Does one repress an unsightly birthmark? One can have it removed by a plastic surgeon, but the skin that is transplanted in its place is not the skin with which one feels naturally at ease.

One can shake off torture as little as the question of the possibilities and limits of the power to resist it. I have spoken with many comrades about this and have attempted to relive all kinds of experiences. Does the brave man resist? I am not sure. There was, for example, that young Belgian aristocrat who converted to Communism and was something like a hero, namely in the Spanish civil war, where he had fought on the Republican side. But when they subjected him to torture in Breendonk, he "coughed up," as it is put in the jargon of common criminals, and since he knew a lot, he betrayed an entire organization. The brave man went very far in his readiness to cooperate. He drove with the Gestapo men to the homes of his comrades and in extreme zeal encouraged them to confess just everything, but absolutely everything, that was their only hope, and it was, he said, a question of paying any price in order to escape torture. And I knew another, a Bulgarian professional revolutionary, who had been subjected to torture compared to which mine was only a somewhat strenuous sport, and who had remained silent, simply and steadfastly silent. Also the unforgettable Jean Moulin, who is buried in the Pantheon in Paris, shall be remembered here. He was arrested as the first chairman of the French Resistance Movement. If he had talked, the entire Résistance would have been destroyed. But he bore his martyrdom beyond the limits of death and did not betray one single name.

Where does the strength, where does the weakness come from? I don't know. *One* does not know. No one has yet been able to draw distinct borders between the "moral" power of resistance to physical pain and "bodily" resistance (which likewise must be placed in quotation marks). There are more than a few specialists who reduce the entire problem of bearing pain to a purely physiological basis. Here only the French professor of surgery and member of the Collège de France, René Leriche, will be cited, who ventured the following judgment:

"We are not equal before the phenomenon of pain," the professor says.

> One person already suffers where the other apparently still perceives hardly anything. This has to do with the individual quality of our sympathetic nerve, with the hormone of the parathyroid gland, and with the vasoconstrictive substances of the adrenal glands. Also in the physiological observation of pain we cannot escape the concept of individuality. History shows us that we people of today are more sensitive to pain than our ancestors were, and this from a purely physiological standpoint. I am not speaking here of any hypothetical moral power of resistance, but am staying within the realm of physiology. Pain remedies and narcosis have contributed more to our greater sensitivity than moral factors. Also the reactions to pain by various people are absolutely not the same. Two wars have given us the opportunity to see how the physical sensitivities of the Germans, French, and English differ. Above all,

there is a great separation in this regard between the Europeans on
the one hand and the Asians and Africans on the other. The latter
bear physical pain incomparably better than the former . . .

Thus the judgment of a surgical authority. It will hardly be dis-
puted by the simple experiences of a nonprofessional, who saw many
individuals and members of numerous ethnic groups suffering pain
and deprivation. In this connection, it occurs to me that, as I was able
to observe later in the concentration camp, the Slavs, and especially the
Russians, bore physical injustice easier and more stoically than did, for
example, Italians, Frenchmen, Hollanders, or Scandinavians. As body,
we actually are not equal when faced with pain and torture. But that
does not solve our problem of the power of resistance, and it gives us no
conclusive answer to the question of what share moral and physical
factors have in it. If we agree to a reduction to the purely physiological,
then we run the risk of finally pardoning every kind of whiny reaction
and physical cowardice. But if we exclusively stress the so-called moral
resistance, then we would have to measure a weakly seventeen-year-
old gymnasium pupil who fails to withstand torture by the same standards as an athletically built thirty-year-old laborer who is accustomed
to manual work and hardships. Thus we had better let the question
rest, just as at that time I myself did not further analyze my power to
resist, when, battered and with my hands still shackled, I lay in the cell
and ruminated.

For the person who has survived torture and whose pains are
starting to subside (before they flare up again) experiences an ephem-
eral peace that is conducive to thinking. In one respect, the tortured
person is content that he was body only and because of that, so he
thinks, free of all political concern. You are on the outside, he tells
himself more or less, and I am here in the cell, and that gives me a
great superiority over you. I have experienced the ineffable, I am filled
with it entirely, and now see, if you can, how you are going to live with
yourselves, the world, and my disappearance. On the other hand,
however, the fading away of the physical, which revealed itself in pain
and torture, the end of the tremendous tumult that had erupted in the
body, the reattainment of a hollow stability, is satisfying and soothing.
There are even euphoric moments, in which the return of weak powers
of reason is felt as an extraordinary happiness. The bundle of limbs that
is slowly recovering human semblance feels the urge to articulate the

experience intellectually, right away, on the spot, without losing the least bit of time, for a few hours afterward could already be too late.

Thinking is almost nothing else but a great astonishment. Astonishment at the fact that you had endured it, that the tumult had not immediately led also to an explosion of the body, that you still have a forehead that you can stroke with your shackled hands, an eye that can be opened and closed, a mouth that would show the usual lines if you could see it now in a mirror. What? you ask yourself—the same person who was gruff with his family because of a toothache was able to hang there by his dislocated arms and still live? The person who for hours was in a bad mood after slightly burning his finger with a cigarette was lacerated here with a horsewhip, and now that it is all over he hardly feels his wounds? Astonishment also at the fact that what happened to you yourself, by right was supposed to befall only those who had written about it in accusatory brochures: torture. A murder is committed, but it is part of the newspaper that reported on it. An airplane accident occurred, but that concerns the people who lost a relative in it. The Gestapo tortures. But that was a matter until now for the somebodies who were tortured and who displayed their scars at antifascist conferences. That suddenly you yourself are the Somebody, is grasped only with difficulty. That, too, is a kind of alienation.

If from the experience of torture any knowledge at all remains that goes beyond the plain nightmarish, it is that of a great amazement and a foreignness in the world that cannot be compensated by any sort of subsequent human communication. Amazed, the tortured person experienced that in this world there can be the other as absolute sovereign, and sovereignty revealed itself as the power to inflict suffering and to destroy. The dominion of the torturer over his victim has nothing in common with the power exercised on the basis of social contracts, as we know it. It is not the power of the traffic policeman over the pedestrian, of the tax official over the taxpayer, of the first lieutenant over the second lieutenant. It is also not the sacral sovereignty of past absolute chieftains or kings; for even if they stirred fear, they were also objects of trust at the same time. The king could be terrible in his wrath, but also kind in his mercy; his autocracy was an exercise of authority. But the power of the torturer, under which the tortured moans, is nothing other than the triumph of the survivor over the one who is plunged from the world into agony and death.

Astonishment at the existence of the other, as he boundlessly asserts himself through torture, and astonishment at what one can become oneself: flesh and death. The tortured person never ceases to be amazed that all those things one may, according to inclination, call his soul, or his mind, or his consciousness, or his identity, are destroyed when there is that cracking and splintering in the shoulder joints. That life is fragile is a truism he has always known—and that it can be ended, as Shakespeare says, "with a little pin." But only through torture did he learn that a living person can be transformed so thoroughly into flesh and by that, while still alive, be partly made into a prey of death.

Whoever has succumbed to torture can no longer feel at home in the world. The shame of destruction cannot be erased. Trust in the world, which already collapsed in part at the first blow, but in the end, under torture, fully, will not be regained. That one's fellow man was experienced as the antiman remains in the tortured person as accumulated horror. It blocks the view into a world in which the principle of hope rules. One who was martyred is a defenseless prisoner of fear. It is *fear* that henceforth reigns over him. Fear—and also what is called resentments. They remain, and have scarcely a chance to concentrate into a seething, purifying thirst for revenge.

ROBERT JAY LIFTON, the Distinguished Professor of Psychiatry and Psychology at John Jay College and The Graduate Center of the City University of New York, was born in Brooklyn in 1926. He received the National Book Award for *Death in Life: Survivors of Hiroshima*, which appeared in 1968. His other widely acclaimed books include *Home from the War; The Life of the Self; The Broken Connection;* and *The Future of Immortality*. None of them, however, makes a more lasting contribution than *The Nazi Doctors: Medical Killing and the Psychology of Genocide*, which was published, after many years of research, in 1986.

If Raul Hilberg shows that the Holocaust was not the result of hooliganism and uncoordinated terror but stemmed instead from bureaucratic organization, Lifton underscores that the Holocaust was neither instigated by the uneducated nor sustained by the ill-trained. On the contrary, the skilled and highly educated were at its core—none more so than leaders from the medical profession and its allied fields. Trained in medicine and psychiatry, Lifton details how physicians, in particular, were at the heartlessness of the Holocaust. As the following selection suggests, the "final solution" evolved from and then epitomized a "biomedical vision." That vision called for excising *lebensunwertes Leben* ("life unworthy of life") from Nazi Germany's "superior" society. To do this, genocidal Nazi doctors made "healing" synonymous with "killing" and turned the latter into "*a therapeutic imperative*." Although Lifton notes that "one cannot expect to emerge from a study of this kind spiritually unscathed," he maintains with equal conviction that an avoidance of "the sources of that evil seemed to me, in the end, a refusal to call forth our capacity to engage and combat it."

Robert Jay Lifton

"This World Is Not This World"

Approaching Auschwitz

I gained an important perspective on Auschwitz from an Israeli dentist who had spent three years in that camp. We were completing a long interview, during which he had told me about many things, including details of SS dentists' supervision of prisoners' removal of gold fillings from the teeth of fellow Jews killed in the gas chambers. He looked about the comfortable room in his house with its beautiful view of Haifa, sighed deeply, and said, "This world is not this world." What I think he meant was that, after Auschwitz, the ordinary rhythms and appearances of life, however innocuous or pleasant, were far from the truth of human existence. Underneath those rhythms and appearances lay darkness and menace.

The comment also raises the question of our capacity to approach Auschwitz. From the beginning there has been enormous resistance on the part of virtually everyone to knowledge of what the Nazis were doing and have done there. That resistance has hardly abated, whatever the current interest in what we call "the Holocaust." Nor have more recent episodes of mass slaughter done much to overcome it. For to permit one's imagination to enter into the Nazi killing machine—to begin to experience that killing machine—is to alter one's relationship to the entire human project. One does not want to learn about such things.

From Robert Jay Lifton, *The Nazi Doctors: Medical Killing and the Psychology of Genocide*. New York: Basic Books, Inc., 1986. Copyright © 1986 by Robert Jay Lifton. Reprinted by permission of Basic Books, Inc., Publishers.

Psychologically speaking, nothing is darker or more menacing, or harder to accept, than the participation of physicians in mass murder. However technicized or commercial the modern physician may have become, he or she is still supposed to be a healer—and one responsible to a tradition of healing, which all cultures revere and depend upon. Knowledge that the doctor has joined the killers adds a grotesque dimension to the perception that "this world is not this world." During my work I gained the impression that, among Germans and many others, this involvement of physicians was viewed as the most shameful of all Nazi behavior.

When we think of the crimes of Nazi doctors, what come to mind are their cruel and sometimes fatal human experiments. Those experiments, in their precise and absolute violation of the Hippocratic oath, mock and subvert the very idea of the ethical physician, of the physician dedicated to the well-being of patients. I shall examine those human experiments from the standpoint of the regime's medical and political ideology.

Yet when we turn to the Nazi doctor's role in Auschwitz, it was not the experiments that were most significant. Rather it was his participation in the killing process—indeed his supervision of Auschwitz mass murder from beginning to end. This aspect of Nazi medical behavior has escaped full recognition—even though we are familiar with photographs of Nazi doctors standing at the ramp and performing their notorious "selections" of arriving Jews, determining which were to go directly to the gas chamber and which were to live, at least temporarily, and work in the camp. Yet this medicalized killing had a logic that was not only deeply significant for Nazi theory and behavior but holds for other expressions of genocide as well.

In this book I will examine both the broad Nazi "biomedical vision" as a central psychohistorical principle of the regime, and the psychological behavior of individual Nazi doctors. We need to look at both dimensions if we are to understand more about how Nazi doctors—and Nazis in general—came to do what they did.

The very extremity of Auschwitz and related Nazi murder renders it close to unreality. A distinguished European physician, who had struggled with Nazi brutality for forty years—first as an inmate of Auschwitz and other camps and then as an authority on medical consequences of that incarceration—said to me very quietly at the end of a long interview, "You know, I still can't really believe that it happened—that a group of people would round up all of the Jews in Europe and send them to a special place to kill them." He was saying that the Auschwitz "other world" is beyond belief. The wonder is that there is not an even greater tendency than actually exists to accept the directly false contention that Nazi mass murder did not take place.

Also at issue for us here is the relationship of Nazi doctors to the human species. Another Auschwitz survivor who knew something about them asked me, "Were they *beasts* when they did what they did? Or were they *human beings?*" He was not surprised by my answer: they were and are men, which is my justification for studying them; and their behavior—Auschwitz itself—was a product of specifically *human* ingenuity and cruelty.

I went on to tell this survivor of the ordinariness of most Nazi doctors I had interviewed. Neither brilliant nor stupid, neither inherently evil nor particularly ethically sensitive, they were by no means the demonic figures—sadistic, fanatic, lusting to kill—people have often thought them to be. My friend replied, "But it is *demonic* that they were *not* demonic." He could then raise his second question, really the one he had in mind in the first place: "How did they become killers?" That question can be addressed, and this book is in the way of an answer.

What my survivor friend was struggling with—what I have struggled with throughout this study—is the disturbing psychological truth that participation in mass murder need not require emotions as extreme or demonic as would seem appropriate for such a malignant project. Or to put the matter another way, ordinary people can commit demonic acts.

But that did not mean that Nazi doctors were faceless bureaucratic cogs or automatons. As human beings, they were actors and participants who manifested certain kinds of behavior for which they were responsible, and which we can begin to identify.

There are several dimensions, then, to the work. At its heart is the transformation of the physician—of the medical enterprise itself—from healer to killer. That transformation requires us to examine the interaction of Nazi political ideology and biomedical ideology in their effects on individual and collective behavior. That in turn takes us to the significance of medicalized killing for Nazi mass murder in general—and for large-scale killing and genocide on the part of others. Finally, the work has relevance for broad questions of human control over life and death—for physicians everywhere, for science and scientists and other professionals in general, for institutions of various kinds—and also for concepts of human nature and ultimate human values. I can no more than touch on most of these general issues, having made a decision to focus on Nazi doctors and medicalized killing, and then on issues of mass murder. But my hope is that others will find here experience that might help them explore any of the searing moral issues implicit in this study.

That hope raises the important question of specificity and generality. I believe that one must stress the specificity of the Nazi killing project, especially concerning Jews: its unique characteristics, and the particular forces that shaped it. But having done that, one must also search for larger *principles* suggested by that unique project. No other event or institution can or should be equated with Auschwitz; but nor should we deny ourselves the opportunity to explore its general relevance for genocide and for situations of a very different order in which psychological and moral questions may be considerably more ambiguous. . . .

Medicalized Killing

In Nazi mass murder, we can say that a barrier was removed, a boundary crossed: that boundary between violent imagery and periodic killing of victims (as of Jews in pogroms) on the one hand, and systematic genocide in Auschwitz and elsewhere on the other. My argument in this study is that the medicalization of killing—the imagery of killing in the name of healing—was crucial to that terrible step. At the heart of the Nazi enterprise, then, is the destruction of the boundary between healing and killing.

Early descriptions of Auschwitz and other death camps focused on the sadism and viciousness of Nazi guards, officers, and physicians. But subsequent students of the process realized that sadism and viciousness alone could not account for the killing of millions of people. The emphasis then shifted to the bureaucracy of killing: the faceless, detached bureaucratic function originally described by Max Weber, now applied to mass murder.[1] This focus on numbed violence is enormously important, and is consistent with what we shall observe to be the routinization of all Auschwitz function.

Yet these emphases are not sufficient in themselves. They must be seen in relation to the visionary motivations associated with ideology, along with the specific individual-psychological mechanisms enabling people to kill. What I call "medicalized killing" addresses these motivational principles and psychological mechanisms, and permits us to understand the Auschwitz victimizers—notably Nazi doctors—both as part of a bureaucracy of killing and as individual participants whose attitudes and behavior can be examined.

Medicalized killing can be understood in two wider perspectives. The first is the "surgical" method of killing large numbers of people by means of a controlled technology making use of highly poisonous gas; the method employed became a means of maintaining distance between killers and victims. This distancing had considerable importance for the Nazis in alleviating the psychological problems experienced (as attested over and over by Nazi documents) by the *Einsatzgruppen* troops who carried out face-to-face shooting of Jews in Eastern Europe—problems that did not prevent those troops from murdering 1,400,000 Jews.[2]

I was able to obtain direct evidence on this matter during an interview with a former *Wehrmacht* neuropsychiatrist who had treated large numbers of *Einsatzgruppen* personnel for psychological disorders. He told me that these disorders resembled combat reactions of ordinary troops: severe anxiety, nightmares, tremors, and numerous bodily complaints. But in these "killer troops," as he called them, the symptoms tended to last longer and to be more severe. He estimated that 20 percent of those doing the actual killing experienced these symptoms of psychological decompensation. About half of that 20 percent associated their symptoms mainly with the "unpleasantness" of what they had to do, while the other half seemed to have moral questions about shooting people in that way. The men had greatest psychological difficulty concerning shooting women and children, especially children. Many experienced a sense of guilt in their dreams, which could include various forms of punishment or retribution. Such psychological difficulty led the Nazis to seek a more "surgical" method of killing.

But there is another perspective on medicalized killing that I believe to be insufficiently recognized: *killing as a therapeutic impera-*

tive. That kind of motivation was revealed in the words of a Nazi doctor quoted by the distinguished survivor physician Dr. Ella Lingens-Reiner. Pointing to the chimneys in the distance, she asked a Nazi doctor, Fritz Klein, "How can you reconcile that with your [Hippocratic] oath as a doctor?" His answer was, "Of course I am a doctor and I want to preserve life. And out of respect for human life, I would remove a gangrenous appendix from a diseased body. The Jew is a gangrenous appendix in the body of mankind."[3]

The medical imagery was still broader. Just as Turkey during the nineteenth century (because of the extreme decline of the Ottoman empire) was known as the "sick man of Europe," so did pre-Hitler ideologies and Hitler himself interpret Germany's post-First World War chaos and demoralization as an "illness," especially of the Aryan race. Hitler wrote in *Mein Kampf*, in the mid-1920s, that *"anyone who wants to cure this era, which is inwardly sick and rotten, must first of all summon up the courage to make clear the causes of this disease."*[4] The diagnosis was racial. The only genuine "culture-creating" race, the Aryans, had permitted themselves to be weakened to the point of endangered survival by the "destroyers of culture," characterized as "the Jew." The Jews were agents of "racial pollution" and "racial tuberculosis," as well as parasites and bacteria causing sickness, deterioration, and death in the host peoples they infested. They were the "eternal bloodsucker," "vampire," "germ carrier," "peoples' parasite," and "maggot in a rotting corpse."[5] The cure had to be radical: that is (as one scholar put it), by "cutting out the 'canker of decay,' propagating the worthwhile elements and letting the less valuable wither away, . . . [and] 'the extirpation of all those categories of people considered to be worthless or dangerous.' "[6]

Medical metaphor blended with concrete biomedical ideology in the Nazi sequence from coercive sterilization to direct medical killing to the death camps. The unifying principle of the biomedical ideology was that of a deadly racial disease, the sickness of the Aryan race; the cure, the killing of all Jews.

Thus, for Hans Frank, jurist and General Governor of Poland during the Nazi occupation, "the Jews were a lower species of life, a kind of vermin, which upon contact infected the German people with deadly diseases." When the Jews in the area he ruled had been killed, he declared that "now a sick Europe would become healthy again."[7] It was a religion of the will—the will as "an all-encompassing metaphysical principle";[8] and what the Nazis "willed" was nothing less than total control over life and death. While this view is often referred to as "social Darwinism," the term applies only loosely, mostly to the Nazi stress on natural "struggle" and on "survival of the fittest." The regime actually rejected much of Darwinism; since evolutionary theory is more or less democratic in its assumption of a common beginning for all races, it is therefore at odds with the Nazi principle of inherent Aryan racial virtue.[9]

Even more specific to the biomedical vision was the crude genetic imagery, combined with still cruder eugenic visions. Here Heinrich Himmler, as high priest, spoke of the leadership's task as being "like the plant-breeding specialist who, when he wants to breed a pure new strain from a well-tried species that has been exhausted by too much cross-breeding, first goes over the field to cull the unwanted plants."[10]

The Nazi project, then, was not so much Darwinian or social Darwinist as a vision of absolute control over the evolutionary process, over the biological human future. Making widespread use of the Darwinian term "selection," the Nazis sought to take over the functions of nature (natural selection) and God (the Lord giveth and the Lord taketh away) in orchestrating their own "selections," their own version of human evolution.

In these visions the Nazis embraced not only versions of medieval mystical anti-Semitism but also a newer (nineteenth- and twentieth-century) claim to "scientific racism." Dangerous Jewish characteristics could be linked with alleged data of scientific disciplines, so that a "mainstream of racism" formed from "the fusion of anthropology, eugenics, and social thought."[11] The resulting "racial and social biology" could make vicious forms of anti-Semitism seem intellectually respectable to learned men and women.

One can speak of the Nazi state as a "biocracy." The model here is a theocracy, a system of rule by priests of a sacred order under the claim of divine prerogative. In the case of the Nazi biocracy, the divine prerogative was that of cure through purification and revitalization of the Aryan race: "From a dead mechanism which only lays claim to existence for its own sake, there must be formed a living organism with the exclusive aim of serving a higher idea." Just as in a theocracy, the state itself is no more than a vehicle for the divine purpose, so in the Nazi biocracy was the state no more than a means to achieve *"a mission of the German people on earth"*: that of *"assembling and preserving*

the most valuable stocks of basic racial elements in this [Aryan] *people
. . .* [and] *. . . raising them to a dominant position."*[12] The Nazi biocracy differed from a classical theocracy in that the biological priests
did not actually rule. The clear rulers were Adolf Hitler and his circle,
not biological theorists and certainly not the doctors. (The difference,
however, is far from absolute: even in a theocracy, highly politicized
rulers may make varying claims to priestly authority.) In any case, Nazi
ruling authority was maintained in the name of the higher biological
principle.

Among the biological authorities called forth to articulate and
implement "scientific racism"—including physical anthropologists,
geneticists, and racial theorists of every variety—doctors inevitably
found a unique place. It is they who work at the border of life and
death, who are most associated with the awesome, death-defying, and
sometimes death-dealing aura of the primitive shaman and medicine
man. As bearers of this shamanistic legacy and contemporary practitioners of mysterious healing arts, it is they who are likely to be called
upon to become biological activists.

I have mentioned my primary interest in Nazi doctors' participation in medicalized or biologized killing. We shall view their human
experiments as related to the killing process and to the overall Nazi
biomedical vision. At Nuremberg, doctors were tried only limitedly
for their involvement in killing, partly because its full significance was
not yet understood.[13]

In Auschwitz, Nazi doctors presided over the murder of most of
the one million victims of that camp. Doctors performed selections—
both on the ramp among arriving transports of prisoners and later in
the camps and on the medical blocks. Doctors supervised the killing in
the gas chambers and decided when the victims were dead. Doctors
conducted a murderous epidemiology, sending to the gas chamber
groups of people with contagious diseases and sometimes including
everyone else who might be on the medical block. Doctors ordered
and supervised, and at times carried out, direct killing of debilitated
patients on the medical blocks by means of phenol injections into the
bloodstream or the heart. In connection with all of these killings,
doctors kept up a pretense of medical legitimacy: for deaths of Auschwitz prisoners and of outsiders brought there to be killed, they signed
false death certificates listing spurious illnesses. Doctors consulted
actively on how best to keep selections running smoothly; on how

many people to permit to remain alive to fill the slave labor requirements of the I. G. Farben enterprise at Auschwitz; and on how to burn
the enormous numbers of bodies that strained the facilities of the
crematoria.

In sum, we may say that doctors were given much of the responsibility for the murderous ecology of Auschwitz—the choosing of
victims, the carrying through of the physical and psychological me-
chanics of killing, and the balancing of killing and work functions in the
camp. While doctors by no means ran Auschwitz, they did lend it a
perverse medical aura. As one survivor who closely observed the
process put the matter, "Auschwitz was like a medical operation," and
"the killing program was led by doctors from beginning to end."

We may say that the doctor standing at the ramp represented a
kind of omega point, a mythical gatekeeper between the worlds of the
dead and the living, a final common pathway of the Nazi vision of
therapy via mass murder.

NOTES

1. See Raul Hilberg, *The Destruction of the European Jews* (Chicago: Quad-
rangle, 1967); Richard L. Rubenstein, *The Cunning of History: Mass Death and the
American Future* (New York: Harper & Row, 1975); Hannah Arendt, *Eichmann in
Jerusalem: A Report on the Banality of Evil* (New York: Viking, 1961). Hilberg's
expanded edition of his classic work was too recent to consult fully for this book; see
The Destruction of the European Jews, 3 vols., rev. and definitive ed. (New York:
Holmes & Meier, 1985).

2. Hilberg, *Destruction*, p. 256.

3. A slightly different, published version is found in Ella Lingens-Reiner, *Prisoners of Fear* (London: Gollancz, 1948), pp. 1–2.

4. Adolf Hitler, *Mein Kampf* (Boston: Houghton Mifflin, 1943), p. 435.

5. Ibid., pp. 150, 300–308, 312–13. For scholarly treatments of Hitler's (and
earlier) metaphors for the Jews, see Eberhard Jäckel, *Hitler's Weltanschauung: A
Blueprint for Power* (Middletown, Conn.: Wesleyan University Press, 1972); Rudolph
Binion, *Hitler Among the Germans* (New York: Elsevier, 1976); Lucy S. Dawidowicz,
The War Against the Jews, 1933–1945 (New York: Holt, Rinehart & Winston, 1975),
pp. 19–21, 55–56; Uriel Tal, *Christians and Jews in Germany: Religion, Politics and
Ideology in the Second Reich, 1870–1914* (Ithaca: Cornell University Press, 1975), pp.
259–89.

6. Hans Buchheim, quoted in Helmut Krausnick, "The Persecution of the Jews,"
in Krausnick et al., *Anatomy of the SS State* (New York: Walker, 1968), p. 15.

7. Hilberg, *Destruction*, p. 12.

8. J. P. Stern, *Hitler: The Führer and the People* (Glasgow: Fontana/Collins, 1971), p. 70. The celebration of that religious impulse was epitomized by the gigantic Nuremberg rally of 1934, whose theme, "The Triumph of the Will," became the title of Leni Riefenstahl's noted film. Riefenstahl, in an interview with an assistant of mine, made clear that Hitler himself provided that slogan.

9. George L. Mosse, *The Crisis of German Ideology: Intellectual Origins of the Third Reich* (New York: Grosset & Dunlap, 1964), p. 103.

10. Himmler, quoted in Krausnick, "Persecution," p. 14.

11. George L. Mosse, *Toward the Final Solution: A History of European Racism* (New York: Fertig, 1978), p. 77.

12. Hitler, *Mein Kampf,* pp. 397–98.

13. *Nuremberg Medical Case*, especially vol. I, pp. 8–17 (the indictment) and 27–74 (opening statement by Chief Prosecutor Telford Taylor, 9 December 1946); personal interview with James M. McHaney, prosecutor of the Medical Case.

TERRENCE DES PRES (1939–1987) wrote only one book about the Holocaust, but it is a classic. *The Survivor: An Anatomy of Life in the Death Camps,* which appeared in 1976, explored in detail the written testimonies of those who endured *l'univers concentrationnaire,* as David Rousset called it. The result is Des Pres's own testimony about what it took to be a survivor. His interpretation of the survivors' accounts shows that places such as Auschwitz revealed not only the depravity of human existence but also the grandeur that can be found in the refusal to despair and die.

An accomplished essayist and literary scholar, Des Pres had what Elie Wiesel called a "melancholy way of interpreting despairing tales and [a] sensitive approach to memories of death." But the work of this man—for many years he was professor of English at Colgate University—always serves life. Those characteristics are evident in the selection that follows, in which Des Pres coins a phrase—"excremental assault"—that must remain, lamentably, part of the vocabulary required by the Holocaust.

Des Pres shows how it was no coincidence that Auschwitz has been called *anus mundi.* "The fact is," he rightly concludes, "that prisoners were *systematically* subjected to filth." They were the deliberate targets of excremental assault, which aimed to achieve "complete humiliation and debasement of prisoners." The killers succeeded—too often, too much—but not completely. That realization forms another key factor that Des Pres wants remembered. When the victims recognized excremental assault for what it was, they resisted. That resistance included emphasis on trying, against all odds, to stay clean. But that extraordinary effort might have been the difference between sustaining snatches of dignity to help get one through and the giving up that had death as its conclusion. Nothing, of course, guaranteed survival in the death camps. Des Pres's anatomy of excremental assault makes that fact abundantly clear. Nevertheless he is correct when he writes, "Life itself depends on keeping dignity intact, and this, in turn, depends on the daily, never finished battle to remain *visibly* human."

In the late summer of 1976 there was a conference on the work of Elie Wiesel held on Long Island. Terrence Des Pres's *The Survivor* had recently appeared, and he was there. So was Emil Fackenheim. At one point the discussion turned to Des Pres's book. As Harry James Cargas recalls, Fackenheim referred specifically to the crucial chapter on "Excremental Assault." In his whispery voice, he said: "I never use the word 'shit,' but the way Terrence Des Pres uses it, it becomes a holy word."

Terrence Des Pres

Excremental Assault

*As the column returns from work after a whole day spent in
the open, the stench of the camp is overwhelmingly offensive.
Sometimes when you are still miles away the poisoned air
blows over you.*

SEWERYNA SZMAGLEWSKA, *Smoke over Birkenau*

*He had stopped washing a long time before . . . and now the
last remnants of his human dignity were burning out within
him.*

GUSTAV HERLING, *A World Apart*

It began in the trains, in the locked boxcars—eighty to a hundred
people per car—crossing Europe to the camps in Poland:

> The temperature started to rise, as the freight car was enclosed and
> body heat had no outlet. . . . The only place to urinate was through
> a slot in the skylight, though whoever tried this usually missed,
> spilling urine on the floor. . . . When dawn finally rose . . . we were
> all quite ill and shattered, crushed not only by the weight of fatigue
> but by the stifling, moist atmosphere and the foul odor of excre-
> ment. . . . There was no latrine, no provision. . . . On top of every-
> thing else, a lot of people had vomited on the floor. We were to live
> for days on end breathing these foul smells, and soon we lived in
> the foulness itself (Kessel, 50–51).

Transport by boat, in the case of many Soviet prisoners, was even worse: "most people were seasick and they just had to vomit on those down below. That was the only way to perform their natural functions too" (Knapp, 59). From the beginning, that is, subjection to filth was an aspect of the survivor's ordeal. In Nazi camps especially, dirt and excrement were permanent conditions of existence. In the barracks at night, for example, "buckets of excrement stood in a little passage by the exit. There were not enough. By dawn, the whole floor was awash with urine and feces. We carried the filth about the hut on our feet, the stench made people faint" (Birenbaum, 226). Sickness made things worse:

> Everybody in the block had typhus . . . it came to Belsen Bergen in its most violent, most painful, deadliest form. The diarrhea caused by it became uncontrollable. It flooded the bottom of the cages, dripping through the cracks into the faces of the women lying in the cages below, and mixed with blood, pus and urine, formed a slimy, fetid mud on the floor of the barracks (Perl, 171).

The latrines were a spectacle unto themselves:

> There was one latrine for thirty to thirty-two thousand women and we were permitted to use it only at certain hours of the day. We stood in line to get into this tiny building, knee-deep in human excrement. As we all suffered from dysentery, we could rarely wait until our turn came, and soiled our ragged clothes, which never came off our bodies, thus adding to the horror of our existence by the terrible smell which surrounded us like a cloud. The latrine consisted of a deep ditch with planks thrown across it at certain intervals. We squatted on these planks like birds perched on a telegraph wire, so close together that we could not help soiling one another (Perl, 33).

Prisoners lucky enough to work in one of the camp hospitals, and therefore able to enjoy some measure of privacy, were not thereby exempt from the latrine's special horror: "I had to step into human excreta, into urine soaked with blood, into stools of patients suffering from highly contagious diseases. Only then could one reach the hole, surrounded by the most inexpressible dirt" (Weiss, 69). The new pris-

oner's initiation into camp life was complete when he "realized that
there was no toilet paper"—

> that there was no paper in the whole of Auschwitz, and that I would
> have to "find another way out." I tore off a piece of my scarf and
> washed it after use. I retained this little piece throughout my days
> in Auschwitz; others did likewise (Unsdorfer, 102).

Problems of this kind were intensified by the fact that, at one time
or another, *everyone* suffered from diarrhea or dysentery. And for
prisoners already starved and exhausted, it was fatal more often than
not: "Those with dysentery melted down like candles, relieving themselves in their clothes, and swiftly turned into stinking repulsive skele-
tons who died in their own excrement" (Donat, 269). Sometimes whole
camp populations sickened in this way, and then the horror was overwhelming. Men and women soiled themselves and each other. Those
too weak to move relieved themselves where they lay. Those who did
not recover were slowly enveloped in their own decomposition: "Some
of the patients died before they ever reached the gas chambers. Many
of them were covered all over with excrement, for there were no
sanitary facilities, and they could not keep themselves clean" (Newman, 39).

Diarrhea was a deadly disease and a source of constant befoulment, but it was also dangerous for another reason—it forced prisoners to break rules:

> Many women with diarrhea relieved themselves in soup bowls or
> the pans for "coffee"; then they hid the utensils under the mattress
> to avoid the punishment threatening them for doing so: twenty-five
> strokes on the bare buttocks, or kneeling all night long on sharp
> gravel, holding up bricks. These punishments often ended in the
> death of the "guilty" (Birenbaum, 134).

In another case a group of men were locked day after day in a room
without ventilation or toilet facilities of any kind. Next to a window by
which guards passed they discovered a hole in the floor. But to use it a
man had to risk his life, since those caught were beaten to death. "The
spectacle of these unfortunates, shaking with fear as they crawled on
hands and knees to the hole and relieved themselves lying down, is
one of my most terrible memories of Sachsenhausen" (Szalet, 51).

The anguish of existence in the camps was thus intensified by the mineral movement of life itself. Death was planted in a need which could not, like other needs, be repressed or delayed or passively endured. The demands of the bowels are absolute, and under such circumstances men and women had to oppose, yet somehow accommodate, their own most intimate necessities:

> Imagine what it would be like to be forbidden to go to the toilet; imagine also that you were suffering from increasingly severe dysentery, caused and aggravated by a diet of cabbage soup as well as by the constant cold. Naturally, you would try to go anyway. Sometimes you might succeed. But your absences would be noticed and you would be beaten, knocked down and trampled on. By now, you would know what the risks were, but urgency would oblige you to repeat the attempt, cost what it might. . . . I soon learned to deal with the dysentery by tying strings around the lower end of my drawers (Maurel, 38–39).

With only one exception, so far as I know, psychoanalytic studies of the camp experience maintain that it was characterized by regression to "childlike" or "infantile" levels of behavior. This conclusion is based primarily on the fact that men and women in the concentration camps were "abnormally" preoccupied with food and excretory functions. Infants show similar preoccupations, and the comparison suggests that men and women react to extremity by "regression to, and fixation on, pre-oedipal stages" (Hoppe, 77). Here, as in general from the psychoanalytic point of view, context is not considered. The fact that the survivor's situation was itself abnormal is simply ignored. That the preoccupation with food was caused by literal starvation does not count; and the fact that camp inmates were *forced* to live in filth is likewise overlooked.

The case for "infantilism" has been put most forcefully by Bruno Bettelheim. A major thesis of his book *The Informed Heart* is that in extreme situations men are reduced to children; and in a section entitled "Childlike Behavior" he simply equates the prisoners' objective predicament with behavior inherently regressive. Bettelheim observes, for example—and of course this was true—that camp regulations were designed to transform excretory functions into moments of crisis. Prisoners had to ask permission in order to relieve themselves, thereby becoming exposed to the murderous whim of the SS guard to whom they spoke. During the twelve-hour workday, furthermore, prisoners were often not allowed to answer natural needs, or they were forced to do so *while* they worked and on the actual spot *where* they worked. As one survivor says: "If anyone of us, tormented by her stomach, would try to go to a nearby ditch, the guards would release their dogs. Humiliated, goaded, the women did not leave their places—they waded in their own excrement" (Zywulska, 67). Worst of all were the days of the death marches, when prisoners who stopped for any reason were instantly shot. To live they simply had to keep going:

> Urine and excreta poured down the prisoners' legs, and by nightfall the excrement, which had frozen to our limbs, gave off its stench. We were really no longer human beings in the accepted sense. Not even animals, but putrefying corpses moving on two legs (Weiss, 211).

Under such conditions, excretion does indeed become, as Bettelheim says, "an important daily event"; but the conclusion does not follow, as he goes on to say, that prisoners were therefore reduced "to the level they were at before toilet training was achieved" (132). Outwardly, yes; men and women were very much concerned with excretory functions, just as infants are, and prisoners were "forced to wet and soil themselves" just as infants do—except that infants are not forced. Bettelheim concludes that for camp inmates the ordeal of excremental crisis "made it impossible to see themselves as fully adult persons any more" (134). He does not distinguish between behavior in extremity and civilized behavior; for of course, if in civilized circumstances an adult worries about the state of his bowels, or sees the trip to the toilet as some sort of ordeal, then neurosis is evident. But in the concentration camps behavior was governed by immediate death-threat; action was not the index of infantile wishes but of response to hideous necessity.

The fact is that prisoners were *systematically* subjected to filth. They were the deliberate target of excremental assault. Defilement was a constant threat, a condition of life from day to day, and at any moment it was liable to take abruptly vicious and sometimes fatal forms. The favorite pastime of one *Kapo* was to stop prisoners just before they reached the latrine. He would force an inmate to stand at attention for questioning; then make him "squat in deep knee-bends until the poor man could no longer control his sphincter and 'exploded' "; then beat him; and only then, "covered with his own excrement, the victim would be allowed to drag himself to the latrine" (Donat, 178). In another instance prisoners were forced to lie in rows on the ground, and each man, when he was finally allowed to get up, "had to urinate across the heads of the others"; and there was "one night when they refined their treatment by making each man urinate into another's mouth" (Wells, 91). In Birkenau, soup bowls were periodically taken from the prisoners and thrown into the latrine, from which they had to be retrieved: "When you put it to your lips for the first time, you smell nothing suspicious. Other pairs of hands trembling with impatience wait for it, they seize it the moment you have finished drinking. Only later, much later, does a repelling odor hit your nostrils" (Szmaglewska, 154). And as we have seen, prisoners with dysentery commonly got around camp rules and kept from befouling themselves by using their own eating utensils:

> The first days our stomachs rose up at the thought of using what were actually chamber pots at night. But hunger drives, and we were so starved that we were ready to eat any food. That it had to be handled in such bowls could not be helped. During the night, many of us availed ourselves of the bowls secretly. We were allowed to go to the latrines only twice each day. How could we help it? No matter how great our need, if we went out in the middle of the night we risked being caught by the S.S., who had orders to shoot first and ask questions later (Lengyel, 26).

There was no end to this kind of degradation. The stench of excrement mingled with the smoke of the crematoria and the rancid decay of flesh. Prisoners in the Nazi camps were virtually drowning in their own waste, and in fact death by excrement was common. In Buchenwald, for instance, latrines consisted of open pits twenty-five feet long, twelve feet deep and twelve feet wide. There were railings along the edge to squat on, and "one of the favorite games of the SS, engaged in for many years," was to catch men in the act of relieving themselves and throw them into the pit: "In Buchenwald ten prisoners suffocated in excrement in this fashion in October 1937 alone" (Kogon,

56). These same pits, which were always overflowing, were emptied at night by prisoners working with nothing but small pails:

> The location was slippery and unlighted. Of the thirty men on this assignment, an average of ten fell into the pit in the course of each night's work. The others were not allowed to pull the victims out. When work was done and the pit empty, then and then only were they permitted to remove the corpses (Weinstock, 157–58).

Again, conditions like these were not accidental; they were determined by a deliberate policy which aimed at complete humiliation and debasement of prisoners. Why this was necessary is not at first apparent, since none of the goals of the camp system—to spread terror, to provide slaves, to exterminate populations—required the kind of thoroughness with which conditions of defilement were enforced. But here too, for all its madness, there was method and reason. This special kind of evil is a natural outcome of power when it becomes absolute, and in the totalitarian world of the camps it very nearly was. The SS could kill anyone they happened to run into. Criminal *Kapos* would walk about in groups of two and three, making bets among themselves on who could kill a prisoner with a single blow. The pathological rage of such men, their uncontrollable fury when rules were broken, is evidence of a boundless desire to annihilate, to destroy, to smash everything not mobilized within the movement of their own authority. And inevitably, the mere act of killing is not enough; for if a man dies without surrender, if something within him remains unbroken to the end, then the power which destroyed him has not, after all, crushed everything. Something has escaped its reach, and it is precisely this something— let us call it "dignity"—that must die if those in power are to reach the orgasmic peak of their potential domination.

As power grows, it grows more and more hostile to everything outside itself. Its logic is inherently negative, which is why it ends by destroying itself (a consolation which no longer means much, since the perimeter of atomic destruction is infinite). The exercise of totalitarian power, in any case, does not stop with the demand for outward compliance. It seeks, further, to crush the spirit, to obliterate that active inward principle whose strength depends on its freedom from entire determination by external forces. And thus the compulsion, felt by men with great power, to seek out and destroy all resistance, all spiritual autonomy, all sign of dignity in those held captive. It was not enough just to shoot the Old Bolsheviks; Stalin had to have the show trials. He had to demonstrate publicly that these men of enormous energy and spirit were so utterly broken as to openly repudiate themselves and all they had fought for. And so it was in the camps. Spiritual destruction became an end in itself, quite apart from the requirements of mass murder. The death of the soul was aimed at. It was to be accomplished by terror and privation, but first of all by a relentless assault on the survivor's sense of purity and worth. Excremental attack, the physical inducement of disgust and self-loathing, was a principal weapon.

But defilement had its lesser logic as well. "In Buchenwald," says one survivor, "it was a principle to depress the morale of prisoners to the lowest possible level, thereby preventing the development of fellow-feeling or co-operation among the victims" (Weinstock, 92). How much self-esteem can one maintain, how readily can one respond with respect to the needs of another, if both stink, if both are caked with mud and feces? We tend to forget how camp prisoners looked and smelled, especially those who had given up the will to live, and in consequence the enormous revulsion and disgust which naturally arose among prisoners. Here was an effective mechanism for intensifying the already heightened irritability of prisoners towards each other, and thus for stifling in common loathing the impulse toward solidarity. Within the camp world all visible signs of human beauty, of bodily pride and spiritual radiance, were thereby to be eliminated from the ranks of the inmates. The prisoner was made to feel subhuman, to see his self-image only in the dirt and stink of his neighbor. The SS, on the contrary, appeared superior not only by virtue of their guns and assurance, but by their elegant apartness from the filth of the prisoner's world. In Auschwitz prisoners were forced to march in the mud, whereas the clean roadway was reserved for the SS.

And here is a final, vastly significant reason why in the camps the prisoners were so degraded. This made it easier for the SS to do their job. It made mass murder less terrible to the murderers, because the victims appeared less than human. They *looked* inferior. In Gitta Sereny's series of interviews with Franz Stangl, commandant of Treblinka, there are moments of fearful insight. Here is one of the most telling:

"Why," I asked Stangl, *"if they were going to kill them anyway,
what was the point of all the humiliation, why the cruelty?"*
"To condition those who actually had to carry out the policies,"
he said. "To make it possible for them to do what they did" (101).

In a lecture at the New School (New York, 1974), Hannah Arendt
remarked that it is easier to kill a dog than a man, easier yet to kill a rat
or frog, and no problem at all to kill insects—"It is in the glance, in the
eyes." She means that the perception of subjective being in the victim
sparks some degree of identification in the assailant, and makes his act
difficult in proportion to the capacity for suffering and resistance he
perceives. Inhibited by pity and guilt, the act of murder becomes
harder to perform and results in greater psychic damage to the killer
himself. If, on the other hand, the victim exhibits self-disgust; if he
cannot lift his eyes for humiliation, or if lifted they show only
emptiness—then his death may be administered with ease or even
with the conviction that so much rotten tissue has been removed from
life's body. And it is a fact that in camp the procedure of "selection"—to
the left, life; to the right, death—was based on physical appearance
and on a certain sense of inward collapse or resilience in the prospec-
tive victim. As a survivor of Auschwitz puts it:

> Yes, here one rotted alive, there was no doubt about it, just like the
> SS in Bitterfield had predicted. Yet it was vitally important to keep
> the body clear. . . . Everyone [at a "selection"] had to strip and one
> by one, parade before them naked. Mengele in his immaculate
> white gloves stood pointing his thumb sometimes to the right,
> sometimes to the left. Anyone with spots on the body, or a thin
> *Muselmann*, was directed to the right. That side spelt death, the
> other meant one was allowed to rot a little longer (Hart, 65).

With water in permanent shortage; with latrines submerged in their
own filth; with diarrhea rife and mud everywhere, strict cleanliness
was just not possible. Simply to *try* to stay clean took extraordinary
effort. As one survivor says: "To pick oneself up, to wash and clean
oneself—all that is the simplest thing in the world, isn't it? And yet it
was not so. Everything in Auschwitz was so organized as to make these
things impossible. There was nothing to lean on; there was no place for
washing oneself. Nor was there time" (Lewinska, 43). That conditions
were "so organized" was a dreadful discovery:

At the outset the living places, the ditches, the mud, the piles of excrement behind the blocks, had appalled me with their horrible filth. . . . And then I saw the light! I saw that it was not a question of disorder or lack of organization but that, on the contrary, a very thoroughly considered conscious idea was in the back of the camp's existence. They had condemned us to die in our own filth, to drown in mud, in our own excrement. They wished to abase us, to destroy our human dignity, to efface every vestige of humanity, to return us to the level of wild animals, to fill us with horror and contempt toward ourselves and our fellows (Lewinska, 41–42).

With this recognition the prisoner either gave up or decided to resist. For many survivors this moment marked the birth of their will to fight back:

But from the instant when I grasped the motivating principle . . . it was as if I had been awakened from a dream. . . . I felt under orders to live. . . . And if I did die in Auschwitz, it would be as a human being, I would hold on to my dignity. I was not going to become the contemptible, disgusting brute my enemy wished me to be. . . . And a terrible struggle began which went on day and night (Lewinska, 50).

Or as another survivor says:

There and then I determined that if I did not become the target of a bullet, or if I were not hanged, I would make every effort to endure. No longer would I succumb to apathy. My first impulse was to concentrate on making myself more presentable. Under the circumstances this may sound ludicrous; what real relation was there between my new-found spiritual resistance and the unsightly rags on my body? But in a subtle sense there *was* a relationship, and from that moment onwards, throughout my life in the camps, I knew this for a fact. I began to look around me and saw the beginning of the end for any woman who might have had the opportunity to wash and had not done so, or any woman who felt that the tying of a shoe-lace was wasted energy (Weiss, 84).

Washing, if only in a ritual sense—and quite apart from reasons of health—was something prisoners needed to do. They found it necessary to survival, odd as that may seem, and those who stopped soon died:

> At 4:30, "coffee"—a light mint infusion without nourishment and with a repulsive taste—was distributed. We often took a few swallows and used the rest for washing, but not all of us were able to do without this poor substitute for coffee and consequently many inmates ceased to wash. This was the first step to the grave. It was an almost iron law: those who failed to wash every day soon died. Whether this was the cause or the effect of inner breakdown, I don't know; but it was an infallible symptom (Donat, 173).

Another survivor describes the initial disappearance of concern for his appearance, and the gradual realization that without such care he would not survive:

> Why should I wash? Would I be better off than I am? Would I please someone more? Would I live a day, an hour longer? I would probably live a shorter time, because to wash is an effort, a waste of energy and warmth. . . . But later I understood. . . . In this place it is practically pointless to wash every day in the turbid water of the filthy wash-basins for purposes of cleanliness and health; but it is most important as a symptom of remaining vitality, and necessary as an instrument of moral survival (Levi, 35).

By passing through the degradation of the camps, survivors discovered that in extremity a sense of dignity is something which men and women cannot afford to lose. Great damage has to be borne, much humiliation suffered. But at some point a steady resistance to their obliteration as human beings must be made. They learned, furthermore, that when conditions of filth are enforced, befoulment of the body is experienced as befoulment of the soul. And they came to recognize, finally, that when this particular feeling—of something inwardly untouchable—is ruined beyond repair, the will to live dies. To care for one's appearance thus becomes an act of resistance and a necessary moment in the larger structure of survival. Life itself depends on keeping dignity intact, and this, in turn, depends on the daily, never finished battle to remain *visibly* human:

> So we must certainly wash our faces without soap in dirty water and dry ourselves on our jackets. We must polish our shoes, not because

the regulation states it, but for dignity and propriety. We must walk erect, without dragging our feet, not in homage to Prussian discipline but to remain alive, not to begin to die (Levi, 36).

The basic structure of Western civilization or perhaps of any civilization, insofar as the processes of culture and sublimation are one, is the division between body and the spirit, between concrete existence and symbolic modes of being. In extremity, however, divisions like these collapse. The principle of compartmentalization no longer holds, and organic being becomes the immediate locus of selfhood. When this happens, body and spirit become the ground of each other, each bearing the other's need, the other's sorrow, and each responds directly to the other's total condition. If spiritual resilience declines, so does physical endurance. If the body sickens, the spirit too begins to lose its grip. There is a strange circularity about existence in extremity: survivors preserve their dignity in order "not to begin to die"; they care for the body as a matter of "moral survival."

For many among us, the word "dignity" no longer means much; along with terms like "conscience" and "spirit" it has grown suspect and is seldom used in analytic discourse. And certainly, if by "dignity" we mean the projection of pretense and vainglory, or the ways power cloaks itself in pomp and ritual pride; if, that is, we are referring to the parodic forms of this principle, as men exploit it for justification or gain—just as honor and conscience are exploited and likewise parodied, although real in themselves—then of course the claim to dignity is false. But if we mean an inward resistance to determination by external forces; if we are referring to a sense of innocence and worth, something felt to be inviolate, autonomous and untouchable, and which is most vigorous when most threatened; then, as in the survivor's case, we come upon one of the constituents of humanness, one of the irreducible elements of selfhood. Dignity, in this case, appears as a self-conscious, self-determining faculty whose function is to insist upon the recognition of itself *as such*.

Certainly the SS recognized it, and their attempt to destroy it, while not successful in the survivor's case, was one of the worst aspects of the camp ordeal. When cleanliness becomes impossible and human beings are forced to live in their own excretions, their pain becomes intense to the point of agony. The shock of physical defilement causes spiritual concussion, and, simply to judge from the reports of those

who have suffered it, subjection to filth seems often to cause greater
anguish than hunger or fear of death. "This aspect of our camp life,"
says one survivor, "was the most dreadful and the most horrible ordeal
to which we were subjected" (Weiss, 69). Another survivor describes
the plight of men forced to lie in their own excreta: they "moaned and
wept with discomfort and disgust. Their moral wretchedness was
crushing" (Szalet, 78). In the most bizarre cases, defilement caused a
desperation bordering on madness, as when a group of prisoners were
forced "to drink out of the toilet bowls":

> The men could not bring themselves to obey this devilish order;
> they only pretended to drink. But the blockfuehrers had reckoned
> with that; they forced the men's heads deep into the bowls until
> their faces were covered with excrement. At this the victims almost
> went out of their minds—that was why their screams had sounded
> so demented (Szalet, 42).

But why is contact with excrement unbearable? If actual discomfort is minor, why is the reaction so violent? And why does the sense of
dignity feel most threatened in this particular case? The incident of the
toilet bowls, cited above, has been examined from a psychoanalytic
point of view, the conclusion being this:

> infantile satisfactions . . . could be acquired only by means against
> which culture has erected strong prohibitions. . . . Enforced break-
> down of these barriers was capable of bringing the prisoner near to
> mental disintegration (Bluhm, 15).

The extreme suffering of those men thus resulted from a breach in
cultural taboo. Their demented screams issued from the rending of
subliminal structures, in response to violation of those "cleanliness
habits" which are "enforced by any culture at an early stage of training"
(17). The survivor's struggle against an excremental fate, to speak more
plainly, is a function of "toilet training"—although that term is not used
in the article from which I am quoting, since the degree of reduction it
implies, even from a psychoanalytic perspective, seems altogether
disproportionate to the violence of the prisoners' experience. The
article goes on, however, to suggest that the depth at which the scream
originates may reveal, beyond the relative and flexible demands of

culture, the violation of a limit or boundary not relative in the same sense:

> however, the normal adult of our civilization shares the disgust toward the contact with his excrements with members of tribes who live on the lowest levels of culture. This disgust seems to be a demarkation line, the transgression of which can produce effects much more devastating than the appearance of more or less isolated regressive symptoms (17).

From the psychoanalytic point of view, moral anguish is a product of conflict between cultural demands and the regressive desire to subvert them. But if we keep in mind that all regression is in the service of pleasure, or release from pain (which was Freud's definition of pleasure), then the whole theory of infantile regression, in the survivor's case, becomes absurd. The scream of those desperate men was indeed a defense against dissolution, but to reduce their extraordinary pain to the violation of a taboo, or any restriction merely imposed, seems entirely to miss the point. In any case, the inhibiting authority of toilet training is not so central to selfhood that infraction causes the personality to disintegrate. Only once in Western culture has this been viewed in terms of psychic crisis—among the bourgeois classes in the nineteenth century, with their radical reliance on physical rigidity and, as a consequence, their prurient forms of sexual satisfaction; and I would suggest, finally, that such training is the ritual organization of an inherent biological process. Plenty of taboos went by the board in the concentration camps, but not this one—not, that is, transgression of a "demarkation line" which runs deeper than cultural imposition. What human beings will or will not tolerate depends, up to a point, on training of all kinds. Beyond that, however, there are things absolutely unacceptable because something—let us keep the word "dignity"—in our deepest nature revolts. And on such revolt, life in extremity depends.

In *The Symbolism of Evil*, Paul Ricoeur defines "dread of the impure" as the special kind of fear we feel in reaction to "a threat which, beyond the threat of suffering and death, aims at a diminution of existence, a loss of the personal core of one's being" (41). That, I think, is a good description of what survivors feel when threatened by excremental attack. Ricoeur goes on to argue that the feeling of defilement under-lies concepts like "sin" and "guilt," and finally that as "the oldest of the symbols of evil," defilement "can signify analogically all the degrees of the experience of evil" (336). And indeed, why does imagery of wash-ing and physical purgation underlie our ideas of sanctity and spiritual purification? Why do we use images associated with excrement— imagery of corruption and decay, of dirt and contagion, of things contaminated, rotting or spoiled—to embody our perceptions of evil? Ricoeur concludes that all such imagery is symbolic only, that it repre-sents inner states of being—and for us no doubt he is right. But in the concentration camps, defilement was a condition known by actual sight and touch and smell, and hence this question: when survivors react so violently to contact with excrement, are they responding to what it symbolizes, or is their ordeal the concrete instance from which our symbolism of evil derives?

The implication of Ricoeur's analysis is that "the consciousness of self seems to constitute itself at its lowest level by means of symbolism and to work out an abstract language only subsequently" (9). As far as it goes that is true, yet where does the symbolism originate? How did defilement come to symbolize evil? Ricoeur can only answer that in the beginning was the symbol—that human selfhood became aware of itself through symbolic objectification of its own structure and condi-tion. This kind of starting point, however, is also a culmination; it is nothing less than the goal of civilization, the outcome of a process of sublimation or transcendence or etherealization (call it what you wish) by which actual events and objects become the images, myths and metaphors that constitute man's spiritual universe. Transformation of the world into symbol is perpetual; thereby we internalize actuality and stay in spiritual, if not in concrete, connection with those primal experiences from which, as civilized beings, we have detached our-selves.

But this activity can be reversed. When civilization breaks down, as it did in the concentration camps, the "symbolic stain" becomes a condition of literal defilement; and evil becomes that which causes real "loss of the personal core of one's being." In extremity man is stripped of his expanded spiritual identity. Only concrete forms of existence remain, actual life and actual death, actual pain and actual defilement; and these now constitute the medium of moral and spiritual being. Spirit does not simply vanish when sublimation fails. At the cost of much of its freedom it falls back to the ground and origin of meaning—back, that is, to the physical experience of the body. Which is another way of saying that, in extremity, symbols tend to actualize.

We might say, then, that in extremity symbolism *as symbolism* loses its autonomy. Or, what amounts to the same thing, that in this special case everything is felt to be inherently symbolic, intrinsically significant. Either way, meaning no longer exists above and beyond the world; it re-enters concrete experience, becomes immanent and invests each act and moment with urgent depth. And hence the oddly "literary" character of experience in extremity. . . . It is as if amid the smoke of burning bodies the great metaphors of world literature were being "acted out" in terrible fact—death and resurrection, damnation and salvation, the whole of spiritual pain and exultation in passage through the soul's dark night.

The following event, for example, seems literary to the point of embarrassment. It is the kind of incident we might expect at the climax of a novel, valid less in itself than as a fiction bearing meaning, and therefore acceptable through the symbolic statement it makes, the psychic drama it embodies. This event, however, happens to be real. It occurred during the last days of the Warsaw Ghetto uprising, it was the fate of many men and women. Armed with handguns and bottles of gasoline, the ghetto fighters held out for fifty-two days against tanks, field artillery and air strikes. So stubbornly did they resist that the Germans finally resorted to burning down the ghetto building by building, street by street, until everything—all life, all sign of man—was gone. The last chance for escape was through the sewers, and down into that foul dark went the remnant of the ghetto:

> On the next day, Sunday, April 25, I went down . . . into the underground sewer which led to the "Aryan" side. I will never forget the picture which presented itself to my eyes in the first moment when I descended into the channel. Dozens of refugees . . . sought shelter in these dark and narrow channels awash with filthy water from the municipal latrines and foul refuse flushed down from the private apartments. In these low, narrow channels, only wide enough for one person to crawl forward in a bent position, dozens of people lay jammed and huddled together in the mud and filth (Friedman, 284).

They stayed below, sometimes for days, making their way toward the "free" side, coming up occasionally to see where they were, and then simply waiting. Many died, but through the combined effort of Jewish and Polish partisans, some were rescued and survived:

> On May 10, 1943, at nine o'clock in the morning, the lid of the sewer over our heads suddenly opened, and a flood of sunlight streamed into the sewer. At the opening of the sewer Krzaczek [a member of the Polish resistance] was standing and calling all of us to come out, after we had been in the sewer for more than thirty hours. We started to climb out one after another and at once got on a truck. It was a beautiful spring day and the sun warmed us. Our eyes were blinded by the bright light, as we had not seen daylight for many weeks and had spent the time in complete darkness. The streets were crowded with people, and everybody . . . stood still and watched, while strange beings, hardly recognizable as humans, crawled out of the sewers (Friedman, 290).

If that were from a novel, how easily we might speak of rites of passage; of descent into hell; of journey through death's underworld. We would respond to the symbolism of darkness and light, of rebirth and new life, as, blessed by spring and the sun, these slime-covered creatures arise from the bowels of the earth. And we would not be misreading. For despite the horror, it all seems familiar, very much recalling archetypes we know from art and dreams. For the survivor, in any case, the immersion in excrement marks the nadir of his passage through extremity. No worse assault on moral being seems possible. Yet even here there was life and will, as if these shit-smeared bodies were the accurate image of how much mutilation the human spirit can bear, despite shame, loathing, the trauma of violent recoil, and still keep the sense of something inwardly inviolate. "Only our feverish eyes," said one survivor of the sewers, "still showed that we were living human beings" (Friedman, 289).

REFERENCES

(Page numbers in the preceding essay by Terrence Des Pres refer to the editions listed below.)

Bettelheim, Bruno. *The Informed Heart*. Glencoe, Ill.: Free Press, 1960.

Birenbaum, Halina. *Hope Is the Last to Die*, trans. David Welsh. New York: Twayne, 1971.

Bluhm, Hilde O. "How Did They Survive?" *American Journal for Psychotherapy* 2 (1948): pp. 3–32.

Donat, Alexander. *The Holocaust Kingdom*. New York: Holt, Rinehart and Winston, 1965.

Friedman, Philip. *Martyrs and Fighters*. London: Routledge & Kegan Paul, 1954.

Hart, Kitty. *I Am Alive*. London and New York: Abelard-Schuman, 1962.

Herling, Gustav. *A World Apart*, trans. Joseph Marek. New York: Roy, 1951.

Hoppe, Klaus D. "The Psychodynamics of Concentration Camps Victims," *The Psychoanalytic Forum* 1 (1966); pp. 76–85.

Kessel, Sim. *Hanged at Auschwitz*, trans. Melville and Delight Wallace. New York: Stein and Day, 1972.

Knapp, Stefan. *The Square Sun*. London: Museum Press, 1956.

Kogon, Eugen. *The Theory and Practice of Hell*, trans. Heinz Norden. New York: Farrar, Straus, 1953.

Lengyel, Olga. *Five Chimneys: The Story of Auschwitz*, trans. Paul P. Weiss. Chicago: Ziff-Davis, 1947.

Levi, Primo. *Survival in Auschwitz*, trans. Stuart Woolf. New York: Collier, 1969.

Lewinska, Pelagia. *Twenty Months at Auschwitz*, trans. Albert Teichner. New York: Lyle Stuart, 1968.

Maurel, Micheline. *An Ordinary Camp*, trans. Margaret S. Summers. New York: Simon & Schuster, 1958.

Newman, Judith Sternberg. *In the Hell of Auschwitz*. New York: Exposition, 1964.

Perl, Gisella. *I Was a Doctor in Auschwitz*. New York: International Universities Press, 1948.

Ricoeur, Paul. *The Symbolism of Evil*, trans. Emerson Buchanan. New York: Harper & Row, 1967.

Sereny, Gitta. *Into That Darkness*. New York: McGraw-Hill, 1974.

Szalet, Leon. *Experiment "E"*, trans. Catherine Bland Williams. New York: Didier, 1945.

Szmaglewska, Seweryna. *Smoke over Birkenau*, trans. Jadwiga Rynas. New York: Henry Holt, 1947.

Unsdorfer, S. B. *The Yellow Star*. New York and London: Thomas Yoseloff, 1961.

Weinstock, Eugene. *Beyond the Last Path*, trans. Clara Ryan. New York: Boni and Gaer, 1947.

Weiss, Reska. *Journey Through Hell*. London: Vallentine, Mitchell, 1961.

Wells, Leon. *The Janowska Road*. New York: Macmillan, 1963.

Zywulska, Krystyna. *I Came Back*, trans. Krystyna Cenkalska. London: Dennis Dobson, 1951.

LAWRENCE L. LANGER, professor of English at Simmons College in Boston, Massachusetts, was born in 1929 in New York City. Few literary scholars have done as much to evaluate and advance understanding of the written testimony of Holocaust survivors as well as the prose and poetry penned by creative artists in response to that event. Langer's efforts are well represented in *The Holocaust and the Literary Imagination; The Age of Atrocity: Death in Modern Literature;* and *Versions of Survival: The Holocaust and the Human Spirit.*

If Terrence Des Pres added "excremental assault" to the human vocabulary as he explored the Holocaust, Langer's study provides another crucial concept: "choiceless choice." In the following selection, Langer explores how the Holocaust's human domination put people in positions that strained the boundaries of moral choice again and again. It is not even one where there is much sense in speaking about "the lesser of evils." As Langer understands it, a "choiceless choice" does not "reflect options between life and death, but between one form of abnormal response and another, both imposed by a situation that [is] not of the victim's own choosing." For its victims, the Holocaust made "choiceless choice" commonplace. One lesson that Lawrence Langer drives home is that no one should have to face such bleak options again.

Lawrence L. Langer

The Dilemma of Choice in the Deathcamps

Do you know how one says never *in camp slang?* Morgen
früh *tomorrow morning.*

PRIMO LEVI

Suppose Dante's pilgrim in the *Divine Comedy* had arrived at the exit
from the Inferno to find the way barred by a barbed wire fence, posted
with warnings reading "No trespassing. Violators will be annihilated."
When the spiritual and psychological equivalents of Purgatory and
Paradise are excluded from human possibility, to be replaced by the
daily threat of death in the gas chamber, then we glimpse the negative
implications of survival, especially for the Jews, in the Nazi extermination camps. After we peel from the surface of the survivor ordeal the
veneer of dignified behavior, hope, mutual support and the inner
resolve to resist humiliation, we find beneath a raw and quivering
anatomy of human existence resembling no society we have ever
encountered before. When such an existence transforms the life in-
stinct and forces men and women who would remain alive to suspend
the golden rule and embrace the iron one of "do unto others before it is
done unto you," we must expect some moral rust to flake from the
individual soul. We are left with a spectacle of reality that few would
choose to celebrate, *if* they could tolerate a world where words like
dignity and choice had temporarily lost their traditional meaning because Nazi brutality had eliminated the human supports that usually
sustain them. But such a world so threatens our sense of spiritual

From *Centerpoint* 4 (Fall 1980). Reprinted by permission.

continuity that it is agonizing to imagine or consent to its features without introducing some affirmative values to mitigate the gloom.

For those like Viktor Frankl who see life as a challenge to give meaning to being, the notion that the *situation* in Auschwitz deprived being of meaning is the highest form of impiety. He speaks of the deathcamp as a "living laboratory" or "testing ground" where he witnessed how "some of our comrades behave like swine while others behaved like saints." But this arbitrary division into heroes and villains is misleading, since it totally ignores the even more arbitrary environment that shaped human conduct in Auschwitz. Frankl cannot resist the temptation to incorporate the deathcamp experience into his world view, to make events serve his theory of behavior: "Man has both potentialities within himself: which one is actualized depends on decisions but not on condition."[1] This may be an accurate description of human character in a Dostoevsky novel: we shall see how much evidence Frankl was required to ignore to protect his image of man in the deathcamps as a self-determining creature, no matter how humiliating his surroundings. Auschwitz was indeed a laboratory and testing ground, but if we contemplate the "experiment" without rigid moral preconceptions, we discover that men could not be divided simply into saints and swine, and that self-actualization as a concept evaporates when impossible conditions obliterate the possible decisions we have been trained to applaud. To speak of survival in Auschwitz as a form of self-actualization is to mock language and men, especially those who did not survive.

If we pursue the proposition that some stains of the soul of history—and the Holocaust is such a stain—are indelible, where will it lead us? It will lead us certainly to an unfamiliar version of survival, to the conclusion that after Auschwitz the idea of human dignity could never be the same again. It will force us to reexamine the language of value that we used before the event, and to admit that at least when describing the Holocaust, if not its consequences, such language may betray the spirit and the facts of the ordeal. Perhaps this is what Primo Levi, himself a survivor, was trying to say in *Survival in Auschwitz* when he wrote:

> Just as our hunger is not that feeling of missing a meal, so our way of being cold has need of a new word. We say "hunger," we say "tiredness," "fear," "pain," we say "winter" and they are different

things. They are free words, created and used by free men who
lived in comfort and suffering in their homes. If the Lagers [camps]
had lasted longer a new, harsh language would have been born; and
only this language could express what it means to toil the whole day
in the wind, with the temperature below freezing, and wearing
only a shirt, underpants, cloth jacket and trousers, and in one's
body nothing but weakness, hunger and knowledge of the end
drawing near.[2]

This crucial observation leaves us with a profound dilemma, since no
one has yet invented a vocabulary of annihilation to modify the language of transcendence employed by Frankl and similar commentators. For this reason we must bring to every "reading" of the Holocaust
experience a wary consciousness of the way in which "free words" and
their associations may distort the facts or alter them into more manage-
able events.

The consequences of this predicament may seem threatening to
the conservative ethical intelligence, but they are nonetheless un-
avoidable. They illuminate a version of survival less flattering to the
human creature than more traditional accounts, but their spokesmen
and spokeswomen deserve a hearing if only to clarify our vision of how
utterly the Nazi mentality corrupted moral reality for the victims.
Moreover, this complementary vision may enable us to comprehend
better how little discredit falls to these victims, who were plunged into
a crisis of what might call "choiceless choice," where critical decisions
did not reflect options between life and death, but between one form of
"abnormal" response and another, both imposed by a situation that was
in no way of the victim's own choosing. Consider this brief episode
narrated by Judith Sternberg Newman, a nurse by profession, who was
deported to Auschwitz from Breslau with 197 other Jewish women:
three weeks later, only eighteen of them were still alive:

Two days after Christmas, a Jewish child was born on our block.
How happy I was when I saw this tiny baby. It was a boy, and the
mother had been told that he would be taken care of. Three hours
later, I saw a small package wrapped in cheese cloth lying on a
wooden bench. Suddenly it moved. A Jewish girl employed as a
clerk came over, carrying a pan of cold water. She whispered to me
"Hush! Quiet! Go away!" But I remained, for I could not understand what she had in mind. She picked up the little package—it

was the baby, of course—and it started to cry with a thin little voice. She took the infant and submerged its little body in the cold water. My heart beat wildly in agitation. I wanted to shout "Murderess!" but I had to keep quiet and could not tell anyone. The baby swallowed and gurgled, its little voice chittering like a small bird, until its breath became shorter and shorter. The woman held its head in the water. After about eight minutes the breathing stopped. The woman picked it up, wrapped it up again, and put it with the other corpses. Then she said to me, "We had to save the mother, otherwise she would have gone to the gas chamber." This girl had learned well from the SS and had become a murderess herself.[3]

How is one to pass judgment on such an episode, or relate it to the inner freedom celebrated by other commentators on the deathcamp experience? Does moral choice have any meaning here? The drama involves the helpless infant, whose fate is entirely in someone else's hands (and the fate of the infant Oedipus only reminds us of how far life in Auschwitz had drifted from the moral order, to say nothing of the moral ironies, of art); the absent mother, who may or may not have approved of the action; the "agent" who coolly sacrifices one life to preserve another, as a deed of naked necessity, without appeal, not of moral choice; and the author, sole witness to a crime that is simultaneously an act of charity and perhaps of literal secular salvation to the mother. Conventional vocabulary limps through a situation that allows no heroic response, no acceptable gesture of protest, no mode of action to permit *any* of the participants, including the absent mother, to retain a core of human dignity. The *situation* itself forbids it, together with the Nazi "law" stating that mothers who refuse to surrender their newborn infants to death must accompany them to the gas chamber. This predatory profile of survival, when fear of such death, not affirmation of a basic human dignity, drives men and women to behavior they would not consider under normal circumstances, confirms another moment when reality defeats both a language of judgment and mode of moral behavior: "I wanted to shout 'Murderess!' but I had to keep quiet and could not tell anyone."

In the absence of humanly significant alternatives—that is, alternatives enabling an individual to make a decision, act on it, and accept the consequences, all within a framework that supports personal integrity and self-esteem—one is plunged into a moral turmoil that may silence judgment, as in the above example, but cannot paralyze all action, if one still wishes to remain alive. Ella Lingens-Reiner, another Auschwitz survivor, offers a crude but critical instance of how effectively the optionless anguish of the deathcamp could alienate dignity from choice. In her barracks there was a single limited source of water for washing and for draining excrement from the latrine. If the women took the water for washing, the primitive sewage system would be blocked, creating an intolerably offensive (and unhealthy) situation. Outside the camp, there would be various options to solve this dilemma: complain to the landlord or health department, call a plumber or find a new source of water—or simply change your residence. In Auschwitz they were of course excluded. Lingens-Reiner lucidly sums up the condition of choiceless choice, where the only alternatives are between two indignities: "It is dreadful to be without water; it is impossible to let people take away all the water while feces are piling up in the ditches!"[4] As one wavers between the "dreadful" and the "impossible," one begins to glimpse a deeper level of reality in the deathcamps, where moral choice as we know it was superfluous, and inmates were left with the futile task of redefining decency in an atmosphere that could not support it.

In contradiction to those who argue that the only way of surviving was to cling to the values of civilized living despite the corrupting influence of the deathcamps, Lingens-Reiner insists that those who tried to salvage such moral luggage imposed fatal burdens on themselves. She tells of her own difficulty in ridding herself of such inclinations: shortly after arriving, she says, "I was still under the impression that it was advisable for people in our situation to behave with exemplary correctness. To the very last I could not get rid of this notion, although it was quite absurd. In reality only those prisoners had a chance to survive in the camp—if they were not privileged on account of their profession, beauty, or other specially favorable circumstances—who were determined to do the exact opposite of what they were told to do, on principle to break every rule governing civilian life."[5] This harshly practical view flatters no one, neither the author nor her companions nor the reader, all of whom are confronted by conditions that with very few exceptions *prohibit* the exercise of uncontaminated moral freedom and hence the achievement of a tragic dignity to temper the austerity of human doom in Auschwitz.

We have seen that the sharing which represents a social ideal in normal societies was not necessarily the most effective, and certainly not always the most possible form of behavior in the deathcamps. Even less accessible in that degrading environment was the moral idea which celebrates the dignity of the self through conscious choice. Suppose we suspend our need to discover an ethics of survival, whether based on moral values or social imperatives, and approach the camp ordeal as one from which no familiar or generally acceptable system of cause and effect behavior can be derived. The implications reach far beyond moral ideology to the role of time and history in human destiny, to the structure of character and the very unity of our lives in the twentieth century. History assures us that man is superior to time when retrospectively he can explain the unexpected, account, in this instance, for the extermination of a people, uncover a system for surviving and thus reduce the event to a partial intellectual order that somehow theoretically balances the price in human lives paid for that order. But from the perspective of the victims, who of course far outnumbered the survivors, the disorder of meaningless death contradicts the ordering impulses of time. Those who died for nothing during the Holocaust left the living with the paralyzing dilemma of facing a perpetually present grief. To the puzzled inquiry why interest in the Holocaust seems to grow as the event recedes in time, one answer may be that there is no inner space to bury it in.

Ella Lingens-Reiner helps to illuminate this paradox. As time passed, she says, the sense of the world outside (*our* world still) blurred, and the inner life of people who endured months and years in the camps atrophied. Such people "transferred their ambitions and emotions to the life inside the camp. Therefore they would fight for positions not only because they intended to survive, but also for their own sake, because it satisfied their need to win power, recognition and a following within the precincts. Some of them invested their whole being in these matters, and so lost much of their intellectual and even moral standards." She writes not with contempt, but with compassion, with an effort to convey how subtly a deathcamp-inspired behaviour could infiltrate a common sense of dignity and triumph over the victim's vision of decency. After praising the tremendous achievement of some women for preserving "their personal integrity in spite of everything," she adds with utter frankness: "the truly frightening thing was that women who had striven for that integrity, who still took life and ethics seriously, proved in the end too small for their overwhelming destiny, and never noticed when they acted on principles which were in reality those of National Socialism."[6] She speaks not of habitual criminals, or self-serving collaborators, but of individual women who believe in integrity but find their response to reality determined by a "destiny" that admits no meaningful moral opposition: the threat of death in Auschwitz.

Such a destiny created a situation beyond good and evil that even a Nietzsche could not imagine. How are we to portray or apply ethical measures to that prototypical example of choiceless choice, the mother of three children who reputedly was told by the Nazis that she might save *one* of them from execution? She was free to "choose," but what civilized mind could consider this an exercise of moral choice, or discover in modern history or Jewish tradition a myth to dignify her dilemma? The alternatives are not difficult, they are *impossible,* and we are left with the revelation of a terrifying question posed by a universe that lacks a vision to contain it. How is character to survive *any* decision in such a situation, and retain a semblance of human dignity? The human need *outside* the deathcamps to see the Holocaust as some kind of continuum in the spiritual history of man repeatedly stumbles over the limits of language, to say nothing of the limits of traditional moral theory. An entire ethical vocabulary, which for generations furnished a sanctuary for motive and character, no matter how terrible the external details, has been corrupted by the facts of *this* event.

Against the natural longing for a Moment of Truth in the death-camps, when the human will asserted itself and a reborn dignity prevailed, we must measure moments of truth like the following, narrated by Hermann Langbein in *Menschen in Auschwitz* from a report by David Rousset, who was describing a group of "selectees" being escorted to the gas chamber:

> An old man, who could hardly move his legs any more, sat down along the way. An accompanying guard roared at him: "Get moving, or I'll beat you within an inch of your life!" Quickly the old man exclaimed: "No, don't kill me. I'm going, I'm going!" and rejoined the procession to the gas chamber.[7]

Once again the choice is not between life and death, resistance and submission, courage and cowardice, but between two forms of humiliation, in this instance each leading to the extinction of a life. By shielding himself instinctively from an immediate threat, the victim inadvertently consigns himself to a consequent one: once one's ultimate fate had been decided by the murderers—and for the Jews, extermination was their fate from the moment they entered the camps—freedom of moral decision vanished because the antagonist was in total control of the means of supporting life and the manner of imposing death. One could not escape one's enfolding doom, even temporarily, by pretending that responses from the normal world would be heard with sympathetic ears. Langbein's example dramatically ratifies that. Perhaps this is what one survivor meant when he wrote bitterly: "Only to survive, to survive, everything consists in that, and the forms of survival are extreme and loathsome [*ekelhaft*], they are not worth the price of a life."[8]

The illusion that under the worst of circumstances—and in Auschwitz, for the Jews and Soviet prisoners of war in particular, all but a few of the circumstances were of the "worst"—men and women could meaningfully distinguish between what they did (or suffered) and the attitude they adopted toward their deeds is supported more easily by language than by events. The relation between deed and motive, fate and intent (so vital to familiar moral discourse) collapsed so often in the deathcamps that it ceased to represent an ethical bulwark for the victims. "I lived better than many of my comrades," confessed one of the prisoner functionaries, "without feeling that it was immoral. In the concentration camp, no one has the right to judge himself according to moral rules that would be valid in normal times."[9] This survivor is not *proud* of his behavior, nor is he particularly happy about the suspension of values that dominated the general struggle to survive in the world of Auschwitz. Imagine the desolation of Salmen Lewental, whose diary was literally unearthed from the ashes of Auschwitz in 1962, as he tries to describe what the will to survive has done to prisoners who were forced to live "ill" beyond conception by the daily routine of destruction:

> Why do you do such ignoble work, what do you live for, what is your aim in life, what do you desire . . . what would you like to achieve living this kind of life . . . And here is the crux . . . of our Kommando, which I have no intention to defend as a whole. I must speak the truth here, that some of that group have in the course of

> time so entirely lost themselves that we ourselves were simply ashamed. They simply forgot what they were doing . . . and with time . . . they got so used to it that it was even strange [that one wanted] to weep and to complain: that . . . such normal, average . . . simple and unassuming men . . . of necessity got used to everything so that these happenings make no more impression on them. Day after day they stand and look on how tens of thousands of people are perishing and [do] nothing.[10]

This is description, not judgment: man is a creature who adapts. Lewental's shame does not presume blame, nor do his questions about purpose and goal expect replies. He had already answered his questions in an earlier fragment of the diary: "one wants to live because one lives, because the whole world lives." Members of the Sonderkommando did not choose degradation, any more than the luckier kitchen workers or medical orderlies "chose" decency. Reduced to the condition of choiceless choice, the human creature exists from hour to hour, often from minute to minute. "Do you think, perhaps, that I *volunteered* for this work?" rings out the desperate voice of another Sonderkommando member, who like Lewental did not survive? "What should I have done? . . . You think the members of the Sonderkommando are monsters? I tell you, they're like the others only more unfortunate."[11]

Tadeusz Borowski in *This Way for the Gas, Ladies and Gentlemen,* tells the story of a smaller concentration camp where new prisoners arrived daily. The camp had a limited quantity of supplies, and the Kommandant disliked seeing the prisoners starve to death. But every day the camp seemed to have a few dozen more men than it could feed. "So every evening," he says, "a ballot, using cards or matches, was held in every block, and the following morning the losers did not go to work. At noon they were led out behind the barbed-wire fence and shot."[12] Few examples could illustrate more effectively the notion of choiceless choice. The victims are offered an option that is no option, since the results of a lottery are governed by chance, not choice. And obviously, anyone who refused to participate in the macabre game certified his execution the next day. Refusal to participate in the ritual of extermination was not a meaningful alternative for the victim because he shared no responsibility for the situation which condemned him to such an existence. He lacked the power to act physically in behalf of his own survival, and without this power (which through luck or collaboration or good connections might be *bestowed* on him), no mere control of attitude or feeling of spiritual inviolability could salvage his moral self. Since the deathcamp universe eliminated conditions which support worth, the victim could not "choose" extermination and remain human, while the survivor could not "choose" life and remain human. He could strive for life and, if lucky, remain *alive*: but this was a struggle between states of being, not competing values.

After having "witnessed" some of the agonizing dilemmas confronting prisoners in the deathcamps, we should be less persuaded by comforting halftruths like the following, from Viktor Frankl's version of survival: "Psychological observations of the prisoners have shown that only men who allowed their inner hold on their moral and spiritual selves to subside eventually fell victim to the camp's degenerating influences."[13] How do we present this sanctimonious view to the woman who was forced to drown an infant to save the mother, or the other woman who could only stand by in silence? We have seen that when the environment in Auschwitz supported one person's life, it was often at the cost of another's death—not because victims made wrong choices, or no choices, but because dying was the "purpose" of living in this particular environment: it was the nature of Auschwitz. The need to equate moral activity with continued existence and moral passivity with death reflects a desperate desire to retain some ethical coherence in a chaotic universe. But the "decision to survive" is contradicted by the condition of "choiceless choice," and may betray nothing more than a misuse of what Primo Levi called "free words": using language to create value where none exists. The real challenge before us is to invent a vocabulary of annihilation appropriate to the deathcamp experience; in its absence, we should at least be prepared to redefine the terminology of transcendence—"dignity," "choice," "suffering," and "spirit"—so that it conforms more closely to the way of being in places like Auschwitz, where the situation that consumed so many millions imposed *impossible* decisions on victims not free to embrace the luxury of the heroic life.

NOTES

1. Viktor E. Frankl, *Man's Search for Meaning* (New York: Pocket Books, 1963), pp. 212–213.

2. Primo Levi, *Survival in Auschwitz: The Nazi Assault on Humanity*, trans. Stuart Woolf (New York: Collier Books, 1969), pp. 112–113.

3. Judith Sternberg Newman, *In the Hell of Auschwitz* (New York: Exposition Press, 1963), pp. 42–43.

4. Ella Lingens-Reiner, *Prisoners of Fear* (London: Victor Gollancz, 1948), p. 29.

5. *Ibid.*, p. 22.

6. *Ibid.*, p. 91.

7. Hermann Langbein, *Menschen in Auschwitz* (Wien: Europaverlag, 1972), p. 134. Translation mine.

8. *Ibid.*, p. 112.

9. *Ibid.*, p. 166.

10. Jadwiga Bezwinska, ed., *Amidst a Nightmare of Crime: Manuscripts of Members of Sonderkommando*, trans. Krystyna Michalik (State Museum of Oświęcim, 1973), p. 139.

11. Langbein, p. 225.

12. Tadeusz Borowski, *This Way for the Gas, Ladies and Gentlemen*, trans. Barbara Vedder (New York: Penguin Books, 1976), p. 119.

13. Frankl, p. 110.

DAVID ROUSSET, who spent much of his career as a journalist, was born in Roanne, France, in 1912. After completing his education, he wrote on politics and economics for publications such as *Time* and *Fortune* and also taught philosophy in a Parisian *lycée*. Adamantly opposed to fascism, he became active in the Resistance when France fell to Germany in World War II. His activities included attempts to organize anti-Nazi groups among German soldiers.

The Gestapo arrested Rousset in Paris on October 16, 1943. He endured Nazi concentration camps at Buchenwald, Neuengamme, and Helmstedt, where he worked in the salt mines for a year. A solid man, more than 200 pounds, he weighed less than 120 when he returned to Paris at the war's end. Soon after, however, he was at work on *L'Univers Concentrationnaire*. One of the first studies of the Nazi system of concentration camps, Rousset's book—translated as *The Other Kingdom* (1947)—appeared in France in 1946. In restrained and understated prose, Rousset offered a series of brief but hard-hitting compositions that begin with an ironic epigraph: "There exists a decree issued by Goering protecting frogs."

The camps, Rousset shows, offered no such protection for their human subjects. The camp network was "a universe apart" where "it is only power that counts, power derived from physical strength and guile." *The Other Kingdom*'s concluding chapter—it contains Rousset's most memorable line, "normal men do not know that everything is possible"—forms the selection that follows. The book from which it comes is not only one of the early survivor protests against the *l'univers concentrationnaire* but also one of the most eloquent.

David Rousset

The Dead Stars Pursue Their Courses

The concentrationary universe shrivels away within itself. It still lives
on in the world like a dead planet laden with corpses.

Normal men do not know that everything is possible. Even if the
evidence forces their intelligence to admit it, their muscles do not
believe it. The concentrationees do know. The soldier who has spent
months under fire has made the acquaintance of death. Death lived
among the concentrationees at every hour of their existence. She
showed them all her faces. They came to know all her exigencies. They
lived dread as an ever-present obsession. They knew the humiliation of
beatings, the weakness of the flesh under the lash. They weighed the
ravages of starvation. For years on end they groped their way through
the fantastic scene littered with the ruins of human dignities. They are
set apart from the rest of the world by an experience impossible to
communicate.

The decomposition of a society and of all the classes of that society,
in the fetid stench of destroyed social values, they came to know at first
hand, an immediate reality like an ominous shadow threatening the
entire planet with a fate in which all men must share. The evil far
outweighs any military triumphs. It is the gangrene of a whole economic and social system. Its contamination still spreads far beyond the
ruins of cities.

Few men returned from the concentration camps, and fewer still
with their health. How many of them are living corpses condemned to
a life of vain convalescence!

Yet in every one of the cities of this strange universe, there were

From David Rousset, *The Other Kingdom,* trans. Ramon Guthrie. New York: Reynal & Hitch-
cock, 1947. Reprinted by permission.

those who refused to yield. I am thinking of Hewitt. I am thinking of my comrades: Marcel Hic, who died at Dora; of Roland Filiatre and Philippe, who came through with ravaged bodies but their revolutionary faith intact. Of Walter, Emil, of Lorenz, haunted by the knowledge that his wife also was in a concentration camp, and yet who never wavered. Of Yvonne, Dr. Rohmer, Lestin, and Maurice, the Communist from Villejuif, racked with fever but always firm and serene. Of Raymond, his flesh gouged with blows, yet faithful to his life. Of Claude and Marcel, starving yet bearing high the dignity of their youth. Of Guy, the adolescent, and Robert Antelme, my companion in underground Paris, who came back a ghost yet in love with living. Of Broguet, the baker, who was always able to find escape into childhood dreams. Pierre, who to live built up perilous adventures. Veillard, who died at Neuengamme. Of Paul Faure, so perceptive and poised, expert at working out decisive details. Of Crémieux, who, in the darkest moments of his despair, never betrayed his art. And Martin, my most intimate companion in the days of death, an old man of sixty-six who never weakened and finally came through victorious.

All this is no small recompense.

On the positive side, it is still too soon to reckon the value of our experience as concentrationees, but already it promises to be a rich one. Dynamic awareness of the strength and beauty of the sheer fact of living, in itself, brutal, entirely stripped of all superstructures—living through even the worst of cataclysms and most disastrous setbacks. A cool, sensual thrill of joy founded on the most complete understanding of the wreckage, and consequently incisiveness in action and firmness in decisions, in short, a broader and more intensely creative vigor.

For some it brought confirmation; for most, a discovery—and a compelling one: the mainspring of idealism run down, in the destitution of the concentrationary universe, punctured delusions reveal the dependence of man's condition on economic and social structures, the true material relations that determine behavior. In its ulterior expression, this knowledge tends to translate itself into precise action, knowing how to direct its energy, what to destroy and how to construct.

Finally, the fascinating discovery of humor, not so much as a projection of the personality, but as an objective pattern of the universe.

Ubu and Kafka cease to be literary fantasies and become component elements of the living world.

The discovery of this humor enabled many of us to survive. It is clear that it will command new horizons in the reconstruction of the themes of life and in their interpretation.

The existence of the camps is a warning. German society, both because of the strength of its structure and the violence of the crisis that demolished it, underwent a decomposition that is exceptional even in the present state of world affairs. But it would be easy to show that the most characteristic traits of both the SS mentality and the social conditions which gave rise to the Third Reich are to be found in many other sectors of world society—less pronounced, it is true, and not developed on any such scale as in the Reich. But it is only a question of circumstances. It would be blindness—and criminal blindness, at that—to believe that, by reason of any difference of national temperament, it would be impossible for any other country to try a similar experiment. Germany interpreted, with an originality in keeping with her history, the crisis that led her to the concentrationary universe. But the existence and the mechanism of that crisis were inherent in the economic and social foundations of capitalism and imperialism. Under a new guise, similar effects may reappear tomorrow. There remains therefore a very specific war to be waged. The lessons learned from the concentration camps provide a marvelous arsenal for that war. And the German anti-Fascists, interned for more than ten years, should be our invaluable comrades in arms in such a fight.

JOHN K. ROTH, the Russell K. Pitzer Professor of Philosophy at Claremont McKenna College and the co-editor of this volume, was born in Grand Haven, Michigan, in 1940. A Christian, Roth concentrates on the Holocaust largely because that event indicts—and has fundamental implications for—the Christian tradition. His seventeen books include *A Consuming Fire: Encounters with Elie Wiesel and the Holocaust* and *Approaches to Auschwitz: The Holocaust and Its Legacy* (with Richard L. Rubenstein). In 1982, he was visiting professor of Holocaust studies at the University of Haifa, Israel. Owing significantly to his many years of teaching and writing about the Holocaust, Roth was named the 1988 Professor of the Year for the United States and Canada by the Council for Advancement and Support of Education and the Carnegie Foundation for the Advancement of Teaching.

In his essay "On Losing Trust in the World," Roth meditates on the theme introduced earlier by Jean Améry in his reflections on "Torture." Améry observes that "every day anew I lose my trust in the world," and cites as one reason that "every morning when I get up I can read the Auschwitz number on my forearm." Améry contends that trust in the world, called into question as it was by the Holocaust, can never be regained. Though Améry may be correct, Roth explores the possibility that trust might still be mended.

John K. Roth

On Losing Trust in the World

Jean Améry, lone child of a Catholic mother and a Jewish father, was born in Vienna on October 31, 1912. He fled Nazism by going to Belgium in 1938. There he later joined the Resistance. Captured by the Gestapo in 1943, he was sent to a series of concentration camps, including Auschwitz. Liberated from Bergen-Belsen in 1945, Améry went on to write a series of remarkable essays about his Holocaust experiences. One of them is simply titled "Torture." It drove Améry to the following observation: "The expectation of help, the certainty of help, is indeed one of the fundamental experiences of human beings. . . ." But the gravest loss produced by the Holocaust, he suggested, was that it radically undermined that "element of trust in the world . . . the certainty that by reason of written or unwritten social contracts the other person will spare me—more precisely stated, that he will respect my physical, and with it also my metaphysical, being."[1] Jean Améry took his own life on October 17, 1978. That fact, along with a host of other particularities generated by the Holocaust, compels one to assess what losing trust in the world can mean.

In the spring of 1942, while Améry resisted Nazism, SS officer Ernst Biberstein went east. He had already been involved in deporting Jews to killing centers, but his new assignment would take him from an administrative post into the field to relieve an officer in *Einsatzgruppe* C. One of four Nazi squadrons charged with eliminating Jews behind the lines of the German advance into Russia, *Einsatzgruppe* C policed the Ukraine. Among its credits was the murder

From Alan Rosenberg and Gerald E. Myers, eds., *Echoes from the Holocaust: Philosophical Reflections on a Dark Time*. Philadelphia: Temple University Press, 1988. Copyright © 1988 by Temple University Press. All rights reserved. Reprinted by permission.

of more than 33,000 Jews at Babi Yar the previous September, a task accomplished in only two days. Biberstein missed Babi Yar, but he did nothing to diminish the record of his unit once he assumed command. It was unnecessary to deport thousands of Jews because Biberstein and his men worked efficiently. This Nazi, however, was not bloodthirsty. No evidence shows that he actively sought to lead a crew of killers or that he relished the operations carried out by those under his command. His is only one example within a spectrum of activity that included not only direct participation in murder but also the many sorts of complicity required to make a process of destruction happen. And yet when we think about losing trust in the world, Biberstein's case makes us wonder. It does so because, prior to his joining the SS in 1936, Biberstein had been a Protestant pastor.

As Biberstein moved from killing by administrative decision to killing by ordering executioners to fire machine guns, a young German soldier reached Munich, following orders that transferred him to the university there for training as a medic. Earlier, his letters alluded to events that had shaken him to the core. "I can't begin to give you the details," he wrote, "it is simply unthinkable that such things exist. . . . The war here in the East leads to things so terrible I would never have thought them possible."[2] Willi Graf referred not to combat against Russian troops but to slaughter by the *Einsatzgruppen*.

In Munich two of Graf's closest friends were Hans and Sophie Scholl, both in their early twenties. Motivated by an understanding of Christianity and a love for Germany that were at odds with Hitler's, the Scholls were determined to do more than ask helplessly, "What can we do?" With Hans in charge, their public dissent began. Although they possessed abundant courage, ingenuity, and high ideals, their power was scant. Nonetheless, along with their philosophy professor, Kurt Huber, fifty-one, and fellow students Alex Schmorell, Christoph Probst, and Willi Graf, leaflets from their resistance movement, The White Rose, attacked Nazism.

German resistance to Hitler remained scattered. It did not land many telling blows, as the Scholls' effort seems to demonstrate. Their group operated for less than a year, its output restricted to several thousand copies of seven different flyers. The war and the death camps churned on for more than two years after the White Rose was crushed. The results seem paltry, but a second glance is in order. The war was still in Hitler's favor when the students' protest began in 1942. By the time the Scholls were caught, that tide had turned at Stalingrad. The White Rose could assume no credit for this reversal, but the Nazis did take its activity seriously, all the more so as Hitler's war plans began to collapse. Nazi justice proceeded quickly. On February 22, 1943, only four days after their arrest, the Scholls and Christoph Probst stood trial. Eight hours later they were beheaded. Again the question, What can anyone do? comes to mind. Sophie Scholl's testimony, documented by the court that convicted her, was that "somebody, after all, had to make a start."3

The lives of Jean Améry, Ernst Biberstein, and Hans and Sophie Scholl unfolded in the midst of modernized economic systems, technological capabilities, and political structures that have produced abundant blessings but also surplus people, unique forms of human domination, and unprecedented quantities of mass murder. As the Holocaust exemplified, the modern political state may not flinch from putting its apparatus of destruction into action. If a ruling elite retains control over this overwhelming power, the more ordinary man or woman seems to fall impotently before it.

The truth about the Holocaust cannot be approached unless one grasps the fact that twentieth-century states may progressively squeeze the individual into obedience devoid of dissent. As people become aware of this reality, however, they are tempted to put the Holocaust into a deterministic framework. What happened seems inescapable, individual responsibility recedes, and, as a consequence, trust in the world suffers. Such a deterministic outlook is as dangerous as it is easy, for it is the stuff of which indifference is made. The truth about the Holocaust cannot be taught unless indifference is resisted, and thus the importance of remembering that, from time to time, courageous resistance did save lives and prevent the Nazis from doing their worst. Many Jews resisted. Some Gentiles did, too, including a few from deep within the German system itself. If Jewish losses did not exceed two-thirds of European Jewry and one-third of the Jewish people worldwide, the credit does not belong entirely to Allied military might. Persons acting as individuals or within small groups made their contributions as well.

The immensity of the Holocaust becomes too impersonal and more inevitable than it really was if one overlooks the fact that individuals did make the decisions and obey the orders that destroyed millions. To drive home that lesson is one of the most important philosophical insights to derive from the Holocaust. By exploring realistically, moreover, what people did or could have done in the midst of the destruction process, perhaps we can glimpse ways to redeem at least some fragments of the trust in the world that the Holocaust destroyed. Consider, therefore, the question put to an imprisoned Franz Stangl, formerly the commandant of Sobibor and Treblinka, on June 27, 1971, by the journalist Gitta Sereny. "Do you think," she asked near the end of a long series of interviews, "that that time in Poland taught you anything?"[4] To be more specific, it is crucial to ask, Could Franz Stangl have left the path that took him to Treblinka where he occupied a middle-management position requiring him to see that others carried out the murderous responsibilities handed to him? And if he could have done so, would it have made any difference if he had?

Simon Wiesenthal, the famed Nazi hunter, was once quoted as saying that "if I had done nothing else in life but to get this evil man Stangl, then I would not have lived in vain" (p. 351; page references in this and the following paragraph are to Sereny's *Into That Darkness*). At the time, Stangl was on trial in Düsseldorf, Germany, having been extradited from Brazil, where on February 28, 1967, he was arrested in Brooklin, one of the better residential areas of São Paulo. Although Stangl had never flaunted his past, neither was he in hiding. In 1945 American authorities knew about his activity at Treblinka, but Stangl fled to Rome. Assisted by clergy in the Vatican, he obtained a Red Cross passport—it reversed his name from Franz P. to Paul F. Stangl— and then moved on to Damascus, following a route used before and since by his SS peers. Before long he sent for his wife and children, who traveled under their own names and told the Austrian police of their destination. In 1954 the Stangls openly entered Brazil, register-ing at the Austrian consulate in São Paulo. Eventually employed by Volkswagen, Stangl had made a new beginning.

Although the surprise was less that Stangl had been found than that he had ever been lost, his court appearance brought the darkness of his past to light. On December 22, 1970, he was sentenced by a West German court to life imprisonment. Early in April of the next year, Gitta Sereny met him for the first time. This meeting occurred because Sereny, who had covered Stangl's trial, became convinced that he was "an individual of some intelligence" and that "things had happened to and inside him which had happened to hardly anyone else, ever" (pp. 13, 23). Stangl used the initial interview to rebut accusations made against him, but Sereny was after something more, "some new truth which would contribute to the understanding of things that had never yet been understood" (p. 23). She encouraged Stangl to provide it, promising "to write down exactly what he said, whatever it would be, and that I would try—my own feelings notwithstanding—to understand without prejudice" (pp. 23–24).

After deliberating, Stangl agreed. In fits and starts the layers of his life unfolded in the seventy hours of conversation held in April and June 1971. First published in the *Daily Telegraph Magazine*, these dialogues were later elaborated into book form. In addition to keeping her promise to Stangl, Sereny provides an account more valuable than Rudolf Hoess's autobiographical description of his career as the commandant of Auschwitz.[5] For Sereny went on to interview Stangl's family, many of his associates, and other Holocaust authorities in compiling her narrative. Even after all of the cross-checking, elements of the Stangl story remain open to conjecture, but Sereny's work has the advantage of multiple dimensions missing in Hoess's confession.

Born in 1908 in the small Austrian town of Altmünster, Stangl claimed that he was "scared to death" of his father, a former soldier, who died of malnutrition when his son was eight.[6] Leaving school at fifteen to become an apprentice weaver, he was good at the work and soon supervised others. Music and sailing were his diversions. Looking back, Stangl called these years "my happiest time." In the Austria of the 1930s, however, the young man saw that a lack of higher education would prevent him from further promotions in the textile field. Police work attracted him as an alternative, particularly since it might enable him to assist in checking the turbulence that economic depression had brought to his country. He passed the required entrance examination in 1931 and was notified to report to the Linz barracks for training. Upon announcing his departure, Stangl learned that his textile employer had been planning to send him to Vienna for additional schooling. When Sereny asked whether he still could have seized that opportunity, Stangl responded that his boss "didn't ask me" (pp. 27, 28; page references here and in the following ten paragraphs are to Sereny's *Into That Darkness*).

Stangl's account frequently reveals his passivity, a sense of being conscripted into circumstances beyond his control. A case in point is his early affiliation with the Nazis. It remains unclear whether Stangl was an illegal Nazi in Austria prior to the *Anschluss* (March 1938), but he offered the following story. As a young police officer he was decorated for meritorious service, including special recognition for seizing a Nazi arms cache shortly after Engelbert Dollfuss, the Austrian chancellor, was assassinated in July 1934. That achievement would plague Stangl, but the immediate result was his posting to Wels as a political investigator "to ferret out anti-government activities" (p. 29). Stangl, now married, claims to have had no Nazi sympathies at this time, but in 1938 his situation changed. Early on the National Socialists purged the Austrian police. Among the first victims were three of Stangl's colleagues who had received the same decoration that had come to him for his raid against the Nazis some years before. Out of fear, Stangl told Sereny, he arranged for a friend to enter his name on a list that would certify his having been a Nazi party member for the previous two years.

According to Stangl, the die was cast: "It wasn't a matter of choosing to stay or not stay in our profession. What it had already become, so quickly, was a question of survival" (p. 35). Thus, Stangl remained in police work after his branch was absorbed into the Gestapo in January 1939. Over his wife's objections, he also signed the standard statement that identified him as a *Gottgläubiger*, a believer in God, but severed his ties with the Roman Catholic church. The next decisive step on the path to Treblinka came in November 1940 when Stangl was ordered to Berlin.

These orders, signed by Heinrich Himmler, transferred Stangl to the General Foundation for Institutional Care (Gemeinnützige Stiftung für Heil und Anstaltspflege). This foundation, one unit in the larger network code-named T-4 because its headquarters were at Tiergartenstrasse 4, helped to administer T-4's program of "mercy killing" of the mentally and physically handicapped in Germany and Austria. Stangl was to be a leading security officer in this secret operation. He reports that the assignment was presented to him as a choice, though prudence ruled out the alternatives. Thus, when Stangl returned to Austria, his new post was at a euthanasia center not far from Linz, Schloss Hartheim, which later on would kill Jews from the concentration camp nearby at Mauthausen.

The activities of T-4 were under Hitler's personal control. Moreover, the euthanasia project, which used carbon monoxide gas, had the blessing of influential German scientists and physicians. It lasted many months and claimed some 100,000 lives. Public protest led by prominent German Christians helped stall this death machine in August 1941, but by then the project's goals were virtually achieved. The euthanasia program was probably not consciously devised as a training ground for staff to carry out the Final Solution, but it cannot be sheer coincidence that personnel from Schloss Hartheim and other centers regrouped in Poland to officiate at the death camps. In February 1942, for example, T-4 offered Franz Stangl a new choice: Either report back to Linz, where he would be subject to a superior whom he feared, or take a position in the East near Lublin. This "either or" was no accident either. The Berlin officials were confident that Stangl would choose Poland, and he did. Soon after arriving there, he learned that his commanding officer, SS General Odilo Globocnik, "intended confiding to me the construction of a camp called Sobibor" (p. 103).

Nazi objectives called for much of western Poland to be incorporated into the Reich. Jews from that area would be deported to the Polish interior, an area referred to as the *Generalgouvernement*, where they would be ghettoized with countless other Jews from this region and eventually exterminated. In the *Generalgouvernement*, Globocnik, assisted by Christian Wirth and a team of T-4's euthanasia experts under Wirth's direction, had overall command of "Operation Reinhard," named for its mastermind, Reinhard Heydrich, who had been assassinated in the spring of 1942 by Czech patriots.

The pure death camps opened by Globocnik in the *Generalgouvernement* during 1942—Belzec (March), Sobibor (May), and Treblinka (July)—were in administrative channels that led directly to Hitler's chancellery. In contrast, Auschwitz and Maidanek, the latter also in this zone, remained under the authority of the Main Office of Economic Administration (WVHA, Wirtschaft-Verwaltungshauptamt) because they were labor installations as well. Himmler often sought to intensify the zeal of his underlings through competition, and thus he had given Hoess sole charge of Auschwitz. Rivalry ensued, but if Globocnik, Wirth, and their associates finished second to Hoess as architects of mass death, they certainly were not failures. Before Belzec, Sobibor and Treblinka were shut down less than two years later, they destroyed nearly two million Jews and thousands of Gypsies, children making up one-third of the total. Sereny reports that the survivors of these camps—"work-Jews" who had to help run them—numbered under one hundred.

Stangl claims not to have known at first the purpose of his construction project at Sobibor, but ignorance vanished when he was taken to Belzec to witness the first large-scale extermination with permanent chambers using exhaust gas. He learned that Sobibor would do likewise and that he would be in charge. Back at Sobibor, Stangl discussed the options with a friend: "We agreed that what they were doing was a crime. We considered deserting—we discussed it for a long time. But how? Where could we go? What about our families?" (p. 113). Stangl applied for a transfer. He got no reply, but in June he did receive a letter from his wife. She wrote that his superiors were arranging for her to bring the Stangl children to Poland for a visit.

Sobibor opened in mid-May 1942 and operated for two months. Then the equipment malfunctioned, and exterminations ceased until October. Meanwhile the Stangl family arrived, lodging at an estate about three miles from the camp. Heretofore Stangl had kept his wife in the dark about the particulars of his work at Schloss Hartheim and in Poland. Now she learned the truth about Sobibor from one of her husband's subordinates. Apparently the possibility of an open confrontation that might lead to his wife's rejection of him was more than Stangl could risk. He not only told her that he had no direct responsibility for any killing but also arranged a speedy departure for his family. By the time they were back home in Austria, Stangl had been transferred to Treblinka.

Franciszek Zabecki, one of the persons interviewed by Gitta Sereny, was a member of the Polish underground. As traffic supervisor at the Treblinka railway station, he tracked German military movements and also became "the only trained observer to be on the spot throughout the whole existence of Treblinka camp" (p. 149). Zabecki counted the extermination transports, recording the figures marked on each car. "The number of people killed in Treblinka was 1,200,000," he testifies, "and there is no doubt about it whatever" (p. 250).

Dr. Irmfried Eberl, formerly in charge of a euthanasia center at Bernburg near Hanover, was the builder and first commandant of Treblinka. His administration had been wanting in Globocnik's eyes, and thus Stangl replaced him, describing his arrival there as an entry into Dante's Inferno. Stangl rationalized that his major assignment was to care for the riches left behind by those on their way to the gas. "There were enormous—fantastic—sums involved and everybody wanted a piece of it, and everybody wanted control" (p. 162). Indeed, Stangl argued, the main reason for the extermination of the Jews was that the Nazis were after their money. At least one Jewish survivor, Alexander Donat, does not disagree completely. He credits Stangl with being "sober enough to realize that behind the smokescreen of propaganda and racist mystique there was no sacred mission but only naked greed."[7] In any case, Stangl tried to convince himself that his involvement was limited to handling Treblinka's windfall. Actually he headed the entire extermination process, which destroyed five to six thousand Jews per day. The system worked, says Stangl, "and because it worked, it was irreversible." With unintended irony, he reiterates that his work was "a matter of survival—always of survival." "One did become used to it," he adds.[8]

Stangl made "improvements" at Treblinka, among them a fake railroad station to deceive the arriving victims. It was unveiled at Christmas 1942. Meanwhile Stangl was in Austria on furlough. He obtained such leaves every three or four months, but relations with his wife were strained throughout his time at Treblinka. The gassing and burning continued under Stangl's administration during the first half of 1943. However, on August 2, a Monday, which usually was a light working day because transports were less frequently loaded on Sundays, Treblinka's death machine temporarily jammed when a long-planned revolt broke out among the Jewish workers. Although the camp was set ablaze, the gas chambers remained intact. Transports from Bialystok would still end there, the last one arriving on August 19. Thereafter the camp itself was liquidated, disguised with plantings and a small farm "built from the bricks of the dismantled gas chambers" (p. 249; page references here and in the following six paragraphs are to Sereny's *Into That Darkness*). Stangl was reassigned to Trieste.

That same Christmas of 1942, Stangl had become fully assimilated into the SS, and at the war's end his SS uniform led to his arrest by Americans in an Austrian village on the Attersee. Two years later, as Austrian officials investigated Schloss Hartheim's euthanasia campaign, Stangl came to their attention. They requested jurisdiction, which was granted. Interned in an "open" prison at Linz, Stangl walked away as the Hartheim trial proceeded. Twenty years passed before he was brought to justice.

In conversation with Sereny, Stangl never stopped implying that he was himself a victim of the Holocaust. He reckoned that he was caught in a web from which he could not escape. And yet his excuses were less than ironclad, even in his own eyes. Responding to Sereny's question, "Do you think that that time in Poland taught you anything?" Stangl's final words included these: "Yes, that everything human has its origin in human weakness" (p. 363). Not twenty-four hours later, Franz Stangl died of heart failure.

Could anything have strengthened Stangl's heart enough to divert him from the course he took? That issue forms the climax of *Into That Darkness,* and at this point, surprisingly, not Franz but Theresa Stangl takes center stage. In October 1971, Sereny ended her last conversation with Frau Stangl by inquiring:

> Would you tell me what you think would have happened if at any time you had faced your husband with an absolute choice; if you had said to him: "Here it is; I know it's terribly dangerous, but either you get out of this terrible thing, or else the children and I will leave you." What I would like to know is: if you had confronted him with these alternatives, which do you think he would have chosen?

Theresa Stangl contemplated that painful question for a long time. At last she expressed the belief that given the choice—Treblinka or his wife—her husband "would in the final analysis have chosen me" (p. 361).

The next day Sereny received a note from Frau Stangl qualifying her previous statement. Franz Stangl, wrote his wife, "would never have destroyed himself or the family" (p. 362). Sereny, however, believes that the first appraisal contains the greater truth, no matter how difficult it may have been for Frau Stangl to accept it. If Sereny is correct, the web of responsibility, and of human frailty, too, spreads out. Yet one also must ask a second question, Would resistance really have made any difference? Franz Stangl, for one, had his doubts. Quizzed about what might have happened if he had refused his orders, Stangl replied: "If I had sacrificed myself, if I had made public what I felt, and had died . . . it would have made no difference. Not an iota. It would all have gone on just the same, as if it and I had never happened." Sereny accepted the answer but pressed on to ask whether such action might at least have given courage to others. "Not even that," insisted Stangl. "It would have caused a tiny ripple, for a fraction of an instant—that's all" (pp. 231–32).

Such testimony cannot be discounted. Fear and insecurity are never easily dislodged, and even if every SS man had shared Stangl's professed ambivalence about the Final Solution, an isolated defection from the ranks would hardly have halted the destruction process. Those truths, however, detract nothing from others that should be stressed as well. First, Sobibor and Treblinka testify that Stangl's despair, however realistic, does not deserve to be the last word. Second, those death camps, as Theresa Stangl helps to show, also signify that such despair moves closer to self-perpetuation whenever people, especially those nearest and dearest to each other, fail to help one another oppose the weakness that enables those in power to consign defenseless victims to misery and death. Third, had more individuals done for each other what was very much within their power, namely, to call each other to account for their actions, the Holocaust need not have gone on just the same. We are and must be responsible for each other as well as for ourselves. We must be born again as men and women blessed with the capacity to confront each other and care for each other here and now. If those points are obvious, they are anything but trivial. Not to underscore them is to create a silence in which personal responsibility can be too easily shirked and in which helpless people can be too easily found redundant and killed.

Gitta Sereny's encounters with Franz Stangl drove home to her "the fatal interdependence of all human actions" (p. 15). If those actions are to forestall progress that culminates tragically in a paralyzing doom, Theresa Stangl must be taken no less seriously than her husband, his superiors, and their obedient underlings. To discern what she and other individuals, ordinary ones like ourselves, could and could not do, including the ways in which her voice dissolves sanguine illusions about the costs of resistance, contains vital lessons about trust to be learned from that time in Poland.

On October 9, 1974, some three years after Franz Stangl's heart finally failed in a German prison, advanced hardening of the arteries felled a person who played a Holocaust role quite different from the Treblinka commandant's. Black marketeer and bon vivant, Oskar Schindler had a "life of the party" style that frequently made him an unfaithful husband.[9] By some moral conventions, Stangl was a better man than this tall, blond Czech-German who pursued his fortune in the Polish city of Kraków in 1939. Before the war, Schindler joined the Sudeten German party. Wearing its swastika lapel pin proved good for business. Hence, this industrial speculator followed the Wehrmacht

into Poland and took over an expropriated enamelware factory. Soon
he realized handsome returns by using Jewish labor, which cost him
practically nothing—at first. That qualification, however, spells the
difference between Schindler's remaining a pleasure-seeking profiteer
and his becoming an individual whose personal initiative saved more
than a thousand Jews from annihilation.

The tyranny that followed Hitler's seizure of Bohemia and Mo-
ravia in March 1939 both surprised and disillusioned Schindler but not
completely. Indeed, Schindler would go on to lend his services to
Admiral Wilhem Canaris's *Abwehr* (the foreign and counterin-
telligence department of the German High Command). What decisively changed Schindler's mind was the violence he witnessed as
special squads recruited from Heydrich's *Sicherheitsdienst* began to
attack Kraków's Jews. Insofar as those tactics targeted productive laborers, Schindler found them utterly counterproductive to the war
effort. More than that, this wasting of human life struck him as profoundly morally wrong. Deciding that he could intercede from within
the German system itself, Schindler negotiated a daring series of
bargains. If his initial purpose was to keep healthy the labor he needed
to sustain his factory's productivity, before the war ended Schindler's
obsession was more fundamental. He was determined that the hundreds of workers in his care would survive and have a future.

Schindler kept a list. It contained the names of some 1,300 men
and women who came to call themselves *Schindlerjuden*. As liberation
approached in the spring of 1945, Schindler promised he would "continue doing everything I can for you until five minutes past midnight."[10] His promise was good, just as his word had been for years.
During that time in Poland, when his Jewish workers had been forced
to live in a slave labor camp under the sadistic Amon Goeth, Schindler
spent a fortune in bribes to set up his own subcamp haven at the
factory. With the dedicated help of his wife, Emily, that practice continued when Schindler had to relocate his factory in Czechoslovakia as
the Red Army advanced. Schindler's efforts even plucked from Auschwitz some of those whose names were written in his list of life.

With the war's end, Oskar and Emily Schindler were refugees.
They had lost everything, except that they were not forgotten by the
Schindlerjuden. Under the leadership of Leopold and Mila Pfeffer-
berg, they rallied to help him when their own recovery permitted.
Among many other kindnesses, they saw that Schindler's last wish, a

Jerusalem burial, was granted. Today in Jerusalem a tree at Yad
Vashem, the Israeli memorial to the Holocaust, grows in honor of
Oskar Schindler. It testifies that he took to heart the Talmudic verse he
heard in Kraków in 1939 from Yitzhak Stern, a Jewish accountant: "He
who saves the life of one man saves the entire world." Even now,
however, the *Schindlerjuden* do not know exactly why Oskar Schindler performed his lifesaving missions.

Hoping to revive at least some of the trust that Jean Améry lost,
there are social scientists who are trying to determine why people like
Schindler helped the defenseless while so many others did not.[11] Just
as it is clear that very few of the rescuers regard themselves as moral
heroes, it may be that an "altruistic personality" will emerge from
these Holocaust studies. Whatever we can learn on that score is important. As another Jewish survivor, Pierre Sauvage, aptly puts the
point:

> If we do not learn how it is possible to act well even under the most
> trying circumstances, we will increasingly doubt our ability to act
> well even under less trying ones. If we remember solely the horror
> of the Holocaust, we will pass on no perspective from which mean-
> ingfully to confront and learn from that very horror. If we remem-
> ber solely the horror of the Holocaust, it is we who will bear the
> responsibility for having created the most dangerous alibi of all:
> that it was beyond man's capacity to know and care. If Jews do not
> learn that the whole world did not stand idly by while we were
> slaughtered, we will undermine our ability to develop the friend-
> ships and alliances that we need and deserve. If Christians do not
> learn that even then there were practicing Christians, they will be
> deprived of inspiring and essential examples of the nature and
> requirements of their faith. If the hard and fast evidence of the
> possibility of good on earth is allowed to slip through our fingers
> and turn into dust, then future generations will have only dust to
> build on. If hope is allowed to seem an unrealistic response to the
> world, if we do not work towards developing confidence in our
> spiritual resources, we will be responsible for producing in due
> time a world devoid of humanity—literally.[12]

If we neither deny our century's wounds nor submit meekly to the
Holocaust scars that deface humankind, perhaps we can have more
than dust to build on. The mending of trust in the world depends on

the determination to resist the world's horror with undeceived lucidity. Few have done as well on that score as the winner of the 1986 Nobel Peace Prize, Holocaust survivor Elie Wiesel. Speaking of the Holocaust, Wiesel says, "I'm afraid that the horror of that period is so dark, people are incapable of understanding, incapable of listening."[13] And yet Wiesel's work, including his thirty books, testifies that he does not despair. Hatred, indifference, even history itself, may do their worst, but that outcome does not deserve to be the final word. Such themes permeate Wiesel's writings. In his recent novel, *The Fifth Son*, which he dedicates to his son Elisha, "and all the other children of survivors," those themes take on nuances of special significance for all students and teachers who try to listen and understand more than forty years after Auschwitz.

The story introduces us to Wolfgang Berger, but that is not his name. He should be dead; yet he lives. This man, who is actually Richard Lander, dwells in Reshastadt, a German town. His real home, the place where he became the *Angel*, is farther east. Its name has been Davarowsk as long as anyone can remember. But Davarowsk is not the same place now that it was before. No place is. Nor is any person, whether he knows it or not. *The Fifth Son* shows as much by exploring "an ontological Event" that cannot be reduced to a word: the Holocaust. [14]

Ariel is the fifth son. But who is Ariel? That question makes him wonder. It makes him suffer, too, and not least because the dilemma drives him toward Reshastadt where he intends to be "the bearer of a message." Although Richard Lander is "not aware of either message or messenger," the *Angel* must reverse his customary role and receive both. Whether either reaches him remains unclear. Still, no reader of this novel is likely to be unmoved by Ariel's testimony.

"Was it dawn or dusk? The town of Reshastadt appears crouched and unreal under a steady slow drizzle. . . . Here is the station. In my confusion, I did not know whether I had just arrived or was preparing to leave again. Was I awake?" (p. 13; page references here and in the following paragraphs are to Wiesel's *The Fifth Son*). Linked stylistically to the work of Borges, Camus, and Kafka, this book creates intense personal encounters. Past, present, and future collide within them as the characters interrogate appearance and reality to see what sense life makes during and after the Final Solution. The resulting art—complex and simple at once—transmutes despair into determination by converting revenge into renewal.

At the outset, the author reminds us of the Torah tradition that refers to "four sons: one who is wise and one who is contrary; one who is simple and one who does not even know how to ask a question" (p. 9). But here Wiesel writes to, for, and about the fifth son. This son is different—not because he lacks qualities the others possess but because he is not there. Death explains the absence, and yet it does not because death explains nothing. Besides, even if it has everything to do with death, the fifth son's absence is not a matter of death alone.

The fifth son is Ariel. In a dual sense, he is both dead and alive, for Ariel is not one son but two. The Ariel born in 1949, who seeks and then bears his message by narrating Wiesel's story, is today a professor "in a small university in Connecticut" (p. 218). Raised in New York, a college student during the sixties, he has experienced the tumult of America during the years of Vietnam. Lisa, his girlfriend, initiates him. Sex, drugs, politics, love—they share them all. But just as "Lisa has left me," though at thirty-five he misses her, so Ariel is shaped less by the American Dream than by the Kingdom of Night he never knew in Davarowsk (p. 217).

Ariel has a brother. That fact was long unknown to him because his brother is also Ariel, the fifth son. If such facts are puzzling, puzzlement only begins to tell the tale. For there is much more to the relationship between Ariel and his brother than questions about a name might suggest. In the case of either of these Ariels, for example, it is an issue whether one or the other is truly the elder or the younger brother.

Though he is eleven years older, the professor's brother will be six forever. That was his age when the *Angel* and his SS cohort hunted Ariel down and took his life in Davarowsk. His Jewish parents, Rachel and Reuven Tamiroff, tried their best for him, although the best was not to be in Davarowsk. Ghettoized with the other Jews, Reuven led the Jewish Council there. He did so fairly, with dignity, and he paid the price. Once he learned the fully murderous intent of Richard Lander and the Nazis, Tamiroff resigned his post and told the ghetto what he knew. The *Angel* allowed Reuven to live but took the lives of six members of the Council and then readied the entire ghetto for deportation to the gas chambers.

The Tamiroffs had to board the death train. Before doing so, they took two other steps. First, Reuven met with Simha Zeligson, Tolka Friedman, and Rabbi Aharon-Asher. He invited them together to share secretly an avenging oath: " 'Whoever among us shall survive this ordeal swears on his honor and on the sanctity of our memory to do all he can to kill the killer, even at the cost of his life' " (p. 155). All save the rabbi agreed. Second, Rachel and Reuven located "some good honest people" who would hide Ariel from the killers (p. 184). Then they left him behind. Eventually Reuven learned that Lander, too, took an oath and kept it. Later he also must contend with the realization that his own resolution to kill was no match for the Nazi's.

Lander knew the Tamiroffs too well. When he spied them boarding the train without Ariel, he disbelieved their story that the child had died from ghetto disease. Keeping his word to Rachel and Reuven, the *Angel* found the boy. His vengeance was "terrible and cruel, people spoke of it in all the ghettos near and far." Since learning of it, Ariel's New York brother "cannot tolerate hot milk" (p. 185).

Learning of it—that is what obsesses the American Ariel, the fifth Jewish son who is alive but not there because he is the child of Holocaust survivors whose Ariel did not survive Davarowsk. If Rachel and Reuven endured, reunited, and crossed the ocean, they could not make the new beginnings for which America is famous. Burdened by a past too heavy, they wanted new life, even gave Ariel a second birth to affirm it, and yet they found that a second Ariel might double their sadness more than their joy. For what identity could they give him, and what identity did they give him by naming him Ariel?

No one is better equipped than Elie Wiesel to probe such issues. The two Ariels, their father, and the encounters they have—all are encompassed by his own experience. In the words of Ariel, who in this case seems to speak for Wiesel himself, "I have said 'I' in their stead. Alternately, I have been one or the other" (p. 219). Surviving the extinction of his own childhood in Auschwitz, Wiesel found his way to New York and then to marriage and fatherhood. This book is wrung from his soul. Together they give voice to the silence that threatens to dominate when a life suffers more than anybody's should. Elie Wiesel lives. So does Ariel. And so must *The Fifth Son*, because the tale has to be told. Even Reuven Tamiroff knows as much, although the second Ariel cannot fully extract the story from him until his mother is gone and he discovers the letters that his father has written to the Ariel who is not there. In the discovery, those letters become his as well, and they lead the New York Ariel to strike up a correspondence of his own with the brother in Davarowsk.

Ariel's letters to Ariel are also prompted by discovery of another kind. Part of Reuven Tamiroff's melancholy derives from the conviction that he and Simha Zeligson made good their attempt to assassinate Richard Lander in 1946. For years they meet weekly to study and debate, seeking to determine in retrospect whether their action was indeed just. Their inquiry does little to assuage the guilt whose persistence troubles them in more ways than one. Ariel's discovery goes further. It comes to include the knowledge that the *Angel* lives, prosperous and happy, as Wolfgang Berger, the Reshastadt businessman.

The business Richard Lander started must not remain unfinished. So Ariel Tamiroff, his appointment made with death, heads for Germany to encounter the Herr Direktor. Ariel reaches the station where he must change trains for Reshastadt. It is Graustadt, that gray city where one "can buy anything: a woman for the morning, insurance with a suicide clause or a lifetime ticket on the German Railroad System" (p. 200).

What happened in Graustadt and not long after is not for an article to say. Nor may it be for Elie Wiesel to determine completely. No one but Ariel is Ariel. And yet that is not where we should leave *The Fifth Son*, for the message that Ariel bears in the novel is that he did not kill. The reason he did not, moreover, has everything to do with Ariel's being Jewish, with his being the fifth son, with his being human.

How does that work? Wiesel gives us hints: Ariel, for example, receives advice from his neighbor and friend, Rebbe Zvi-Hersh, who says, " 'To punish a guilty man, to punish him with death, means linking yourself to him forever: is that what you wish?' " (p. 190). In this case, however, the question is just as important as the traditional counsel that precedes it. If "yes" is not the best answer, "no" does not follow without pain. For anyone who cares, as Ariel's "sad summing up" implies, the truth is that a life lived after Auschwitz cannot be one's own alone but instead will be permeated by "the memory of the living and the dreams of the dead" (p. 220).

That fact may account for the name Elie Wiesel bestowed on the two fifth sons. Ariel is a biblical name. It appears more than once in Scripture, and its meanings are diverse. The name can mean "lion of God" and also "light of God," which could explain why a later tradition thought of Ariel as an angel altogether different from the *Angel*. Unfortunately, a darker side haunts the name as well. For instance, in Isaiah's prophecy the following words can be found: "Yet I will distress Ariel, and there shall be moaning and lamentation, and she shall be to me like an Ariel" (Isa. 29:2). The first Ariel signifies Jerusalem; the second suggests that Ariel will become like an altar, a scene of holocaust. But the oracle sees more. In time, "the nations that fight against Ariel" will themselves be quelled by "the flame of devouring fire" (Isa. 29:6–7). Perhaps that is true—or will be—but having met the *Angel*, Ariel Tamiroff remembers an old saying: "The Lord may wish to chastise, that is His prerogative; but it is mine to refuse to be His whip" (p. 213). For both his brother's sake and his own, Ariel, whose American life has also been a scene of holocaust, will identify with his people, with Jerusalem, even though he chooses to live in the Diaspora, and thereby with the well-being of humankind. Thus, he seems most like his namesake in another part of Scripture.

The biblical book of Ezra only mentions Ariel. His name is nonetheless important and vital. For Ariel is called a "leading" man (Ezra 8:16). His leadership urges remembrance and return from exile. It means to respond to devastation and sadness by acts of restoration that rebuild Jerusalem, mend the world, and make trust possible again. Masterfully recounting the history of the Holocaust and its aftermath, *The Fifth Son* leads the same way. It is therefore fitting that Eliezer is also among Ezra's "leading men." His namesake, the author of this book, urges us all to respond by becoming like Ariel—lions, if not angels, of light who resist a losing of trust that Jean Améry equated with arrival at "the end of the world."[15]

These reflections began with the proposition that the Holocaust compels us to assess what losing trust in the world can mean. Jean Améry's testimony warns that, if unreversed, such a loss portends humankind's demise. Just because we may be closer to that outcome than we care to imagine, a crucial point of this essay is that there still can be a mending of the world. That mending, however, will not occur unless we replace the trust-destroying paths of Ernst Biberstein, Franz Stangl, and "the *Angel*" with the trust-creating ways of the Scholls, Oskar Schindler, Elie Wiesel, and *The Fifth Son*. Determination to take those steps—assessing what losing trust in the world can mean deserves nothing less than that conclusion.

NOTES

1. Jean Améry, *At the Mind's Limits: Contemplations by a Survivor on Auschwitz and Its Realities*, trans. Sidney Rosenfeld and Stella P. Rosenfeld (New York: Schocken, 1986), p. 28. See also his *Radical Humanism: Selected Essays*, ed. and trans. Sidney Rosenfeld and Stella P. Rosenfeld (Bloomington: Indiana University Press, 1984).

2. Cited by Richard Hanser, *A Noble Treason: The Revolt of the Munich Students Against Hitler* (New York: G.P. Putnam's Sons, 1979), p. 152. See also Annette E. Dumbach and Jud Newborn, *Shattering the German Night: The Story of the White Rose* (Boston: Little, Brown, 1986).

3. Hanser, *A Noble Treason*, p. 274.

4. Gitta Sereny, *Into That Darkness: An Examination of Conscience* (New York: Vintage Books, 1983), p. 363.

5. See Rudolf Hoess, *Commandant of Auschwitz: The Autobiography of Rudolf Hoess*, trans. Constantine Fitzgibbon (London: Pan Books, 1974).

6. Sereny, *Into That Darkness*, p. 25.

7. Alexander Donat, ed., *The Death Camp Treblinka: A Documentary* (New York: Holocaust Library, 1979), p. 14. Donat's book, which features eyewitness accounts by survivors of Treblinka, is a valuable complement to Sereny's work. See also Claude Lanzmann, *Shoah: An Oral History of the Holocaust* (New York: Pantheon, 1985), which is the complete text from Lanzmann's epic film about the Holocaust.

8. Sereny, *Into That Darkness*, pp. 202, 164, 200. For an important study of Nazi rationalization, especially as it pertained to the euthanasia and death camp enterprises in which Stangl participated, see Robert Jay Lifton, *The Nazi Doctors: Medical Killing and the Psychology of Genocide* (New York: Basic Books, 1986).

9. For more detail on Oskar Schindler, see Thomas Keneally, *Schindler's List* (New York: Penguin Books, 1983). The title of this account is apt, for in addition to referring to Schindler's record about his Jewish workers, the German word *List* means "cunning." Schindler possessed it abundantly and for good ends. Another remarkable story—that of Hermann "Fritz" Graebe—is told by Douglas K. Huneke, *The Moses of Rovno* (New York: Dodd, Mead, 1985). Graebe, the only German citizen who volunteered to testify against the Nazis at Nuremberg, was a structural engineer during World War II. Assigned to the Ukraine by the Railroad Administration of the Third Reich, he was horrified by the murder of nearly 1,500 Jewish men by Nazi killing squads. His response was to build a rescue network that protected hundreds of Jews. At the war's end, he used his own train to bring scores of them across Allied lines to freedom.

10. Keneally, *Schindler's List*, p. 371.

11. Perhaps the most ambitious and promising work of this kind is the Study of the Altruistic Personality Project, which is headed by Samuel P. Oliner. This sociologist is a Holocaust survivor who was hidden by Polish Catholics during World War II. His important autobiography, *Restless Memories: Recollections of the Holocaust Years* (Berkeley: Judah L. Magnes Museum, 1986), tells that story. Oliner has interviewed

hundreds of rescuers and survivors to clarify the factors and motivations that led people to save Jewish lives during the Nazi era. The findings of his study appear in *The Altruistic Personality: Rescuers of Jews in Nazi Europe* (New York: The Free Press, 1988). Although exceptions to them exist, among Oliner's more important discoveries are the following: (1) Rescuers, women and men alike, came from different social classes and diverse occupations. (2) They had learned and deeply internalized values such as helpfulness, responsibility, fairness, justice, compassion, and friendship. (3) They had friends in groups outside of their own family circles or immediate communities. (4) They had high levels of self-confidence and self-esteem and were not afraid to take calculated risks. (5) They knew what was happening around them, and, in addition, benefited from a supportive emotional network—their rescue efforts met with approval from family members or others who could be trusted. Oliner believes that, if he were in trouble and could identify persons with these qualities, his chances of receiving assistance would be excellent.

12. Pierre Sauvage was born during the Holocaust in the French village of Le Chambon, Haute-Loire, where many Jews were hidden and saved. A distinguished filmmaker, he has produced *Weapons of the Spirit* (1987), a documentary about that place. He also heads "The Friends of Le Chambon," an organization that honors those who saved Jews during the Holocaust. His words are quoted by permission.

13. Cited by Richard Zoglin, "Lives of Spirit and Dedication," *Time*, October 27, 1986, p. 66.

14. Elie Wiesel, *The Fifth Son*, trans. Marion Wiesel (New York: Summit Books, 1985), p. 208.

15. Améry, *At the Mind's Limits*, p. 29.

SUGGESTIONS FOR FURTHER READING

Czerniakow, Adam. *The Warsaw Diary of Adam Czerniakow: Prelude to Doom.* Edited by Raul Hilberg, Stanislaw Staron, and Josef Kermisz. Translated by Stanislaw Staron et al. New York: Stein and Day, 1979.

Delbo, Charlotte. *None of Us Will Return.* Translated by John Githens. Boston: Beacon Press, 1978.

Dinur, Yehiel (Ka-tzetnik 135633). *Star Eternal.* Translated by Nina Dinur. New York: Arbor House, 1971.

Eisen, George. *Children and Play in the Holocaust: Games Among the Shadows.* Amherst: The University of Massachusetts Press, 1988.

Ezrahi, Sidra Dekoven. *By Words Alone: The Holocaust in Literature.* Chicago: The University of Chicago Press, 1980.

Furet, François, ed. *Unanswered Questions: Nazi Germany and the Genocide of the Jews.* New York: Schocken Books, 1989.

Hallie, Philip P. *Lest Innocent Blood Be Shed: The Story of the Village of Le Chambon and How Goodness Happened There.* New York: Harper & Row, 1979.

Hillesum, Etty. *An Interrupted Life: The Diaries of Etty Hillesum, 1941–1943.* Translated by J.B. Gaarlandt. New York: Washington Square Press, 1985.

Lanzmann, Claude. *Shoah: An Oral History of the Holocaust.* New York: Pantheon Books, 1985.

Levi, Primo. *Survival in Auschwitz: The Nazi Assault on Humanity.* Translated by Stuart Woolf. New York: Collier Books, 1958.

Müller, Filip. *Eyewitness Auschwitz: Three Years in the Gas Chambers.* Edited and translated by Suzanne Flatauer. New York: Stein and Day, 1979.

Müller-Hill, Benno. *Murderous Science: Elimination by Scientific Selection of Jews, Gypsies, and Others, Germany 1933–1945.* Translated by George R. Fraser. Oxford and New York: Oxford University Press, 1988.

Proctor, Robert. *Racial Hygiene: Medicine under the Nazis.* Cambridge, Mass.: Harvard University Press, 1988.

Rosenfeld, Alvin H. *A Double Dying: Reflections on Holocaust Literature.* Bloomington: Indiana University Press, 1980.

Sereny, Gitta. *Into That Darkness: An Examination of Conscience.* New York: Vintage Books, 1983.

Young, James E. *Writing and Rewriting the Holocaust: Narrative and the Consequences of Interpretation.* Bloomington: Indiana University Press, 1988.

PART THREE

"Where Is God Now?"

(ELIE WIESEL, *Night*)

> Where are we going?
> *To the end of the world, little girl. We are going to the*
> *end of the world.*
> Is that far?
> *No, not really.*
> You see, I am really tired. Is it wrong, tell me, is it
> wrong to be so tired?
> *Everybody is tired, my little girl.*
> Even God?
> *I don't know. You will ask Him yourself.*

ELIE WIESEL, "A Mother and Her Daughter," *A Jew Today*

Some questions are as old as creation: Why is there something rather than nothing? Other questions are as ancient as human civilization: Why do the righteous suffer and the wicked prosper?

Some questions are new and unprecedented: Will human beings end the world as we know it by using nuclear weapons? Will we exercise our capacity to destroy ourselves and all life on earth?

In the aftermath of the Holocaust, old questions are asked anew and new questions are asked with greater urgency and intensity. The question from Elie Wiesel's *Night*—"Where is God now?"—provides a case in point. In it we hear the echo of the biblical Job, but the echo resounds with a contemporary voice of its own.

Judaism and Christianity maintain that God is benevolent, omnipotent, and immanent (though transcendent, God is also involved in history). Biblical religions deny that history is absurd or meaningless.

These faiths regard history as the domain in which the divine expresses its plan for humanity and for all creation.

The Biblical prophets spoke of reward and punishment and of a just God. They spoke of a loving and merciful deity and of the unique bond that linked God and Israel. Political defeat, military victory, famine, or prosperity were accepted as the expression of divine will. All made sense over the long range of divine time. Only the limited, temporal understanding of humanity failed to comprehend God's plan for history and our unique place in that drama.

But even the most devout believer was not without doubt or anguish. The Psalmist could ask: "Why dost Thou stand afar off, O Lord? Why dost Thou hide Thyself in times of trouble? . . . For the wicked boasts of his heart's desire; and the greedy man curses and spurns the Lord. . . . He says to himself 'God has forgotten; He has hidden His face. He will never see it.' " (Psalms 10)

Job could contend with his friends demanding to know the nature of his iniquity, the reason for his suffering. In the end, however, Job yielded—not to an answer he could comprehend but to a sense of God's presence that gave his pain a purpose.

Judaism and Christianity parted company over their understanding of the covenant between God and Israel, the meaning of the people Israel, the content of revelation, the identity of Jesus, and the timing of redemption. But both religions affirmed the ultimate meaning of cosmos and history.

For Judaism, the covenant at Sinai with the ancient Israelites bound generation after generation of Jews. The commandments are expressed in a way of life transmitted from parent to child. The revelation was to continue until the end of days, the end of history. The Messiah has not yet come.

For Christianity, Sinai was replaced by Golgotha, Moses the master by Jesus the Son of God, and the covenant with the people Israel (descendants of those who stood at Sinai) by a covenant with the new Israel (those who accept Jesus as the Christ and follow his teaching). According to Christianity, the Jews have been superseded by Christians as the people of the covenant. They, too, live in expectation of redemption—of the return of a redeemer who was once present and would come again to complete his messianic mission.

Despite these monumental differences—which have been the source of antisemitism, conflict, and murder throughout centuries of peaceless coexistence—both Christianity and Judaism stood together in their view that history expressed God's plan for the world. History was the map upon which we were to read the impressions of God's will.

Although the pious Jew and the faithful Christian might differ in their ways of life, their religious observances, their understanding of the past, and their expectations for the future, both presumed— though the former might often be the victim of the latter—that they lived in a world suffused with God's presence. This world was ultimately—and fundamentally—meaningful.

Naturally, the Holocaust was a shock to the Jewish people. Six million Jews—one third of the corpus of the people Israel—were murdered; one and half million of the slain were children. Entire communities perished, among them the most pious and righteous; eighty percent of the rabbis in the world were killed, as were ninety percent of the full-time students of the Torah.

Not only the fact but the manner of death stunned the Jewish psyche; the victims were subjected to a process of dehumanization and bureaucratic killing that robbed them of all identity and defiled their humanity prior to murder. Jewish history had seen much suffering— from the sacrifice of Isaac to the martyrdom of Hannah and her seven sons; from the Crusaders of medieval Europe to the Cossacks of late seventeenth-century Russia—but nothing in the past compared with the Holocaust.

Jewish liturgy speaks of God as a merciful father, but the cruelty of the Nazis overwhelmed even the memory of mercy. Jewish prayers speak of a God who answered His people in their time of need, but never had the Jews needed God more and never was the God of Israel less available to them than in the years between 1939 and 1945.

Jewish leaders could appeal to the attribute of God's justice, but that justice loses meaning when the nearly-achieved goal of the persecutor is biological obliteration of Jewish blood defined by the identity of one's grandparents. For those Jews living after the Holocaust, it became more difficult to speak of God as good, loving, merciful, or powerful. More difficult still is it to speak of a meaningful human history expressing a divine plan for the people Israel.

The Holocaust forces Judaism (and Christianity) to reexamine its most fundamental beliefs. As Lawrence Langer argues, "From the perspective of the victims, who far outnumber the survivors, the disorder of meaningless death contradicts the ordering impulses of time. Those who died for nothing in the Holocaust left the living with a paralyzing dilemma of facing a perpetually present grief."

As an event, the Holocaust cannot be reduced to an order, to a system for survival, or even to a sense of overriding meaning. For many, the Holocaust defies meaning and negates hope. The scope of victimization reduces even survival to a nullity.

At the end of the book of Lamentations, a scroll read in the synagogue on the ninth day of Av (the anniversary of the destruction of the first and second Temples—in 586 B.C.E. and 70 C.E. respectively—and of the exile of the Jewish people), two verses are chanted: "Return us unto Thee, oh Lord, and we shall return; renew our days as of old. Unless You have abandoned us entirely, have been angry with us to the extreme." Tradition mandates that the book not end in utter abandonment but that the verse of return be repeated so that the lament can end with the possibility of hope.

We will read five Jewish theologians in this section of the anthology, five thinkers who must contend with the problem of abandonment and divine absence. How does one find a way to end the lament with the possibility of hope? How does one speak of God, of the Jewish people and humanity, in a time of despair? The answers of these men will differ radically, as they should, because such anguishing questions cannot yield simple answers.

Elie Wiesel, whose dialogues have framed the questions we ask, speaks in the voice of the young boy he was when he was transported from the world of the Yeshiva to the gates of Birkenau. We hear him think of God in the camps, when he observes a praying congregation during the High Holidays, when he encounters a dying child hanging on the gallows.

We read of Richard Rubenstein's moment of conversion when he faced the full implications of covenantal faith in the world of the Holocaust. So, too, we hear Emil Fackenheim try to articulate the Commanding Voice of Auschwitz in a world where God was absent. Eliezer Berkovits paints a portrait of the survivors who must redeem God and Jewish history in the end of days. And Irving Greenberg speaks of the dialectics of faith when he suggests a principle of truth after the Holocaust. "No statement, theological or otherwise, should be made that would not be credible in the presence of the burning children."

We have collected significant essays by major Jewish thinkers not because the question of God's presence in history is restricted to Jews, nor because the theological issues raised by the Holocaust apply only to one faith community and not the other. On the contrary, the Holocaust raises as many questions for the content of Christian faith as it does for Judaism. The Jewish thinkers we present do not speak to their own faith community alone, nor do they confine their insights to the world of Jewish existence.

Richard Rubenstein's moment of truth came in his encounter with Heinrich Grüber, dean of the Evangelical Church of East and West Berlin, a courageous anti-Nazi whose passion for justice made him testify against Adolf Eichmann in Jerusalem but whose Christian commitments led him to assert without embarrassment that Auschwitz was the will of God. "For some reason, it was part of God's plan that the Jews died. God demands our death daily. He is the Lord, He is the Master, all is in His keeping and ordering," Grüber said. Rabbi and pastor discussed the ultimate meaning of mass murder and systematic, bureaucratic genocide; the pastor found meaning in the teaching of his faith, but the rabbi could not. Rubenstein repudiated his faith in the God of history.

Irving Greenberg, an Orthodox rabbi, speaks of the challenge of the Holocaust to Christian faith. He asks whether religions of redemption are credible in a world where, as Hegel put it, history is "the slaughter-bench at which the happiness of peoples, the wisdom of states, and the virtue of individuals have been sacrificed." Greenberg asks what faith in Jesus means in a world so distant from redemption.

After the Holocaust, Christian thinkers have been forced to confront Christian antisemitism and the fact that the Holocaust took place within the heart of Christian Europe. The perpetrators were Christians, they acted in part out of the teachings—latent if not manifest in their tradition. Important work has been done by Christian scholars—such as James Parkes, Alice and A. Roy Eckhart, Franklin Littell, Rosemary Ruether, and Paul van Buren—exploring the theological roots of Christian antisemitism. In Vatican II, the Roman Catholic Church boldly reevaluated its teaching on the Jews, altering sacred liturgy, recrafting the understanding of the crucifixion and the relationship of the daughter religion to its mother faith.

In Elie Wiesel's dialogue between "A Mother and Her Daughter" with which Part Three begins, the little girl wonders where they are going. She is tired. She wonders whether God is tired, too. A child's question, it is anything but childish when asked on the way to Auschwitz, on the way to the end of the world. The little girl's mother does not know the answer, but she knows the question deserves to be asked, confronted, and shared.

As we have seen, any confrontation with the Holocaust has the power to raise the most basic of all questions: Why creation? Why evil? How do we speak of God, and how do we speak to God? Is religious integrity to be found in obedience or in defiance? Is the religious vocation of this generation to find answers or to wrestle with the appropriate questions—those questions that are without answers?

Once the most basic questions are asked, Christians and Jews can find a common ground with each other because they need each other. The struggle for truth robs each faith of the arrogance of its certitude. Humility is the prerequisite for dialogue.

WELL BEFORE Elie Wiesel was awarded the 1986 Nobel Peace Prize, both of the editors of this anthology had written a book on his significance as a thinker. So we find it odd to write a brief introduction to only a small selection of the first of his books. There is more to the man and his work than you will read here—much more. But any reader of Wiesel's work must begin somewhere. It is best to begin with *Night*.

Wiesel only started to write after a decade of self-imposed silence. The result was his first book, *Un di Velt Hot Geshvign* (*And the World Was Silent*). Written in Yiddish, this work was condensed, refined, and intensified (dare we say purified?) into Wiesel's classic memoir published in French as *La Nuit* with an introduction by the distinguished French and Roman Catholic writer, François Mauriac. Of his decade of silence, Wiesel says: "I felt that I needed ten years to collect the words and the silence in them."

According to Wiesel, *Night* is the only book in which he writes about the Holocaust directly. His experience in "the kingdom of night" has cast its shadow on the avalanche of words he has written and spoken since he ended his silence.

What Wiesel uniquely offers is entry into an experience, into the darkness of the Holocaust and the darkness that remains in its aftermath. The sacred mystery of our time may not be the face of God, but of the anti-God and the "evil side of man." Through Wiesel's work and his persona, the non-survivor is offered a glimpse at what was and is no longer, the darkness of unspeakable horror, and of the painful but productive process of regeneration after destruction.

Night, a memoir of the kingdom of darkness, is the story of a young boy reared in the ways of Torah and fascinated by the eternity of Israel. The boy is rudely shocked by history as he is transported from Sighet to Auschwitz, from a world infused with God's presence to a universe apart—a world without God and without humankind. In the following sections, Wiesel first experiences the incongruity between the teachings of Jewish tradition and the experience of Auschwitz. As *Night* unfolds, Wiesel describes how his faith was painfully consumed by the flames that sent the bodies of the innocent and the young skyward. Wiesel writes of his move from religious rebellion to defiance and from defiance to an encounter with the void—the void of God's absence from history and from the author's personal life, the emptiness where His presence once had been.

Throughout his early work, Wiesel struggles to find meaning in his suffering, to endow his fate and the history of the Jewish people with a transcendent purpose. Only in his fourth work, *The Town Beyond the Wall*, does he succeed. The major character is a young Holocaust survivor who has made his way to Paris after the war. His mentor, the man who teaches him the meaning of survival, is not a Jew with memories of Sinai and Auschwitz, but a Spaniard, who learned of death and love during the Spanish Civil War. From Pedro, the young survivor learns two lessons that have shaped Wiesel's writings ever since. Pedro tells the young man:

> You frighten me. You want to eliminate suffering by pushing it to its extreme: to madness. To say 'I suffer therefore I am' is to become the enemy of man. What you must say is 'I suffer, therefore you are.' Camus wrote somewhere that to protest against a universe of unhappiness you had to create happiness. That's an arrow pointing the way: it leads to another human being. And not via absurdity.

Wiesel knows that suffering can shatter men and women or heal them. It can be used to unite people or to divide them. The only way to redeem suffering, and to endow it with meaning, is to treat its memory as a source of healing. In his public career, Wiesel has remained faithful to this insight.

Whether writing about the struggle of Soviet Jewry or of the meaning of the Bible, whether depicting pious Hasidim or alienated young Jews, Wiesel never dwells on suffering. Instead he invokes its memory in order to teach, to rouse from indifference, to urge that more be done, to plead for Jewish pride or human solidarity, to challenge complacency.

Wiesel is a master of the spoken word. He is the premier Jewish orator of our time, a traveling *maggid* appearing in synagogues and universities, on television, and at scholarly forums with a message that is compelling; his demeanor and voice evoke tears and laughter, melancholy and nostalgia.

Wiesel was born in Sighet, Rumania, on Simchat Torah in 1928. When his hometown—it had become part of Hungary in 1940—was occupied by the Germans in the spring of 1944, Wiesel and his family were subsequently deported to Auschwitz. His mother and little sister, Tzipora, were killed there, and Wiesel's father died at Buchenwald. Liberated from Buchenwald in April 1945, Wiesel made France his postwar home, studying at the Sorbonne and working as a journalist for an Israeli newspaper. He came to the United States in 1956 to cover the United Nations and became an American citizen in 1963. Wiesel continues to write in French and his works are translated into English, most often by his wife, Marion. He is currently the Andrew Mellon University Professor of the Humanities at Boston University and has served as chairman of the United States Holocaust Memorial Council. Wiesel's awards are too numerous to mention. In addition to the Nobel Peace Prize awarded in 1986, he has been awarded national medals in the United States and France as well as honorary degrees by more than a score of universities on three continents.

As you read his words, you will enter an awesome world. Lawrence Cunningham has described *Night* as the anti-Exodus, the journey from freedom to slavery, from light to darkness, from God to the anti-God. Begin the journey with Wiesel. He has been the guide for so many in this generation.

Elie Wiesel

Selections from Night

A week later, on the way back from work, we noticed in the center of the camp, at the assembly place, a black gallows.

We were told that soup would not be distributed until after roll call. This took longer than usual. The orders were given in a sharper manner than on other days, and in the air there were strange undertones.

"Bare your heads!" yelled the head of the camp, suddenly.

Ten thousand caps were simultaneously removed.

"Cover your heads!"

Ten thousand caps went back onto their skulls, as quick as lightning.

The gate to the camp opened. An SS section appeared and surrounded us: one SS at every three paces. On the lookout towers the machine guns were trained on the assembly place.

"They fear trouble," whispered Juliek.

Two SS men had gone to the cells. They came back with the condemned man between them. He was a youth from Warsaw. He had three years of concentration camp life behind him. He was a strong, well-built boy, a giant in comparison with me.

His back to the gallows, his face turned toward his judge, who was the head of the camp, the boy was pale, but seemed more moved than afraid. His manacled hands did not tremble. His eyes gazed coldly at the hundreds of SS guards, the thousands of prisoners who surrounded him.

From Elie Wiesel, *Night,* trans. Stella Rodway. New York: Bantam Books, 1986. Copyright © 1960 by MacGibbon & Kee. Reprinted by permission of Hill and Wang, a division of Farrar, Straus and Giroux, Inc.

The head of the camp began to read his verdict, hammering out each phrase:

"In the name of Himmler . . . prisoner Number . . . stole during the alert. . . . According to the law . . . paragraph . . . prisoner Number . . . is condemned to death. May this be a warning and an example to all prisoners."

No one moved.

I could hear my heart beating. The thousands who had died daily at Auschwitz and at Birkenau in the crematory ovens no longer troubled me. But this one, leaning against his gallows—he overwhelmed me.

"Do you think this ceremony'll be over soon? I'm hungry. . . ." whispered Juliek.

At a sign from the head of the camp, the Lagerkapo advanced toward the condemned man. Two prisoners helped him in his task—for two plates of soup.

The Kapo wanted to bandage the victim's eyes, but he refused.

After a long moment of waiting, the executioner put the rope round his neck. He was on the point of motioning to his assistants to draw the chair away from the prisoner's feet, when the latter cried, in a calm, strong voice:

"Long live liberty! A curse upon Germany! A curse . . .! A cur—"

The executioners had completed their task.

A command cleft the air like a sword.

"Bare your heads."

Ten thousand prisoners paid their last respects.

"Cover your heads!"

Then the whole camp, block after block, had to march past the hanged man and stare at the dimmed eyes, the lolling tongue of death. The Kapos and heads of each block forced everyone to look him full in the face.

After the march, we were given permission to return to the blocks for our meal.

I remember that I found the soup excellent that evening. . . .

I witnessed other hangings. I never saw a single one of the victims weep. For a long time those dried-up bodies had forgotten the bitter taste of tears.

Except once. The Oberkapo of the fifty-second cable unit was a

Dutchman, a giant, well over six feet. Seven hundred prisoners worked under his orders, and they all loved him like a brother. No one had ever received a blow at his hands, nor an insult from his lips.

He had a young boy under him, a *pipel*, as they were called—a child with a refined and beautiful face, unheard of in this camp.

(At Buna, the *pipel* were loathed; they were often crueller than adults. I once saw one of thirteen beating his father because the latter had not made his bed properly. The old man was crying softly while the boy shouted: "If you don't stop crying at once I shan't bring you any more bread. Do you understand?" But the Dutchman's little servant was loved by all. He had the face of a sad angel.)

One day, the electric power station at Buna was blown up. The Gestapo, summoned to the spot, suspected sabotage. They found a trail. It eventually led to the Dutch Oberkapo. And there, after a search, they found an important stock of arms.

The Oberkapo was arrested immediately. He was tortured for a period of weeks, but in vain. He would not give a single name. He was transferred to Auschwitz. We never heard of him again.

But his little servant had been left behind in the camp in prison. Also put to torture, he too would not speak. Then the SS sentenced him to death, with two other prisoners who had been discovered with arms.

One day when we came back from work, we saw three gallows rearing up in the assembly place, three black crows. Roll call. SS all round us, machine guns trained: the traditional ceremony. Three victims in chains—and one of them, the little servant, the sad-eyed angel.

The SS seemed more preoccupied, more disturbed than usual. To hang a young boy in front of thousands of spectators was no light matter. The head of the camp read the verdict. All eyes were on the child. He was lividly pale, almost calm, biting his lips. The gallows threw its shadow over him.

This time the Lagerkapo refused to act as executioner. Three SS replaced him.

The three victims mounted together onto the chairs.

The three necks were placed at the same moment within the nooses.

"Long live liberty!" cried the two adults.

But the child was silent.

"Where is God? Where is He?" someone behind me asked.

At a sign from the head of the camp, the three chairs tipped over.

Total silence throughout the camp. On the horizon, the sun was setting.

"Bare your heads!" yelled the head of the camp. His voice was raucous. We were weeping.

"Cover your heads!"

Then the march past began. The two adults were no longer alive. Their tongues hung swollen, blue-tinged. But the third rope was still moving; being so light, the child was still alive. . . .

For more than half an hour he stayed there, struggling between life and death, dying in slow agony under our eyes. And we had to look him full in the face. He was still alive when I passed in front of him. His tongue was still red, his eyes were not yet glazed.

Behind me, I heard the same man asking:

"Where is God now?"

And I heard a voice within me answer him:

"Where is He? Here He is—He is hanging here on this gallows. . . ."

That night the soup tasted of corpses.

The summer was coming to an end. The Jewish year was nearly over.

On the eve of Rosh Hashanah, the last day of that accursed year, the whole camp was electric with the tension which was in all our hearts. In spite of everything, this day was different from any other. The last day of the year. The word "last" rang very strangely. What if it were indeed the last day?

They gave us our evening meal, a very thick soup, but no one touched it. We wanted to wait until after prayers. At the place of assembly, surrounded by the electrified barbed wire, thousands of silent Jews gathered, their faces stricken.

Night was falling. Other prisoners continued to crowd in, from every block, able suddenly to conquer time and space and submit both to their will.

"What are You, my God," I thought angrily, "compared to this afflicted crowd, proclaiming to You their faith, their anger, their revolt? What does Your greatness mean, Lord of the universe, in the face of all this weakness, this decomposition, and this decay? Why do You still trouble their sick minds, their crippled bodies?"

Ten thousand men had come to attend the solemn service, heads of the blocks, Kapos, functionaries of death.

"Bless the Eternal. . . ."

The voice of the officiant had just made itself heard. I thought at first it was the wind.

"Blessed be the Name of the Eternal!"

Thousands of voices repeated the benediction; thousands of men prostrated themselves like trees before a tempest.

"Blessed be the Name of the Eternal!"

Why, but why should I bless Him? In every fiber I rebelled. Because He had had thousands of children burned in His pits? Because He kept six crematories working night and day, on Sundays and feast days? Because in His great might He had created Auschwitz, Birkenau, Buna, and so many factories of death? How could I say to Him: "Blessed art Thou, Eternal, Master of the Universe, Who chose us from among the races to be tortured day and night, to see our fathers, our mothers, our brothers, end in the crematory? Praised be Thy Holy Name, Thou Who hast chosen us to be butchered on Thine altar?"

I heard the voice of the officiant rising up, powerful yet at the same time broken, amid the tears, sobs, the sighs of the whole congregation:

"All the earth and the Universe are God's!"

He kept stopping every moment, as though he did not have the strength to find the meaning beneath the words. The melody choked in his throat.

And I, mystic that I had been, I thought:

"Yes, man is very strong, greater than God. When You were deceived by Adam and Eve, You drove them out of Paradise. When Noah's generation displeased You, You brought down the Flood. When Sodom no longer found favor in Your eyes, You made the sky rain down fire and sulphur. But these men here, whom You have betrayed, whom You have allowed to be tortured, butchered, gassed, burned, what do they do? They pray before You! They praise Your name!"

"All creation bears witness to the Greatness of God!"

Once, New Year's Day had dominated my life. I knew that my sins grieved the Eternal; I implored his forgiveness. Once, I had believed profoundly that upon one solitary deed of mine, one solitary prayer, depended the salvation of the world.

This day I had ceased to plead. I was no longer capable of lamentation. On the contrary, I felt very strong. I was the accuser, God the accused. My eyes were open and I was alone—terribly alone in a world without God and without man. Without love or mercy. I had ceased to be anything but ashes, yet I felt myself to be stronger than the Almighty, to whom my life had been tied for so long. I stood amid that praying congregation, observing it like a stranger.

The service ended with the Kaddish. Everyone recited the Kaddish over his parents, over his children, over his brothers, and over himself.

We stayed for a long time at the assembly place. No one dared to drag himself away from this mirage. Then it was time to go to bed and slowly the prisoners made their way over to their blocks. I heard people wishing one another a Happy New Year!

I ran off to look for my father. And at the same time I was afraid of having to wish him a Happy New Year when I no longer believed in it.

He was standing near the wall, bowed down, his shoulders sagging as though beneath a heavy burden. I went up to him, took his hand and kissed it. A tear fell upon it. Whose was that tear? Mine? His? I said nothing. Nor did he. We had never understood one another so clearly.

The sound of the bell jolted us back to reality. We must go to bed. We came back from far away. I raised my eyes to look at my father's face leaning over mine, to try to discover a smile or something resembling one upon the aged, dried-up countenance. Nothing. Not the shadow of an expression. Beaten.

Yom Kippur. The Day of Atonement.

Should we fast? The question was hotly debated. To fast would mean a surer, swifter death. We fasted here the whole year round. The whole year was Yom Kippur. But others said that we should fast simply because it was dangerous to do so. We should show God that even here, in this enclosed hell, we were capable of singing His praises.

I did not fast, mainly to please my father, who had forbidden me to do so. But further, there was no longer any reason why I should fast. I no longer accepted God's silence. As I swallowed my bowl of soup, I saw in the gesture an act of rebellion and protest against Him.

And I nibbled my crust of bread.

In the depths of my heart, I felt a great void.

SOME BOOKS ARE GOOD—they warrant attention and are well worth reading—but a few distinguished works become classics that shape the intellectual heritage of generations. A few important works are revolutionary. They change the way in which we speak about issues and set the agenda for subsequent scholarship. Richard L. Rubenstein's *After Auschwitz: Radical Theology and Contemporary Judaism* determined the nature of Jewish theological debate for the past quarter-century. Rubenstein's central premise, seemingly so obvious now, was that Jewish theology must grapple with the two radical events of modern Jewish life: the Holocaust and the rise of the State of Israel.

After Auschwitz, Rubenstein argues, the belief in a redeeming God—one who is active in history and will bring an end to the vicissitudes of the human condition—is no longer credible. Belief in such a God ultimately implies that Hitler was part of a divine plan and that the Jewish people were being punished for their sins.

Two decades following the publication of this book, Rubenstein's views may have lost some of their original sting; a consciousness of the Holocaust and its devastating implications have become central to Jewish identity. As a result, Israel and the Jewish community—rather than the synagogue and God—have come to dominate Jewish life. However, in 1966, Rubenstein's words were explosive.

For the first decades after the Holocaust, Jews responded to the catastrophe with silence. Survivors were stunned and grief-stricken. What they had seen seemed beyond communication. Furthermore, few people were interested in hearing their tale. Survivors intuitively knew that to look back too soon or too intently could be dangerous. American Jewry in particular was unprepared to listen to the survivor (then called a refugee) or to accept its current or past responsibilities. A sense of the tragic was antithetical to the American sensibilities of a post-immigrant generation.

There were a few breaches in the wall of silence, but not many. Some testimony had been given by survivors, a few works of literature had been written, such as Elie Wiesel's memoir *Night*, and an occasional book of scholarship had been completed, such as Raul Hilberg's classic, *The Destruction of European Jews*. But these pieces were read by only a limited audience. Meanwhile, suburban religious life continued to grow at a record pace. Seemingly, nothing earth-shattering had happened—either at Auschwitz or in Jerusalem—that should challenge religious belief.

The silence was broken by *After Auschwitz*. This book was accorded a significant gentile audience since Rubenstein was considered to be the Jewish participant in the then-fashionable death-of-God debate. He was featured in *Time* magazine, and soon the subject of God and the Holocaust was too timely to be ignored. Even if the messenger was denied a hearing by his own people, his message had to be pondered.

However, it was history, and not solely Rubenstein's literary achievement, that gave *After Auschwitz* its lasting impact.

Within a year of the book's publication, the Six-Day War had broken out; both Israel and the Holocaust suddenly and irreversibly returned to Jewish consciousness. In 1967, Israel—and with it the Jewish people—once again faced destruction. While the stunning victory, including the triumphant reunification of Jerusalem, reduced the level of anxiety, American Jews have never forgotten the lessons of vulnerability and abandonment.

The linkage between Israel and the Holocaust has intensified rather than diminished with time. *After Auschwitz* was the first work to connect the two events as revolutions that required a rethinking of conventional wisdom and a redirection of Jewish—and Christian— religious life.

In this part's selections Rubenstein's influence on Jewish theology can be measured. Each thinker—Emil Fackenheim, Eliezer Berkovits, Irving Greenberg, and Elie Wiesel—feels obliged to counter Rubenstein's challenge. While his work may not have provided the answers that either Jews or Christians seek for their religious life, Rubenstein has certainly raised the questions they must confront.

It is also a measure of our ecumenical age that the conversionary moment for an American-born rabbi came in the privacy of a German minister's study as the two sought to find common ground at a frightening moment—when the Berlin Wall was being constructed and the major powers appeared at the brink of conflict. The rabbi and the anti-Nazi pastor parted as friends. But if the latter seems to have been unchanged by their meeting, the former left with his faith shattered.

The echo of this encounter has reshaped Jewish thought for our time.

Rubenstein, the Robert O. Lawton Distinguished Professor of Religion at Florida State University, was born in New York City in 1924. He serves as president of the Washington Institute for Values in Public Policy, in Washington, D.C.

A prolific author, Rubenstein has many other books to his credit; the best known include: *The Religious Imagination; Morality and Eros; The Cunning of History; The Age of Triage;* and *Approaches to Auschwitz* (with John K. Roth); as well as *Power Struggle,* his autobiography.

Richard L. Rubenstein

The Dean and the Chosen People

I went to Germany in August 1961 as the guest of the *Bundes-presseamt* to make a two-week survey of religious and cultural trends. I was scheduled to enter Germany on Sunday the 13th, the day of the closing of the border between East and West Berlin. Because of the international situation, I changed my plans and proceeded to Berlin so that I could observe the crisis directly.

The *Bundespresseamt* was extremely helpful. They arranged a series of interviews for me with religious and cultural leaders. I shall never forget my interview with Heinrich Grüber, Dean of the Evangelical Church of East and West Berlin. He dramatized the consequences of accepting the normative Judaeo-Christian theology of history in the light of the death camps. After my interview, I reached a theological point of no return—If I believed in God as the omnipotent author of the historical drama and Israel as His Chosen People, I had to accept Dean Grüber's conclusion that it was God's will that Hitler committed six million Jews to slaughter. I could not possibly believe in such a God nor could I believe in Israel as the chosen people of God *after Auschwitz*.

In the spring of 1965, Dean Grüber wrote to *Christianity and Crisis* denying the words I had ascribed to him. I replied that I did not bear the Dean any ill-will nor did I have any reason to falsify his words. The significance of the Dean's assertion of God's Lordship over the death camps is precisely the fact that he was not a Nazi or an anti-Semite but a very decent human being who believed in the historic doctrines of the election of Israel and of God as the final author of the historical drama.

From Richard L. Rubenstein, *After Auschwitz: Radical Theology and Contemporary Judaism.* Indianapolis: Bobbs-Merrill, 1966. Reprinted by permission.

There is an enlarged photograph in the Jewish Historical Museum in Amsterdam which epitomizes much that Jews feel concerning Christianity's role in the "final solution." The picture was taken in Westerbroek Concentration Camp in the Netherlands at a Christmas party celebrated by the SS and their women. Those responsible for the death of over one hundred and ten thousand Dutch Jews took time out of their grisly labors to celebrate the birth of their Jewish God in the very place where they were sealing the doom of every single Jew they could find. The plain fact is that those who murdered the Jews were, if not believing communicants of the Christian faith, at least men and women whose only exposure to religion was derived from Christian sources. Furthermore, the people directly involved in the murder enterprise were not gutter riff-raff. More often than not, they were men with university or professional training behind them. In some instances, former pastors were active leaders in the work of death.

Christian thinkers very frequently point out that Nazism was an anti-Christian explosion which departed utterly from Christian morality. This is undeniably true. It does, however, gloss over the difference between those anti-Christian feelings which are rooted in a competing value system such as Islam, and the anti-Christian explosion of Christians against their own value system. Nazism was an anti-Christian movement. It was, nevertheless, dialectically related to Christianity. It was the *negation* of Christianity as *negation* was understood by Hegel and Freud. It could have as little existed without Christianity as the Black Mass of medieval satanism could have existed without the Mass of Catholicism. Assuredly the classic villains of Christianity, the Jews, became the prime objects of extermination of the anti-Christian Christians, the Nazis.

The more one studies the classical utterances of Christianity on Jews and Judaism, while at the same time reviewing the terrible history of the Nazi period, the more one is prompted to ask whether there is something in the logic of Christian theology, *when pushed to a metaphysical extreme,* which ends with the justification of, if not the incitement to, the murder of Jews. Though there is much pain in the exploration of this question, neither the Christian nor the Jew can avoid it.

Given the question of the relationship between Christianity and the Holocaust, I considered myself very fortunate when, during the summer of 1961 while on a visit to Western Germany, the *Bundes-*

esseamt, the Press and Information Office of the German Federal Republic, made it possible for me to visit and interview Dr. Heinrich Grüber, Dean of the Evangelical Church in Berlin, at his home in Berlin-Dahlem. It was my third visit to Germany in thirteen months. The first two visits were private. On this occasion the *Bundespresseamt* helped me to understand something of the complex reality that is contemporary Germany.

Thousands of Germans could have testified against Eichmann and offered relevant testimony. Only one actually testified in Jerusalem. Dean Grüber is a Protestant clergyman with a very long and heroic record of opposition to the Nazis on Christian grounds, and of friendship and succor for Nazism's chief victims. In the end, his courage brought him to Dachau and near-martyrdom. His resistance was especially meritorious because it incurred the possibility of great danger to his wife and children as well as to himself.

Since the war Dean Grüber has devoted himself to the work of healing and reconciliation. He has been instrumental in creating the Heinrich Grüber Haus in Berlin-Dahlem, an old-age residence for victims of the Nuremberg laws. These included Germans who had married Jews, Jews who had converted to Christianity, and a few old Jews who, in spite of the fury which had disrupted their lives, wanted to end their days in Berlin. With public and government support, a very spacious and attractive home has been built for these people who were the very special concern of the Dean.

In addition to testifying at the Eichmann trial, Dean Grüber has been instrumental in fostering the work of reconciliation between Germany and Israel on the political level, and between German Christianity and Judaism at the religious level. At his suggestion, on his seventieth birthday his German friends and admirers contributed well over one hundred thousand marks for the planting of a forest in his honor in Israel. He rejected all gifts. He insisted instead that the money be given to build Israel. He is also active in a German-Israel organization devoted to the exchange of visits between the youth of the two countries. He has visited Israel three times.

The Dean is over seventy, but there is a healthiness and a heartiness to his person which is noticeable immediately. He has a very attractive and spacious home, something very rare in Berlin today where, of necessity, apartment-house living is all that most people can hope for. He met me at the door and brought me to his study which was lined with books, a rather attractive oil copy of Rembrandt's *Flora*, and all sorts of relics and souvenirs of a long and distinguished career. In one corner, there was also a very impressive sculpture of the Dean's head.

After many sessions of interviewing Germans in all walks of life, I had learned to expect the interviewee to undergo a warm-up period before the initial reserve wore off. In the case of the Dean, this was unnecessary. There was an admirable bluntness and candor to his manner which revealed that the man means exactly what he says. This thoroughgoing honesty was present to the point of pain throughout the interview. It was not a quality the Nazis valued.

The most obvious point of departure for the conversation was the Eichmann trial. He explained that he went to Jerusalem with the greatest reluctance, and only after his name had come up so frequently that he felt he had no decent alternative. He also asserted that he went as a German, a member of the people who had perpetuated the injustice, and as a member of the Christian Church which had remained silent before it.

"Did testifying cause you any harm with your own people?" I asked.

He replied that it had not and went on to say that he did not really see much difference between himself and Eichmann, that he too was guilty, that, in fact, the guilt was to be shared by all peoples rather than by Eichmann alone.

"If there had only been a little more responsibility all around, things would have been different."

He complained bitterly of how the governments of practically every civilized country turned their backs on the Jews, making it impossible for them to leave. He spoke of his own efforts to secure immigration visas and complained of how seldom he succeeded.

I asked him about the Heinrich Grüber Haus. He explained that he had helped hundreds of people, many of whom were victims of the Nuremberg laws, to leave Germany. In recent years some wanted to return. Originally he had founded his home for twenty people, most of whom were Christians who had lost Jewish relatives during the persecutions. He felt that these people deserved a more comfortable life in their remaining years than most old people. It was also extremely difficult to place them successfully in the average German old-age home as many German old people were still bitterly anti-Semitic and would have objected. To meet these problems, he had built, with much public support, this very unique and very beautiful home.

Without being asked, the Dean informed me that he had never converted Jews and did not want to do so now. On the contrary, he wanted Christians to become better Christians and Jews to become better Jews. I quickly learned that the Dean had very decided ideas on what Jews ought to be and how they ought to behave.

Again continuing without being questioned on the matter, the Dean informed me that Germany's Jews today were in great danger. He said that once again Jews are influential in the banks, the press, and other areas of public interest. This surprised me, as I had been informed that there are only eight thousand employed or self-employed Jews in a nation of fifty million.

"The problem in Germany is that the Jews haven't learned anything from what happened to them," he informed me. "I always tell my Jewish friends that they shouldn't put a hindrance in the way of our fight against anti-Semitism."

In view of his long established friendship for the Jewish people, I asked him to clarify his statement. He replied that many of the brothels and risqué night clubs, for example, are now in Jewish hands, especially those in close proximity to the army camps.

"For hundreds of years, there has been a virulent tradition of anti-Semitism among the Germans. Hitler exploited that tradition for his own ends. It is very difficult for us to wipe it out. After the Eichmann trial, this is one of my tasks. I am involved in one or two meetings a week to help end anti-Semitism, but it is very difficult because of the Jews in prominent positions and those who are engaged only in seeking money no matter what they do."

In reply, I told the Dean of the feelings of many Israelis that one of the most wonderful things about Israel is that there Jews have the right to be anything they want without relating it to the Jewish problem. I put the problem to him in terms of the freedom of every man to make his own life-choices and to pay the price for his personal decisions.

"Look, I don't understand why you are so troubled about a pitifully small number of Jews in shady positions or being interested in making money rather than following edifying pursuits. It seems to me that every person pays a price for the kind of life he leads. Why should Germans be upset about the life-decisions of these Jews unless they are unduly envious or overly involved in other people's lives? Must every Jew make himself so pale, so inconspicuous, even invisible, that he will give no offense? Is that the lesson Jews must learn from the death camps, that they must prove to the Germans their pre-eminent capacity for virtue? Wouldn't it seem a far better solution for all Jews left in Germany to leave and go where they could be anything they wished, without worrying about what the Germans thought or felt about them? After what has happened, why should any Jew remain and worry about German approval?"

The Dean was not prepared to let go. He was disturbed at the thought of the few remaining Jews leaving Germany. He felt that I was correct that Jews had as much right to be anything they pleased as the Germans, but he also felt that, after what had happened, they ought not to do these things, as it made the work of ending anti-Semitism so much harder. It was evident that in his mind there is an objective relationship between Jewish behavior and anti-Semitism.

Having asserted that the Jews had as much right to produce scoundrels or ne'er-do-wells as any other people, the Dean quickly retracted. He spoke of the ancient covenant between God and Israel and how Israel as the chosen people of God was under a very special obligation to behave in a way which was spiritually consistent with Divine ordinance.

"I don't say this about Israel; God says this in the Bible and I believe it!" he insisted with considerable emotion.

The Dean was not the first German clergyman who had spoken to me in this vein. I had previously met a number of others in Berlin and Bonn. All insisted that there was a very special providential relationship between Israel, what happened to it, and God's will, that this had been true in the time of the Bible and that the *Heilsgeschichte*, the "salvation history," of the Jewish people had continued to unfold to this very day. In fairness, it should be pointed out that this belief has been shared by the vast majority of religious Jews throughout history. The theological significance of the Zionist movement and the establishment of the State of Israel lay largely in the rejection of *Heilsgeschichte* and the assertion that Jewish misfortune had been made by men and could be undone by men. For the pastors the conviction remained—it should be said that the conviction has been strengthened—that nowhere in the world were the fruits of God's activity in history more evident than in the life and the destiny of the Jewish people. In each instance I very quickly rejoined that such thinking had as its inescapable conclusion the idea that the Nazi slaughter of the Jews was somehow God's will, that God really wanted the Jewish People to be exterminated. In every instance before meeting Dr. Grüber, I was met by an embarrassed withdrawal.

Countess Dr. von Rittberg, the representative of the Evangelical Church to the Bonn Government, a charming and learned lady, was one of the German religious leaders with whom I discussed this issue. She had offered the customary interpretation of Israel's destiny as being guided by a special Divine concern, but she partially withdrew it in the face of my objection.

"Theologically this may be true, but humanly speaking and in any terms that I can understand, I cannot believe that God wanted the Nazis to destroy the Jews," she said.

Her reluctance to follow the logic of her theology to its hideous conclusion, which made the Nazis the accomplices of a righteous God, was, humanly speaking, understandable. I found a similar reluctance in the other clergymen with whom I spoke, though, because I was a rabbi and a guest, there is a distinct possibility that I did not get a truly representative sampling of theological opinion.

The same openness and lack of guile which Dean Grüber had shown from the moment I met him was also manifest in his reaction to my question concerning God's role in the death of the six million, a question which I believe is decisive for contemporary Jewish theology.

"Was it God's will that Hitler destroyed the Jews?" I repeated. "Is that what you believe concerning the events through which we have lived?"

Dr. Grüber arose from his chair and rather dramatically removed a Bible from a bookcase, opened it and read: *"Um deinetwillen werden wir getotet den ganzen Tag* . . . for Thy sake are we slaughtered every day . . ." (Ps. 44:22)

"When God desires my death, I give it to him!" he continued. "When I started my work against the Nazis I knew that I would be killed or go to the concentration camp. Eichmann asked me, 'Why do you help these Jews? They will not thank you.' I had my family; there were my wife and three children. Yet I said, 'Your will be done even if You ask my death.' For some reason, it was part of God's plan that the Jews died. God demands our death daily. He is the Lord, He is the Master, all is in His keeping and ordering."

Listening to the Dean, I recalled Erich Fromm's descriptions of the authoritarian personality in *Escape From Freedom*. All the clergy-men had asserted the absolute character of God's Lordship over man-kind and of mankind's obligation to submit unquestioningly to that Lordship, but none had carried the logic of this theology as far as did the Dean.

The Dean's disturbing consistency undoubtedly had its special virtues. No consideration of personal safety could deter the Dean from total obedience to his Heavenly Master; this contrasted starkly with too many of his fellow countrymen who gave lip-service to a similar ideal but conveniently turned the other way in the crisis. Neverthe-less, there was another side to this stance which was by no means as pleasant. Eichmann also had served his master with complete and utterly unquestioning fidelity. Even sixteen years after the close of hostilities, not only Eichmann, but apparently his defense counsel, seemed to feel that such servitude was self-justifying. Furthermore, in both the Dean and his demonic antagonist, the will of the master, in the one case God, in the other case Hitler, was unredeemed by a saving empiricism. Neither man preferred an inconsistency in logic to the consistency of accepting the gratuitous murder of six million. In neither individual was there even a trace of personal autonomy.

When Dr. Grüber put down his Bible, he could not stop himself. He told me that he looked at the Holocaust from a Biblical perspective. In the past, the Jews had been smitten by Nebuchadnezzar and other "rods of God's anger." Hitler was simply another such rod. The incon-gruity of Hitler as an instrument of God never seemed to occur to him. Of course, he granted that what Hitler had done was immoral and he insisted that Hitler's followers were now being punished by God.

"At different times," he said, "God uses different peoples as His whip against His own people, the Jews, but those whom He uses will be punished far worse than the people of the Lord. You see it today here in Berlin. We are now in the same situation as the Jews. My church is in the East sector. Last Sunday (August 13, 1961, the day of the border closing) I preached on Hosea 6:1 ('Come, and let us return unto the Lord: For He hath torn, and He will heal us; He hath smitten, and He will bind us up'). God has beaten us for our terrible sins; I told our people in East Berlin that they must not lose faith that He will reunify us."

I felt a chill at that instant. There was enormous irony in the Dean's assertion that the Germans had become like Jews. I was listening to a German clergyman interpret German defeat as the rabbis had interpreted the fall of Jerusalem almost two thousand years before. For the rabbis, Jerusalem fell because of the sins of the Jewish people. For Dean Grüber, Berlin had fallen because of the sins of the German people. When he sought words of consolation with which to mollify the wounding of his imprisoned church he turned to the very same verses from Hosea which had consoled countless generations of Israel.

He pursued the analogy between Germany and Israel: "I know that God is punishing us because we have been the whip against Israel. In 1938 we smashed the synagogues; in 1945 our churches were smashed by the bombs. From 1938 we sent the Jews out to be homeless; since 1945 fifteen million Germans have experienced homelessness."

The feeling of guilt was very apparent; so too was the fact that for him German suffering appeased and ameliorated this feeling. Everything he said reiterated his belief that God was ultimately responsible for the death of the Jews. It may have been a mystery to him, but it was nevertheless taken as unshakable fact.

The Dean had asserted that God had been instrumental in the Holocaust. He had not identified the nature of the crime for which God was supposed to have smitten the Jews. During the Eichmann trial, Dr. Robert Servatius, the defense counsel, had offered the suggestion that the death of the six million was part of a "higher purpose," and in recompense for an earlier and greater crime against God, thereby joining the modern trial in Jerusalem with one held twenty centuries before. Time was running short. I did not have the opportunity to question Dean Grüber concerning the nature of the enormous crime for which six million Jews had to perish. His thinking was so thoroughly drenched in New Testament and Prophetic categories that there is little reason to believe that he would have disagreed with Dr. Servatius. Stated with theological finesse it comes to pretty much the same thing as the vulgar thought that the Christ-killers got what was coming to them.

At a number of American Protestant seminaries, there have been attempts to study and tone down some of the more patently anti-Semitic teachings in religious textbooks and literature. Similar efforts are today being made within Catholicism. The Jewish declaration of the Vatican Council is the outstanding example. Many thoughtful Christians assert that *all* men, insofar as they are sinners, killed Christ and that the blame must therefore not be placed on the Jews alone. In the face of a crime so hideous as the Holocaust, decent men recoil and attempt to do what they can to root out the incitement to further evil. These attempts have been rightly appreciated in Jewish circles. Yet one is forced to ask whether there is much efficacy in these efforts. The fundamental issue transcends the question of whether Jews are regarded as Christ-killers. At the heart of the problem is the question of whether it is possible for Christians to remain Christians without regarding Jews in mythic, magic, and theological categories. Jews alone of all the people in the world are regarded as actors and participants in the divine drama of sin and innocence, guilt and salvation, perdition and redemption. If the Jews are an utterly normal people like any other, capable of the same virtues and vices, then there is no reason to assert that Jesus had more than a human significance. The Christian Church must insist on the separate and special character of the Jewish people in order that its claims concerning the significance of Jesus may be credible. As long as Jews are thought of as set apart from humanity by God, they are going to be the object of both the abnormal demands and hatreds of which the Dean spoke.

It would seem that as long as there is Christianity, Jews will be the potential objects of a special and ultimately pernicious attention which will always have the potentiality of exploding in violence. Even were all the textbooks "corrected," there would still be the Gospels, which contain enough material alleging the Jews to be Christ-killers—and, hence, deicides—to assure the ever-present threat of a murderous hatred of Jews by Christians. Even when Christians assert that all men are guilty of the death of the Christ, they are asserting a guilt more hideous than any known in any other religion, the murder of the unique incarnate manifestation of the Lord of Heaven and Earth. On the Jewish side, we would say that not only are the Jews not guilty of this alleged deicide, but that no man is guilty because it never happened. Here again there is an unbridgeable wall. The best that Christians can do for the Jews is to spread the guilt, while always reserving the possibility of throwing it back entirely upon the Jews. This is no solution for the Jews, for they must insist that this dimension of guilt exists for no man in reality, although they might be willing to admit that it exists for every man in fantasy.

What made the visit to Dean Grüber so memorable and so interesting was the fact that here was a Christian who had almost died because of his efforts on behalf of Jews—the Nazis kicked out his teeth and at one point he was left for dead in Dachau—yet he was incapable of seeing Jews simply as normal human beings with the same range of failings and virtues as any other group. It may be argued that the Dean's opinions prove nothing, that he exhibited a typically German incapacity to place the concrete, empirical facts of day-to-day life before an overwhelming ideology. There is undoubtedly some truth in this. Nevertheless, the Dean's attitudes, especially in view of what he has done, intensify the question of Christian theology and the extermination of Europe's Jews.

My visit did suggest one element of hope. Most Americans and Britons simply don't think the way Dean Grüber does. There seems to be something in the German mentality which demands utter metaphysical consistency. This has often been productive of much good. It has resulted in some of the greatest and most imaginative uses of the human intellect. The system of Hegel comes to mind immediately. Nevertheless, the existentialist and pragmatic protests have a validity which can be justified at least on human grounds. Human relations cannot, must not be absolutely consistent with ideological necessities. When they are, life is lost and a dead, murdering logic destroys what it cannot countenance.

Out of my interview I came away with a question for the Jewish community. Can we really blame the Christian community for viewing us through the prism of a mythology of history when we were the first to assert this history of ourselves? As long as we continue to hold to the doctrine of the election of Israel, we will leave ourselves open to the theology expressed by Dean Grüber, that because the Jews are God's Chosen People, God wanted Hitler to punish them.

There is a way out; religious uniqueness does not necessarily place us at the center of the divine drama of perdition, redemption, and salvation for mankind. All we need for a sane religious life is to recognize that we are, when given normal opportunities, neither more nor less than any other men, sharing the pain, the joy, and the fated destiny which Earth alone has meted out to all her children.

We began with a question: Does the Christian Church's attitude toward Jews and Judaism involve it in a process which, in times of stress, can lead to the murder of Jews? We must now append a further question: Does the way Jews regard themselves religiously contribute to the terrible process? The tendency of the Church to regard Jews in magic and theological terms encourages the view that the vicissitudes of Jewish history are God's will. If we accept his theological premises, there is no way of avoiding Dean Grüber's conclusion that God sent Hitler. But how can we ask Christians to give up these premises if we Jews continue to regard ourselves as the Chosen People and as the special object of God's concern in history? No man can predict the way the matter will end. There is, however, no doubt that the simple capacity of Jew and Christian to accept their own and each other's humanity lies at the core of any possibility of reconciliation between these two great faiths of the Western world.

FOR MORE THAN twenty years, Emil Fackenheim tried to establish that nothing between the revelation at Mount Sinai and the Messianic Redemption could decisively challenge Jewish faith. Like Franz Rosenzweig, the distinguished German-Jewish philosopher of the early twentieth century, Fackenheim tried to insulate Jewish faith from history. In his own estimation, he failed.

Fackenheim could not shield Jewish faith from the ashes of Auschwitz or the stones of Jerusalem. In the middle of the twentieth century, Jewish history was assaulted by events unequalled in magnitude by any other generation of Jews—save perhaps the slaves who escaped Egypt, crossed the sea, and stood at Sinai.

Once Fackenheim recognized the failure of his theological endeavor to establish an ahistorical faith, he embarked upon a long and distinguished confrontation with Jewish fate. The result was a series of important works: *God's Presence in History*, Fackenheim's initial attempt to define a theology of the Holocaust; *The Jewish Return into History: Reflections in the Age of Auschwitz and a New Jerusalem*, a theology for the generation that experienced both tragedy and triumph; and *To Mend the World: Foundations for Future Jewish Thought*, the mature statement by a senior scholar who acknowledged the rupture of the Holocaust.

In retrospect, Fackenheim's initial effort to detach faith from history appears incomprehensible. Born in Halle, Germany, in 1916, Fackenheim was trained as a Reform rabbi. A survivor of Sachsenhausen concentration camp, which he entered at the age of 22, Fackenheim came to Canada two years after *Kristallnacht* (the burning of synagogues, Jewish businesses, and homes that took place on November 9–10, 1938). After serving as a rabbi for a number of years, Fackenheim moved to the University of Toronto where he swiftly established himself as the preeminent Jewish philosopher and a brilliant interpreter of Hegel, the revolutionary German thinker who united philosophy and history.

In 1983 Fackenheim observed, "Ever since 1933, or shortly thereafter, I have been trying to respond through philosophical understanding and Jewish religious thought, to what gradually emerged as being a catastrophe without precedent, the Nazi assault on God and Man, on the human family in general and, in particular, on the Jewish people, the most radically singled out victim. And, after fifty years, I believe that the bulk of the task still lies ahead."

In the essay reprinted here, Fackenheim first articulates his view of the Holocaust's implications. Judaism maintains that God is present in history, but Fackenheim asks how one can speak of God at Auschwitz or Treblinka? If God was not present at the death camps, perhaps Judaism's faith claims are invalid.

Though such is the conclusion of Richard Rubenstein in *After Auschwitz* and Elie Wiesel in *Night*, Fackenheim disagrees.

In order to speak of God's presence in history, Fackenheim turns to the midrashic tradition—the body of rabbinic legend, myth, allegory, and exegesis—which daringly affirms God's presence in history "in full awareness of the fact that the affirmation is strange, extraordinary, even paradoxical." Fackenheim distinguishes between two root experiences of the Jewish people: the Exodus and Sinai. In the Exodus, Israel (the Jewish people) experienced God's saving presence; at Sinai, Israel heard God's commanding presence which proclaimed the Ten Commandments. Surely, God's saving presence was tragically absent at Auschwitz, but in its aftermath the Jewish people felt duty bound to obey what Fackenheim calls the "Commanding Voice of Auschwitz."

Fackenheim has captured—perhaps more intensely than any of his contemporaries—the modern Jewish response to the Holocaust. He has developed the intellectual justification for the ideology of survival. *"Jews are forbidden to grant Hitler posthumous victories,"* Fackenheim proclaims. In the following essay—first presented in the late sixties at a symposium on "Jewish Values in the Post-Holocaust Future"—Fackenheim explains the implications of this commandment. Subsequently Fackenheim has followed a path that has taken him from Toronto to Jerusalem, from political and religious liberalism to militant Zionism and Orthodox Judaism.

Emil L. Fackenheim

The 614th Commandment

Our topic today has two presuppositions which, I take it, we are not going to question but will simply take for granted. First, there is a unique and unprecedented crisis in this period of Jewish history which needs to be faced by all Jews, from the Orthodox at one extreme to the secularists at the other. (Thus I take it that we are not going to discuss the various forms of Judaism and Jewishness as though nothing had happened.) Second, whatever our response to the present crisis, it will be, in any case, a stubborn persistence in our Jewishness, not an attempt to abandon it or escape from it. (Thus I take it that we shall leave dialogues with Jews who do not want to be Jews for another day.)

How shall we understand the crisis of this period in Jewish history? We shall, I think, be misled if we think in the style of the social sciences which try to grasp the particular in terms of the universal. We shall then, at best, understand the present Jewish crisis only in terms of the universal Western or human crisis, thus failing to grasp its uniqueness; at worst we shall abuse such an understanding as a means of escaping into the condition of contemporary-man-in-general. Instead of relying on the sociological mind, we must rely on the historical mind, which moves from the particular to the universal. But the historical mind, too, has its limitations. Thus no contemporary Jewish historian at the time of the destruction of the First or the Second Temple could have fully understood the world-historical significance of that event, if only because, in the midst of the crisis, he was not yet on the other side of it. We, too, are in the midst of the contemporary crisis, and hence unable fully to understand it. As for our attitude

From "Jewish Values in the Post-Holocaust Future: A Symposium," *Judaism* 16 (Summer 1967). Reprinted by permission.

toward the future, this cannot be one of understanding or prediction, but only one of commitment and, possibly, faith.

How shall we achieve such fragmentary understanding of our present crisis as is possible while we are still in the midst of it? A crisis as yet unended can only be understood in terms of contradictions as yet unresolved. Jewish existence today is permeated by three main contradictions:

1) The American Jew of today is a "universalist," if only because he has come closer to the full achievement of equal status in society than any other Jew in the history of the Diaspora; yet this development coincides with the resurrection of Jewish "particularism" in the rebirth of a Jewish nation.

2) The Jew of today is committed to modern "secularism," as the source of his emancipation; yet his future survival as Jew depends on past religious resources. Hence even the most Orthodox Jew of today is a secularist insofar as, and to the extent that, he participates in the political and social processes of society. And even the most secularist Jew is religious insofar as, and to the extent that, he must fall back on the religious past in his struggle for a Jewish future.

3) Finally—and this is by far the most radical contradiction, and one which threatens to engulf the other two—the Jew in two of the three main present centers of Jewry, America and Israel, is at home in the modern world, for he has found a freedom and autonomy impossible in the pre-modern world. Yet he is but twenty-five years removed from a catastrophe unequaled in all of Jewish history—a catastrophe which in its distinctive characterizations is modern in nature.

These are the three main contradictions. Merely to state them is to show how false it would be for us to see our present Jewish crisis as nothing more than an illustration of the general Western or human crisis. I will add to the general point nothing more than the mere listing of two specific examples. First, we may have a problem with "secularity," like our Christian neighbors. But our problem is not theirs, if only because for us—who have "celebrated" the secular city since the French Revolution—the time for such celebrating is past since the Holocaust. Second, while we have our problems with academically inspired atheism and agnosticism, they are central at best only for Jews who want to be men-in-general. For the authentic Jew who faces up to his singled-out Jewish condition—even for the authentic agnostic or atheistic Jew—a merely academically inspired doubt in

God must seem sophomoric when he, after Auschwitz, must grapple with despair.

We must, then, take care lest we move perversely in responding to our present crisis. We must first face up and respond to our Jewish singled-out condition. Only thus and then can we hope to enter authentically into an understanding of and relation with other manifestations of a present crisis which is doubtless universal.

In groping for authentic responses to our present Jewish crisis, we do well to begin with responses which have already occurred. I believe that there are two such responses: first, a commitment to Jewish survival; second, a commitment to Jewish unity.

I confess I used to be highly critical of Jewish philosophies which seemed to advocate no more than survival for survival's sake. I have changed my mind. I now believe that, in this present, unbelievable age, even a mere collective commitment to Jewish group-survival for its own sake is a momentous response, with the greatest implications. I am convinced that future historians will understand it, not, as our present detractors would have it, as the tribal response-mechanism of a fossil, but rather as a profound, albeit as yet fragmentary, act of faith, in an age of crisis to which the response might well have been either flight in total disarray or complete despair.

The second response we have already found is a commitment to Jewish unity. This, to be sure, is incomplete and must probably remain incomplete. Yet it is nonetheless real. Thus the American Council for Judaism is an anachronism, as is, I venture to say, an Israeli nationalism which would cut off all ties with the Diaspora. No less anachronistic is a Jewish secularism so blind in its worship of the modern secular world as wholly to spurn the religious resources of the Jewish past; likewise, an Orthodoxy so untouched by the modern secular world as to have remained in a pre-modern ghetto.

Such, then, are the responses to the present crisis in Jewish history which we have already found, in principle however inadequately in practice. And their implications are even now altogether momentous. Whether aware of what we have decided or not, we have made the collective decision to endure the contradiction of present Jewish existence. We have collectively rejected the option, either of "checking out" of Jewish existence altogether or of so avoiding the present contradictions as to shatter Jewish existence into fragments.

But the question now is whether we can go beyond so fragmentary a commitment. In the present situation, this question becomes: can we confront the Holocaust, and yet not despair? Not accidentally has it taken twenty years for us to face this question, and it is not certain that we can face it yet. The contradiction is too staggering, and every authentic escape is barred. We are bidden to turn present and future life into death, as the price of remembering death at Auschwitz. And we are forbidden to affirm present and future life, as the price of forgetting Auschwitz.

We have lived in this contradiction for twenty years without being able to face it. Unless I am mistaken, we are now beginning to face it, however fragmentarily and inconclusively. And from this beginning confrontation there emerges what I will boldly term a 614th commandment: *the authentic Jew of today is forbidden to hand Hitler yet another, posthumous victory.* (This formulation is terribly inadequate, yet I am forced to use it until one more adequate is found. First, although no anti-Orthodox implication is intended, as though the 613 commandments stood necessarily in need of change, we must face the fact that something radically new has happened. Second, although the commandment should be positive rather than negative, we must face the fact that Hitler did win at least one victory—the murder of six million Jews. Third, although the very name of Hitler should be erased rather than remembered, we cannot disguise the uniqueness of his evil under a comfortable generality, such as persecution-in-general, tyranny-in-general, or even the-demonic-in-general.)

I think the authentic Jew of today is beginning to hear the 614th commandment. And he hears it whether, as agnostic, he hears no more, or whether, as believer, he hears the voice of the *metzaveh* (the commander) in the *mitzvah* (the commandment). Moreover, it may well be the case that the authentic Jewish agnostic and the authentic Jewish believer are closer today than at any previous time.

To be sure, the agnostic hears no more than the *mitzvah*. Yet if he is Jewishly authentic, he cannot but face the fragmentariness of his hearing. He cannot, like agnostics and atheists all around him, regard this *mitzvah* as the product of self-sufficient human reason, realizing itself in an ever-advancing history of autonomous human enlightenment. The 614th commandment must be, to him, an abrupt and absolute *given*, revealed in the midst of total catastrophe.

On the other hand, the believer, who bears the voice of the *metzaveh* in the *mitzvah*, can hardly hear anything more than the *mitzvah*. The reasons which made Martin Buber speak of an eclipse of God are still compelling. And if, nevertheless, a bond between Israel and the God of Israel can be experienced in the abyss, this can hardly be more than the *mitzvah* itself.

The implications of even so slender a bond are momentous. If the 614th commandment is binding upon the authentic Jew, then we are, first, commanded to survive as Jews, lest the Jewish people perish. We are commanded, second, to remember in our very guts and bones the martyrs of the Holocaust, lest their memory perish. We are forbidden, thirdly, to deny or despair of God, however much we may have to contend with Him or with belief in Him, lest Judaism perish. We are forbidden, finally, to despair of the world as the place which is to become the kingdom of God, lest we help make it a meaningless place in which God is dead or irrelevant and everything is permitted. To abandon any of these imperatives, in response to Hitler's victory at Auschwitz, would be to hand him yet other, posthumous victories.

How can we possibly obey these imperatives? To do so requires the endurance of intolerable contradictions. Such endurance cannot but bespeak an as yet unutterable faith. If we are capable of this endurance, then the faith implicit in it may well be of historic consequence. At least twice before—at the time of the destruction of the First and of the Second Temples—Jewish endurance in the midst of catastrophe helped transform the world. We cannot know the future, if only because the present is without precedent. But this ignorance on our part can have no effect on our present action. The uncertainty of what will be may not shake our certainty of what we must do.

ELIEZER BERKOVITS' "In the Beginning Was the Cry: A Midrash for Our Times" is presented for the first time in this anthology. Like its author, this contemporary midrash is bold and brave, wrestling with the two central questions of Jewish mysticism: why did God create the world, and why do the righteous suffer?

These questions have preoccupied Berkovits for a quarter of a century. For many years the Rumanian-born scholar taught at the Hebrew Theological College in Skokie, Illinois, an Orthodox rabbinical seminary that unites secular learning and traditional Talmudic study. A distinguished Talmudist and student of Jewish law, Berkovits is equally well-versed in Jewish philosophy. Among his other works are *Toward Historic Judaism; God, Man and History; Major Themes in Modern Jewish Thought,* which won the National Jewish Book Award in 1975; and *With God in Hell.*

Berkovits is the first Orthodox thinker who responded to Richard Rubenstein's *After Auschwitz* with a book-length work reassessing traditional Jewish theodicy. "Man can only exist," Berkovits writes in *Faith after the Holocaust,* "because God renounces the use of power on him. . . . History is the arena of human responsibility and its product." For Berkovits, the question raised by the Holocaust is not "where was God?" but "what is man?" How can we believe in human goodness after Auschwitz? Man—not God—must bear chief responsibility for the event.

How, then, are we to understand divine omnipotence? According to Berkovits, God shackles His might so that history may be possible. For Berkovits, history is the domain of human activity: "Yet all this does not exonerate God for all the suffering of the innocent in history. God is responsible for having created a world in which man is free to make history." Berkovits maintains that there must be a dimension beyond history where all suffering finds its redemption through God.

While the responsibility for history belongs to humanity, the responsibility for the *creation* of history belongs to God. In effect, Berkovits has deferred the problem of history to the end of days. His attitude toward that end is one of trust—and of expectation. He trusts "that in God the tragedy of man may find its transformation."

More than two decades after writing *Faith after the Holocaust*, Berkovits has presented a visionary image for the end of days. This midrash invites interpretation.

Like many of the scholars who have wrestled with Holocaust questions, Berkovits' images of the divine and human predicament have grown more bleak over time. As we read his modern midrash, let us ask ourselves about the end of history: Why is resurrection not the answer? What is the limit to God's power? What is the role of those who have experienced the absurdity of existence? What must they do for humanity and God?

Eliezer Berkovits

In the Beginning Was the Cry

Finally the end came. The *aharit hayamim*. Not exactly the "End of Days" of which the prophets of Israel had spoken, but the end of life on earth. Scientists had never been able to decide whether or not the world had come into being as the result of the "Big Bang," but life on earth had certainly disappeared in a big bang. Human genius had penetrated into the remotest recesses of nature and had unraveled its sources of energy. Man had gained control over unlimited stores of power. The choice was in his hand—to use this power for good or for evil. Confusing scientific advancement with human progress, he had become more and more alienated from the human aspects of his own existence. Unavoidably, he fashioned the big bang and with it his own destruction.

Before creating man, God had taken counsel with His angels. Angels, pointing to the evil that would inhere in human nature, advised Him against bringing man into the world. But God refused to accept their advice. He explained that He, the Infinite One, was in need of a Good that could not be found in the heavenly spheres, one that only man could provide.

At first it was difficult to understand the divine reasoning, but God insisted—His Good was His divine Being. It existed because He was. It could not be otherwise. So with His Truth. It could never be challenged. God could never be tempted. But He desired a different kind of Good, one that could be challenged by Evil. God wanted a truth that maintained itself against all adversaries. He needed the Good and the Truth that would be fruits of the earth. So He took the

Previously unpublished, this essay is printed by permission of the author.

chance and made man. Now that all was over, perhaps the risk had been too high. Would it have been better if He had listened to the counsel of the angels and not created man?

But all was not lost. There was still Resurrection. God had built a safety valve into the risky adventure of making man. Man's saga of self-destruction might yet be redeemed. Resurrection would be the New Beginning designed to reveal and to justify the meaning and purpose of God's old creation.

After the long age of darkness and death, new life was breathed into earth's ruins. Once again the Light of Creation lit up the sky. New plants and trees covered the earth. Rivers again flowed with living waters. Birds and animals returned to their rebuilt nests and lairs. Then, the trumpets sounded and slowly the graves opened. Millions of people emerged, clothed in new dignity. Would all the hopes of man now find their fulfillment?

Suddenly all was silent. It was like the silence of the Old World, when all nature held its breath waiting for the word from Sinai. Now the hallelujahs of the New World had ended in the stillness of expectation. All awaited the New Word, the Ultimate Revelation. But gradually the silence of the New Hope was invaded by a silence of divine embarrassment. The New Word was not heard. Was Resurrection faulty, too?

The New Man looked around searchingly. Then he beheld the blemish in all that new glory. There they stood—the Girl, the Sister, the Mother, the Man—motionless, in complete separateness, indifferent to the new life, to its hope and promise. Indignation rose against the Four. They were delaying the ultimate fulfillment. As each continued in his isolation, indignation gave way to anger. Was it the beginning of hatred? Was mankind, awakened to new life, reverting to the vices of the old Adam? Something must be done to resolve the mystery. As the tension approached its breaking point, the heavenly court asked for the records. Who were the Four? Was some experience haunting their memory? Was it a memory from the hour of their death?

The records were brought and the members of the court began reading.

The Girl was sixteen years old. She had met her death in a German death camp by a bullet fired at her head by a member of the Sonderkommando. Among the millions forced into the gas chambers, she alone had survived. By some freak chance, she was pushed face down into a pool of water which protected her against the poisonous fumes. She heard and saw it all. The cries, the despair, the chaos. As the bodies piled up around her, the stronger climbed over the weaker towards the air not as yet contaminated. Many lost control of their bodily functions, their excrements covering those below. When all was over and the Sonderkommando came to remove the bodies, they found the Girl still breathing. They took and hid her for several days, but the moment came when they had to rid themselves of the incriminating burden.

The Sister lived in the Warsaw ghetto. Of her entire family only she and her brother had survived. Together they found refuge in an attic. During the day they searched for food; at night they clung to each other for warmth against the cold. One afternoon as they were climbing the stairs to their room, the brother collapsed and died. It was late Friday afternoon, Erev Shabbat. The men whose task it was to collect the bodies of the dead could no longer be called. The dead boy remained lying on the stairs until Sunday. Every time the Sister left the attic to find food, she had to step over her dead brother. One day the Sister's turn came.

The Mother with her baby were hiding in a bunker with some other Jews. German police were hunting them down. When they approached the bunker, the baby started to cry. There was no other way. The Mother strangled her child.

The Man had gone through the same hell that millions of others had endured. What was known about him was learned from diary entries scrawled in the cover pages of an old prayer book. The diary contained nothing that was not known from a multitude of similar records. It concluded with the words, "I was standing behind the electrically charged barbed wire fence. In front of me I saw the road to Warsaw. I looked at the road . . ."

Was it the strange behavior of the Four that was preventing completion of the miracle of Resurrection? The New World was longing for the New Word, without which all would be vanity. What did the Four want? True, the Girl had witnessed horror no human could comprehend, but did she not see that all death had been redeemed:— that from deepest degradation man had risen to new dignity and beauty—that alive around her were the companions from the gas chamber? And why the indifference of the Sister to her brother? He stood there clothed in new strength, waiting for a sign of joyous welcome. But none came. And the Mother—how heartless she seemed! Her child had been returned, all the promises of babyhood blooming in a maturing beauty. It was longing for a motherly embrace. How could she ignore her child! But the darkest blemish was cast by the Man. He stood behind the electrified barbed wire. Why remember such banality?

The New Word was still not heard. God remained speechless. The tension was becoming unbearable. Suddenly, Father Abraham stepped forward to the divine throne with a daring that astonished the heavenly court. He who had once boldly pleaded the cause of Sodom was pleading once again.

"Almighty God, do you not understand? The Four did not die of bullets, of lethal fumes, of bodily hurt. They died of contempt for what used to be called life—like the Man who stood behind the barbed wire fence, in front of him the road to Warsaw. 'I looked at the road,' he wrote. Why did he remember it? Perhaps it was important to remember it in order to save his last words for a surviving generation. What was he saying to you, God?

"Was it not this? 'I looked at the road. All I wanted was to be able to go for a walk along that road to Warsaw. What kind of a world is it, God, where human wickedness will not let you go for a little walk?' It was then that he died, overwhelmed by the absolute absurdity of life. What is it they want? What can you give, God, to those who want nothing? The Four want nothing. They have lost all desire for life, for existence, even for Resurrection.

"Almighty God, you are omnipotent. You restored life to the dead earth. You resurrected the human race which inhabited the earth through many generations. Your utterance, 'Let there be!' restored to life the millions of Jews whose ashes had been scattered to all the winds of time. But the Four ceased to be because their souls died. They died of absurdity.

"Almighty God. You are omnipotent! But how do you resurrect dead souls?"

Once again complete silence filled the universe. At last, God spoke: "Abraham, my beloved son, I cannot."

A wailing filled the New Creation. God's cry reached the Four like a pleading embrace. The child, frightened, turned to her mother: "Mother, do you hear? Who is crying?" The Mother, seeing her child as if for the first time, hugged and kissed her and explained: "That is poor God crying. But never fear, my child. There will be another day and another and another, and we all will yet make Him smile."

At THE CORE of Irving Greenberg's work is a genuine confrontation with the Holocaust. More than any other Orthodox thinker of our age, Greenberg attempts to deal with the implications of this critical event in human history. He does not shy away from the task even when it challenges his faith and puts him at odds with his community.

The co-editor (with Alvin H. Rosenfeld) of *Confronting the Holocaust: The Impact of Elie Wiesel*, Greenberg is most closely identified with the issue of pluralism in Jewish life. His widely publicized, award-winning essay "Will There Be One Jewish People in the Year 2,000?" catapulted the problem of Jewish unity to the forefront of communal concerns. Although he was not the first to note the dangers of a schism, his essay drew significant attention. Having left the comfort of a secure academic appointment at New York's City College, Greenberg created CLAL—the National Jewish Center for Learning and Leadership—in order to promote intra-Jewish dialogue.

Although a popular theologian, the form of Greenberg's many publications often masks an intensive, systematic theological endeavor in which Jewish thought is reformulated in the aftermath of the Holocaust and the rise of the State of Israel. With exceptions such as "Cloud of Smoke, Pillar of Fire" (a condensed version of this seminal work follows), the bulk of Greenberg's works has appeared in pamphlets, oral presentations, and newspapers articles—odd but important forums for serious theological discourse.

With each publication, Greenberg refines the implications of his original insight that the Holocaust and the State of Israel have initiated the third great era in Jewish history. The very nature of the divine-human relationship is being transformed before our eyes, according to Greenberg. Even though the *content* of that covenant has been altered and the relationship between God and the Jewish people has changed, continuity remains in the covenant that binds Israel and God.

The descendant of a distinguished rabbinic family, Greenberg was born in New York City in 1933. An ordained rabbi, Greenberg is also a

Harvard-trained American historian. Unlike most of his Orthodox colleagues who speak of the simultaneity of Biblical and Rabbinic teaching—written and oral revelation—Greenberg daringly writes of transformations and discontinuities, of the shifting role between Israel and God and the revolutionary impact of history.

According to Greenberg, in the Biblical era God is more active. Divine intervention includes commandment and historical reward. The human role is essentially passive and obedient. The symbol of the covenant, circumcision, is "sealed into Jewish physical existence, and thus is experienced in part as 'involuntary.'"

In the Rabbinic era, Jews were called by God to a new level of covenantal existence. "God had 'constricted' or imposed self-limitation to allow the Jews to take on true partnership in the covenant." Direct revelation ceased, Greenberg argues, "yet even as Divine Presence became more hidden, it became more present; the widening of ritual contact with the Divine goes hand in hand with increased hiding." Divine presence is to be found in Torah study and in deeds of kindness and graciousness; God is not only in the Temple but in a seemingly secular environment.

Greenberg also speaks of a shattered covenant in the Holocaust. Following Elie Wiesel and Jacob Glatstein, Greenberg recognizes that the Holocaust has altered our perceptions of God and humanity. He offers a powerful verification principle, which must become the test of religious integrity after the Holocaust. "No statement, theological or otherwise, should be made that would not be credible in the presence of the burning children."

Greenberg argues that the covenant was broken in the Holocaust, but the Jewish people chose voluntarily to renew it. "We are in the age of the renewal of the covenant. God is no longer in a position to command, but the Jewish people are so in love with the dream of redemption that they volunteered to carry out the mission." The choice to remain Jews, Greenberg argues, is a response to the covenant with God and between generations of Jews.

Greenberg gives new meaning to the religious vocation of our age. The task of Jewish existence—and of all authentic religious existence after the Holocaust—is to recreate the divine and human images that were destroyed in the Holocaust, to respond to death by creating life, and to continue the Jewish people's journey in history. Jews must labor to bring redemption.

Unlike other Jewish theologians who denounce Christianity for its indifference and its participation in the Holocaust, Greenberg also explores the implications of the Holocaust for the Christian vision of God, humanity, and redemption. This theological treatment paved the way for authentic Christian encounters with the Holocaust, such as those found in the work of Paul van Buren and Robert McAfee Brown. The following essay was originally the keynote address for an international symposium on the Holocaust held at the Cathedral of Saint John the Divine, in New York City, June 3–6, 1974.

Paul Tillich once wrote that the theologian must stand both inside and outside the theological circle of faith. He must describe the spirituality that is the hallmark of a religious tradition while also understanding the world beyond the circle of faith. A denizen of two worlds, the theologian must explain one domain to another.

Greenberg clearly follows Tillich's dictum. He describes the power, passion, and poignancy of traditional Judaism to assimilated Jews and gentiles—his 1988 book *The Jewish Way: Living the Holidays* is one splendid example—and he translates the attraction and the danger of modernity to those inside the circle of faith. To Greenberg's credit, he speaks to both groups without losing the ability to live meaningfully in either world.

Irving Greenberg

Cloud of Smoke, Pillar of Fire

To the memory of my father,
Rabbi Eliyahu Chaim Greenberg,
1894–1975

I. Judaism and Christianity: Religions of Redemption and the Challenge of History

Both Judaism and Christianity are religions of redemption. Both religions come to this affirmation about human fate out of central events in history. For Jews, the basic orientating experience has been the Exodus. Out of the overwhelming experience of God's deliverance of His people came the judgment that the ultimate truth is not the fact that most humans live nameless and burdened lives and die in poverty and oppression. Rather, the decisive truth is that man is of infinite value and will be redeemed. Every act of life is to be lived by that realization.

For Christians, the great paradigm of this meaning is the life, death, and resurrection of Jesus Christ. By its implications, all of life is lived.

The central events of both religions occur and affect humans in

Work on this article was supported by a fellowship from The National Endowment for the Humanities in 1974–75 and research support from the Meinhardt Spielman Fund for the Department of Jewish Studies, City College, CUNY. The author wishes to thank Professor Alvin Rosenfeld of Indiana University for his most helpful close reading and extensive editorial comments on this text as well as for a series of conversations in Jerusalem which affected the final content of this essay.

From Eva Fleischner, ed., *Auschwitz: Beginning of a New Era? Reflections on the Holocaust.* New York: Ktav, 1977. Reprinted by permission.

history. The shocking contrast of the event of salvation come and the cruel realities of actual historical existence have tempted Christians to cut loose from earthly time. Yet both religions ultimately have stood by the claim that redemption will be realized in actual human history. This view has had enormous impact on the general Western and modern view that human liberation can and will be realized in the here and now.

Implicit in both religions is the realization that events happen in history which change our perception of human fate, events from which we draw the fundamental norms by which we act and interpret what happens to us. One such event is the Holocaust—the destruction of European Jewry from 1933 to 1945.

The Challenge of the Holocaust

Both religions have always sought to isolate their central events—Exodus and Easter—from further revelations or from the challenge of the demonic counter-experience of evil in history. By and large, both religions have continued since 1945 as if nothing had happened to change their central understanding. It is increasingly obvious that this is impossible, that the Holocaust cannot be ignored.

By its very nature, the Holocaust is obviously central for Jews. The destruction cut so deeply that it is a question whether the community can recover from it. When Adolf Eichmann went into hiding in 1945, he told his accomplice, Dieter Wisliceny, that if caught, he would leap into his grave laughing. He believed that although he had not completed the total destruction of Jewry, he had accomplished his basic goal—because the Jews could never recover from this devastation of their life center. Indeed, Eichmann had destroyed 90 percent of East European Jewry, the spiritual and biological vital center of prewar world Jewry. Six million Jews were killed—some 30 percent of the Jewish people in 1939; but among the dead were over 80 percent of the Jewish scholars, rabbis, full-time students and teachers of Torah alive in 1939. Since there can be no covenant without the covenant people, the fundamental existence of Jews and Judaism is thrown into question by this genocide. For this reason alone, the trauma of the Holocaust cannot be overcome without some basic reorientation in light of it by the surviving Jewish community. . . .

The Holocaust as Radical Counter-Testimony To Judaism and Christianity

For Christians, it is easier to continue living as if the event did not make any difference, as if the crime belongs to the history of another people and faith. But such a conclusion would be and is sheer self-deception. The magnitude of suffering and the manifest worthlessness of human life radically contradict the fundamental statements of human value and divine concern in both religions. Failure to confront and account for this evil, then, would turn both religions into empty, Pollyanna assertions, credible only because believers ignore the realities of human history. It would be comparable to preaching that this is the best of all possible worlds to a well-fed, smug congregation, while next door little children starve slowly to death.

Judaism and Christianity do not merely tell of God's love for man, but stand or fall on their fundamental claim that the human being is, therefore, of infinite and absolute value. ("He who saves one life it is as if he saved an entire world"—B.T. Sanhedrin 37a; "God so loved the world that He gave His only begotten son"—John 3:16.) It is the contradiction of this intrinsic value and the reality of human suffering that validates the absolute centrality and necessity of redemption, of the Messianic hope. . . .

In short, the Holocaust poses the most radical counter-testimony to both Judaism and Christianity. Elie Wiesel has stated it most profoundly:

> Never shall I forget the little faces of the children, whose bodies I saw turned into wreaths of smoke beneath a silent blue sky.
>
> Never shall I forget those flames which consumed my faith forever.
>
> Never shall I forget that nocturnal silence which deprived me, for all eternity, of the desire to live.
>
> Never shall I forget those moments which murdered my God and my soul and turned my dreams to dust.
>
> Never shall I forget these things, even if I am condemned to live as long as God Himself. Never.[1]

The cruelty and the killing raise the question whether even those who believe after such an event dare talk about God who loves and cares without making a mockery of those who suffered.

Further Challenge of the Holocaust to Christianity

THE MORAL FAILURE AND COMPLICITY OF ANTI-SEMITISM. Unfortunately, however, the Holocaust poses a yet more devastating question to Christianity: What did Christianity contribute to make the Holocaust possible? The work of Jules Isaac, Norman Cohn, Raul Hilberg, Roy Eckardt, and others poses this question in a number of different ways. In 1942, the Nietra Rebbe went to Archbishop Kametko of Nietra to plead for Catholic intervention against the deportation of the Slovakian Jews. Tiso, the head of the Slovakian government, had been Kametko's secretary for many years, and the rebbe hoped that Kametko could persuade Tiso not to allow the deportations. Since the rebbe did not yet know of the gas chambers, he stressed the dangers of hunger and disease, especially for women, old people, and children. The archbishop replied: "It is not just a matter of deportation. You will not die there of hunger and disease. They will slaughter all of you there, old and young alike, women and children, at once—it is the punishment that you deserve for the death of our Lord and Redeemer, Jesus Christ—you have only one solution. Come over to our religion and I will work to annul this decree."[2]

There are literally hundreds of similar anti-Semitic statements by individual people reported in the Holocaust literature. As late as March 1941—admittedly still before the full destruction was unleashed—Archbishop Grober (Germany), in a pastoral letter, blamed the Jews for the death of Christ and added that "the self-imposed curse of the Jews, 'His blood be upon us and upon our children' had come true terribly, until the present time, until today."[3] Similarly the Vatican responded to an inquiry from the Vichy government about the law of June 2, 1941, which isolated and deprived Jews of rights: "In principle, there is nothing in these measures which the Holy See would find to criticize."[4]

In general, there is an inverse ratio between the presence of a fundamentalist Christianity and the survival of Jews during the Holocaust period. This is particularly damning because the attitude of the local population toward the Nazi assault on the Jews seems to be a critical variable in Jewish survival. (If the local population disapproved of the genocide or sympathized with the Jews, they were more likely to hide or help Jews, resist or condemn the Nazis, which weakened the effectiveness of the killing process or the killer's will to carry it out.) We must allow for the other factors which operated against the Jews in the countries with a fundamentalist Christianity. These factors include Poland and the Baltic nations' lack of modernity (modernity = tolerance, ideological disapproval of mass murder, presence of Jews who can pass, etc.); the isolation and concentration of Jews in these countries, which made them easy to identify and destroy; the Nazis considered Slavs inferior and more freely used the death penalty for any help extended to Jews; the Nazis concentrated more of the governing power in their own hands in these countries. Yet even when all these allowances are made, it is clear that anti-Semitism played a role in the decision not to shield Jews—or to actually turn them in. If the Teaching of Contempt furnished an occasion—or presented stereotypes which brought the Nazis to focus on the Jews as the scapegoat in the first place; or created a residue of anti-Semitism in Europe which affected the local populations' attitudes toward Jews; or enabled some Christians to feel they were doing God's duty in helping kill Jews or in not stopping it—then Christianity may be hopelessly and fatally compromised. The fact is that during the Holocaust the church's protests were primarily on behalf of converted Jews. At the end of the war, the Vatican and circles close to it helped thousands of war criminals to escape, including Franz Stangl, the commandant of the most murderous of all the extermination camps, Treblinka, and other men of his ilk. Finally in 1948, the German Evangelical Conference at Darmstadt, meeting in the country which had only recently carried out this genocide, proclaimed that the terrible Jewish suffering in the Holocaust was a divine visitation and a call to the Jews to cease their rejection and ongoing crucifixion of Christ. May one morally be a Christian after this?[5]

EVEN SOME CHRISTIANS WHO RESISTED HITLER FAILED ON THE JEWISH QUESTION. Even the great Christians—who recognized the danger of idolatry, and resisted the Nazi government's takeover of the German Evangelical Church at great personal sacrifice and risk—did not speak out on the Jewish question.[6] All this suggests that something in Christian teaching supported or created a positive context for anti-Semitism, and even murder. Is not the faith of a gospel of love, then, fatally tainted with collaboration with genocide— conscious or unconscious? To put it another way: If the Holocaust challenges the fundamental religious claims of Christianity (and Judaism), then the penumbra of Christian complicity may challenge the credibility of Christianity to make these claims.

IS THE WAGER OF CHRISTIAN FAITH LOST? There is yet a third way in which this problem may be stated. In its origins, Christianity grew out of a wager of faith. Growing in the bosom of Judaism and its Messianic hope, Jesus (like others), could be seen either as a false Messiah or as a new unfolding of God's love, and a revelation of love and salvation for mankind. Those who followed Jesus as the Christ, in effect, staked their lives that the new orientation was neither an illusion nor an evil, but yet another stage in salvation and a vehicle of love for mankind. "The acceptance . . . of Jesus as the Messiah means beholding him as one who transforms and will transform the world."7 As is the case with every vehicle, divine and human, the spiritual record of this wager has been mixed—comprising great inspiration for love given and great evils caused. The hope is that the good outweighs the evil. But the throwing into the scales of so massive a weight of evil and guilt raises the question whether the balance might now be broken, whether one must not decide that it were better that Jesus had not come, rather than that such scenes be enacted six million times over—and more. Has the wager of faith in Jesus been lost? . . .

II. The Challenge to Modern Culture

. . . For the world, too, the Holocaust is an event which changes fundamental perceptions. Limits were broken, restraints shattered, that will never be recovered, and henceforth mankind must live with the dread of a world in which models for unlimited evil exist. . . .

The Demonic in the Modern World

. . . No assessment of modern culture can ignore the fact that science and technology—the accepted flower and glory of modernity—now climaxed in the factories of death; the awareness that the unlimited, value-free use of knowledge and science, which we perceive as the great force for improving the human condition, had paved the way for the bureaucratic and scientific death campaign. There is the shock of recognition that the humanistic revolt, celebrated as the liberation of humankind in freeing man from centuries of dependence upon God and nature, is now revealed—at the very heart of the enterprise—to sustain a capacity for death and demonic evil. . . .

One of the most striking things about the Einsatzgruppen leadership makeup is the prevalence of educated people, professionals, especially lawyers, Ph.D.'s, and yes, even a clergyman.[8] How naive the nineteenth-century polemic with religion appears to be in retrospect; how simple Feuerbach, Nietzsche, and many others. The entire structure of autonomous logic and sovereign human reason now takes on a sinister character. . . .

As Toynbee put it, "a Western nation, which for good or evil, has played so central a part in Western history . . . could hardly have committed these flagrant crimes had they not been festering foully beneath the surface of life in the Western world's non-German provinces. . . . If a twentieth-century German was a monster, then, by the same token a twentieth-century Western civilization was a Frankenstein guilty of having been the author of this German monster's being."[9] This responsibility must be shared not only by Christianity, but by the Enlightenment[10] and democratic cultures as well. Their apathy and encouragement strengthened the will and capacity of the murderers to carry out the genocide, even as moral resistance and condemnation weakened that capacity.

The Moral Failure and Complicity of Universalism

Would that liberalism, democracy, and internationalism had emerged looking morally better. But, in fact, the democracies closed their doors to millions of victims who could have been saved. America's record is one of a fumbling and feeble interest in the victims which allowed anti-Semites and provincial economic and patriotic concerns to rule the admission—or rather the nonadmission—of the refugees. Indeed, the ideology of universal human values did not even provide sufficient motivation to bomb the rail lines and the gas chambers of Auschwitz when these were operating at fullest capacity, and when disruption could have saved ten thousand lives a day. Thus the synthetic rubber factory at Buna in the Auschwitz complex was bombed, but the death factory did not merit such attention. [11] The ideology of universalism did have operational effects. It blocked specifying Jews as victims of Nazi atrocities, as in the Allied declaration of January 1942, when the Nazis were warned they would be held responsible for their cruel war on civilians. In this warning, the Jews were not mentioned by name on the grounds that they were after all humans, not Jews, and citizens of the countries in which they lived. The denial of Jewish particularity—in the face of the very specific Nazi war on the Jews—led to decisions to bomb industrial targets to win the war for democracy, but to exclude death factories—lest this be interpreted as a *Jewish* war! The very exclusion of specifying Jews from warnings and military objectives was interpreted by the Nazis as a signal that Jews were expendable. They may have read the signal correctly. In any event, liberalism and internationalism became cover beliefs—designed to weaken the victims' perception that they were threatened and to block the kind of action needed to save their lives. . . . [12]

Especially disastrous was the victims' faith in universalism and modern humanitarian values. It disarmed them. [As Alexander Donat wrote:]

> The basic factor in the Ghetto's lack of preparation for armed resistance was psychological; we did not at first believe the Resettlement Operation to be what in fact it was, systematic slaughter of the entire Jewish population. For generations East European Jews had looked to Berlin as the symbol of law, order, and culture. We could not now believe that the Third Reich was a government of gangsters embarked on a program of genocide "to solve the Jewish problem in Europe." We fell victim to our faith in mankind, our belief that humanity had set limits to the degradation and persecution of one's fellow man. . . . [13]

III. The Holocaust as Orienting Event and Revelation

Not to Confront Is to Repeat

For both Judaism and Christianity (and other religions of salvation—both secular and sacred) there is no choice but to confront the Holocaust, because it happened, and because the first Holocaust is the hardest. The fact of the Holocaust makes a repetition more likely—a limit was broken, a control or awe is gone—and the murder procedure is now better laid out and understood. Failure to confront it makes repetition all the more likely. So evil is the Holocaust, and so powerful a challenge to all other norms, that it forces a response, willy-nilly; not to respond is to collaborate in its repetition. This irony of human history which is already at work, is intensified by the radical power of the Holocaust. Because the world has not made the Holocaust a central point of departure for moral and political policy, the survivors of the Holocaust and their people have lived continually under the direct threat of another Holocaust throughout the past thirty years. Muslims who feel that the event is a Western problem and that Christian guilt has been imposed on them have been tempted to try to stage a repeat performance. They lack the guilt and concern, and that in itself leads to guilt.

The nemesis of denial is culpability. Pope John XXIII, who tried strongly to save Jews in the Holocaust (he made representations and protests, issued false baptismal papers, helped Jews escape), felt guilty and deeply regretted the Catholic Church's past treatment of Jews. This pope did more than any other pope had ever done to remove the possibility of another destruction (through the Vatican II Declaration, revising Catholic instruction and liturgy with reference to the Jews, dialogue, etc.).* Pope Paul VI, who denied the complicity or guilt of Pius XII in the Holocaust, was tempted thereby into a set of policies (he watered down the Declaration, referred to Jews in the old Passion story terms, refused to recognize Israel's de jure political existence, maintained silence in the face of the threat of genocide), which brings the dreadful guilt of collaboration in genocide so much closer.

This principle applies to secular religions of salvation as well. Thus, the German Democratic Republic (East Germany) has denied any responsibility for the Holocaust, on the grounds that it was carried

---

*Writing under a pseudonym, a priest who had served as ghost writer for Pope John published a report on Vatican II which stated that John had composed a prayer about the Jews. The text, to be read in all Catholic churches, said: "We are conscious today that many centuries of blindness have cloaked our eyes so that we can no longer see the beauty of Thy chosen people. . . . We realize that the mark of Cain stands on our foreheads. Across the centuries our Brother Abel has lain in blood which we drew, or shed tears we caused, forgetting Thy love. Forgive us for crucifying Thee a second time in their flesh. For we knew not what we did . . ."[14] While the prayer is apocryphal (no trace of it has been found in John's papers), widespread acceptance of its attribution reflects John's known regret and concern.

out by fascist and right-wing circles, whereas East Germany is socialist. As a result, it has allowed Nazis back into government with even
more impunity than West Germany. Whereas West Germany has
given back billions of dollars of Jewish money in the form of reparations
(it is estimated that many more billions were directly stolen and
spoiled), the GDR, having no guilty conscience, has yielded up none of
the ill-gotten gains of mass murder. In fact, East Germany and its
"socialist" allies have pursued policies which have kept the genocide of
the Jewish people in Israel a live option to this day. Thus, failure to
respond to the Holocaust turns a hallowed ideology of liberation into a
cover for not returning robbed goods and for keeping alive the dream
of another mass murder. . . .

The Holocaust cannot be used for triumphalism. Its moral challenge must also be applied to Jews. Those Jews who feel no guilt for the
Holocaust are also tempted to moral apathy. Religious Jews who use
the Holocaust to morally impugn every other religious group but their
own are the ones who are tempted thereby into indifference at the
Holocaust of others (cf. the general policy of the American Orthodox
rabbinate on United States Vietnam policy). Those Israelis who place
as much distance as possible between the weak, passive Diaspora
victims and the "mighty Sabras" are tempted to use Israeli strength
indiscriminately (i.e., beyond what is absolutely inescapable for self-
defense and survival), which is to risk turning other people into victims
of the Jews. Neither faith nor morality can function without serious
twisting of perspective, even to the point of becoming demonic, unless
they are illuminated by the fires of Auschwitz and Treblinka.

The Dialectical Revelation of the Holocaust

The Holocaust challenges the claims of all the standards that compete
for modern man's loyalties. Nor does it give simple, clear answers or
definitive solutions. To claim that it does is not to take burning children
seriously. This surd will—and should—undercut the ultimate ade-
quacy of any category, unless there were one (religious, political,
intellectual) that consistently produced the proper response of resistance and horror at the Holocaust. No such category exists, to my
knowledge. To use the catastrophe to uphold the univocal validity of
any category is to turn it into grist for propaganda mills. The Nazis
turned their Jewish victims into soap and fertilizer after they were

dead. The same moral gorge rises at turning them into propaganda. The Holocaust offers us only dialectical moves and understandings— often moves that stretch our capacity to the limit and torment us with their irresolvable tensions. In a way, it is the only morally tenable way for survivors and those guilty of bystanding to live. Woe to those so at ease that they feel no guilt or tension. Often this is the sign of the death of the soul. I have met many Germans motivated by guilt who came to Israel on pilgrimages of repentance. I have been struck that frequently these were young people, too young to have participated in the geno- cide; or, more often, persons or the children of persons who had been anti-Nazi or even imprisoned for resistance. I have yet to meet such a penitent who was himself an SS man or even a train official who transported Jews. Living in the dialectic becomes one of the verifica- tion principles for alternative theories after the Holocaust.

Let us offer, then, as working principle the following: No state- ment, theological or otherwise, should be made that would not be credible in the presence of the burning children. In his novel *The Accident,* Elie Wiesel has written of the encounter of a survivor with Sarah, a prostitute who is also a survivor. She began her career at twelve, when she was separated from her parents and sent to a special barracks for the camp officers' pleasure. Her life was spared because there were German officers who liked to make love to little girls her age. Every night she reenacts the first drunken officer's use of a twelve- year-old girl. Yet she lives on, with both life feeling and self-loathing. And she retains enough feeling to offer herself to a shy survivor boy, without money. "You are a saint," he says. "You are mad," she shrieks. He concludes, "Whoever listens to Sarah and doesn't change, whoever enters Sarah's world and doesn't invent new gods and new religions, deserves death and destruction. Sarah alone has the right to decide what is good and what is evil, the right to differentiate between what is true and what usurps the appearance of truth."[15]

In this story Wiesel has given us an extraordinary phenomenology of the dialectic in which we live after the Holocaust. Sarah's life of prostitution, religiously and morally negative in classic terms, under- goes a moral reversal of category. It is suffering sainthood in the context of her life and her ongoing response to the Holocaust experi- ence. Yet this scene grants us no easy Sabbatianism, in which every act that can wrap itself in the garment of the Holocaust is justified and the old categories are no longer valid. The ultimate tension of the dialectic is maintained, and the moral disgust which Sarah's life inspires in her (and Wiesel? and us?) is not omitted either. The more we analyze the passage the more it throws us from pole to pole in ceaseless tension. The very disgust may, in fact, be the outcome of Sarah's mistaken judgment; she continues to judge herself by the categories in which she was raised before the event. This is suggested in the narrator's compassion and love for her. Yet he himself is overcome by moral nausea—or is it pity?—or protest?—until it is too late and Sarah is lost. There is no peace or surcease and no lightly grasped guide to action in this world. To enter into Sarah's world in fear and trembling, and to remain there before and in acting and speech, is the essence of religious response today, as much as when normative Judaism bids us enter into the Exodus, and Christianity asks we enter into Easter and remain there before and in acting or speaking. The classic normative experiences themselves are not dismissed by Wiesel. They are tested and reformulated—dialectically attacked and affirmed—as they pass through the fires of the new revelatory event. [16]

Resistance to New Revelation: Jewish and Christian

Much of classic Jewish and Christian tradition will resist the claim that there have been new revelatory events in our time. Judaism has remained faithful to the covenant of Sinai and rejected this claim when expressed in the life of Jesus as understood by St. Paul and the Christian church, or in the career of Sabbatai Zevi and others. . . . [17] The very quality of faithfulness to the covenant resists acceptance of new revelation—as it should. Human nature's love for the familiar conspires with faithfulness to keep new norms out. But no one said that the Holocaust should be simply assimilable. For traditional Jews to ignore or deny all significance to this event would be to repudiate the fundamental belief and affirmations of the Sinai covenant: that history is meaningful, and that ultimate liberation and relationship to God will take place in the realm of human events. Exodus-Sinai would be insulated from all contradictory events—at the cost of removing it from the realm of the real—the realm on which it staked its all—the realm of its origin and testimony. However much medieval Judaism was tempted to move redemption to the realm of eternal life, it never committed this sacrilege. It insisted that the Messianic Kingdom of God in this world was not fulfilled by the salvation of the world to come. . . . [18] There is an alternative for those whose faith can pass through the demonic, consuming flames of a crematorium: it is the willingness and ability to hear further revelation and reorient themselves. That is the way to wholeness. Rabbi Nachman of Bratzlav once said that there is no heart so whole as a broken heart. After Auschwitz, there is no faith so whole as a faith shattered—and re-fused—in the ovens.

Since this further revelation grows in the womb of Judaism, it may be asked whether it speaks only to Jews, or to Christians also. Classic Christianity is tempted to deny further revelation after Easter. Christianity testified and built itself on the finality of revelation in Christ's life and teaching. Yet, at its core, Christianity claims that God sent a second revelation, which grew out of the ground of acknowledged covenant, superseded the authority of the first revelation, and even supplied a new, higher understanding of the first event. Christian polemic has mocked and criticized the people of Israel for being so blinded by the possession of an earlier revelation and by pride in its finality that Israel did not recognize the time of its visitation. However unjust the polemic against Judaism was (as I believe it was), it ill behooves Christianity to rule out further revelation a priori—lest it be hoist by its own petard. Rather, it should trust its own faith that God is not owned by anyone and the spirit blows where it lists. The very anguish and harsh judgments which the Holocaust visits on Christianity (see above, pp. 307–310) open the possibility of freeing the Gospel of Love from the incubus of evil and hatred.

The desire to guarantee absolute salvation and understanding is an all too human need which both religions must resist as a snare and temptation. Just as refusal to encounter the Holocaust brings a nemesis of moral and religious ineffectiveness, openness and willingness to undergo the ordeal of reorienting by the event could well save or illuminate the treasure that is still contained in each tradition. . . .

IV. Jewish Theological Responses to the Holocaust

A Critique

There have been some notable Jewish theological responses that have correctly grasped the centrality of the Holocaust to Jewish thought and faith. The two primary positions are polar. One witness upholds the

God of History. Emil Fackenheim has described the Commanding Voice of Auschwitz, which bids us not to hand Hitler any posthumous victories, such as repudiating the covenant and retrospectively declaring Judaism to have been an illusion. Eliezer Berkovits has stressed that Jewish survival testifies to the Lord of History. The other witness affirms the death of God and the loss of all hope. Richard Rubenstein has written: "We learned in the crisis that we were totally and nakedly alone, that we could expect neither support nor succor from God nor from our fellow creatures. Therefore, the world will forever remain a place of pain, suffering, alienation and ultimate defeat."[19] These are genuine important responses to the Holocaust, but they fall afoul of the dialectical principle. Both positions give a definitive interpretation of the Holocaust which subsumes it under known classical categories. Neither classical theism nor atheism is adequate to incorporate the incommensurability of the Holocaust; neither produced a consistently proper response; neither is credible alone—in the presence of the burning children.

Rubenstein's definitiveness is part of this writer's disagreement with him. Rubenstein concluded that "Jewish history has written the *final chapter* in the terrible story of the God of History"; that "the world will *forever* remain a place of pain . . . and *ultimate defeat*," and that the "pathetic hope (of coming to grips with Auschwitz through the framework of traditional Judaism) *will never be realized*" (italics supplied).[20] After the Holocaust, there should be no final solutions, not even theological ones. I could not be more sympathetic to Rubenstein's positions, or more unsympathetic to his conclusions. That Auschwitz and the rebirth of Israel are normative; that there are traditional positions which Auschwitz moves us to repudiate (such as "We were punished for our sins") is a profoundly, authentically Jewish response. To declare that the destruction closes out hope forever is to claim divine omniscience and to use the Holocaust for theological grist. Contra Rubenstein, I would argue that it is not so much that any affirmations (or denials) cannot be made, but that they can be made authentically only if they are made after working through the Holocaust experience. In the same sense, however, the relationship to the God of the covenant cannot be unaffected.

Dialectical Faith, or "Moment Faiths"

Faith is living life in the presence of the Redeemer, even when the world is unredeemed. After Auschwitz, faith means there are times when faith is overcome. Buber has spoken of "moment gods": God is known only at the moment when Presence and awareness are fused in vital life. This knowledge is interspersed with moments when only natural, self-contained, routine existence is present. We now have to speak of "moment faiths," moments when Redeemer and vision of redemption are present, interspersed with times when the flames and smoke of the burning children blot out faith—though it flickers again. Such a moment is described in an extraordinary passage of *Night*, as the young boy sentenced to death but too light to hang struggles slowly on the rope. Eliezer finally responds to the man asking, "Where is God now?" by saying, "Here He is—He is hanging here on this gallows . . ."[21]

This ends the easy dichotomy of atheist/theist, the confusion of faith with doctrine or demonstration. It makes clear that faith is a life response of the whole person to the Presence in life and history. Like life, this response ebbs and flows. The difference between the skeptic and the believer is frequency of faith, and not certitude of position. The rejection of the unbeliever by the believer is literally the denial or attempted suppression of what is within oneself. The ability to live with moment faith is the ability to live with pluralism and without the self-flattering, ethnocentric solutions which warp religion, or make it a source of hatred for the other.

Why Dialectical Faith Is Still Possible

THE PERSISTENCE OF EXODUS. Of course, the question may still be asked: Why is it not a permanent destruction of faith to be in the presence of the murdered children?

One reason is that there are still moments when the reality of the Exodus is reenacted and present. There are moments when a member of the community of Israel shares the reality of the child who was to have been bricked into the wall but instead experienced the liberation and dignity of Exodus. (The reference here is to the rabbinic legend that in Egypt, Jewish children were bricked into a wall if their parents did not meet their daily quota of bricklaying.) This happens even to those who have both literally and figuratively lived through the Holocaust. Wiesel describes this moment for us in *The Gates of the Forest,* when Gregor "recites the Kaddish, the solemn affirmation . . . by which man returns to God his crown and his scepter."[22] Neither Exodus nor Easter wins out or is totally blotted out by Buchenwald, but we encounter both polar experiences; the life of faith is lived between them. And this dialectic opens new models of response to God, as we shall show below.

THE BREAKDOWN OF THE SECULAR ABSOLUTE. A second reason is that we do not stand in a vacuum when faith encounters the crematoria. In a real sense, we are always choosing between alternative faiths when we make a decision about ultimate meaning. In this culture the primary alternative to religion is secular man in a world closed off from any transcendence, or divine incursion. This world grows out of the intellectual framework of science, philosophy, and social science, of rationalism and human liberation, which created the enterprise of modernity. This value system was—and is—the major alternative faith which Jews and Christians joined in large numbers in the last two centuries, transferring allegiance from the Lord of History and Revelation to the Lord of Science and Humanism. In so many ways, the Holocaust is the direct fruit and will of this alternative. Modernity fostered the excessive rationalism and utilitarian relations which created the need for and susceptibility to totalitarian mass movements and the surrender of moral judgment. The secular city sustained the emphasis on value-free sciences and objectivity, which created unparalleled power but weakened its moral limits. (Surely it is no accident that so many members of the Einsatzgruppen were professionals.) Mass communication and universalization of values weakened resistance to centralized power, and served as a cover to deny the unique danger posted to particular, i.e. Jewish, existence.

In the light of Auschwitz, secular twentieth-century civilization is not worthy of this transfer of our ultimate loyalty. . . . Nothing in the record of secular culture on the Holocaust justifies its authority claims. The victims ask us, above all, not to allow the creation of another matrix of values that might sustain another attempt at genocide. The absence of strong alternative value systems gives a moral monopoly to the wielders of power and authority. Secular authority unchecked becomes absolute. Relative values thus become the seedbed of absolute claims, and this is idolatry. This vacuum was a major factor in the Nazi ability to concentrate power and carry out the destruction without protest or resistance. (The primary sources of resistance were systems of absolute alternative values—the Barmen Conference in the Confessional Church, Jehovah's Witnesses, etc.)[23] After the Holocaust it is all the more urgent to resist this absolutization of the secular. . . .

If nothing else sufficed to undercut this absolute claim of nonaccessibility of the divine, it is the knowledge that the absence of limits or belief in a judge, and the belief that persons could therefore become God, underlay the structure of *l'univers concentrationnaire*. Mengele and other selectors of Auschwitz openly joked about this. I will argue below that the need to deny God leads directly to the assumption of omnipotent power over life and death. The desire to control people leads directly to crushing the image of God within them, so that the jailer becomes God. Then one cannot easily surrender to the temptation of being cut off from the transcendence, and must explore the alternatives. Surely it is no accident that in the past forty years language analysts like Wittgenstein, critics of value-free science and social sciences, existentialists, evangelical and counter-culture movements alike, have fought to set limits to the absolute claims of scientific knowledge and of reason, and to ensure the freedom for renewed encounter with the transcendental.

THE LOGIC OF POST-HOLOCAUST AND, THEREFORE, POST-MODERN FAITH. A third reason to resist abandoning the divine is the moral urgency that grows out of the Holocaust and fights for the presence of the Lord of History. Emil Fackenheim has articulated this position in terms of not handing Hitler posthumous victories. I prefer an even more traditional category, and would argue that the moral necessity of a world to come, and even of resurrection, arises powerfully out of the encounter with the Holocaust. Against this, Rubenstein and others would maintain that the wish is not always father to the fact, and that such an illusion may endanger even more lives. To this last point I would reply that the proper belief will save, not cost, lives. . . .

Moral necessity validates the search for religious experience rather than surrender to the immediate logic of nonbelief. Thus, if the Holocaust strikes at the credibility of faith, especially unreconstructed faith, dialectically it also erodes the persuasiveness of the secular option. If someone is told that a line of argument leads to the conclusion that he should not exist, not surprisingly the victim may argue that there must be alternative philosophical frameworks. Insofar as the Holocaust grows out of Western civilization, then, at least for Jews, it is a powerful incentive to guard against being overimpressed by this culture's intellectual assumptions and to seek other philosophical and historical frameworks. . . .

The moral light shed by the Holocaust on the nature of Western culture validates skepticism toward contemporary claims—even before philosophic critiques emerge to justify the skepticism. It is enough that this civilization is the locus of the Holocaust. The Holocaust calls on Jews, Christians, and others to absolutely resist the total authority of this cultural moment. The experience frees them to respond to their own claim, which comes from outside the framework of this civilization, to relate to a divine other, who sets limits and judges the absolute claims of contemporary philosophic and scientific and human political systems. To follow this orientation is to be opened again to the possibilities of Exodus and immortality.

This is a crucial point. The Holocaust comes after two centuries of Emancipation's steadily growing domination of Judaism and the Jews. Rubenstein's self-perception as a radical breaking from the Jewish past is, I think, misleading. A more correct view would argue that he is repeating the repudiation of the God of History and the Chosen that was emphasized by the modernizing schools, such as Reconstructionism. This position had become the stuff of the values and views of the majority of Jews. "Being right with modernity" (defined by each group differently) has been the dominant value norm of a growing number of Jews since 1750, as well as Christians. Despite the rear-guard action of Orthodox Judaism and Roman Catholicism (until the 1960s) and of fundamentalist groups, the modern tide has steadily risen higher. The capacity to resist, criticize, or break away from these models is one of the litmus tests of the Holocaust as the new orienting experience of Jews, and an indication that a new era of Jewish civilization is under way. This new era will not turn its back on many aspects of modernity, but clearly it will be freer to reject some of its elements, and to take from the past (and future) much more fully.

THE REVELATION IN THE REDEMPTION OF ISRAEL. I have saved for last the most important reason why the moment of despair and disbelief in redemption cannot be final, at least in this generation's community of Israel. Another event has taken place in our lifetime which also has extraordinary scope and normative impact—the rebirth of the State of Israel. As difficult to absorb in its own way and, like the Holocaust, a scandal for many traditional Jewish and Christian categories, it is an inescapable part of the Jewish historical experience in our time. And while it is a continuation and outgrowth of certain responses to the Holocaust, it is at the same time a dialectical contradiction to many of its implications. If the experience of Auschwitz symbolizes that we are cut off from God and hope, and that the covenant may be destroyed, then the experience of Jerusalem symbolizes that God's promises are faithful and His people live on. Burning children speak of the absence of all value—human and divine; the rehabilitation of one-half million Holocaust survivors in Israel speaks of the reclamation of tremendous human dignity and value. If Treblinka makes human hope an illusion, then the Western Wall asserts that human dreams are more real than force and facts. Israel's faith in the God of History demands that an unprecedented event of destruction be matched by an unprecedented act of redemption, and this has happened.[24]

This is not simply a question of the memories of Exodus versus the experience of Auschwitz. If it were a question of Exodus only, then those Jews already cut off from Exodus by the encounter with modern culture would be excluded and only "religious" Jews could still be believers.

But almost all Jews acknowledge this phenomenon—the event of redemption and the event of catastrophe and their dialectical interrelationship—and it touches their lives. Studies show that the number of those who affirm this phenomenon as central (even if in nontheological categories) has grown from year to year; that its impact is now almost universal among those who will acknowledge themselves as Jews, and that its force has overthrown some hierarchies of values that grew as modernity came to dominate Jewish life.[25] In fact, the religious situation is explosive and fermenting on a deeper level than anyone wishes to acknowledge at this point. The whole Jewish people is caught between immersion in nihilism and immersion in redemption—both are present in immediate experience, and not just historical memory. To deny either pole in our time is to be cut off from historical Jewish experience. In the incredible dialectical tension between the two we are fated to live. Biblical theology already suggested that the time would come when consciousness of God out of the restoration of Israel would outweigh consciousness of God out of the Exodus. In the words of Jeremiah: "The days will come, says the Lord, when it shall no longer be said: 'as God lives who brought up the children of Israel out of the land of Egypt' but 'as God lives who brought up the children of Israel from the land of the north and from all the countries whither He had driven them,' and I will bring them back into their land that I gave to their fathers" (Jer. 16:14–15).

DESPITE REDEMPTION, FAITH REMAINS DIALECTICAL. But if Israel is so redeeming, why then must faith be "moment faith," and why should the experience of nothingness ever dominate?

The answer is that faith is living in the presence of the Redeemer, and in the moment of utter chaos, of genocide, one does not live in His presence. One must be faithful to the reality of the nothingness. Faith is a moment truth, but there are moments when it is not true. This is certainly demonstrable in dialectical truths, when invoking the truth at the wrong moment is a lie. To let Auschwitz overwhelm Jerusalem is to lie (i.e., to speak a truth out of its appropriate moment); and to let Jerusalem deny Auschwitz is to lie for the same reason.

The biblical witness is that a permanent repudiation of the covenant would also have been a lie. "Behold, they say: our bones are dried up and our hope is lost; we are cut off entirely" (Ezek. 37:11). There were many who chose this answer, but their logic led to dissolution in the pagan world around them. After losing hope in the Lord of History, they were absorbed into idolatry—the faith of the gods of that moment. In the resolution of the crisis of biblical faith, those who abandoned hope ceased to testify. However persuasive the reaction may have been at that time, every such decision in Israel's history—until Auschwitz—has been premature, and even wrong. Yet in a striking talmudic interpretation, the rabbis say that Daniel and Jeremiah refused to speak of God as awesome or powerful any longer in light of the destruction of the Temple.[26] The line between the repudiation of the God of the covenant and the Daniel-Jeremiah reaction is so thin that repudiation must be seen as an authentic reaction even if we reject it. There is a faithfulness in the rejection; serious theism must be troubled after such an event. . . .

V. Explorations in Post-Holocaust Theological Models

Job and Renewed Divine Encounter

What, then, are the theological models that could come to the fore in a post-Holocaust interpretation of the relationship between God and man?

One is the model of Job, the righteous man from whom everything is taken: possessions, loved ones, health. It is interesting that his wife proposes that Job "curse God and die"; his friends propose that he is being punished for his sins. Job rejects both propositions. (At the end, God specifically rebukes the friends for their "answer.") The ending of the book, in which Job is restored and has a new wife and children, is of course unacceptable by our principle. Six million murdered Jews have not been and cannot be restored. But Job also offers us a different understanding. His suffering is not justified by God, nor is he consoled by the words about God's majesty and the grandeur of the universe surpassing man's understanding. Rather, what is meaningful in Job's experience is that in the whirlwind the contact with God is restored. That sense of Presence gives the strength to go on living in the contradiction.[27]

The theological implications of Job, then, are the rejection of easy pieties or denials and the dialectical response of looking for, expecting, further revelations of the Presence. This is the primary religious dimension of the reborn State of Israel for all religious people. When suffering had all but overwhelmed Jews and all but blocked out God's Presence, a sign out of the whirlwind gave us the strength to go on, and the right to speak authentically of God's Presence still.

Rabbi Joseph B. Soloveichik has presented a related image, "the knock on the door" of history. The image is taken from the Song of Songs. Shulamit has been taken to the king's court, is separated from her lover for so long that she begins to waver and to doubt the reality of her past love. Suddenly there is a knock on the door. It must be her beloved, but she hesitates to answer—she is too tired from the experience of separation and defeat. Then the emotional realization that it may be her lover fires her and she goes to the door. By the time she does open the door, he is not to be seen (Song of Songs 5:1 ff.). The entire episode is so ambiguous that it can be dismissed as the reaction

of an overheated imagination, of romantic longing. But the knock has
so keenly recrystallized her feelings for her beloved that she will not
betray the relationship again.[28] As ambiguous as the secularity and
flawed character of the reborn state is, it is enough to confirm the
conviction not to "sell out to the court" and deny the past—or future—
relationship with the beloved.

Israel's relationship to the Holocaust enormously intensifies the
theological weight and testimony of both events. In turn, this deepens
the irony of Jewish history and its dialectical impact on Christianity.
Christian resistance to the possible new revelatory events in Judaism's
history stems from the desire to be faithful to the finality of Christ. But
inability to hear new revelation may be one of the signs of the death of
the soul. (The phrase "may be one of the signs of the death of the soul"
is used advisedly. It may be, in fact, that there is no revelation here.
Those who deem it revelation may be mistaken, or it may be heard
only by those for whom it is intended; those who do not hear it may not
hear it because it is not addressed to them at all.)

One of the classic Christian self-validations has been the claim
that the Old Covenant is finished; the old olive tree is blasted and
bears no more fruit. New revelation in Judaism is perceived as incompatible with Christianity's superseding nature; the admission could
destroy the structure of Christian authority. Yet confession by Christians of Judaism's ongoing life and acceptance in gratitude of a new
harvest of revelation would, at one stroke, undercut the whole Teaching of Contempt tradition in Christianity. . . . In light of the Holocaust,
classical Christianity is called "to die" to be reborn to new life; or it
lives unaffected, to die to God and man.

The Suffering Servant and the Limits of Modernity

There is a second theological model that seems destined for a greater
role in Jewish theology and, I dare say, for new meaning in Christianity: the Suffering Servant. Hitherto, this image has been played
down by Jews because of its centrality in Christian theology. We are
indebted to J. Coert Rylarsdaam for opening our eyes to this neglected
model. Rylarsdaam once said that if being a Christian meant taking up
the cross and being crucified for God, then the only practicing Christians were the Jews.

The Suffering Servant in Isaiah 53 sounds like a passage out of

Holocaust literature. He is led as a sheep to slaughter (a term much and unfairly used in reference to the Holocaust). He is despised and forsaken of men. The term "despised" is repeated twice in verse 3. He is not only held in contempt, but there is a contempt-evoking element in him: he stinks. He is a man of pain and disease, with no comeliness. Men look away from him. (The chapter reads like an eyewitness description of the inmates of concentration camps after a month or two.) The Suffering Servant is smitten by God, but not for his sins. He is struck for the sins of all men. (In biblical language, in which all human actions have their source in God, it is stated: "The Lord hath made to light on him the iniquity of us all."). . .

To borrow a homely metaphor: The old coal mines had no gas detectors. Instead, canaries and parakeets were kept in the mines. When coal gas escaped, it would poison the birds, for they were much more sensitive to it than humans. When the birds were poisoned, the miners knew it was time to go to another vein or move in a different direction.

The Holocaust was an advance warning of the demonic potential in modern culture. If one could conceive of Hitler coming to power not in 1933 but in 1963, after the invention of nuclear and hydrogen bombs, then the Holocaust would have been truly universal. It is a kind of last warning that if man will perceive and overcome the demonism unleashed in modern culture, the world may survive. Otherwise, the next Holocaust will embrace the whole world.

Unfortunately, the strain of evil is deeply embedded in the best potentials of modernity. The pollution is in the liberating technology; the uniformity in the powerful communication and cultural explosion; the mass murder in the efficient bureaucracy. This suggests a desperate need to delegitimatize the excessive authority claims of our culture. Yet some of its most attractive features may be the ones to lead us into the path of no return.

From this fact comes a call to Jews and Christians to resist the overwhelming attractions of the secular city even at its best. For as much as humanity needs immersion in the pluralism of its humanizing communications, and the freedom from fixed roles of its extraordinary options, and the liberating materialism of the city, it also needs groups to stay in spiritual tension with these same forces. The analogy may be to Ulysses, who must strap himself to the mast to make sure that, no matter how beautiful the siren song, he would not let himself be swept into the whirlpool of absolute commitment—and shipwreck. Christians and Jews are called upon to preserve their inner community and its testimony, out of the past and future. Their task is harder than Ulysses', for they are also called by the Holocaust to correct that very testimony's faults through participation in the new, open civilization. Let Gunter Lewy's and Gordon Zahn's studies of Catholics in Germany serve as warning.[29] The price of commitment to a *Kulturreligion* may be the inability to resist the worst moral possibilities in an otherwise good society. Once the center of loyalty is placed in that structure and there is absolute commitment to that society's values, then religion is powerless to check the excesses.

The Holocaust warns us that our current values breed their own nemesis of evil when unchecked—even as Nazi Germany grew in the matrix of modernity. To save ourselves from such error, we will have to draw on the warning of the experiences of the Suffering Servant. The Holocaust suggests a fundamental skepticism about all human movements, left and right, political and religious—even as we participate in them. Nothing dare evoke our absolute, unquestioning loyalty, not even our God, for this leads to possibilities of SS loyalties. SS Reichsführer Himmler could speak of "honor" and "decency" in carrying out the slaughter of millions. "By and large, however, we can say that we have performed this task in love of our people. And we have suffered no damage from it in our inner self, in our soul, in our character."[30]

At the same time, the Holocaust demands a reinterpretation of the Suffering Servant model, especially for Christians, who have tended to glorify this role. It is a warning that when suffering is overwhelming, then the servant may be driven to yield to evil. . . . The redemptive nature of suffering must be in absolute tension with the dialectical reality that it must be fought, cut down, eliminated. I once visited a great Christian, who had gone to India and devoted his life to a community caring in extraordinary sacrificial love for brain-damaged little children. Yet the community had never thought of bringing in a doctor to diagnose what treatment might be available to improve the condition of the children.

The Controversy with God—and with the Gospels

There is yet a third theological model which comes to the forefront after the Holocaust. I would call it the Lamentations 3 model (finding it in Chapter 3 of the Lamentations). It is the dominant theme in the writings of Elie Wiesel.

The early chapters of Lamentations are full of the "obvious" biblical solution: punishment for sins. Chapter 3 sounds a different note: "I am the man who has seen suffering." "God ate up my flesh and skin." "He [God] is a bear who stalks, and attacks me like a lion . . ." The agony is inflicted by God, but there is no note of sinfulness. There is only anger and pain. "And I said: my eternity and my hope from God has been lost." The climax is not guilt, but control, anger, and a feeling of being cut off from God.

Says Wiesel on Rosh Hashanah: "This day I had ceased to plead . . . on the contrary, I felt very strong. I was the accuser, God the accused. . . . I had ceased to be anything but ashes, yet I felt myself to be stronger than the Almighty . . ." Or again, "man is very strong, greater than God. When You were deceived by Adam and Eve, You drove them out of Paradise. . . . But there are men here whom You have betrayed, whom You have allowed to be betrayed, gassed, burned; what do they do? They pray before You. They praise Your name!"[31]

In Lamentations, what pulls the narrator through is the sudden memory of past goodness. "This I recall to mind, therefore I have hope: the Lord's mercies, for they are not consumed." The Exodus memory is sustaining.

Wiesel teaches us that in the very anger and controversy itself is the first stage of a new relationship, perhaps the only kind of relationship possible with God at this point in history. Could it be that the banal quality of prayer in our time is due to the fact that there are not enough prayers that, in our anger, we can say? Is it because we lack a prayer on the Holocaust that expresses the anger—that, at least, blames God? Anger is more compatible with love and involvement than pleasant niceties and old compliments.

Again, these are direct implications of this model. Centrally: it is to justify human beings, not God. It suggests a total and thoroughgoing self-criticism that would purge the emotional dependency and self-abasement of traditional religion and its false crutch of certainty and security. It involves a willingness to confess and clear up the violations of the image of God (of women, Jews, blacks, others) in our values, and a willingness to overcome the institutionalism that sacrifices God to self-interest. (One of the defenses of Pius XII's silence is that he felt he should not endanger the church and the faithful by stopping genocide.[32] If true faith means taking up the cross for God, then when will there ever be a truer time to be crucified, if necessary? Even if the attempt to help is doomed to failure, when will it ever be more appropriate to risk one's life or the church's life than to stop the crucifixion of children?) Justifying people means the fullest willingness, in both Judaism and Christianity, to defend the revolt against God and the faith that grows out of the desire to liberate man. Yet here too, the Holocaust demands a dialectical capacity from us. Rebels are not usually good at conserving; but if we simply validate the contemporary, we fall into idolatry and prepare the legitimization of another Holocaust.

In this model we find the source for one of the fundamental steps Christianity must take after the Holocaust: to quarrel with the Gospels themselves for being a source of anti-Semitism. For the devout Christian, the New Testament is the word of God. Yet even the word of God must be held to account for nourishing hatred, as well as for culpability in, or being an accessory to, the fact of genocide. Nothing less than a fundamental critique and purification of the Gospels themselves can begin to purify Christianity from being a source of hatred. The Holocaust reveals that Christianity has the stark choice of contrition, repentance, and self-purification, or the continual temptation to participate in genocide or pave the way for it. If Christianity has barely survived the first Holocaust, I do not believe that it can survive a second with any real moral capital at all. As painful as is the prospect, then, of a surrender of missionary enterprise to the Jew or a critique of the Gospels, this is possible out of a faith purged by the flames of the Holocaust. Ultimately it will be less painful than the alternative, of being accessory to the once and future fact of genocide. It will take extraordinary sacrificial effort to achieve this. But extraordinary catastrophes are not mastered by routine treatment or evasion. Only extraordinary outbursts of life or creativity can overcome them. To overwhelming death one must respond with overwhelming life. . . .

VI. The Central Religious Testimony after the Holocaust

Recreating Human Life

In the silence of God and of theology, there is one fundamental testimony that can still be given—the testimony of human life itself. This was always the basic evidence, but after Auschwitz its import is incredibly heightened. In fact, it is the only testimony that can still be heard.

The vast number of dead and morally destroyed is the phenomenology of absurdity and radical evil, the continuing statement of human worthlessness and meaninglessness that shouts down all talk of God and human worth. The Holocaust is even model and pedagogy for future generations that genocide can be carried out with impunity—one need fear neither God nor man. There is one response to such overwhelming tragedy: the reaffirmation of meaningfulness, worth, and life—through acts of love and life-giving. The act of creating a life or enhancing its dignity is the counter-testimony to Auschwitz. To talk of love and of a God who cares in the presence of the burning children is obscene and incredible; to leap in and pull a child out of a pit, to clean its face and heal its body, is to make the most powerful statement—the only statement that counts.

In the first moment after the Flood, with its testimony of absurd and mass human death, Noah is given two instructions—the only two that can testify after such an event. "Be fruitful and multiply and replenish the earth" (Gen. 9:1–7), and "but your life blood I will hold you responsible for"—"who sheds man's blood, shall his blood be shed; for in the image of God made He man" (Gen. 9:5–6). Each act of creating a life, each act of enhancing or holding people responsible for human life, becomes multiplied in its resonance because it contradicts the mass graves of biblical Shinar—or Treblinka.

Recreating the Image of God

This becomes the critical religious act. Only a million or billion such acts can begin to right the balance of testimony so drastically shifted by the mass weight of six million dead. In an age when one is ashamed or embarrassed to talk about God in the presence of the burning children, the image of God, which points beyond itself to transcendence, is the only statement about God that one can make. And it is human life itself that makes the statement—words will not help.

Put it another way: the overwhelming testimony of the six million is so strong that it all but irretrievably closes out religious language. Therefore the religious enterprise after this event must see itself as a desperate attempt to create, save, and heal the image of God wherever it still exists—lest further evidence of meaninglessness finally tilt the scale irreversibly. Before this calling, all other "religious" activity is dwarfed.

But where does one find the strength to have a child after Auschwitz? Why bring a child into a world where Auschwitz is possible? Why expose it to such a risk again? The perspective of Auschwitz sheds new light on the nature of childrearing and faith. It takes enormous faith in ultimate redemption and meaningfulness to choose to create or even enhance life again. In fact, faith is revealed by this not to be a belief or even an emotion, but an ontological life-force that reaffirms creation and life in the teeth of overwhelming death. One must silently assume redemption in order to have the child—and having the child makes the statement of redemption. . . .

The Context of an Image of God

In a world of overpopulation and mass starvation and of zero population growth, something further must be said. I, for one, believe that in the light of the crematoria, the Jewish people are called to re-create life. Nor is such testimony easily given. One knows the risk to the children.

But it is not only the act of creating life that speaks. To bring a child into a world in which it will be hungry and diseased and neglected, is to torment and debase the image of God. We also face the challenge to create the conditions under which human beings will grow as an image of God; to build a world in which wealth and resources are created and distributed to provide the matrix for existence as an image of God.

We also face the urgent call to eliminate every stereotype discrimination that reduces—and denies—this image in the other. It was the ability to distinguish some people as human and others as not that enabled the Nazis to segregate and then destroy the "subhumans"

(Jews, Gypsies, Slavs). The ability to differentiate the foreign Jews from French-born Jews paved the way for the deportation first of foreign-born, then of native, French Jews. This differentiation stilled conscience, stilled the church, stilled even some French Jews. The indivisibility of human dignity and equality becomes an essential bulwark against the repetition of another Holocaust. It is the command rising out of Auschwitz.

This means a vigorous self-criticism, and review of every cultural or religious framework that may sustain some devaluation or denial of the absolute and equal dignity of the other. This is the overriding command and the essential criterion for religious existence, to whoever walks by the light of the flames. Without this testimony and the creation of facts that give it persuasiveness, the act of the religious enterprise simply lacks credibility. To the extent that religion may extend or justify the evils of dignity denied, it becomes the devil's testimony. Whoever joins in the work of creation and rehabilitation of the image of God is, therefore, participating in "restoring to God his scepter and crown." Whoever does not support—or opposes—this process is seeking to complete the attack on God's presence in the world. These must be seen as the central religious acts. They shed a pitiless light on popes who deny birth control to starving millions because of a need to uphold the religious authority of the magisterium; or on rabbis who deny women's dignity out of loyalty to divinely given traditions.

VII. Religious and Secular after the Holocaust

THE END OF THE SECULAR-RELIGIOUS DICHOTOMY. This argument makes manifest an underlying thrust in this interpretation. The Holocaust has destroyed the meaning of the categories of "secular" and "religious." Illuminated by the light of the crematoria, these categories are dissolved and not infrequently turned inside out.

We must remember the many "religious" people who carried out the Holocaust. There were killers and murderers who continued to practice organized religion, including Christianity. There were many "good Christians," millions of respectable people, who turned in, rounded up, and transported millions of Jews. Some sympathized with or were apathetic to the murder process, while perceiving themselves as religiously observant and faithful—including those who did an extra measure of Jew-hunting or betrayal because they perceived it as an appropriate expression of Christian theology. Vast numbers of people practiced religion in this period, but saw no need to stand up to or resist the destruction process. . . .

IF "ALL IS PERMITTED," WHAT IS THE "FEAR OF GOD"? The Holocaust is overwhelming witness that "all is permitted." It showed that there are no limits of sacredness or dignity to stop the death process. There were no thunderbolts or divine curses to check mass murder or torture. The Holocaust also showed that one can literally get away with murder. After the war a handful of killers were punished, but the vast majority were not. Catholic priests supplied disguises and passports for mass murderers to help them escape punishment. German and Austrian officials cleared them of guilt—or imposed a few years of prison for killing tens of thousands. Men in charge of legally ostracizing Jews and clearing them for destruction became secretaries to cabinet ministers. Men who owned gas-producing companies, those who had built crematoria, were restored to their full ownership rights and wealth. Thirty years later, an anti-Nazi woman was imprisoned for seeking to kidnap and deliver for extradition a mass murderer, while he went free. Austrian juries acquitted the architects of the Auschwitz gas chambers. If all is permitted, why should anyone hold back from getting away with whatever one can? The prudential argument, that it is utilitarian not to do so, surely is outweighed by the reality that one can get away with so much. And the example of millions continually testifies against any sense of reverence or dignity to check potential evil.

I would propose that there is an explanation; a biblical category applies here. Whoever consistently holds back from murder or human exploitation when he could perpetrate it with immunity—or any person who unswervingly devotes himself to reverence, care, and protection of the divine image which is man, beyond that respect which can be coerced—reveals the presence within of a primordial awe—"fear of God"—which alone evokes such a response.

The biblical category suggests that fear of God is present where people simply cannot do certain things. It is, as it were, a field of force that prevents certain actions. . . . When fear of God is not present, there are no limits.

RELIGIOUS AND SECULAR SELF-DEFINITION IN LIGHT OF AUSCHWITZ. Nor can we take self-definitions seriously. During the Holocaust, many (most?) of the church's protests were on behalf of Jews converted to Christianity. Consider what this means. It is not important to protest the murder of Jews; only if a person believes in Jesus Christ as Lord and Savior is there a moral need to protest his fate.33 Can we take such self-definitions of religious people as reflection of belief in God?

When, in May and June 1967, it appeared that another Holocaust loomed, men of God remained silent. Pope Paul VI, moved by all sorts of legitimate or normal considerations (concern for Christian Arabs, concern for holy places, theological hang-ups about secular Israel) remained silent. A self-avowed atheist, root source of much of modern atheism, Jean-Paul Sartre, spoke out against potential genocide—even though he had to break with his own deepest political alliances and self-image in his links to Arabs and Third World figures to do so. He knew that there is one command: Never another Holocaust. Which is the man of God, which the atheist? By biblical perspective? By Auschwitz perspective? Are title, self-definition, official dress, public opinion—even sincere personal profession—more significant than action?

If someone were to begin to strangle you, all the while protesting loudly and sincerely: "I love you!" at what point would the perception of that person's sincerity change? At what point would you say, "Actions speak louder than words"? As you turn blue, you say, "Uh . . . pardon me, are you sure that I am the person you had in mind . . . when you said, 'I love you'?"

One must fully respect the atheist's right to his own self-definition. But from the religious perspective, the action speaks for itself. The denial of faith has to be seen as the action of one determined to be a secret servant, giving up the advantages of acknowledged faith, because at such a time such advantages are blasphemous. Perhaps it reveals a deeper religious consciousness that knows there must be a silence about God—if faith in Him is not to be fatally destroyed in light of the Holocaust and of the abuse of faith in God expressed by a Himmler. Thus, the atheist who consistently shows reverence for the image of God, but denies that he does so because he is a believer in God, is revealed by the flames to be one of the thirty-six righteous—the hidden righteous, whom Jewish tradition asserts to be the most righteous, those for whose sake the world exists. Their faith is totally inward and they renounce the prerequisites of overt faith; and for their sake the world of evil is borne by God.[34]

THE STATE OF ISRAEL: A STUDY IN SECULARITY AND RELIGION AFTER AUSCHWITZ.

By this standard, the "secular" State of Israel is revealed for the deeply religious state that it is. Both its officially nonreligious majority as well as its official and established religious minority are irrelevant to this judgment. The real point is that after Auschwitz, the existence of the Jew is a great affirmation and an act of faith. The re-creation of the body of the people, Israel, is renewed testimony to Exodus as ultimate reality, to God's continuing presence in history proven by the fact that his people, despite the attempt to annihilate them, still exist.

Moreover, who show that they know that God's covenant must be upheld by re-creating his people? Who heard this overriding claim and set aside personal comfort, cut personal living standards drastically, gave life, health, energy to the rehabilitation of the remnants of the covenant people? Who give their own lives repeatedly in war and/or guard duty to protect the remnant? Surely the secular Jews of Israel as much as, or more than, the religious Jew, or non-Jews anywhere.

The religious-secular paradox goes deeper still. Instead of choosing to flee at all costs from the terrible fate of exposure to genocide, instead of spending all their energy and money to hide and disappear, Jews all over the world—secular Jews included—renewed and intensified their Jewish existence and continued to have and raise Jewish children. Knowing of the fate to which this choice exposes them (a fate especially dramatically clear in Israel, where year after year the Arabs have preached extermination); aware of how little the world really cared, or cares, and that the first time is always the hardest—what is one to make of the faith of those who made this decision and who live it every day, especially in Israel? The answer has been given most clearly by Emil Fackenheim. To raise a Jewish child today is to bind the child and the child's child on the altar, even as father Abraham bound Isaac. Only, those who do so today know that there is no angel to stop the process and no ram to substitute for more than one and one-half million Jewish children in this lifetime. Such an act then, can only come out of resources of faith, of ultimate meaningfulness—of Exodus trust—on a par with, or superior to, father Abraham at the peak of his life as God's loved and covenanted follower. Before such faith, who shall categorize in easy categories the secular and the devout Israeli or Jew?

A classic revelation of the deeper levels can be found in the "Who is a Jew" controversy, and in the Israeli "Law of Return," which guarantees every Jew automatic admittance into Israel. This law has been used against Israel, in slogans of "racism," by those who say that if Israel only de-Zionizes and gives up this law she would have peace from her Arab neighbors, and by Christians and other non-Jews who then assess Israel as religiously discriminatory. All these judgments cost the secular Israelis a great deal—not least because any weakening of public support means a heightened prospect of genocide for themselves and their children. In turn, the secular Israeli is bitterly criticized by observant Jews for not simply following the traditional definition of who is a Jew. In 1974 this issue even disrupted attempts to form a government, at a time when life-and-death negotiations hung in the balance. Why, then, has the law been stubbornly upheld by the vast majority of secular Israelis?

It reveals the deepest recesses of their souls. They refuse to formally secularize the definition of "Israeli" and thereby cut the link between the covenant people of history and the political body of present Israel—despite their own inability to affirm, or even their vigorous denial of, the covenant! They see Auschwitz as revelatory and commanding, normative as great events in covenant history are, and they are determined to guarantee automatic admission to every Jew—knowing full well he is always exposed (by covenantal existence) to the possibility of another Holocaust with no place to flee. The lesson of Auschwitz is that no human being should lack a guaranteed place to flee again, just as the lesson of the Exodus was that no runaway slave should be turned back to his master (Deut. 23:16). (Needless to say, there is self-interest involved also—more Jews in Israel strengthen the security of Israel. But the admixture of self-interest is part of the reality in which religious imperatives are acted upon by all human beings.)

In light of this, Zionism, criticized by some devout Jews as secular revolt against religion and by other observant Jews for its failures to create a state that fully observes Jewish tradition, is carrying out the central religious actions of the Jewish people after Auschwitz. Irony piles upon irony! The re-creation of the state is the strongest suggestion that God's promises are still valid and reliable. Thus the secularist phenomenon gives the central religious testimony of the Jewish people today. In the Holocaust many rabbis ruled that every Jew killed for being Jewish has died for the sanctification of the name of God. In death as in life, the religious-secular dichotomy is essentially ended.

Dialectical Reflections on the End of the Secular-Religious Difficulty

CONTRA HUMANISM. Once we establish the centrality of the reverence for the image of God and the erosion of the secular-religious dichotomy after Auschwitz, then the dialectic of the Holocaust becomes visible. Such views could easily become embodied in a simple humanism or a new universalist liberation that is totally absorbed in the current secular option. To collapse into this option would be to set up the possibility of another idolatry. True, it would be more likely a Stalinist rather than a fascist idolatry; but it reopens the possibility of the concentration of power and legitimacy which could carry out another Holocaust. We are bidden to resist this temptation. Indeed, there is a general principle at work here. Every solution that is totally at ease with a dominant option is to be seen as an attempt to escape from the dialectical torment of living with the Holocaust. If you do escape, you open up the option that the Holocaust may recur. A radical self-critical humanism springing out of the Holocaust says no to the demons of Auschwitz; a celebration of the death of God or of secular man is collaboration with these demons.

CONTRA PROTEAN MAN. The fury of the Holocaust also undercuts the persuasiveness of another modern emphasis—the sense of option and choice of existence. This sense of widespread freedom to choose identity and of the weakening of biological or inherited status is among the most pervasive values of contemporary culture. It clearly grows out of the quantum leap in human power and control through medicine and technology, backed by the development of democratic and universalist norms. It has generated a revolt against inherited disadvantage, and even genetic or biological limitations. The freedom of being almost protean is perceived as positive—the source of liberation and human dignity. In light of the Holocaust, we must grapple with the question anew. Is the breaking of organic relationships and deracination itself the source of the pathology which erupted at the heart of modernity? Erich Fromm has raised the issue in *Escape from Freedom*. Otto Ohlendorf—the head of D Einsatzgruppe, and one of the very few war criminals willing to admit frankly what he did and why—stressed the search for restored authority and rootedness (e.g., the failure to conserve the given as well as the freely chosen in modern culture) as a major factor in the scope and irrationality of the Nazis' murderous enterprise. Since the attack started against the people of Israel, but planned to go on to Slavs and other groups, it poses a fundamental question to the credibility of modern culture itself. There has not been enough testing and study of this possibility in the evidence of the Holocaust yet, but it warrants a serious study and an immediate reconsideration of the persuasiveness of the "freedom-of-being" option in modernity. The concept is profoundly challenged by the Jewish experience in the Holocaust.[35] For the demonic assault on the people of Israel recognized no such choice. Unlike the situation that prevailed in medieval persecutions, one could not cease to be a Jew through conversion. In retrospect, liberation turned out to be an illusion that weakened the victims' capacity to recognize their coming fate or the fact that the world would not save them—because they were Jews.

CONTRA THE SUPERIORITY OF THE SPIRIT OVER THE FLESH. This insight also reverses the historical, easy Christian polemic concerning the "Israel of the flesh" versus "Israel of the spirit." After all, is not Israel of the spirit a more universal and more committed category, a more spiritually meaningful state, than the status conferred by accident of birth? Yet the Holocaust teaches the reverse. When absolute power arose and claimed to be God, then Israel's existence was antithetical to its own. Israel of the flesh by its mere existence gives testimony, and therefore was "objectively" an enemy of the totalitarian state. By the same token neither commitment to secularism, atheism, or any other faith—nor even joining Christianity— could remove the intrinsic status of being Jewish, and being forced to stand and testify. Fackenheim, Berkovits, Rubenstein, and others have spoken of the denial of significance to the individual Jew by the fact that his fate was decided by his birth—whatever his personal preference. But classical Jewish commentators had a different interpretation. The mere fact that the Jew's existence denies the absolute claims of others means that the Jew is testifying. The act of living speaks louder than the denial of intention to testify, as I have suggested in my comments on fear of God above. During the Holocaust, rabbis began to quote a purported ruling by Maimonides that a Jew killed by bandits—who presumably feel freer to kill him because he is a Jew—has died for the sanctification of the Name, whether or not he was pressured before death to deny his Judaism and his God.[36] This testimony, voluntarily given or not, turns out to be the secret significance of "Israel of the flesh." A Jew's life is on the line and therefore every kind of Jew gives testimony at all times.

Israel of the spirit testifies against the same idolatry and evil. Indeed, there were sincere Christians who stood up for their principles, were recognized as threats, and sent to concentration camps. However, Israel of the spirit only has the choice of being silent; with this measure of collaboration, it can live safely and at ease. Not surprisingly, the vast majority chose to be safe. As Franklin Littell put it, when paganism is persecuting, Christians "can homogenize and become mere gentiles again; while the Jews, believing or secularized, remain representatives of another history, another providence."[37] It suggests that from now on one of the great keys to testimony in the face of the enormously powerful forces available to evil, will be to have given hostages, to be on the line because one is inextricably bound to this fate. The creation of a forced option should be one of the goals of moral pedagogy after the Holocaust. It is the meaning of chosenness in Jewish faith. The Christian analogy of this experience would be a surrender of the often self-deceiving universalist rhetoric of the church and a conception of itself as people of God—a distinct community of faith with some identification—that must testify to the world. . . .

VIII. Living with the Dialectic

The dialectic I have outlined is incredibly difficult to live by. How can we reconcile such extraordinary human and moral tensions? The classical traditions of Judaism and Christianity suggest: by reenacting constantly the event which is normative and revelatory. Only those who experience the normative event in their bones—through the community of the faith—will live by it.[38] I would suggest, then, that in the decades and centuries to come, Jews and others who seek to orient themselves by the Holocaust will unfold another sacral round. Men and women will gather to eat the putrid bread of Auschwitz, the potato-peelings of Bergen-Belsen. They will tell of the children who went, the starvation and hunger of the ghettoes, the darkening of the light in the Mussulmen's eyes. To enable people to reenact and relive Auschwitz there are records, pictures, even films—some taken by the murderers, some by the victims. That this pain will be incorporated in the round of life we regret; yet we may hope that it will not destroy hope but rather strengthen responsibility, will, and faith.

After Auschwitz, one must beware of easy hope. Israel is a perfect symbol for this. On the one hand, it validates the right to hope and speak of life renewed after destruction. On the other hand, it has been threatened with genocide all along. At the moment it is at a low point—yet prospects for a peace also suddenly emerge. Any hope must be sober, and built on the sands of despair, free from illusions. Yet Jewish history affirms hope.

I dare to use another biblical image. The cloud of smoke of the bodies by day and the pillar of fire of the crematoria by night may yet guide humanity to a goal and a day when human beings are attached to each other; and have so much shared each other's pain, and have so purified and criticized themselves, that *never again will a Holocaust be possible*. Perhaps we can pray that out of the welter of blood and pain will come a chastened mankind and faith that may take some tentative and mutual steps toward redemption. Then truly will the Messiah be here among us. Perhaps then the silence will be broken. At the prospect of such hope, however, certainly in our time, it is more appropriate to fall silent.

NOTES

1. Elie Wiesel, *Night* (New York: Hill & Wang, 1960), pp. 43–44.

2. Michael Dov Weissmandl, *Min Hametzar* (1960; reprint ed., Jerusalem, n.d.) p. 24. See also Weissmandl's report of his conversation with the papal nuncio in 1944. He quotes the nuncio as saying: "There is no innocent blood of Jewish children in the world. All Jewish blood is guilty. You have to die. This is the punishment that has been awaiting you because of that sin [deicide]." Dr. Livia Rotkirchen of Yad Vashem has called my attention to the fact that the papal nuncio tried to help save Jews and used his influence to do so. Weissmandl's quote appears to be incompatible with that image. Dr. Rotkirchen speculates that Weissmandl, in retrospect, attributed the statement to the wrong person. In any event, this judgment that the Jews deserved

their fate as punishment for deicide or rejecting Christ is a strong and recurrent phenomenon. On the papal nuncio's work, see Livia Rotkirchen, "Vatican Policy and the Jewish 'Independent' Slovakia (1939–1945)," *Yad Vashem Studies* 6 (1967): pp. 27–54.

3. Pastoral letter of March 25, 1941, A.B. Freiburg, no. 9, March 27, 1941, p. 388; quoted in Günter Lewy, *The Catholic Church and Nazi Germany* (New York: McGraw-Hill, 1964), p. 294.

4. Saul Friedländer, *Pius XII and the Third Reich: A Documentation* (New York: Knopf, 1966), p. 97. Cf. the whole discussion of the decrees by the Vatican, ibid., pp. 92–99.

5. "Ein Wort zur Judenfrage, der Reichsbruderrat der Evangelischen Kirche in Deutschland," issued on April 8, 1948 in Dietrich Goldschmidt and Hans-Joachim Kraus, eds., *Der Ungekundigte Bund: Neue Begegnung von Juden und christlicher* (Stuttgart, 1962), pp. 251–54. The extent to which Vatican circles helped Nazi war criminals escape is only now becoming evident. See on this Gitta Sereny, *Into That Darkness* (London: Andre Deutsch, 1974), pp. 289–323. See also Ladislav Farago, *Aftermath: Martin Bormann and the Fourth Reich* (New York: Simon & Schuster, 1974).

6. Cf. memorandum submitted to Chancellor Hitler, June 4, 1936, in Arthur C. Cochrane, *The Church's Confession Under Hitler* (Philadelphia: Westminster Press, 1962), pp. 268–79; J. S. Conway, *The Nazi Persecution of the Churches* (London: Weidenfeld & Nicolson, 1968), pp. xx, xxiii, 84–85, 261–65.

7. A. Roy Eckardt, *Elder and Younger Brothers* (New York: Scribner's, 1967), p. 107.

8. The trial record of the Einsatzgruppen leaders shows that of twenty-four defendants, Herren Schubert, Lindow, Schulz, Blume, Braune, Sandberger, Haensch, Strauch, and Klingelhoefer were lawyers. Other professionals included architect Blobel, economist Sieberg, professor Six, banker Noske, secondary-school instructor Steimle, economist Ohlendorf, dentist Fendler, and last but not least, clergyman Biberstein.

9. Arnold Toynbee, *A Study of History*, vol. 60, p. 433, quoted in Eliezer Berkovits, *Faith After the Holocaust* (New York: Ktav, 1973), p. 18.

10. Arthur Herzberg, *The French Enlightenment and the Jews* (New York: Columbia University Press, 1968); Uriel Tal, *Yahadut V'Natzrut BaReich Ha-Sheni* [Jews and Christians in the Second Reich], *1870–1914* (Jerusalem: Magnes Press, 1969); and Eleanore Sterling, *Er Ist Wie Du: Fruh Geschichte des Anti Semitismus in Deutschland, 1915–1850* (Munich: Chr. Kaiser, 1956). One should also note Elie Wiesel's biting words on the moral collapse in the camps of "the intellectuals, the liberals, the humanists, the professors of sociology and the like." Elie Wiesel, "Talking and Writing and Keeping Silent," in Franklin H. Littell and Hubert G. Locke, *The German Church Struggle and the Holocaust* (Detroit: Wayne State University Press, 1974), p. 273. It could be that relativism and tolerance, in themselves good or neutral moral qualities, combine with excessive rationalism and functionalism to weaken the capacity to take absolute stands against evil: they rationalize that everything is relative and there is no need to say no! at all costs.

11. Henry Feingold, *The Politics of Rescue* (New Brunswick: Rutgers University Press, 1970), passim and summary, pp. 295–307; David Wyman, *Paper Walls* (Amherst: University of Massachusetts Press, 1968).

12. *Punishment for War Crimes: The Inter-Allied Declaration Signed at St. James's Palace, London on 13th January, 1942 and Relative Documents* (New York: United Nations Information Office, [1943], pp. 5–6. See also U.S. Department of State, *Foreign Relations of the United States: Diplomatic Papers, 1942* (Washington: Government Printing Office, 1960), vol. 1, p. 45, and *Foreign Relations of the United States: Diplomatic Papers, 1941* (Washington, Government Printing Office, 1958), vol. 1, p. 447.

13. Alexander Donat, *The Holocaust Kingdom: A Memoir* (New York: Rinehart, 1965), p. 103.

14. F.E. Cartus [pseud.], "Vatican II and the Jews," *Commentary*, January 1965, p. 21.

15. Elie Wiesel, *The Accident* (New York: Hill & Wang, 1962), p. 91.

16. Elie Wiesel, "The Death of My Father," in *Legends of our Time* (New York: Holt, Rinehart & Winston, 1968), pp. 2, 4, 5, 6, 7; idem, *The Gates of the Forest* (New York: Holt, Rinehart & Winston, 1966), pp. 194, 196, 197, 198, 224, 225–26.

17. Gershom Scholem, *Sabbatai Zevi: The Mystical Messiah* (Princeton: Princeton University Press, 1973).

18. Cf. Maimonides, *Commentary on the Mishnah*, Sanhedrin, chap. 10, mishnah 1.

19. Eliezer Berkovits, *Faith after the Holocaust* (New York: Ktav, 1973); Emil Fackenheim, *God's Presence in History* (New York: New York University Press, 1970); Richard Rubenstein, *After Auschwitz* (Indianapolis: Bobbs-Merrill, 1968), especially pp. 128–29.

20. Richard Rubenstein, "Homeland and Holocaust," in *The Religious Situation 1968* (Boston: Beacon Press, 1969), pp. 39–111.

21. Wiesel, *Night*, p. 71.

22. Wiesel, *The Gates of the Forest*, pp. 225–26.

23. Cf. Rudolf Hoess, *Commandant of Auschwitz* (London: Weidenfeld & Nicolson, 1959), pp. 88–91; Saul Friedlander, *Counterfeit Nazi: The Ambiguity of Good*, (London: Weidenfeld & Nicolson, 1969); p. 21–22, 36, 59, 64.

24. Cf. I. Greenberg, *The Rebirth of Israel: Event and Interpretation* (forthcoming).

25. Compare and contrast Marshall Sklare (with Joseph Greenblum), *Jewish Identity on the Suburban Frontier* (New York: Basic Books, 1967), especially pp. 214–49, 322–26, with T. I. Lenn and Associates, *Rabbi and Synagogue in Reform Judaism* (Hartford: Lenn and Associates, 1972), especially chap. 13, pp. 234–52. Note especially the younger age shift on p. 242. Cf. also how low Israel rates in the "essential" category of being a good Jew, in respondents in Sklare, p. 322.

26. Cf. B.T. Yoma 68b.

27. Jose Faur, "Reflections on Job and Situation Morality," *Judaism* 19, no. 2 (Spring 1970): 219–25, especially p. 220; André Neher, "Job: The Biblical Man," *Judaism* 13, no. 1 (Winter 1964): 37–47; Robert Gordis, "The Lord Out of the

Whirlwind," ibid., especially pp. 49–50, 55–58, 62–63. See also Margarethe Susman, *Das Buch Hiob und das Schicksal des jüdischen Volkes* (Zurich: Steinberg, 1946).

28. Joseph B. Soloveichik, "Kol Dodi Dofek," in *Torah U'Meluchah*, ed. Simon Federbush (Jerusalem: Mossad Harav Kook, 1961), pp. 11–44, especially pp. 21–25.

29. Günter Lewy, *The Catholic Church and Nazi Germany;* Gordon C. Zahn, *German Catholics and Hitler's Wars: A Study in Social Control* (New York: Sheed & Ward, 1962); idem, *In Solitary Witness: The Life and Death of Franz Jägerstätter* (London: Chapman, 1966).

30. *Trial of the Major War Criminals before the International Military Tribunal* (Nuremberg, 1947–49), vol. 29, 1919. PS printed in *Nazi Conspiracy and Aggression* vol. 4, pp. 518–72 especially pp. 559, 563–64, 566 ff., quoted in Joachim C. Fest, *The Face of the Third Reich* (London: Weidenfeld & Nicolson, 1970), p. 119.

31. Wiesel, *Night*, pp. 73–74.

32. Falconi, *The Silence of Pius XII* (Boston: Little, Brown, 1970), pp. 74–80; Saul Friedländer, *Pius XII and the Third Reich*, pp. 123, 139 ff.

33. J. S. Conway, *The Nazi Persecution of the Churches*, pp. 261–65; Saul Friedlander, *Counterfeit Nazi*, pp. 37, 38, 145–49; Falconi, *Silence of Pius XII*, p. 87; Friedlander, *Pius XII and the Third Reich*, pp. 92–102, but see also pp. 114 ff.; Gitta Sereny, *Into That Darkness*, pp. 276 ff., 292–303. See also Weissmandl, *Min Hametzar*, pp. 21–22, 23–24. Cf. also Karl Barth's mea culpa on the Jewish Issue in a letter to Eberhard Bethge quoted in E. Bethge, "Troubled Self-Interpretation and Uncertain Response in the Church Struggle," in Littell and Locke, *German Church Struggle*, p. 167.

34. Cf. Irving Greenberg, "A Hymn to Secularists" (Dialogue of Irving Greenberg and Leonard Fein at the General Assembly in Chicago, November 15, 1974 [cassette distributed by Council of Jewish Federations and Welfare Funds, New York, 1975]).

35. Cf. Erich Fromm, *The Fear of Freedom* (American title, *Escape from Freedom*), 1st ed. (London; Routledge & Kegan Paul, 1942). See George Stein, *The Waffen SS* (Ithaca: Cornell University Press, 1970); for Ohlendorf's testimony, see *Trials of War Criminals Before the Nuremberg Military Tribunals Under Control Council Law No. 10, October 1946–April 1949* (Washington: Government Printing Office, 1952), vol. 4; *United States of America v. Otto Ohlendorf et al.*, case No. 9, pp. 384–91.

36. The purported Maimonides ruling is quoted in Rabbi Simon Huberband's essay on Kiddush Hashem (Sanctification of God's name), found in the collection of his Holocaust writings printed under the title *Kiddush Hashem* (Tel Aviv: Zachor 1969), p. 23. Rabbi Menachem Ziemba, the great rabbinical scholar of Warsaw, is quoted as citing the same Maimonides ruling in Hillel Seidman, *Yoman Ghetto Varsha* (New York: Jewish Book, 1959), p. 221. An exhaustive search of Maimonides' work (including consultation with Dr. Haym Soloveichik, who has edited a mimeographed collection of Maimonides' writings on Kiddush Hashem for the Hebrew University) makes clear that there is no such ruling in Maimonides. The acceptance during the Holocaust of the view that Maimonides issued such a ruling—even by scholars of Maimonides such as Ziemba—only shows the urgency of the need for such a ruling. The Rabbis instinctively recognized that every Jew was making a statement when killed in the Holocaust—the very statement that the Nazis were so frantically trying to silence by killing all the Jews. This is contra Richard Rubenstein's comments in "Some Perspec-

tives on Religious Faith After Auschwitz," in Littell and Locke, *German Church Struggle*, p. 263.

37. Franklin H. Littell, *The German Phoenix: Men and Movements in the Church in Germany* (Garden City, N.Y., 1960), p. 217.

38. Haggadah of Pesach; Exod. 12:13, 20:1–14, 22:21; Lev. 11, esp. v. 45, 19:33–36, 23:42–43, 25:34–55; Deut. 4:30–45, 5:6–18, 15:12–18, 16:1–12, 26:1–11; Josh. 24; Judg. 2:1–5, 11–12; Jer. 2:1–9, 7:22–27, 11:1–8, 16:14–15, 22:7–8, 31:3–33, 32:16–22, 34:8–22; Ezek. 20; Neh. 9.

MOST GOOD SCHOLARSHIP is objective and detached. The object of experience is examined under a microscope or kept at a distance. In the study or laboratory, the scholar ponders a subject, sheds preconceptions, and searches for clarity and truth. The dialogues of such scholars are learned tomes, meticulous exchanges of research. Their work is to be admired.

Occasionally, another form of learning takes place in dialogue. People who have struggled with an issue for years present their deepest, most personal, or painful insights in the hope that these inner struggles may illuminate the views of their audience, inform and recast the confrontation with truth. In these cases, theological dialogue becomes confession, a cathartic cleansing. Dare one say a sacrament?

One such dialogue occurred at the first International Scholars' Conference on the German Church Struggle and the Holocaust, which was held at Wayne State University in 1970. Organized by Franklin H. Littell, Hubert G. Locke, and others, this ongoing annual conference continues to produce ground-breaking scholarship about the Holocaust. None of the work from these meetings, however, has sustained more attention than the encounter between two titans in the field of Holocaust studies: Richard Rubenstein, whose work *After Auschwitz: Radical Theology and Contemporary Judaism* had forced the Jewish community to confront the theological issues raised by the Holocaust and Israel; and Elie Wiesel, then a young writer who had emerged after a decade of silence and another fifteen years of relative obscurity to become the spokesman for those who were murdered in the Holocaust. Both men testified about the truths they had lived.

One man spoke of the outer dimension of the Holocaust—of power and mastery, politics and technology. The other spoke of the inner world of the concentration camp—of defiance and spiritual resistance, of divinity and humanity, of despair and Jewish resilience.

In this encounter both men prefigured books they would write. Rubenstein anticipated the theme of *The Cunning of History*, in which he presents the Holocaust as an extreme expression of the mainstream

346

of Western civilization. Wiesel spoke of silence, a theme that has come to haunt many of his works.

One man spoke of the God who abandoned His people and must consequently be abandoned by that people if Jews are to live with integrity and transmit a truthful legacy to the post-Holocaust generation. The other writer could neither abandon God nor affirm Him. He wrestled with the mystery of faith and admired the believer he once had been.

One man broke with tradition; the other could not. "If you want difficulties," Wiesel writes, "chose to live with God. Can you compare the tragedy of the believer to that of the nonbeliever? The real tragedy, the real drama is the drama of the believer."

The encounter was direct and unexpected. Littell and Locke, who edited the book that first contained the exchange between Rubenstein and Wiesel, write: "On Wednesday evening of the conference, the distinguished novelist, Elie Wiesel, was to speak on "The Literature of the Holocaust." As indicated in his opening remarks, Mr. Wiesel chose not to speak on the announced topic, but, instead, to address himself in part to the lecture previously given by Dr. Richard Rubenstein as well as the larger, more basic questions about the Holocaust: What can be told, what can be written, where must silence be kept, what can be witnessed only by living?"

Those who attended the conference still speak of that dialogue. Such interactions are the essence of intellectual engagement. They are part of the lore of Holocaust scholarship.

Writing in 1987, for example, Christian theologian Michael D. Ryan, one of the younger scholars in attendance, recalls "the brilliant and intense conversations that I had with my luncheon companion for four days, Rabbi Richard Rubenstein. . . . It is significant in view of what I am going to report that Rubenstein was the first to tell me about the works of Elie Wiesel. He said among other things that his was the most important voice to be heard today."

Ryan goes on to recount how Rubenstein's talk on the fourth afternoon of the conference left "a certain mood of disquietude" that was still "noticeable in the auditorium as Elie Wiesel rose to speak on that evening." Setting aside most of his prepared address, Wiesel offered a moving rejoinder to Rubenstein. Many in the audience— including a number of Ryan's fellow Christians—preferred Wiesel's view, but Ryan especially cautioned the Christians not to "use Wiesel's faith as a way to dismiss the doubt that Rubenstein's address raised for you. You must not try to get around it, for his is the brook of fire for you to pass through on your way to meaningful faith."

Ryan's point was that "to have a Jew [Rubenstein] question the existence of the God of Torah, as the God of history, was even more threatening [to Christian tradition and belief] than Jewish statements of faith, for it attacked the fundamental premise of all Biblical faith."

Ryan is not alone in reporting that he still ponders "the issue between Wiesel who spoke with the authority of a survivor and Rubenstein who spoke with the authority of complete honesty and from his own rational perception of an irrational universe." Ryan concludes: "Richard Rubenstein's resignation to life in this absurd world of power without benefit of consolation of traditional religious faith is just as authentic as Wiesel's affirmation of religious faith as a kind of holy madness appropriate for our time."

Those who were not there can still listen and learn—the reader can wrestle with these men and against them. The issues that permeate religious discussions of the Holocaust were all raised in this critical debate.

Perhaps the answers too—but most certainly all the questions.

Richard L. Rubenstein and Elie Wiesel

An Exchange

I.
Rubenstein: Some Perspectives on Religious Faith after Auschwitz

One of the oldest tasks confronting a father in the Jewish tradition is that of deciding what he will hand down to his children. Personality is very largely a distillation of memory. A very significant part of the personality children take with them is dependent upon what they receive from their father. I therefore begin this discussion of theology by sharing with my audience some things that have happened to me within the family circle. I do so because of my conviction that theology can no longer be an interpretation of the received Word of God. It may have been that at one time. Since Sören Kierkegaard, a certain subjectivity has entered the discipline. The theologian must share with his readers his own personal religious existence. It is no longer possible for the theologian to be primarily the spokesman for or the defender of institutionally defined faith. If one wishes to be a theologian in our time, one must begin with the personal equation.

In the summer of 1960 I visited Europe for the first time. I spent the summer partly in Amsterdam and partly at a Dutch North Sea resort, Wyk aan Zee. I had just completed my doctorate and wanted to visit my wife's native land. She was the same age that Anne Frank would have been had she survived. She had escaped from Holland

From Franklin H. Littell and Hubert G. Locke, eds., *The German Church Struggle and the Holocaust*. Detroit: Wayne State University Press, 1974. Reprinted by permission of Franklin H. Littell and Hubert G. Locke.

during the four days of the German invasion of May 1940. Her family was among the very few Dutch Jewish survivors of the Holocaust. We wanted to visit her childhood home as well as to come to know those of her relatives who had been fortunate enough to survive.

At first it did not occur to me that I might have any interest in meeting Germans or visiting Germany in spite of the fact that Germany was only a few hours away. Then I began to notice German visitors, especially at Wyk aan Zee. There were signs everywhere in German advertising *Zimmer frei*, "room available." I remember my first contact with a German. An elderly man thought I was Dutch and asked me for directions. I did not know whether to be courteous or react in rage. At the time I could only see Germans as cold-blooded, mass murderers of my people.

Things became more complicated on the beach. My children often played ball with their Dutch cousins. Occasionally, the ball would roll near a German family. They would invariably return it. Eventually, I had to face the question: Could I permit my children to play with Germans? This may seem trivial, but the question had great existential import for me at the time. And, I was not able to resolve it satisfactorily.

In August of that year, I took my eleven-year-old son Aaron into Germany to see the country that had caused our family and our people so much horror. When I first crossed the border, I had the distinct feeling that I was entering enemy territory. The town we first visited was Düsseldorf. By accident we met Dr. Hans Lamm and the editors of the *Allgemeine Wochenzeitung der Juden in Deutschland*. Through Dr. Lamm's good offices, we were invited to attend a briefing which was being given by the *Bundespresseamt*, the Press and Information Office of the Federal Republic, in Bonn. This followed the season of the *"Schmiererei,"* the defacing of synagogues which had just taken place throughout West Germany.

My son listened intently during the briefings. He was understandably very curious. As we drove back to Holland, he began to ask me questions about Auschwitz. They were not the kind of questions I had expected. I thought my son would ask me about the Germans. He did not. He took it for granted that the murders had been the will of the German people and their legally constituted government. Most of his questions were about the United States.

"Daddy," he said, "didn't the Americans know there was an Auschwitz?"

"Yes, they did," I replied.

"Well, if that's so, couldn't they have done anything about it?"

"I'm not sure."

"Well, didn't we have any German prisoners of war?"

"Yes, we did."

"Couldn't they have been used as hostages to make the Germans behave?" he asked.

I couldn't answer and I would not today suggest that we could have effectively held German prisoners hostage to Nazi good behavior. What is important was that my son perceived that more was involved in the Holocaust than the Nazis and their victims. As I wrote in *After Auschwitz*, a shadow of alienation entered that eleven-year-old boy which has never left him. One of the most important effects of my taking my son into Germany was that both of us had to face the question of what kind of human community might be possible for him—not only with Germans but also with his fellow Americans. Both of us had to ask ourselves what sense of community we might have with our fellowmen, especially since we refused to delude ourselves that only the Germans thought the world would be better off without Jews.

Above all, I did not want him to hate Germans, not for the sake of Germans but for his own sake. I understood that hatred is a poison which eats away at the soul. If hatred cannot be directed against an external object in realistic action, it will sooner or later turn against the subject who possesses the hate. It was not my wish to see my son grow up possessed of a hatred against Germans which he would be compelled to expend against himself.

Nor did I want his image of himself as a Jew to be controlled by that of the helpless victim going up in smoke. There was nothing in any way dishonorable or degrading about those who were compelled to become victims. Nevertheless, it was not an identity which any man ought to be compelled to choose if he were not compelled by fate so to do.

The problem of my children's developing identities was further intensified by the fact that they knew that their mother had literally escaped by the skin of her teeth. One day during that 1960 sojourn, I chanced upon my nine-year-old daughter Hannah. She was walking near the Westerkerk opposite the Anne Frank House. I noticed that she was reading and was oblivious of everything around her.

"What are you reading, Hannah?" I asked.

"Anne Frank's Diary."

In June 1969, nine years later, I again visited Germany, this time to take delivery of a new Volkswagen at the factory in Wolfsburg. We were visiting Paris at the time. The day before I was scheduled to go, my younger son Jeremy who was then eleven, the same age his older brother had been nine years before, asked,

"Daddy, can I come with you?"

After thinking it over, I replied, "Yes, Jeremy, you may."

The two of us took the night train to Hanover and thence to Wolfsburg where we picked up the car. We were impressed by the enormous industrial chimneys which towered above the Volkswagen plant, but somehow they made us think of the chimneys of the crematoria of yesteryear. We returned to Paris by way of Cologne where we spent the night. While in Cologne, Jeremy began to ask me almost the same questions his brother had nine years before. Jeremy was aware of the family history. His reaction was, however, slightly different.

As we stood in the plaza before the great Cologne Cathedral at about nine in the evening, Jeremy suddenly turned to me and shrieked.

"Daddy, get me out of here. I don't want to be near these people."

I understood his reaction. It was a shudder of utter horror when he realized the enormity of what the people around him had done. Nevertheless, as a father, it was my responsibility to help him mature as an individual who was beyond both hatred and resentment, the fruitless aggression of the powerless, so that he could deal realistically not only with Germans but with all non-Jews in the years to come.

Regrettably, there is more to the problem. I am not unaware of the history of the Nazi period. Although I would certainly defer to historians of the period for some precise details—I am painfully aware of the relations between both the Evangelical and the Catholic Church and the Nazis. There were, of course, individual and group resistance; but, in general, the record of the Christian Church towards the specific issue of the extermination of the Jews was less than heroic. The mystery of Pope Pius XII's reaction to the events remains a painful question to this very day. It is clear that the Pontiff knew in great detail what was happening. For considerations which remain unknown to this day, he was unwilling to utter any protest. How shall I interpret this to my children? Shall I simply say that the fraternal bond, problematic as it has been throughout history, between Jew and Christian broke down completely? Could I encourage my children to look for a reconciliation some day based upon Christian repentance and Jewish acceptance of the Christian confession? To look for such a result would be neither realistic nor even desirable. Were Christians made to feel guilty, they might someday be driven to justify the very thing that made them feel guilty. Any human encounter based upon the idea that one side bears some kind of mark of Cain and must forever do penance to the other precludes genuine reconciliation, especially between rival religious traditions.

Another way of handling the problem might be simply for Jews to avoid, wherever possible, all relations with Christians. One important Jewish theologian is reported to have declared that he will abstain from dialogue with Christians until they repent. It is difficult to take such a position seriously. The theologian in question has willingly accepted many invitations to appear before Christian audiences. Such speaking is already an act of dialogue and encounter. The man's actions simply belie his words. It is no more possible for Jew and Christian to break off dialogue than for the various segments of the family of man to become totally exclusive, non-communicating atomic units. It simply will not work.

The question of what I, as a father, can hand down to my sons and daughter involves another visit to Germany, one which I describe in *After Auschwitz*. On August 15, 1961, two days after the DDR (*Deutsche Demokratische Republik*) erected the wall between East and West Berlin, I arrived in Bonn from Amsterdam to survey political and cultural trends in West Germany. At the urging of my hosts, the *Bundespresseamt*, the Press and Information Office of the Federal Republic, I decided to fly immediately to Berlin.

On August 17, 1961, at 4:30 in the afternoon, I had a two-hour conversation with Probst Dr. Heinrich Grüber at his home in Berlin-Dahlem. Dean Grüber had been the only German to testify in Jerusalem against Adolf Eichmann at the celebrated trial earlier that summer. He had a distinguished record in the defense of Jewish rights, or at least, the rights of Christians of "non-Aryan" origin, during the Nazi period. He had himself been a concentration camp inmate. We talked under almost apocalyptic conditions. American army tanks rumbled outside his home. He was pastor of a church in East Berlin. Living in West Berlin he was very upset that he was cut off from his flock. He began to use the imagery of the biblical theology of history to describe what was happening.

God was punishing a sinful Germany, he declared. He asserted that God was making Germans refugees as the Germans had made others homeless. Having commenced with his biblical interpretation of recent history, he could not stop until he asserted that it had been God's will to send Adolf Hitler to exterminate Europe's Jews. At the moment that I heard Grüber make that assertion, I had what was perhaps the most important single crisis of faith I have ever had. I recognized that Grüber was not an Antisemite and that his assertion that the God of the Covenant was and is the ultimate Author of the great events of Israel's history was no different from the faith of any traditional Jew. Grüber was applying the logic of Covenant Theology to the events of the twentieth century. I appreciated his fundamental honesty. He recognized that, if one takes the biblical theology of history seriously, Adolf Hitler is no more nor less an instrument of God's wrath than Nebuchadnezzar.

If I were a fundamentalist Christian I might be tempted to say to the Jewish community, "See here, you deluded people. When are you going to see the light? When are you going to stop being punished by God and accept his supreme gift to you, by confessing that Jesus Christ is the Redeemer of Israel?"

Nor do I regard such a question by an evangelical Christian as Antisemitic. If one accepts the doctrine that God is distinctively involved in the history of Israel, the fundamentalist Christian may indeed be right in asserting that the sorrows of the Jews have been inflicted upon them for rejecting Jesus. Whether one is a fundamentalist Christian or a traditional Jew, it is impossible to regard the sorrows of Jewish history as mere historical accidents. They must in some sense express the will of God as a just and righteous Creator. Either such a God is a sadist who inflicts pain because he enjoys it or he has a reason for the misfortune he inflicts. The only morally defensible motive for a superior to inflict pain on an inferior would be punitive chastisement which has as its purpose altering the victim's mode of behavior. If one takes Covenant Theology seriously, as did Dean Grüber, Auschwitz must be God's way of punishing the Jewish people in order that they might better see the light, the light of Christ if one is a Christian, the light of Torah if one is a traditional Jew.

I have often stated that the idea that a God worthy of human adoration could have inflicted Auschwitz on what was allegedly his people is obscene. But, notice the terrible price one must pay if one rejects the God of the Covenant. If the God of the Covenant exists, at Auschwitz my people stood under the most fearsome curse that God has ever inflicted. If the God of history does not exist, then the Cosmos is ultimately absurd in origin and meaningless in purpose. We have been thrust into the world in which life proliferates, has its hour, only to disappear amidst the further proliferation of life. As human beings we are divided by historical and geographical accident into the tribes of mankind, to no ultimate reason or purpose. We simply are there for but a moment only to disappear into the midnight silence of Eternal Chaos. Like Kierkegaard, I have had to choose between a world without the biblical God and the leap into faith. I have had a slightly different "Either-Or" than Kierkegaard. I have had to decide whether to affirm the existence of a God who inflicts Auschwitz on his guilty people or to insist that nothing the Jews did made them more deserving of Auschwitz than any other people, that Auschwitz was in no sense a punishment, and that a God who would or could inflict such punishment does not exist. In other words, I have elected to accept what Camus has rightly called the courage of the absurd, the courage to live in a meaningless, purposeless Cosmos rather than believe in a God who inflicts Auschwitz on his people.

I have done so as a rabbi and a theologian in the full knowledge that my choice has been rejected by my people. Nevertheless, I would rather be rejected by my people than affirm their guilt at Auschwitz.

Nor does Israel's victory in the Six Day War of 1967 alter that judgment. It might be argued that the same God who delivered the Jews to the ovens also gave them Jerusalem in 1967. When I stood at the Wall for the first time during the summer of 1967, people who knew me came up to me and asked,

"What do you think now? God has given us all of Jerusalem!"

"God is not on the side of the Jews," I replied, "nor is he against the Arabs. The Jews and the Arabs both love this place and consider it their own. We have a terrible conflict. But, to treat the Arab as *villain* rather than *enemy* is to misconceive the nature of the conflict. I refuse to say *Gott mit uns* under any circumstances."

The Six Day War, tentative as its conclusions may have been, is no royal road back to the God of History.

Nor can I make sense out of Auschwitz by regarding it as the latest of a long series of Antisemitic acts inflicted upon Jews by Christians. Auschwitz represents something altogether novel and materially distinct from previous Jewish misfortunes. There is, for example, a difference between the "civilized" Antisemitism of earlier ages and what must be called the Antisemitism of the technological barbarians of the twentieth century. As bitter as was the hostility of Ferdinand and Isabella, the Catholic monarchs of Spain in 1492, against the Jews, they must be seen as civilized Antisemites. They reigned at a time when 781 years of Islamic presence was coming to an end on the Iberian peninsula. Once the Moors had departed, the monarchs had to face the problem of whether they had achieved the religious unity for which their people had fought. As long as there were non-Christians in Spain, that nation's sacred consensus eluded them. At the time, the idea of a secular society was totally unthinkable in Spain. There were several hundred thousand Jews in Spain. The way the monarchs dealt with them highlights the difference between civilized Antisemitism and modern Antisemitism.

They gave the Jews three options: The first was to be baptized and become part of Christian Spain; the second was to leave the country if baptism was impossible. Jews who left were permitted to take what they could carry with them. The choice was a harsh one, but it is crucial that we understand that Ferdinand and Isabella had no interest in exterminating Jews simply because they were Jews. Their interest was in the creation of a Christian Spain, not the extermination of the Jews.

The Jews had a third, tragic option: they could remain on Spanish soil as Jews, but they would be killed if they did so. Nevertheless, this option of extremity was not without dignity. Let us imagine a Jew saying to himself, "I can neither leave this place which I love nor become a Christian."

By his decision such a man elected martyrdom. His death was freely chosen. It served as a witness both to his love of place and his Jewish faith. This is in stark contrast to what took place in the Nazi death camps. One of Hitler's greatest victories was that he deprived the Jews of *all* opportunity to be martyrs. There can be no martyrdom without free choice. In the camps it made no difference whether you were Dr. Edith Stein, who had become a Carmelite nun, or a Hasidic rabbi. All Jews were slaughtered without distinction. Even baptism provided no escape. It must sadly be noted that the pathetic attempts of the Jewish community to see the six million as martyrs is a tragic albeit understandable misperception.

Unfortunately, Auschwitz can be seen as the first triumph of technological civilization in dealing with what may become a persistent human problem, the problem of the waste disposal of superfluous human beings in an overpopulated world. I hope that my deliberate use of language indifferent to the moral dimension is noted. I have attempted to use language as did the Nazis when they spoke of exterminating people as *Sonderbehandlung*, special handling. Part of the technology of mass slaughter involves a process of so laundering the language used to describe the process that it appears to be a technological problem and not an act which takes place between human beings.

When I visited Poland in 1965, it was immediately apparent that, for all of their hatred of the Jews, the Poles could not have created Auschwitz. They simply did not have the technological competence required for the rationalized, bureaucratic structures employed so successfully by the Germans. It is because the Germans were so much at home in technological civilization that they were able to succeed so well in their experiment in human waste disposal.

Hitler has demonstrated how superfluous people can be dispatched with an extraordinary economy of means. He has also demonstrated that such a project need have few, if any, lasting, undesirable effects on the perpetrating group. The Germans are today a healthy, prosperous community. As a frequent visitor to that country, I have often been struck with how healthy Germany is—for Germans. Having gotten rid of the disturbing presence of the Jews, the Germans have solved a problem which had plagued them since the emancipation. Germany today is closer to being the *Volksgemeinschaft*, the homogenous Volk community, the Nazis sought than at any time since the emancipation. If we dismiss all moral considerations, as did the Germans themselves, Hitler's project can be seen as a superlative success. It also invites repetition, if not against the Jews then against other minorities which disturb the harmonious existence of a dominant majority.

Furthermore, as Hannah Arendt has pointed out in *The Origins of Totalitarianism*, there is today no longer any credible intellectual basis for affirming the existence of *human rights*. Such rights in the abstract are meaningless. The only rights an individual has are those he possesses by virtue of his membership in a concrete community which has the power to guarantee him those rights. Without such a community, a man can rely on no residue of universally accepted human rights. Such isolated individuals can easily find themselves in a situation of total rightlessness, as did the death camp inmates.

Miss Arendt's observations are profoundly important theologically. If an individual has no rights beyond those granted to him by his political or kinship community, then all talk about natural, moral law or about a God who endows man with a certain irreducible dignity has been demonstrated by the Germans to be of no consequence when such talk might really matter. Theologians or moralists may argue that all men possess some God-given irreducible measure of dignity, but such talk will neither deter future emulators of the Nazis nor comfort realistically their victims. The Germans have proven their point in the most effective way possible, by successfully dispatching their victims with no countervailing force to impede them until it was too late. Even the verbal impediment of denouncing the Nazis was withheld by those religious authorities who have been most insistent in their assertion of the existence of natural law and the reality of human rights under God. It is not I who have rejected human rights. The German success in ridding themselves of population elements they deemed undesirable has made those rights no longer credible.

A very interesting example is cited by Miss Arendt in support of her argument that human rights are no longer credible. At the conclusion of the war in 1945, the Italian government offered all Jews on Italian soil immediate Italian citizenship. Almost all of the Jews involved instinctively understood that such an offer, as generous and well-intentioned as it may have been, was nevertheless an illusory solution to their problem. They knew that they could not possibly achieve instantaneous affiliation in one of the many primary communities which together constitute the larger Italian community. In good times their citizenship and the rights which accrued to it might be undisturbed; in times of stress their citizenship would prove as worthless as had that of the Jews of Germany. If any reason for the establishment of the State of Israel makes sense to the survivors of the camps, it is that the survivors understood that neither divine sanction nor abstract assertions about civic equality and human decency has any practical credibility to *any* group of people any longer. This is no longer primarily a Jewish problem. Human rights and dignity can only be attained by membership in a community that has the *power* to guarantee those rights. Regrettably, the word *power* must be underscored.

Paradoxically, this insight has made it possible for me and, hopefully, my children to encounter the non-Jewish world, especially the Christian world, without anger or resentment: *we could only be angry or resentful if we expected some standard of conduct from the Christian world which it failed to observe.* But if Auschwitz has taught us anything, it is that in times of stress rights and dignity are most likely to be operative within one's primary or kinship group, if indeed they are operative at all. I earnestly wish it were otherwise. It is my conviction that in pre-modern societies it often was otherwise. Nevertheless, I do not see how one can escape the sorrowful conclusion that he alone has rights and dignity who has the power to enforce those rights or belongs to a group that possesses such power. The possession of power is indispensable for human dignity.

In 1967 there was disappointment and even anger in the Jewish community that most Christians did not share their fears for Israel's survival. It was my conviction that the Jewish attitude was fundamentally mistaken. Because of my background and religious commitments, the fate of Israel is of overwhelming importance to me. Nevertheless, I have no right to expect that what was decisive for me has to be decisive for Christians as well. The fundamental issue for Israel is whether it has the capacity to survive. Reluctantly, I have come to the conclusion that, in the long run, Israel will survive only if it has the capacity to do so unaided by any other power. Without such a capacity, there will be no credible moral deterrent to the extermination of its Jewish population by the surrounding Arabs were they ever to be victorious.

As bleak as this view may seem, it nevertheless makes human fellowship possible for me and, again, hopefully, for my children. I have no unrealistic expectation that human beings will act contrary to their nature. I believe in the psychological reality of the Fall. I am neither disappointed nor resentful when people behave in a way which is both predictable and consistent with their nature. In times of stress, it is unrealistic to expect much virtue or magnanimity from the generality of men, no matter how praiseworthy such behavior may be when it surfaces unexpectedly.

This does not mean that Hitler was right in his leadership of the German people. On the contrary, had Hitler really taken power seriously, he would have recognized the *limits* of German power. Had he acted more circumspectly, Germany would not today be a divided country caught between Russia and the United States. The German catastrophe took place because Hitler did not have the ancient pagan understanding that all action which overreaches itself—all *hubris*—is sooner or later defeated by Almighty *Nemesis*.

The German catastrophe was, I believe, largely due to the fact that Nazism was never a *genuine* paganism but a kind of Judeo-Christian heresy. In *After Auschwitz* I cite an observation of Jean-Paul Sartre in his biography of *Baudelaire* which is relevant to this point. Sartre contends that the priest who celebrates a black mass, thereby inverting Christian ritual and belief, is by no means indifferent to Christianity as might be a genuine pagan. He hates Christianity, but he is dialectically related to the religious system he both accepts and rejects at the same time. Thus, Nazism cannot be understood as neo-paganism, as it has been by the distinguished Jewish theologian, Emil Fackenheim. Nazism dialectically negated heretical Christianity. Had the Germans been true pagans, they would have practiced the ancient pagan virtues of moderation and respect for limits.

In conclusion, I would like to offer my own confession of faith after Auschwitz. I am a pagan. To be a pagan means to find once again one's roots as a child of Earth and to see one's own existence as wholly and totally an earthly existence. It means once again to understand that for mankind the true divinities are the gods of earth, not the high gods of the sky; the gods of space and place, not the gods of time; the gods of home and hearth, not the gods of wandering, though wanderers we must be. Though every single establishment Jewish theologian rejects this position, the Jewish people have given their assent—with their feet. They have gone home. The best part of that people has ceased to be wanderers. They have once again found a place of their own on this earth. That is paganism.

In spite of the apprehensions of the Jewish theological mainstream, paganism does not mean the rejection of one's people's ancestral dance, its distinctive rituals, or its ancestral story. Both the dance and the story have their place within the renewed affirmation of earthly existence. Before the return to Israel, the story seemed to point to a linear progression of the Jewish people in exile. In reality, the story was always about a cyclical movement. Exiled from their land for two thousand years, after Auschwitz they have come home. Auschwitz was indeed the terminal expression of exile. After Auschwitz the Jews of Europe had no viable alternative save homecoming if they were to survive with dignity. The deepest and the most profound of all strivings in the individual and the group may indeed be the striving to return to one's place of origin. Theologically, that striving may be conjoined with a return to the archaic gods of the place of origin.

I should like to conclude with an anecdote about my maternal grandmother. She came to the United States as a young woman from Lithuania. She was an Orthodox Jewish woman who never learned to speak English. Once settled in New York City, she never moved from what was then the Jewish ghetto in the Lower East Side.

I remember one day in 1936 when, as a twelve-year-old, I went to visit her. This was difficult for me because I could not speak Yiddish. Our communication was, of necessity, almost completely non-verbal. I accidentally opened up one of her drawers where I discovered a paper bag filled with dirt. On the outside of the bag, there was the stamp of the British government of Palestine. The bag, with its dirt, had been sent to her from the Holy Land. My own Jewish training was exceedingly limited but I had the good sense not to ask her any questions about the bag. I shut the drawer and did not see the bag until years later. As they lowered my grandmother's coffin into her grave, her oldest son took that paper bag containing the earth of the land of Israel and poured it on the head of the coffin. At that moment I understood something about my grandmother for the first time. My grandmother was a wandering Jew all of her life, but she did not want to wander forever. Somewhere deep within her psyche, she wanted to go home. Her way of going home, at least symbolically, was to return to the earth of her ultimate place of origin as a Jew, the Holy Land. She was a child of earth. In death she wanted her dust to mingle with the dust of the home of her ancestors. I am also convinced that she was returning to the Great Goddess of that earth. In her own way, my grandmother was as thoroughgoing a pagan as I am.

II. Wiesel: Talking and Writing and Keeping Silent

In truth, I think I have never spoken about the Holocaust except in one book, *Night*—the very first—where I tried to tell a tale directly, as though face to face with the experience. All my subsequent books are built around it. I tried to communicate a secret, a kind of an eclipse, and in the Kafka tradition even the eclipse is eclipsed. The secret itself is a secret.

Let me, therefore, not stick to the subject I have been given but rather tell you a few stories. One of them I heard was told not by a Jew but by Jean Cocteau, a French surrealist. It is only an anecdote, but it fits me and us very well. Jean Cocteau was asked, "Mr. Cocteau, if your house were on fire, what would you take away?" And he said, "The fire, naturally." I think what we took away from our tales and from our burning houses in European history was the fire.

A second story, not by Cocteau and not about him was about a *shammes*. A *shammes* means, in English, a beadle, someone who performs certain tasks in the synagogue. In American synagogues there is no beadle—they are all very high officials, very elegantly dressed. The *shammes* is one type that has completely disappeared from our American Jewish scene. Usually the *shammes*, the beadle, was a poor man, often hunchbacked, usually taciturn. I speak about one in my "Moishe-the-Beadle," and there is an authentic story about another: Somewhere in Russia, in a ghetto, a *shammes* called Moishe went mad; day after day he would come to the synagogue, ascend the *bima*, a kind of podium, bang his fist on the pulpit, and say to God, "*Ribbono shel Olam*, Master of the Universe, I want you to know that we are still here." Day after day. Then began the transports. The ghetto was decimated; it had fewer and fewer Jews. Still the beadle came, mad as he was, and with anger or was it laughter, he would pound his fist on the table, saying, "Master of the Universe, I want you to know, we are still *here*." Finally came the last transport, and he was the only Jew who remained in the ghetto. For some reason, the madmen were left behind, as they remained behind in my own town. He was alone in the ghetto. He came to the synagogue, again ascended the *bima*, opened the sanctuary, and banged his fist against the sanctuary, "Master of the Universe, I want you to know, *I* am still here." And then he stopped, only to murmur: "But *you*—where are *you*?"

I don't know what happened to Moishe-the-beadle. I don't even know what happened to Him, the One he addressed. I don't even know whether *I* am here. I say it because, when I think back twenty-five years—one generation, a quarter of a century—sometimes I wonder whether the person inside me who was a child during the war comes from the same root as I, has lived the same experiences, has seen what I have seen. I wonder whether there was a Holocaust at all.

The first three days of the war—in 1944—when the child entered the Kingdom of Night, I remember that the child did not believe—for three days he did not believe that there was a war; that there was such a thing as war. And for three days I didn't believe that the Jews were being killed. I still remember the dream I thought I had: I was with my father, and for three days and three nights the child I was kept saying to his father over and over, "It's not true; it cannot be. It is impossible that Jews could be killed in such a manner, and the world remain silent?" That was my question: Could the world remain silent? Later I found out that the world was silent and that the things which I *thought* happened did indeed occur.

But during the war all the Jews who were trapped inside had no idea that the outside world was aware of what was happening. I listened today to Dick Rubenstein. Of course I share his anger and his despair. Indeed you must know it was fortunate that Jews in the camps didn't realize what was happening in the world. Had the Jews in the camps known that Roosevelt and Churchill and De Gaulle and the Pope and everybody knew, and no one cared, I think they would have committed suicide. I think they would have chosen *not* to survive.

The only ones who *did* know were those who went to their death. I don't know whether you have ever had an occasion to see albums—albums of pictures taken as souvenirs by German officers, amateur photographers, to entertain their guests. It is unbelievable: they were taking pictures. I spent hours looking at those pictures, wondering how any man could have taken them, and how the life immobilized there is still there.

When you look at those pictures, what strikes you are the eyes. And then when you see the eyes, you understand what they were thinking. They went to their deaths without anger, without hate, without sadness, and without shame. I think that they went to their deaths with a terrible feeling of pity. They felt pity—pity for those in the outside world who could go on living with the knowledge of what was happening inside. And here I must disassociate myself from Dick. His was a very moving, eloquent, and disturbing address, in which he tried to explain his philosophy of how one survives or lives in a cruel, cold world of absurdity, what he termed the "God-is-dead world." I never spoke of God in that way, Dick. I never spoke of God at all. Maybe because I come from a little *shtetl* and because I was a *Yeshiva Bocher*—and still am, in a way. And maybe because, for years and years throughout my childhood, I learned that before I said "God is alive," I had to be prepared. I remember we had to go to the *Mikvah*—the ritual bath—in order to be worthy of affirming something as important as "God is blessed"; God is God.

Therefore, I never speak of God now. I rather speak of men who believed in God or men who denied God. How strange that the philosophy denying God came not from the survivors. Those who came out with the so-called God is dead theology, not one of them had been in Auschwitz. Those who had never said it. I have my problems with God, believe me. I have my anger and I have my quarrels and I have my nightmares. But my dispute, my bewilderment, my astonishment is with men. I didn't understand how men could be so "barbarian," as you called it, Dick. I still don't understand it. Maybe because I come from a Yeshiva and that all I learned at the Sorbonne was nothing comparable to what I studied in the Yeshiva. I also don't understand how so many Jews remained human inside the camps. I will never understand it. You spoke of hate—that you don't want your children to hate. Let me reassure you, Dick, a Jew is incapable of hate. In the Bible, wherever hate is mentioned, it always refers to self-hate. The only hate that a Jew is capable of—unfortunately—is self-hate. But then he does it well. We cannot hate our neighbors; we cannot even hate our enemies. Look at Israel; Israelis do not hate the Arabs.

Let me tell you something else. Strange as it may sound, there was no hate involved in the relationship between Jew and German. We didn't hate the Germans, and the Germans didn't hate us. It was worse. You can hate only a human being. To them we were objects. Man doesn't hate objects. And we didn't hate them because we are incapable of hate, especially as they then represented the *Malach Hamavet*, the Angel of Death. How can you hate death? How can you hate something which is beyond you and which sometimes wears the mask of God? How can you? We didn't.

Furthermore, when I think of the Jews in the camps, what astonishes me is that so many of them remained human despite everything. I'll give you an example. As I told you, I came from a Yeshiva taken away straight from the Talmud. All of us—I wasn't the only one; when I say "I," I mean all of us—were taken away from the Yeshiva, from the Talmud, straight to Birkenau. And for three days I was in a daze, I couldn't believe what I saw. Then I awakened and I remember that immediately after, it must have been on the fourth or fifth day, I was sent to a commando. I have never told this story, because I consider it too personal. I was sent to a commando to carry stones. The man with whom I carried stones—I never saw his face, only his neck and I remember only his voice—the very first day he asked me, "Where do you come from?" I told him. "What do you do at home?" I said I was a *Yeshiva Bocher*; I studied. He said, "What tractate did you study?" I told him. He said, "What page?" I told him. He said, "Let's continue." I said, "Are you mad? *Here?* Without books, without anything and *why?*" He said, "We must continue. That is the only way." And believe it or not, we continued. He was a famous *Rosh Yeshiva*, the famous head of a famous Yeshiva Talmudic school in Galicia. He used to recite a passage and I would repeat it, day after day. We studied Talmud to the very end. That a man like this not only studied but also taught Talmud in Auschwitz, that is a source of wonder to me. Also the fact that he was not the only one.

There was a man who smuggled in a pair of *tefillin*, phylacteries. It cost him I don't know how many rations, portions of bread. He smuggled them in and there were at least two hundred Jews who got up every day one hour before everybody to stand in line and to perform the Mitzvah. Absurd! Yes, it was absurd to put on the phylacteries. Do you know there were Jews there who fasted on Yom Kippur! There were Jews who said prayers! There were Jews who sanctified the name of Israel, of their people, simply by remaining human!

Within the system of the concentration camp, something very strange took place. The first to give in, the first to collaborate—to save their lives—were the intellectuals, the liberals, the humanists, the professors of sociology, and the like. Because suddenly their whole concept of the universe broke down. They had nothing to lean on. Very few Communists gave in. There were some, but very few. They had their own church-like organization—a secular church, but very well organized. They were the resisters. Even fewer to give in were the Catholic priests. There were very few priests who, when the chips were down, gave in and collaborated with the torturer. Yet there were exceptions. But you could not have found one single rabbi—*I dare you*—among all the *kapos* or among any of the others who held positions of power in the camps.

You say, Dick, that Hitler deprived the Jew of martyrdom. That is not true. Many Jews, especially the rabbis, could have saved their lives. In my town all the rabbis could have saved their lives, and do you know who wanted to save them? The priests. It's not the first time in history that they wanted alibis. The priests came to our rabbis—we had some thirty of them in our center—offering them refuge in the monastery, in the church. But, of course, what rabbi would choose it? I think there were two, out of at least fifty thousand rabbis in Eastern Europe, two who chose to escape individually. All the others preferred voluntarily, knowingly, to go with their Jews. How did these rabbis maintain their Jewishness and their humanity? *That* is the wonder! After all the system was so strong and the whole world was an accomplice!

What the Germans wanted to do was not only to exterminate the Jewish people physically; first of all, they wanted to exterminate them *spiritually*. Therefore, they invented this whole society—what we call in France *univers concentrationnaire*—with its princes and priests and high priests. The Germans wanted to deprave, to debase the Jew, to have him give up all values and dehumanize him. That was the first thing. Even the language in the camp—what kind of language was it? The most obscene language you could imagine, meant to create a climate, to impose an inhuman concept of man and of the universe upon the Jewish people.

There is a joke which is not funny. The joke is that, in one ghetto an SS officer tortured a Jew, and at one point clobbered him on the head while at the same time firing a blank shot. When the Jew came to, there was the SS man laughing, saying, "You are dead. But you don't know it. You think that you escaped us? We are your masters, even in the other world." It's a macabre joke, but it contains some truth. What the Germans wanted to do to the Jewish people was to substitute themselves for the Jewish God. All the terminology, all the vocabulary testifies to that. And in spite of all, here were these men who remained human and who remained Jewish and went on praying to God.

And here I will tell you, Dick, that you don't understand *them* when you say that it is more difficult to live today in a world without God. NO! If you want difficulties, choose to live *with* God. Can you compare today the tragedy of the believer to that of the nonbeliever?! The real tragedy, the real drama, is the drama of the believer.

It took me ten years to write my first book. It was not a coincidence; it was deliberate. I took a vow of silence in 1945, to the effect that I would wait ten years to be sure that what I would say would be true. In the beginning people did not talk about what happened over there. Those who survived refused to reveal the darkness they had seen. Today you have novelists and sociologists, you have everybody writing about it. In the early days, those who were there did not touch on it: it was fire. Why didn't they? For many reasons.

First, because they were afraid that no one would believe them. Second, they were afraid that, in the very process of telling the tale, they would betray it. Certain tales must be transmitted orally or not at all, must be transmitted like secrets, as a whole, from mouth to ear, in whispers—like the real oral tradition which was never transmitted, never written down according to the Kotzker rabbi. I think it was Braque who said that literature is a wound turned fire; and we were afraid to invite that fire. You remember in the Bible what happened to the two children of Aaroni Hacohen, the high priest? One doesn't play with fire!

So we didn't speak about it because we were afraid of committing a sin. Even today all of my friends have the feeling that, when we write books and publish them, we have committed a sin. Don't ask me why. It's irrational. Something is wrong, something is impure. The real story, perhaps, will never be told. The real truth will never be communicated. The real vision can never be shared, so why speak about it?

I'll go even farther. Today, twenty-five years after the event, I wonder whether we shouldn't have chosen silence then. For some reason, I believe that had all the survivors gathered in a secret conclave, somewhere in a forest, and decided together—I know it's a poetic image, unfeasible, but I feel this sense of loss of this opportunity—if we had then all of us decided never to say a word about it, I think we could have changed man by the very weight of our silence. But then I also believe that mankind wouldn't have been able to bear it. It would have driven man and peoples to madness. That is why, I think, we spoke.

Then we also spoke for a different reason. Somehow the Jew in us is so strong that we believe in communication, we believe in transmission, we believe in sharing. I think the single factor in Jewish existence is this need to communicate. Therefore, we begin always with names; the Bible is full of names. Why do we have all these names—the father and the son, the father of the son—why? To give us this feeling of being linked, of having to continue. We must communicate. This is the central theme of Jewish existence and has been—always—throughout the four thousand years of our history. During World War II it was even more so. Hundreds of people in ghettos sacrificed themselves to enable one of them to get out of the ghetto and tell the tale.

When Shimon Dubnov, probably the greatest historian we have had, was led to the mass grave in Riga together with all the Jews, he shouted, "Jews, open your ears and open your eyes! Take in every cloud; take in every smile; take in every sound. Don't forget!" He was even then, even there, obsessed with the need to communicate, to tell *us* certain tales. In Auschwitz—worse, in Birkenau, in the Sonderkommando, the commando that worked in the crematoria—there were historians; men who wrote down, day after day, fact after morbid fact, dryly and soberly. They were conscious of the necessity to transmit. Why? Why did they do it? And what for? In whom could they believe? In man? That is what bewilders me and astonishes me: that they could still think of man and of God and of us, while they lived and died in an age in which both Jew and man were betrayed by man and God. This story of spiritual strength—I won't call it "resistance" because the word itself was devaluated—of the Jew has to be told. I think this is what makes us so humble. But here we touch, I believe, the very substance of what I call *Jewishness*—because I don't like the word *Judaism*. There are too many *isms* in this world. What do I call *Jewishness?*

There is a story in the Talmud, a very beautiful one. And it's relevant, because you spoke of martyrs, and we speak of martyrs. The story goes: When Rabbi Ishmael, one of the ten martyrs of the faith in Roman times, was led to his death, a heavenly voice was heard, saying, "Ishmael, Ishmael, should you shed one tear, I shall return the universe to its primary chaos." And the Midrash says that Rabbi Ishmael was a gentleman and did not cry. And I couldn't understand for quite a while: why didn't he cry? The hell with it! If this is the price to pay, who needs it? Who wants this kind of world? Who wants to live in it? Yet there are many reasons why he didn't cry.

One, he was a martyr. Two, he obeyed. Three, the last and most poetic ultimate reason why he didn't cry is because he wanted to teach us a lesson in Judaism. Rabbi Ishmael—contrary to his classical opponent, Rabbi Akiba—was a rationalist. Even while dying, he wanted to teach us a lesson: Yes, I could destroy the world, and the world deserves to be destroyed. But to be a Jew is to have all the reasons in the world to destroy and *not to destroy!* To be a Jew is to have all the reasons in the world to hate the Germans and *not to hate them!* To be a Jew is to have all the reasons in the world to mistrust the church and *not to hate it!* To be a Jew is to have all the reasons in the world not to have faith in language, in singing, in prayers, and in God, but *to go on telling the tale, to go on carrying on the dialogue,* and to have my own silent prayers and quarrels with God.

That is the lesson that Rabbi Ishmael, when he died, taught me; but then he was Rabbi Ishmael and I am only a teller of his tales. But then, perhaps, that is the meaning of Jewish existence, especially for a storyteller, to tell tales lived so many times by so many Jews, and I am only one of them.

Postscript

On September 29, 1988, Harry James Cargas convened a symposium on "Elie Wiesel: The Man and His Work." Held at Webster University in St. Louis, Missouri, the symposium celebrated both the thirtieth anniversary of Wiesel's *Night* and the writer's sixtieth birthday. The proceedings included a paper by Franklin Littell, who referred back to the original exchange between Rubenstein and Wiesel. When it was Wiesel's turn to respond to the presentations he had heard all day long, he told a story about that first conference in 1970:

After finishing his response to Rubenstein that evening, Wiesel recalls, Rubenstein stood up and stated that he wished to say something. Wiesel's expectation was that Rubenstein would try to refute him. Instead, Rubenstein's reply to Wiesel was simply: "I as a rabbi want to give you my blessing."

SUGGESTIONS FOR FURTHER READING

Brown, Robert McAfee. *Elie Wiesel: Messenger to All Humanity.* Notre Dame, Ind.: University of Notre Dame Press, 1983.

Brenner, Reeve Robert. *The Faith and Doubt of Holocaust Survivors.* New York: The Free Press, 1980.

Cargas, Harry James. *Harry James Cargas in Conversation with Elie Wiesel.* New York: Paulist Press, 1976.

Cohen, Arthur A. *The Tremendum: A Theological Interpretation of the Holocaust.* New York: Crossroad Publishing Company, 1981.

Eckardt, A. Roy. *For Righteousness' Sake: Contemporary Moral Philosophies.* Bloomington: Indiana University Press, 1987.

Eckardt, Alice L., and A. Roy Eckardt. *Long Night's Journey into Day, A Revised Retrospective on the Holocaust.* Detroit: Wayne State University Press, 1988.

Eliach, Yaffa. *Hasidic Tales of the Holocaust: The First Original Hasidic Tales in a Century.* New York: Vintage Books, 1988.

Haas, Peter J. *Morality after Auschwitz: The Radical Challenge of the Nazi Ethic.* Philadelphia: Fortress Press, 1988.

Katz, Steven T. *Post-Holocaust Dialogues: Critical Studies in Modern Jewish Thought.* New York: New York University Press, 1983.

Maybaum, Ignaz. *The Face of God after Auschwitz.* Amsterdam: Polak & Van Gennep, 1965.

Rosenbaum, Irving J. *The Holocaust and Halakhah.* New York: Ktav, 1976.

Roskies, David G. *Against the Apocalypse: Responses to Catastrophe in Modern Jewish Culture.* Cambridge, Mass.: Harvard University Press, 1984.

Van Buren, Paul M. *A Theology of the Jewish-Christian Reality.* 4 vols. New York: Harper and Row, 1980–89.

Epilogue

Why?

One more thing.
Yes?
When you speak of your little sister leaving you like that, without a hug, without a goodbye, without wishing you a good journey, will you say that it was not her fault?
It was not your fault.
Then whose fault was it?
I shall find out. And I shall tell. I swear it to you, little sister. I shall.

ELIE WIESEL, "A Man and His Little Sister," A *Jew Today*

May 1944: a transport arrives at Auschwitz-Birkenau. Bewildered Jews from Sighet and other Transylvanian towns emerge from train-car prisons into midnight air fouled by burning flesh. Elie Wiesel, age fifteen, his father, mother, and little sister, Tzipora, are among them. Separated by the SS, the boy loses sight of his mother and sister, not fully aware that the parting is forever.

The parting was forever. Thus, the above dialogue, like some other ones by Elie Wiesel found here, did not happen—indeed could not have happened. And yet happen it did—and must, repeatedly. To find out "whose fault was it?" is not easy. A complete answer to that question depends on more than knowing who, what, where, when, and how. It depends on *why* as well.

Why did the Holocaust happen? Although this book and many others respond to that question, they also suggest that it is important to question every answer. Rightly, the question "Why?" asks endlessly, and it can be raised everywhere. Far from obscuring what is clear, such lines of reflection mystify nothing. On the contrary, underscoring the limits of human comprehension, they drive one back to history, back to the fatal interdependence of all human actions, and what is known about it.

In *The Rebel*, the French novelist-philosopher, Albert Camus, aptly writes, "Man is not entirely to blame; it was not he who started history; nor is he entirely innocent, since he continues it." Human actions, and perhaps some of God's as well, took the world to Auschwitz and beyond. But how far beyond remains uncertain, especially if memory fails to emphasize that the Holocaust happened largely because human minds became convinced they could figure everything out and understand why.

In his book *Survival in Auschwitz*, Primo Levi describes his camp initiation. On one occasion, he reached out a window to slake his painful thirst with an icicle. An SS guard immediately snatched it away from him. *"Warum?,"* Levi asked him, only to be told with a shove, *"Hier ist kein warum."* ("Here there is no why.") Levi's question "Why?" sought explanation. He got none, because questions of life and death were already settled there. No asking was permitted for the likes of Levi; in Auschwitz no "why" existed—not as a question and certainly not as satisfying explanation, either.

If Auschwitz raises every "Why?" it did not tolerate the kind Levi posed. Paradoxically, the Holocaust was beyond the question "Why?" because the minds that produced it thought they "understood" why. They "recognized" that one religion had superseded another. They "comprehended" that one race was superior to every other. They "saw" what nature's laws decreed, namely, that there was *lebensunwertes Leben* ("life unworthy of life"). Thus, they "realized" who deserved to live and who deserved to die.

Hitler and his Nazi followers were beyond asking "Why?" because they "knew" why. Knowing they were "right," their "knowing" made them killers. One can argue, of course, that such "knowing" perverted rationality. It did. And yet to say that much is too little, for one must ask about the sources of such perversion. When that asking occurs, part of its trail leads to the tendency of human reason to presume that indeed it can, at least in principle, figure everything out and understand why.

People are less likely to savage and annihilate each other when they ask "Why?" instead of "knowing" why, when their minds are not made up but opened up through questioning. Fault for the Holocaust lies primarily with those who did not question—or at least with those who did not ask "Why?" soon enough, and long enough.

Before it was too late, asking the question "Why?" might have redeemed those who became the killers and their victims. Well taken from Elie Wiesel's dialogue with his little sister, indeed from every page of this book, no point about the fatal interdependence of all human actions can be more important than that.

Suggestions for Further Reading

Arad, Yitzhak, Yisrael Gutman, and Abraham Margaliot, eds. *Documents on the Holocaust*. Oxford: Pergamon Press, 1987.

Cargas, Harry James. *The Holocaust: An Annotated Bibliography*. 2d ed. Chicago: American Library Association, 1985.

Charny, Israel W., et al., eds. *Genocide: A Critical Bibliographic Review*. London: Mansell, 1988.

Dawidowicz, Lucy S., ed. *A Holocaust Reader*. New York: Behrman House, 1976.

Edelheit, Abraham J., and Hershel Edelheit, eds. *Bibliography on Holocaust Literature*. Boulder, Colo.: Westview Press, 1986.

Hilberg, Raul, ed. *Documents of Destruction: Germany and Jewry 1933–1945*. Chicago: Quadrangle Books, 1971.

Laska, Vera. *Nazism, Resistance & Holocaust in World War II: A Bibliography*. Metuchen, N.J.: Scarecrow Press, 1985.

Remak, Joachim, ed. *The Nazi Years: A Documentary History*. New York: Simon and Schuster, 1986.

Shermis, Michael. *Jewish-Christian Relations: An Annotated Bibliography and Resource Guide*. Bloomington: Indiana University Press, 1988.

Szonyi, David M., ed. *The Holocaust: An Annotated Bibliography and Resource Guide*. New York: Ktav, 1985.

Index